FREEDOM A
IN KANT, S
AND KIER

CW00969842

The book traces a set of issues surrou⌐   ⌐
Schelling to Kierkegaard. It aims to clarify the contours of German idealism as a
philosophical movement by examining the motivations not only of its beginning,
but also of its dissolution in the work of the later Schelling, and tracing both to the
same complex of issues in Kant. It then builds a new understanding of
Kierkegaard's theory of agency and his criticisms of idealist ethics and metaphysics
upon this revised account of the historical background.

Michelle Kosch is Associate Professor of Philosophy at the Sage School of
Philosophy at Cornell University.

Freedom and Reason in Kant, Schelling, and Kierkegaard

MICHELLE KOSCH

CLARENDON PRESS · OXFORD

OXFORD
UNIVERSITY PRESS

Great Clarendon Street, Oxford OX2 6DP

Oxford University Press is a department of the University of Oxford.
It furthers the University's objective of excellence in research, scholarship,
and education by publishing worldwide in

Oxford New York

Auckland Cape Town Dar es Salaam Hong Kong Karachi
Kuala Lumpur Madrid Melbourne Mexico City Nairobi
New Delhi Shanghai Taipei Toronto

With offices in

Argentina Austria Brazil Chile Czech Republic France Greece
Guatemala Hungary Italy Japan Poland Portugal Singapore
South Korea Switzerland Thailand Turkey Ukraine Vietnam

Oxford is a registered trade mark of Oxford University Press
in the UK and in certain other countries

Published in the United States
by Oxford University Press Inc., New York

© Michelle Kosch 2006

First published 2006

First published in paperback 2010

British Library Cataloguing in Publication Data

Data available

Library of Congress Cataloging in Publication Data

Kosch, Michelle.
Freedom and reason in Kant, Schelling, and Kierkegaard / Michelle Kosch.
p. cm.
ISBN: 978–0–19–928911–0 (Hbk.)
978–0–19–957794–1 (Pbk.)
1. Free will and determinism—History—19th century. 2. Ethics,
Modern—19th century. 3. Kant, Immanuel, 1724–1804. 4. Schelling,
Friedrich wilhelm Joseph von, 1775–1854. 5. Kierkegaard, Søren,
1813–1855. I. Title.
BJ1461.K67 2006
123′.50922—dc22
2005036616

Typeset by Newgen Imaging Systems (P) Ltd., Chennai, India
Printed in the UK
by
MPG Books Group

ISBN 978–0–19–928911–0(Hbk.), 978–0–19–957794–1 (Pbk.)

1 3 5 7 9 10 8 6 4 2

for Theodore

Acknowledgements

This book began as a dissertation project at Columbia University in 1995, and the intervening decade has brought intellectual and financial support from very many people and institutions. Funding for research and writing has come from Columbia University, the German Academic Exchange Service, the Søren Kierkegaard Research Centre in Copenhagen, and the University of Michigan; additional logistical support and library resources have been provided by Eberhard Karls Universität Tübingen and the Institute for Philosophy of the Humboldt-Universität zu Berlin. My colleagues at the University of Michigan have provided a wonderfully stimulating intellectual environment and unflagging moral support. Colleagues at the Søren Kierkegaard Research Centre provided much thoughtful feedback during my time there. Thanks also to Manfred Frank for sharing his time and expertise during my stay in Tübingen. Charles Larmore, Wolfgang Mann, and Wayne Proudfoot advised the dissertation in which this book had its source, and without their guidance, criticism, and above all patience, it could not have come into being. Special thanks are due to Wolfgang Mann, to whom I owe the original impetus to work on Schelling and without whose encouragement that dissertation would never have become this book. Finally, thanks to Fred Neuhouser, for the nineteenth-century survey that first sparked my interest in German philosophy, and for his generous support and guidance in the intervening years.

Parts of this work have been presented at the Søren Kierkegaard Research Centre and to philosophy and theology departments at a number of universities. The general idea behind chapter 5 was first published as an article in the Palgrave volume *Kierkegaard and Freedom* in 2000, and the first half of that chapter appeared as an article in the *Journal of the History of Philosophy* in January 2006. Thanks to audiences at those talks, and to reviewers at *JHP* and at Oxford University Press for invaluable comments and criticisms. Thanks also to Cambridge University Press and Princeton University Press for permission to reproduce material under copyright.

Contents

List of Abbreviations

WORKS BY KANT

KrV   *Kritik der reinen Vernunft* (*Critique of Pure Reason*)

GMS   *Grundlegung zur Metaphysik der Sitten* (*Groundwork of the Metaphysics of Morals*)

KpV   *Kritik der praktischen Vernunft* (*Critique of Practical Reason*)

KU   *Kritik der Urtheilskraft* (*Critique of the Power of Judgment*)

R   *Religion innerhalb der Grenzen der blossen Vernunft* (*Religion within the Boundaries of Mere Reason*)

MS   *Metaphysik der Sitten* (*The Metaphysics of Morals*)

WORKS BY SCHELLING

StI   *System des transzendentalen Idealismus* (*System of Transcendental Idealism*)

SgP   *System der gesamten Philosophie und der Naturphilosophie insbesondere* (*System of Philosophy as a Whole and of the Philosophy of Nature in Particular*)

FS   *Philosophische untersuchungen über das Wesen der menschlichen Freiheit und die damit zusammenhängenden Gegenstände* (*Philosophical Investigations into the Essence of Human Freedon and Related Matters*)

WA   *Weltalter* (*Ages of the World*)

VC   *Vorrede zu einer philosophischen Schrift Victor Cousins* (*Preface to a Philosophical Work of Victor Cousin*)

GpP   *Grundlegung der positiven Philosophie* (*Groundwork for the Positive Philosophy*) (transcript of Schelling's Münich lectures from 1832–3)

DpE   *Darstellung des philosophischen Empirismus* (*Presentation of Philosophical Empirism*) (Munich lectures from 1836, from Schelling's *Nachlass*)

GnP   *Zur Geschichte der neueren Philosophie* (*On the History of Modern Philosophy*) (Munich lectures from the 1830s, from Schelling's *Nachlass*)

Paulus   *Paulus Nachschrift* (unofficial transcript of Schelling's first course of lectures in Berlin)

PO   *Philosophie der Offenbarung* (*Philosophy of Revelation*) (Schelling's own version of the Berlin lectures from the mid-1840s, published posthumously)

EPM   *Philosophische Einleitung in die Philosophie der Mythologie oder Darstellung der reinrationalen Philosophie* (*Philosophical Introduction to the Philosophy of Mythology or Presentation of Pure Rational Philosophy*)

WORKS BY KIERKEGAARD

BI   *Om Begrebet Ironi* (*On the Concept of Irony*)

EE   *Enten/Eller* (*Either/Or, two volumes*)

FB	*Frygt og Bæven* (*Fear and Trembling*)
PS	*Philosophiske Smuler* (*Philosophical Fragments*)
BA	*Begrebet Angest* (*The Concept of Anxiety*)
SLV	*Stadier paa Livets Vei* (*Stages on Life's Way*)
AE	*Afsluttende uvidenskabelig Efterskrift* (*Concluding Unscientific Postscript*)
LA	*En Litterair Anmeldelse* (*A Literary Review*)
SD	*Sygdommen til Døden* (*The Sickness unto Death*)

NOTE ON CITATIONS AND TRANSLATIONS

In the Kant chapters quotations from the *Critique of Pure Reason* are taken from the Kemp Smith translation. Quotations from Kant's other works are taken from the Wood/Guyer edition where that is possible. Where I reproduce quotations that are part of neither edition, the translations are my own. Citations of the *Critique of Pure Reason* are to the A/B editions and of other works are to the Akademie Ausgabe.

In the Schelling chapters I have supplied only my own translations. When I began this project little of Schelling's work had been translated, and even less was available in print. Since then several new translations of Schelling's works have appeared. However, they are far from covering the range of Schelling's works that I use (none of the text from *Grundlegung der positiven Philosophie* or the *Paulus Nachschrift* that I use in chapter 4 has been translated, for instance), are not of uniform quality, and (if one is entitled to infer anything from the history of Schelling translations) may not be in print for very long. In such circumstances, the additional convenience to the reader of citing and quoting from a specific English edition is likely to be minimal. Except where noted, citations refer to the first (1856–61) edition of Schelling's works (although in some cases I have had to use Schröter's reprint edition, which rearranges the texts but reproduces the first edition pagination in the margins).

In the Excursus all translations are my own and all citations are to the original (usually, the only) edition of the works in question, none of which are available in English translation.

In the Kierkegaard chapters all translations are taken from the Princeton University Press edition of Kierkegaard's works, and from the Princeton edition of the journals where possible. Where I have quoted from journal entries not used in the Princeton edition, translations are mine. Citations to Kierkegaard's published works are to the first Danish edition followed by the fourth Danish edition of Kierkegaard's writings (e.g. II: 144; 3: 156)—except in those cases in which the fourth edition volume is not yet available as this book goes to press. The pagination of the first Danish edition can be found in the margin of the Princeton edition of Kierkegaard's writings from which the translations are taken; future translations will probably refer to the fourth Danish edition. Citations of journals and papers refer to the first complete edition of journals and papers (*Søren Kierkegaards Papirer*) and where possible also to the fourth edition of Kierkegaard's writings (*Søren Kierkegaards Skrifter*).

Introduction

What else, then, can freedom of the will be but autonomy, i.e., the property that the will has of being a law to itself?

Kant, 1785[1]

We can also see that freedom can never be located in a rational subject's being able to choose in opposition to his (lawgiving) reason, even though experience proves often enough that this happens (though we still cannot comprehend how this is possible).... Only freedom in relation to the internal lawgiving of reason is really an ability; the possibility of deviating from it is an inability.

Kant, 1797[2]

If the moral law announces to us no other freedom than that which consists in the self-activity of reason, then the ability to act *immorally* is not only an *inability*, but is simply *impossible*.

Reinhold, 1797[3]

The real and living concept [of freedom] is that it is a capacity for good and evil.

Schelling, 1809[4]

The criterion of the self is always that before which it is a self... everything is qualitatively that by which it is measured, and that which is its qualitative criterion is ethically its goal; the criterion and goal are what define something, what it is, with the exception of the condition in the world of freedom, where by not qualitatively being that which is his goal and his criterion a person must himself have merited this disqualification.

Kierkegaard, 1849[5]

Kant thought that the human being was a law to itself (autonomy)—that is, binding himself under the law he gives himself. What this means in the true or deeper sense is: lawlessness or experimentation.... If there is nothing higher than me that is binding, and I am supposed to bind myself, whence shall I, as A who does the binding, acquire the strictness that I lack as B, who is the one bound—when after all A and B are the same self.

Kierkegaard, 1850[6]

---

[1] *Groundwork* III (4: 447).   [2] *Metaphysics of Morals* (6: 226).
[3] This excerpt from Reinhold, *Auswahl vermischter Schriften*, is reproduced in Bittner and Cramer (1975, 323–4).
[4] 'Philosophische Untersuchungen über das Wesen der menschlichen Freiheit' (VII: 352).
[5] *The Sickness unto Death* (*SD* XI: 191).   [6] Kierkegaard 1909–78 X,2 A 396, 280–1.

This book examines the early history of the idea that moral agency is self-legislating through the lens of one of its central difficulties, that of accounting for the possibility of moral evil. Its primary aim is to shed light on the history of philosophy in the German-language realm between Kant (who first articulated the idea) and Kierkegaard (who best articulated the difficulty). I argue that this was one of the main issues shaping the contours of debate during that period, shaping (if one may put it this way) the rise and fall of German idealism. Let me offer a brief sketch of the philosophical problem before introducing the historical project.

The fundamental idea of the ethics of autonomy is the idea that the moral law is normative for the will in virtue of being the will's own law. The key is the connection between the will or agency and the law that governs it. This is the source both of the interest in the idea—its explanation of why we are bound by moral requirements—and its difficulty. The difficulty lies in saying what it means for the moral law to be the will's own in a way that does not rule out the possibility of intentionally thwarting the law. The idea of autonomy has been cashed out in many ways in the contemporary literature, but all of these ways share the difficulty, insofar as for all of them morality ends up being a constitutive aim of intentional action.[7] Now, many moral psychological accounts (not just the Kantian one) construe the relation between action and morality in this way—the Platonic doctrine that one chooses the worse only in those cases in which one (falsely) believes it to be the better is an instance. And many moral philosophers find this unproblematic.[8] They are concerned with accounting for how ethical demands can seem compelling; that these demands might literally compel would be a good result, not a bad one. Kantians, though, are committed to this whether they like it or not, since there is no apparent way of detaching the aim of morality from intentional action while maintaining that the moral law is binding in virtue of being the will's own. Some Kantians are happy with this result. For them, morality *is* freedom—the only sort of freedom one should want, at any rate—and the idea of freely chosen immorality is unintelligible.[9] Kant himself recognized the problems with this idea, which have to do with both (backward-looking) ascriptions of blame and (forward-looking) constraints on practical deliberation. That it rules out a view of any past behaviour as both imputable and immoral seems a bad result, but those convinced that blame ascriptions have ethical interest only in so far as they inform future deliberations can accept it. Less palatable are the problems that arise from the forward-looking perspective of practical deliberation. In grounding the normativity of morality in my interest in my freedom, the Kantian conception of autonomy rules out

---

[7] For criticisms of the idea that the good is a constitutive end of intentional action and desire, cf. Railton (2003) and Velleman (1992). Velleman (1996) himself endorses a form of autonomism, however, and may face the same difficulty (cf. Clark 2001).

[8] Stocker (1979) offers what are now taken to be standard reasons for resisting this idea.

[9] Korsgaard (1989, 1996a: 159–87) discusses the problem and accepts that for Kantians evil must be unintelligible (cf. Korsgaard 1996a: 171ff.).

a view of my possible future actions as imputably immoral.[10] But that seems an answer to the questions raised in practical deliberation that drains practical deliberation of any properly moral significance.

I do not propose to answer, in this book, the systematic question of the extent to which it is possible to avoid this set of problems in a broadly Kantian framework. What I propose instead is to trace the *history* of the problem in Kant's works and those of the post-Kantian idealists—to trace it through to Kierkegaard who, I argue, rejects the ethics of autonomy on the grounds that it distorts the practical perspective in just this way. One might think that, though central to Kantian moral psychology, this is rather too narrow an issue to be, as I have claimed, the issue that determined the contours of German idealism. But it is larger than it first appears, since it overlaps (as it must) with the Kantian, and later the idealist, account of the place of human agency in nature and of the relation between moral freedom and natural scientific explanation. The conception of freedom operative in German idealism was one in which the equation of morality or rationality and freedom was embraced. The moral law was conceived as (in some sense) a descriptive law, one of a set of laws governing mind and nature. Of course it was still conceived as self-given, a law that mind or agency (now on a cosmic scale) gives itself, and so quite different in character from the mechanistic laws that had made the place of moral agency in nature seem problematic. But, when systematized into a theory of nature and history, this idealist conception of the autonomy of rational nature required seeing individual human beings as pieces in a larger rational structure—moments in the self-development of world-spirit—in a way that was not ultimately different, in its moral implications, from the modern mechanistic conception of nature it sought to replace. Schelling, in his later work, and Kierkegaard articulated a criticism of the idealist conception of agency along these lines that was both the logical conclusion of the idealist experiment with autonomy and the historical transition to mid-nineteenth-century post-idealism.

Contributions to the existing literature

This book tells a single story, but in doing so it makes contributions to two rather different fields, and so has something to convey to two different sets of readers. The first set includes those with an interest in the nineteenth century or in

---

[10] That is, the moral evil problem is a problem even from the practical standpoint as described, for instance, in chapter 2 of Bok (1998). Korsgaard accepts something like the same description (attributing it to the Kant of the *Groundwork*) in chapter 6 of Korsgaard (1996a), but fails to see that if moral wrong is unintelligible then it cannot be relevant to my practical deliberation and so cannot be, for example, something I set out to avoid. The complaint here is not that for something to be a norm for an agent the objective probability of the agent conforming to it must actually be less than one (as, e.g., Lavin (2004) assumes in making a related criticism of Korsgaard). It is rather that nothing can function as a norm in practical deliberation for an agent who believes himself in possession of a demonstration that the probability of his conforming to it (or not acting at all) is one—and who therefore cannot in principle see it as something he must *try* to approximate.

German idealism and a curiosity about how the idealist systems of the post-Kantian period gave rise to the apparently profoundly different approaches characteristic of the most important thinkers of the middle of the nineteenth century. Since this is among the most fertile periods in the history of philosophy for questions in value theory and moral psychology, I think this set of readers should be larger than it is, and hope this book will contribute to enlarging it. The second set consists of those with a thematic interest in Kierkegaard's moral psychology and conception of ethics and religion (and a willingness to assume that a better grasp of these things is to be had by reading his work against the relevant philosophical background). Let me say something about what each of these two sets of readers should expect from the book.

The scholarly literature on the German philosophy of this period contains a growing wealth of narratives that link Kant with his successors Fichte, Schelling and Hegel (through such intermediaries as Reinhold, Maimon, Schulze, Jacobi and the Jena circle of romantics) and offer competing ways of sorting out how problems in each view gave rise to its successor.[11] These narratives generally end with Hegel—or, if they do not, the post-Hegelian part is presented as a denouement[12]—and the story they tell is that of the genesis, rise and eventual hegemony of the idea of autonomy.[13] The post-Hegelian period is a dark age in which this ideal (rather inexplicably) lost its force. The conception of the period from about 1760 to about 1830 as dominated by a unified development that culminated in Hegel has its source, as we know, in Hegel's own account of the period in his lectures on the history of modern philosophy. The specifics of Hegel's account have been challenged—for instance, the Jena circle is now seen as having had an important influence on Fichte's development rather than just being a set of followers of Fichte[14]—but not to the extent that the admission of the concerns of mid-century figures such as Kierkegaard and Marx into the basic storyline seems natural. At least, this has been true of basically all such scholarship in the English-speaking world, and the greater part of that in Germany.

Some scholars of Schelling have challenged this Hegelian view of the period, pointing out that Schelling was not only Hegel's predecessor (having risen to prominence already in the late 1790s) but also his successor (having been called in 1841 to the chair of philosophy in Berlin that had been empty since Hegel's death in 1831). They point out that Schelling's lectures in Berlin (and, in the 1830s, in Munich) were heard by a generation of students working to resolve apparent contradictions in Hegel's system, or trying to see what part of Hegelianism they could salvage, or looking to get beyond Hegel for reasons fundamentally Kantian in spirit—and they point out that this generation of auditors included many of the young Hegelians

[11] For the best treatments in English, cf. Ameriks (2000b), Beiser (1987, 2002), Beiser (2002), Henrich (2003), Pinkard (2002), and Pippin (1997).   [12] Cf. Pinkard (2002).
[13] These stories also generally begin with Kant, even though they really ought to begin with Rousseau—as Neuhouser has set about showing in his recent work. Cf., e.g., Neuhouser (2000).
[14] Cf. Frank (1997).

who were Marx's associates (including Engels, Arnold Ruge, and Feuerbach),[15] as well as Kierkegaard. If the mid-century developments are to be integrated into the history of the idealist period, it has seemed reasonable to think that is to be done via the thought of the later Schelling. Indeed, a convincing case for Schelling's importance for mid-century materialism and Marx has been made.[16]

That a similar case can be made for Schelling's importance for mid-century (for want of a less anachronistic term) personalism and Kierkegaard has often been suggested (even if, for reasons I will discuss, the possibility of such a link has too often been discounted on mistaken historical grounds). The existence of clear textual links between Kierkegaard's *Concept of Anxiety* and Schelling's 1809 essay 'Philosophische Untersuchungen über das Wesen der menschlichen Freiheit' (hereafter, the *Freiheitsschrift*) has been pointed out,[17] and there have been suggestions that both the turn to philosophical anthropology in Kierkegaard and the specifics of his view owe something to that essay.[18] Similarly, links between Schelling's late conception of revelation and Kierkegaard's account of knowledge of God have been explored.[19] Kierkegaard's thesis that actuality somehow eludes philosophical thinking[20] and his claim that the Hegelian system rests on presuppositions that it cannot itself defend[21] have been traced to similar views expressed by Schelling in his lectures.

What has been absent in the literature is a plausible account of the underlying concern that unites these isolated points of agreement (which are sometimes presented as surprising correspondences between two thinkers who otherwise had nothing in common).[22] That underlying concern, I argue here, is with the nature and requirements of moral agency, the possibility of autonomy, and the compatibility of the sort of freedom required for moral responsibility with the demands of systematic philosophy. So abstractly stated, this claim should not be all that surprising, given the centrality of these concerns to all involved. This complex of concerns is already central in the more standard accounts of the period—the ones that end with Hegel. Where my account differs from those is that they—like Hegel—take the idea of autonomy to be itself unproblematic in ethical terms.[23] The only problems to which they take it to give rise are those of articulating a

---

[15] Marx, though not himself present, had read the notes from Schelling's lectures that Paulus published in 1843. Cf. editor's introduction to Schelling (1977).   [16] Frank (1992).

[17] Cf. Theunissen (1965), Figal (1980), and Hennigfeld (1987).

[18] Cf. Theunissen (1965). Theunissen tends to accept the general schema, 'either metaphysics or philosophical anthropology', and contends that Schelling's anthropological concern began and ended with the *Freiheitsschrift*, replaced in the later work with a new metaphysical theology, one far removed from any anthropological concerns. I disagree about both the schema and the relation between Kierkegaard and Schelling.   [19] Also by Theunissen (1964–5).

[20] Cf. Koktanek (1962) and Kosch (2003).   [21] Cf. Schulz (1975).

[22] Cf. Koktanek (1962).

[23] Better put, they take the idea of autonomy to be problematic in only those ethical terms that Hegel himself pointed out in the *Philosophy of Right*—that it leaves the content of ethics underspecified and must be supplemented by the concrete ethical life of a people, which in turn must receive a partially independent philosophical justification. The concerns Schelling and Kierkegaard raised with the ethics of autonomy were distinct from this one.

philosophy of nature, of history and of the social world consistent with the possibility of human autonomy on some recognizable descendant of the Kantian conception, and of solving the Kantian problem of the unity of the practical and
theoretical employments of reason (which in Kant himself had involved radically
different principles, presuppositions, and conclusions about such fundamental
topics as human nature and the existence of God). Of course I do not mean to
suggest that those problems are trivial. But Schelling and Kierkegaard took the
notion of autonomy to give rise to properly ethical problems as well—chiefly the
problems of how such a view can be consistent with the phenomenology of
agency, and of how we are to avoid a certain pernicious ethical self-satisfaction if
we embrace such a view. Focusing on these problems gives one a different view of
the contours of the period, one in which Schelling's later work, that of his students
(the circle of late-idealist philosophers whose students were the first neo-Kantians)
and of Kierkegaard are a natural part of the picture. So the first set of readers to
whom this book is addressed will get a new take on how the story of this period is
to be told.

In telling that story, this book also contributes to what has so far, at least in
English, been a quite distinct body of philosophical literature, the interpretive
literature on Kierkegaard. German-language Kierkegaard scholarship has always
recognized the importance of classical German philosophy and theology as the
background against which Kierkegaard's texts are to be interpreted. But historically oriented scholarship in Britain and America (and even in Denmark) has
generally been less sensitive to the details of the German context (despite its
concern with the details of the Danish context, and despite the fact that German
philosophy clearly set the terms of the Danish debates of the time). Although
Kant's importance for Kierkegaard has generally been recognized, Schelling's has
most often been overlooked, and Hegel has been the major focus among the
post-Kantians—with remarkably unfruitful results in some central areas.[24] The
argument I advance here—that the development in thinking about freedom
from Kant through the early Schelling to the later Schelling and the late idealists
is fundamental both to Kierkegaard's theory of agency and to the place of that
theory in the larger project Kierkegaard undertakes in the pseudonymous
works—can serve as an example of what is to be gained when historically oriented
Kierkegaard interpretation shifts its focus away from Hegel and towards other
figures and arguments with more positive significance for Kierkegaard's core views.

I take Kierkegaard's project to involve a comparative examination of a number
of forms of life (or 'stages' or existential perspectives), with special attention to

---

[24] To take one example salient to the topic here, the very idea of thinking in terms of 'stages of
existence' does seem to have its source in Hegel, as has been repeatedly emphasized. (The best place to
look in the English-language literature for a discussion of the Hegelian background to the idea of the
stages is Taylor (1980)). But despite some substantial overlap between Hegel's and Kierkegaard's
treatments of romanticism, for the most part the content of the Kierkegaardian stages does not have
its source in Hegel, and so comparing them with Hegelian prototypes is of limited use.

spelling out the features peculiar to the Christian one, and with some (often only implicit) criticism of the others. I also take the criticism of these others to be directed not at their particular content or at the goals characteristically pursued by those who embrace them, but rather at the account of the foundation of that content and the justification of those goals implicit in them. The criticized views have presuppositions that sit badly alongside ineliminable features of the situation of agency (of what Kierkegaard calls 'existing subjectivity'), such that it is ultimately impossible for someone to understand her practical situation in the terms they provide. Finally, I take it that part of what is supposed to set the Christian view apart is that it does not pose any of the same problems as the other views (though it may pose new problems of its own), and that this is what makes it a better fit with the situation of existing subjectivity than the others—even though nothing else can be said in its defence. Given this conception of the project in the pseudonymous works, it is uncontroversial that whatever the details of Kierkegaard's theory of agency are, they will be central to that project.[25] Where I disagree with other interpreters is in my estimation of the details of the theory, and therefore of the substance of the criticisms of the aesthetic, ethical and philosophical-religious views of life.

My disagreement with the available interpretations is sharpest in my estimation of the complaint against the non-religious ethical view—an area in which, I believe, no remotely plausible account has so far been advanced. A plausible account needs to explain what unites the views named as targets of the criticism (and since these include a number of modern and ancient figures, this is no trivial task) in such a way that whatever that unifying feature is can be seen as a reasonable target of the criticisms Kierkegaard offers. In order not to be question-begging, such an account needs to do that without presupposing the truth of particular religious commitments or even the applicability of religious concepts. Kierkegaard's texts have not seemed to offer a clear and plausible criticism of the targets he names. I contend that this is because the large argumentative gaps left by certain well-known peculiarities of Kierkegaard's mode of presentation can be filled only by placing the texts against a historical background with the right general contours—and that other interpreters have not got the contours right. In providing what I take to be the proper background, then, the early chapters of this book set the stage for a reading of this part of the project in the pseudonymous works that is more compelling than any presently available in the literature.

This re-drawing of the background has implications that go beyond the interpretation of the theory of stages, however. It is important for understanding the attack on academic metaphysics and epistemology that take up much of the central sections of *Concluding Unscientific Postscript*, and has implications for the interpretation of the sceptical position enunciated there and in the Interlude

---

[25] Parts of this conception of Kierkegaard's project in the pseudonyms are widely shared among interpreters, but parts are not. I will argue for the controversial parts in chapters 5 and 6; I assume them here only for the sake of brevity.

of *Philosophical Fragments*. It also bears significantly on Kierkegaard's epistemology of religion—his account of how we arrive at religious belief, and of what its implications are for our other beliefs and our conduct. I do not think that the material presented in the first four chapters of this book comes close to painting a complete background picture for *that* set of claims. But I do believe that Kierkegaard's religious epistemology was very substantially informed by his conception of agency, and that a rather broad swathe of interpretations of his account of religious belief (for example, all those according to which religious belief is directly or indirectly willed) can be ruled out on the grounds that they conflict with that conception. So although I present only a fairly narrow segment of the philosophical background behind Kierkegaard's thought in this book, it is a central one, and ought therefore to be of interest to many students of his thought.

Chapter outline and abbreviated itineraries

The broad outlines of the story I tell here are as follows.

I begin with an analysis of Kant's attempt to reconcile what is essentially a libertarian position on free will with the claims of theoretical explanation. The stepwise reconciliation begins with the solution to the first *Critique's* third antinomy (which leaves room for transcendental spontaneity even if experience is of a deterministic world) and ends with the third *Critique's* conception of an overarching teleology of nature (which suggests a strategy for integrating practical and theoretical uses of reason on a large scale). I then show that the only argument for the reality of human freedom this reconciliation allows Kant to offer (from the second *Critique's* fact of reason, coupled with ought-implies-can) is one that connects freedom too closely to practical reason, turning freely chosen immorality into a problem he struggles with through the 1790s. In the first two chapters, then, I outline the evolution of Kant's thinking about transcendental freedom, rational self-determination and the possibility of freedom for evil, and examine some early criticisms of Kant in Schmid and Reinhold.

Then I turn to Schelling, whose early systematic philosophy took its start from Kant's third *Critique* and consisted in part in an attempt to replace Kant's combination of phenomenal determinism and noumenal libertarianism with a new form of compatibilism founded on a new conception of natural causality, one consistent with the Kantian aspiration for rational self-determination on the part of human beings. His guiding idea, in that early work, was that seeing actions as necessary does not conflict with seeing them as free—only seeing them as mechanistically produced by a nature that is fundamentally mindless does. If we can see nature as an expression of spirit (or at least an expression of something that we can also coherently see spirit as an expression of) then there is no motivation for dualism in the philosophy of mind and no free-will problem in the traditional sense. Now, this solution makes sense only if the question about moral responsibility in the traditional sense (what causal and rational powers must we attribute to human beings if we are to see them as morally responsible agents?) has been replaced by a question about autonomy (what causal and rational powers must we attribute to human beings if we are to see them as self-determining agents?). These questions are similar and can even look the same; the idealist programme relied on equating them. But morally responsible agents are capable of good *and* evil, and accounts of freedom that reduce freedom to rational self-determination and equate practical rationality with morality have difficulty accounting for this. By 1809 Schelling had come to the conclusion that the investigation into the conditions of possibility of rational self-determination could shed no further light on the question of the conditions of possibility of moral agency in a more general sense, because it could shed no light on the possibility of moral evil. His effort (in the *Freiheitsschrift*) to provide a new theory of moral agency that would do so determined the major features of his later system (which was post-idealist in its epistemology and its emphasis on the contingency of the reality it claimed to explain). Consideration of the problem of evil motivated the rejection both of the ethics of autonomy and of the (idealistic) metaphysics of autonomy. The third and fourth chapters, then, trace Schelling's trajectory from the classic idealist compatibilism which he was the first to enunciate (and which became a model for Hegel's) to the radical critiques of that view and of the ethics of autonomy which he was again the first to enunciate (and which, I argue, became a model for Kierkegaard's).

In an excursus following the Schelling chapters I deal with the historical question of the transmission of Schelling's ideas to Kierkegaard, arguing that Christian Weiße and Immanuel Hermann Fichte (and their circle) provided the required route of transmission of Schelling's largely unpublished later work.

I then turn to Kierkegaard, beginning with a consideration of the critical project in the pseudonyms and offering new interpretations of the criticisms of the aesthetic viewpoint and of the ethical viewpoint offered in the pseudonymous works. I give an interpretation of the account of Christianity presented in *Philosophical Fragments* and *Concluding Unscientific Postscript* that shows how such a view could provide a solution to the problems raised for the criticized ethical stance. I conclude by offering an interpretation of Kierkegaard's theory of agency as presented in *The Concept of Anxiety* and *The Sickness unto Death* that traces its roots to Fichte and the Schelling of the *Freiheitsschrift*. So in the fifth and sixth chapters I place Kierkegaard's pseudonymous corpus against the background outlined in the first four chapters, and present what I take to be the main results for Kierkegaard scholarship of that undertaking.

I have made the reader's itinerary substantially shorter by focusing only on major milestones in the period I have covered. This has meant leaving out discussions of figures who played important intermediary roles. J. G. Fichte was a major figure in the background of Kierkegaard's construal of the ethical standpoint,[26] but I have

---

[26] Cf. Kosch (forthcoming) for a discussion.

omitted a discussion of Fichte's ethics, because it presents no new problems over and above those already present in Kant (despite what Martensen seems to have thought).[27] Likewise, though Hegel had clearly overshadowed the early Schelling as a representative of idealistic metaphysics by the time Kierkegaard was writing (even if this shift happened substantially later in Denmark than it had in Germany—the process was still not complete while Kierkegaard was a student),[28] I have omitted an independent treatment of Hegel's compatibilism, since on this topic Hegel added nothing significant to Schelling's innovations. Kierkegaard's teachers in Denmark likewise do not figure prominently because the roles they played, important as they may have been biographically, were minimally important philosophically.[29] To readers who would prefer a shorter itinerary still I can offer four suggestions. Each set of two chapters is a relatively autonomous unit; there is no need for readers interested solely in the discussion of Schelling or Kierkegaard (and willing to take my word on the history) to consult preceding chapters. For many readers §§I and II of chapter 1 (on Kant's conception of freedom) will cover familiar territory. Few will be interested in the details of the historical case made in the excursus between chapters 4 and 5. Finally, readers interested exclusively in the moral psychological portion of the story can avoid most of the metaphysics by skipping chapter 1 §I and §III, chapter 3 §I, and chapter 4 §II.

Note on Kierkegaard's pseudonymity

I have focused on Kierkegaard's pseudonymous works since it is in these that Kierkegaard engages most philosophically with issues surrounding moral agency and the foundations of ethics. The various discourses and *Works of Love* speak the

---

[27] In his *Lectures on the History of Modern Philosophy from Kant to Hegel* (1838–9), H. L. Martensen praised Kant for his doctrine of radical evil (Kierkegaard 1909–78 II C 25, 294), whereas Fichte is scolded for his negative view ('he regards sin as a $\mu\eta$ $o\nu$, and so remorse is unnecessary, for as I sinned I was a $\mu\eta$ $o\nu$'—Kierkegaard 1909–1978 II C 25, 300). But Martensen's own view of moral evil—judging from his *Outline to a System of Moral Philosophy*—itself aligns sin with unfreedom and good with genuine willing in the way that Kierkegaard will reject. Cf. Martensen (1997: 259ff.).

[28] Sibbern—a major figure in Danish philosophy in the generation preceding Kierkegaard's, and one of his teachers—had been quite deeply influenced by the early Schelling; his systems look like extrapolations of Schelling's *Identitätssystem* even into the 1840s. See Lübcke (2003) for a concise synopsis of Sibbern's thought; Himmelstrup (1934) for an extended treatment. J. L. Heiberg and H. L. Martensen were the two figures most responsible for bringing Hegelianism to Denmark—Heiberg with a series of works the first of which appeared in 1833; Martensen with a number of publications and lecture courses beginning in the late 1830s (cf. Stewart 2003a). So it is no surprise that Schelling—early as well as late—loomed so large in Kierkegaard's thinking.

[29] Martensen was the proximal source of many of Kierkegaard's interpretations of contemporary philosophers—certainly, as we learn from Stewart (2003b), the inspiration for many of Kierkegaard's specific turns of phrase—but on the whole his portrayals of them in his lectures were, if brief, fairly good. The presentation of the idealist notion of (practical and theoretical) autonomy in his dissertation was likewise pithy and accurate, but the criticisms offered there were unoriginal. So, for the topics of interest to me, Martensen was a source neither of historically interesting misconstruals nor of noteworthy innovations.

language of Christian edifying literature, a language quite foreign to philosophers and their concerns.[30] Working primarily from Kierkegaard's pseudonyms brings with it difficulties, particularly for the interpreter who aims to construct a unified view on the basis of several different works (though working primarily from the signed works does not entirely eliminate these difficulties).[31] I try to steer a middle path, in this book, between two common strategies for dealing with Kierkegaard's pseudonymous authorship.

The first strategy is to attribute none of the claims Kierkegaard makes in the pseudonymous works to Kierkegaard himself. Only the pseudonyms' names are mentioned in attributions, and commonalities between their views are taken to be commonalities between the views of distinct authorial voices. Taken to an extreme, this strategy effectively prevents us from uncovering a unified view (of any subtlety) underlying the pseudonymous corpus. If everything Kierkegaard can be taken to be saying 'through' the pseudonyms is said indirectly and none of their assertions can be part of that view, then whatever view we are able to attribute to Kierkegaard himself must be very coarse-grained, because indirect communication taken on its own is a quite blunt instrument for conveying philosophical content. The second strategy, to attribute all of the pseudonyms' claims to Kierkegaard, is much less popular, and for good reason: it requires the interpreter either to attribute bald self-contradictions to Kierkegaard, or to pick and choose quite arbitrarily which among that set of contradictory claims constitutes Kierkegaard's true view. Both extremes are best avoided. Some of what the pseudonyms say must be taken as a straightforward expression of Kierkegaard's own view, while some of their assertions are to be taken either as parts of views he presented for the purpose of rejecting or refuting or for purposes of contrast, or as a means of conveying a personal message in a covert manner to a particular reader. There is no algorithm for drawing such distinctions, but I have used the following considerations as a guide.

Kierkegaard's attitude towards pseudonymity changed dramatically over the years during which the pseudonymous works were published. *Either/Or, Fear and Trembling*, and *Repetition* were originally conceived as pseudonymous works—the

---

[30] *Works of Love*, Kierkegaard's large work on Christian ethics of 1847, seems like an obvious choice for an extended discussion. But that work is concerned primarily with elaborating the normative ethical concept of Christian neighbour love (what it requires and how the individual can go about removing the various psychological obstacles that stand in the way of loving one's neighbour in the genuinely Christian manner). It does not cover the territory that is my primary concern here (what sorts of things ethico-religious imperatives are, how we come to know them, where their motivational force is supposed to have its source, and how that motivational force relates to our agency). Readers interested in a discussion of Kierkegaard's normative ethics will find one in Ferreira (2001).

[31] The signed works, in fact, are no more expressive of a single unitary view than the pseudonymous works are. The best example of this is *Upbuilding Discourses in Various Spirits*, whose first discourse (on the topic: purity of heart is to will one thing) is more Kantian than Kierkegaardian-Christian in spirit (Kierkegaard himself called it 'ethical-ironical' and 'Socratic' at Kierkegaard 1909–78 VIII,1 A 15 10; Kierkegaard 1997–, vol. 20 NB:129) and whose last section, a set of discourses grouped under the title 'The Gospel of Sufferings', reads more like a description of religiousness A than of the Christian religiousness its title suggests.

first and third with multiple layers of pseudonymous authorship.[32] The reasons for this appear to range from the desire to contrast distinct views of life (*Either/Or*) or distinct interpretations of the same set of events (*Repetition*), to the desire to convey a secret message to his ex-fiancée (parts of all three works). We can confidently attribute claims made in these early pseudonymous works to Kierkegaard himself where they correspond to things written in works published (or intended to be published) under his own name, or where they are repeated in several pseudonymous works with ostensibly different total views. Where neither of these conditions hold, we must think twice before attributing the view to Kierkegaard himself.

Unlike these works, *The Concept of Anxiety* and *Philosophical Fragments* were originally intended by Kierkegaard to be published under his own name. He decided to publish them pseudonymously only at the last minute, with minimal changes to the text, and it seems quite different motivations were in play in this decision than in the case of the early pseudonyms.[33] This means that the contents of these works can be attributed to Kierkegaard himself with as much confidence as those of any of his signed works, and I will attribute statements made in them directly to Kierkegaard. (I realize this is not the majority view, but I believe it should be.)

Concluding Unscientific Postscript is a unique case. First, though it shares a pseudonym with *Philosophical Fragments*—and in fact claims to be a continuation of that work—it expresses views that are in some tension with the views of its predecessor. (One might put this tension in a single sentence by saying that although the Climacus of *Fragments* describes Christianity from a standpoint that is genuinely neutral but incorporates elements that are only accessible from the inside,[34] the Climacus of *Postscript* describes it as a connoisseur who is distinctly an outsider, claiming of himself that he is not a Christian.) Second, while it was composed as something Kierkegaard intended to publish pseudonymously, it was also the work in which Kierkegaard first acknowledged (in the appended 'first and last explanation') authorship of the works of the pseudonyms, including *Postscript* itself. I find the former fact to be more significant than the latter, and so like most interpreters, I see some distance between Kierkegaard's views and those of *Postscript*'s Climacus, and take care in attributing arguments found in that work to Kierkegaard.

The Anti-Climacus works are also pseudonymous works from which Kierkegaard distanced himself to only a limited degree (never, for instance, seriously trying to conceal his authorship of them). I treat them much as I treat *The Concept of Anxiety* and *Philosophical Fragments*.

---

[32] *Stages on Life's Way*, which I discuss only minimally, follows the same model as these three early pseudonyms.

[33] See the helpful discussion of the pseudonyms in Hirsch (1933, vol. 1: 133ff.), as well as the commentary volume accompanying Kierkegaard (1997–, vol. 4).

[34] For instance, he mentions in the first chapter that the idea of rebirth is only thinkable by one who has been reborn—the suggestion being that a complete description of Christianity of the sort found in *Fragments* is available only to someone on the inside.

It seems to me that there is a single view of moral psychology and moral epistemology which the Climacus of *Fragments* attributes to Christianity without endorsing it or distancing himself from it, which the Climacus of *Postscript* attributes to Christianity while distancing himself from it, and which Anti-Climacus attributes to Christianity while endorsing it. This view of the moral psychology and meta-ethics of Christianity I take to be Kierkegaard's own view, which he presents from an outsider's and an insider's perspective because it looks quite different from these two perspectives.

1

Kant's Account of Freedom

Kant wanted to maintain something very close to a traditional libertarian conception of free will[1] while advancing novel accounts of the objectivity of theoretical and moral judgement that stand in tension with freedom so construed. This chapter and chapter 2 explore (respectively) those two sources of tension and Kant's efforts to deal with them over the course of his career. The point of these chapters is not to present a unified interpretation of Kant's thinking on freedom. Were such a unified interpretation readily available, the post-Kantian development could not have taken the form that it did.

The issue of the compatibility of freedom and theoretical objectivity arises in the way that it does for Kant because his case for the objectivity of theoretical claims relies in part on his view of causality—in particular, on the claim that the (phenomenal) universality of deterministic causation is a condition of the possibility of experience. The first *Critique*'s third antinomy shows that the transcendental idealist position might leave space for the possibility of some (non-phenomenal) spontaneous causality, though it leaves a number of questions unanswered. The first concerns the grounds Kant can offer for thinking that human wills are characterized by spontaneous causality. Kant's account of this issue develops over time, though his commitment to the necessity of such an account remains constant: ought implies can, for Kant, and so believing that one is bound by moral laws requires believing that one is actually, not merely possibly, free. Despite suggestions to the contrary in the discussion of the third antinomy, Kant will ultimately deny that there can be theoretical grounds for thinking the human will to be a spontaneous cause in the sense defined there. Instead he offers a practical argument for freedom, based on the moral law as a fact of reason and an inference from a known law to a cause that acts (or can act) in accordance with it. This solution raises two further difficulties, however.

The first arises out of Kant's account of how two entirely different sorts of law (deterministic causal laws and the moral law) can apply to one and the same thing

---

[1] Kant held what today would be called an agent-causal account of free will. The only aspect of the contemporary form of this position he rejects is its denial of the truth of determinism. But, as I will explain, Kant's embrace of determinism was conditional on its not being true of things as they are in themselves (and therefore of agents as they are in themselves). He replaces libertarian indeterminism with transcendental idealism.

(human action). One of the aims of the *Critique of Judgment* is to offer a way of understanding how these two types of laws might fit together in such a way as to be complementary rather than conflicting—a way of conceptualizing nature such that the imperative of human autonomy and the principle of mechanistic determinism can be seen as cooperative. (It is a development of this idea that Schelling will present in his early work. Later, though, Schelling will argue that this solution is one that poses problems for individual freedom at least as serious as those posed by the straightforward mechanistic determinism this view replaced.)

The second difficulty has to do with the compatibility of the sort of moral objectivity that is possible given Kant's theoretical position and freedom in the same (libertarian) sense. The claim that the will is able freely and intentionally to choose the immoral over the moral (a claim that seems to be required if moral wrong is to be imputable) stands in tension with the identification of morality and rationality upon which Kant's argument for the objective validity of the moral law, and hence the validity of the attribution of freedom to human agents, rests. This is the problem of the possibility of moral evil on Kant's account, and it is the topic of chapter 2.

These are, in principle, separate problems. In post-Kantian idealism, however (here the focus will be primarily Schelling's early system, though this is true of Hegel as well), moral and theoretical objectivity are conjoined in such a way that the libertarian conception of freedom Kant originally sought to preserve is eliminated entirely. It is this development against which the later (post-1809) Schelling and Kierkegaard will react. Understanding that reaction requires placing it against the background of the options that Kant's approach to the problem of freedom first made available, and the dilemmas it posed.

The first part of this chapter (§I) will describe the view of freedom and its relation to the claims of theoretical reason that I believe Kant wants to defend. In §II, I will discuss Kant's evolving strategy for demonstrating that we in fact have free will, and in §III, I will discuss challenges mounted by Kant's contemporaries to his transcendental idealist solution to the freedom problem, and examine his effort to solve the unity-of-reason problem in the third *Critique*. Although there is no single account in the literature with which I agree on all points, readers familiar with Kant's account of freedom should nonetheless find little to surprise them in this chapter. Sections I and II are meant to serve as background to the discussion of the problem of evil in Kant's moral psychology in chapter 2, and §III as background to the discussion of idealist metaphysics in chapter 3.

I. OUTLINE OF KANT'S VIEW OF FREEDOM

Kant's view of freedom can be broken down into four main claims. (1) We have freedom construed roughly as libertarians construe it: our actions are causally dependent on us rather than on preceding events, and could at least sometimes be different from what they in fact are.[2] (2) The natural world, of which we are a part, is a mechanistically deterministic system—that is, one in which all events are causally dependent on preceding events and could not be different from what they in fact are. (3) These two claims would be incompatible were transcendental realism true (that is: were the natural world of (2) the world as it is in itself). (4) Since transcendental idealism is true, however, (1) and (2) are compatible after all (as free causality and mechanistic causality belong to different conceptual realms). In this section I will briefly explain these four claims in turn. In the section that follows I examine (1), and in the third section (4), in a bit more detail. A large literature exists on (2) already, and Kant has not much to say about (3) beyond the standard appeal to intuitions about responsibility, so the brief discussions of these I give in this section will suffice.

Causal ultimacy; alternate possibilities

1. We have freedom construed roughly as libertarians construe it: our actions are causally dependent on ourselves (or our acts of will) rather than on preceding events, and could at least sometimes be different from what they in fact are.

Kant employed the term 'freedom' in a number of senses.[3] I will introduce four here: transcendental; practical; comparative; and the freedom of rational self-determination. The first is the one that raises the problem of compatibility with determinism; Kant calls it 'transcendental freedom' or 'absolute spontaneity'. This notion is introduced in the discussion of the third antinomy of the *Critique of Pure Reason*, where it is defined as a causality which is not itself determined by any preceding cause, or the spontaneous creation of a new causal sequence. It is 'a causality through which something takes place, the cause of which is not itself determined, in accordance with necessary laws, by another cause antecedent to it, that is to say, an *absolute spontaneity* of the cause, whereby a series of appearances, which proceeds in accordance with laws of nature, begins *of itself*' (*KrV* A446/ B474). Kant here claims that this spontaneous causality, undetermined by any preceding cause, is a component of our ordinary conception of freedom. Although it is only a part of that ordinary conception, it is a part required for moral responsibility: 'The transcendental idea of freedom does not by any means constitute the whole content of the psychological concept of that name, which is mainly empirical. The transcendental idea stands only for the absolute

---

[2] There are two distinct claims here; Kant holds both and thinks the first entails the second. His view is a species of agent-causal account, though of course it differs from standard agent-causal accounts because of the transcendental idealist story I discuss under (4). It also differs from conventional libertarianism for the same reason: Kant's transcendental idealism allowed him to embrace (phenomenal) determinism. That this does not make him a compatibilist in any recognizable sense, I argue under (3).

[3] Lewis White Beck counted as many as five (in Beck (1987))—a list Allison (1990: 1) thinks 'could easily be expanded with a little fine-tuning'. The list I give here is not meant to be exhaustive, but instead to identify as many senses as I will employ to get clear on the problems in which I am interested.

spontaneity of an action, as the proper ground of its imputability' (*KrV* A448/ B476). Here the suggestion is that transcendental freedom is a sufficient condition of an action's imputability. This does not seem to be Kant's considered view, though; being the action of an agent capable of practical reason seems also to be required. Transcendental freedom is certainly, however, a necessary condition of imputability on Kant's view.

The grounds Kant offers for this assertion are standard ones. To be imputable to an agent an action must have its causal source in that agent. It must be under the agent's control. This means, for Kant, that the agent must have been able to do or refrain from doing it. Being the causal source of an action means being able to act otherwise than we in fact do. Moral blame presupposes not only that an agent's conduct ought to have been different, but also that it could have been different.[4]

This requirement is the source of the *prima facie* problem of the compatibility of free and natural causality.

[T]o ascribe to substances in the world itself such a power [viz. a 'transcendental power of freedom'], can never be permissible; for, should this be done, that connection of appearances determining one another with necessity according to universal laws, which we entitle nature, and with it the criterion of empirical truth, whereby experience is distinguished from dreaming, would almost entirely disappear. Side by side with such a lawless faculty of freedom, nature [as an ordered system] is hardly thinkable; the influences of the former would so unceasingly alter the laws of the latter that the appearances which in their natural course are regular and uniform would be reduced to disorder and incoherence. (*KrV* A451/B479)

Kant remarks in the antinomy discussion that it is *only* freedom in the transcendental sense that poses this problem for speculative reason (at *KrV* A448/B476).

The suggestion is that what Kant calls 'freedom in the practical sense' need not pose the same problem. Kant describes *practical* freedom (the second sense of 'freedom' I will discuss) as a capacity to refrain from acting in accordance with one's immediate inclinations by calling up representations of temporally remote aims or goods. I take it that Kant's description of practical freedom, at least in the first *Critique*, is meant to be the description of a capacity no one denies human beings have—a capacity that distinguishes the wills of morally responsible adults from those of animals or very young children. The description from the antinomy is as follows:

Freedom in the practical sense is the will's independence of coercion through sensuous impulses. For a will is sensuous, in so far as it is *pathologically affected*, i.e. by sensuous motives; it is *animal* (*arbitrium brutum*), if it can be pathologically necessitated. The human will is certainly an *arbitrium sensitivum*, not, however, *brutum* but *liberum*. For

---

[4] See the discussion of the malicious lie at *KrV* A555/B583 and, in the *Critique of Practical Reason*, of the gallows at 5: 30 and of the theft at 5: 95, and finally in the *Groundwork* at 4: 455: 'All human beings think of themselves as having a free will. From this come all judgments upon actions as being such that they *ought to have been done even though they were not done*.'

sensibility does not necessitate its action. There is in man a power of self-determination, independently of any coercion through sensuous impulses. (*KrV* A534/B562)

Kant describes practical freedom in the Canon (at *KrV* A801–2/B829–30) in similar, slightly more explicit, terms. He adds, for instance, that a practically free will is one which can be determined 'through motives which are represented only by reason', though his specification of this claim makes it clear that this is not to be read as equivalent to 'through moral motives alone'—for the deliverances of reason at issue here are imperatives of prudence: 'representations of what, in a more indirect manner, is useful or injurious', considerations 'as to what is desirable in respect of our whole state'.

Kant's view of the relationship between practical and transcendental freedom is obscure. In the antinomy discussion, he writes that practical freedom is 'based in' transcendental freedom, and that:

The denial of transcendental freedom must, therefore, involve the elimination of all practical freedom. For practical freedom presupposes that although something has not happened, it *ought* to have happened, and that its cause, [as found] in the [field of] appearance, is not therefore, so determining that it excludes a causality of our will—a causality which, independently of those natural causes, and even contrary to their force and influence, can produce something that is determined in the time-order in accordance with empirical laws, and which can therefore begin a series of events *entirely of itself.* (*KrV* A534/B562)

The suggestion is that, were it not for transcendental freedom, our wills would be no different, from the moral point of view, from those of animals or small children. In the discussion in the Canon, however, he remarks, 'Whether reason is not, in the actions through which it prescribes laws, itself again determined by other influences, and whether that which, in relation to sensuous impulses, is entitled freedom, may not, in relation to higher and more remote operating causes, be nature again, is a question which in the practical field does not concern us' (*KrV* A803/B831). The suggestion here is the opposite, namely that practical freedom *may* be compatible with natural determinism. That is, in both the practical and transcendental conceptions, freedom requires that reason have causal force in the determination of the will; but the transcendental sense adds a further requirement: that reason be an *uncaused* cause.[5] One standard explanation for the discrepancy between the two accounts appeals to the fact that the Canon was written earlier than the antinomy section, and not revised to reflect changes in Kant's thinking about freedom.[6] The fact that the discussion of the issue in the *Critique*

---

[5] 'While we thus through experience know practical freedom to be one of the causes in nature, namely, to be a causality of reason in the determination of the will, transcendental freedom demands the independence of this reason—in respect of its causality, in beginning a series of appearances—from all determining causes of the sensible world. Transcendental freedom is thus, as it would seem, contrary to the law of nature, and therefore to all possible experience; and so remains a problem' (*KrV* A803/B831).

[6] For discussions of this 'patchwork' explanation cf., e.g., Carnois (1987: 29), Allison (1990: 54ff.) and Allison (1996: 109ff.).

of Practical Reason agrees with the antinomy discussion is taken as evidence for this interpretation.

In that work, Kant speaks of a 'comparative' concept of freedom (the third sense I mentioned above) in the context of a discussion of the compatibilist approach to freedom dominant among his contemporaries. This comparative concept is that:

> according to which that is sometimes called a free effect, the determining natural ground of which lies within the acting being, e.g., that which a projectile accomplishes when it is in free motion, in which case one uses the word 'freedom' because while it is in flight it is not impelled from without; or as we also call the motion of a clock a free motion because it moves the hands itself, which therefore do not need to be pushed externally; in the same way the actions of the human being, although necessary by their determining grounds which preceded them in time, are yet called free because the actions are caused from within, by representations produced by our own powers, whereby desires are evoked on occasion of circumstances and hence actions are produced at our own discretion. (*KpV* 5: 96)

This description of comparative freedom seems to match the description of practical freedom in the Canon very closely, except that here what is at issue is an *explicitly* compatibilist conception. That is, comparative freedom is not presented as something we might have regardless of whether we have transcendental freedom; it is described as a sort of freedom had by beings who do not have transcendental freedom. Kant explicitly opposes it to transcendental freedom (now freedom 'in the proper sense') in this discussion, and compares the being who has it with Leibniz's *automaton spirituale* (at *KpV* 5: 97). The agnosticism of the Canon discussion (where we could know from experience that we have practical freedom without bothering ourselves with the question of whether we have transcendental freedom)[7] has been replaced by explicit soft determinism in Kant's characterization of *comparative* freedom.

Does reason have causal force in the case of comparative freedom? Kant's discussion in the second *Critique* suggests that it might not. Although the 'inner mechanism' that results in actions on the comparative conception is one that proceeds by means of representations (used to evoke desires and so produce actions 'at our discretion'), there is no suggestion that comparative freedom requires anything *more* than the capacity to get oneself to do something (or prevent oneself from doing it) by means of a representation (e.g. of a temporally remote effect of the action). Such a capacity can be produced even in beings (trained animals, for example) which lack the capacity to reason, even merely prudentially. Acting on both prudential and moral reasons surely requires the capacity Kant here describes, but there is no such requirement in the other direction. Tellingly, Kant fails to contrast human wills and animal wills in the discussion of comparative freedom at *KpV* 5: 95ff.[8]

---

[7] 'The question of transcendental freedom is a matter for speculative knowledge only, and when we are dealing with the practical we can leave it aside as being an issue with which we have no concern' (*KrV* A803–4/B831–2).

[8] Though his early commentator Bernhardi does, on the grounds that comparative freedom requires both the capacity to represent and the capacity to deliberate, only the former of which he sees Kant as ascribing to animals. Cf. Bernhardi (1796: 245–6).

This is one reason to think that practical and comparative freedom cannot be different names for the same capacity according to Kant, as some commentators have maintained.[9] A second reason is that beings who are practically free are subject to oughts of some sort (cf. *KrV* A534/B562, quoted above), whereas beings with merely comparative freedom cannot be (cf. *KpV* 5: 95, where Kant wonders how it is possible to say of a causally necessitated action that it *ought* to have been omitted, and *KpV* 5: 97, where he remarks that merely comparatively free beings can be subject to no moral law). A third reason to think these two senses of 'freedom' must be different is that Kant actually begins the second *Critique* discussion of comparative freedom by *contrasting* it with practical freedom.

I think we should see comparative and transcendental freedom as competing accounts of the metaphysical commitments we make when we assert that we are free in the practical sense. Ultimately, Kant rejects the former and embraces the latter account. 'Practical freedom' means the same thing in each of the different discussions of it: the capacity to act for reasons rather than from (immediate) desires. This is (in each case) a capacity we are directly aware of having: we know it through experience (*KrV* A803/B831), presumably the experience of practical deliberation. The discrepancies in the account of whether practical freedom requires transcendental freedom reflect a process of determination of Kant's view on that matter. Kant starts off with the view that claims about practical freedom might be independent of claims about transcendental freedom (that is, we might be able to speak about freedom from a practical point of view without making any metaphysical commitments). This view is expressed even more clearly in Kant's review of Schulz's *Attempt at an introduction to a doctrine of morals for all human beings regardless of different religions*:

> In fact, the practical concept of freedom has nothing to do with the speculative concept, which is abandoned entirely to metaphysicians. For I can be quite indifferent as to the origin of my state in which I am now to act; I ask only what I now have to do, and then freedom is a necessary practical presupposition and an idea under which alone I can regard commands of reason as valid. Even the most obstinate sceptic grants that, when it comes to acting, all sophistical scruples about a universally deceptive illusion must come to nothing. (8: 13)

In the *Groundwork* Kant's effort to deduce the reality of moral obligation (from the reality of freedom) makes it clear that this agnosticism is untenable. (Kant's unclarity on this point explains the strange 'circle' discussion, to which I will return in §II.) His final view is the one given in the second *Critique* (and prefigured in the antinomy discussion): the assertion of practical freedom *does* require a positive stance on the question of transcendental freedom. The freedom required for practical purposes can*not* be 'mere nature again'. The second *Critique* also contains the justification for such a stance (because now Kant's view has shifted to one in which

---

[9] Cf., e.g., Ameriks (2000c: 193ff.). Allison is correct to distinguish the two. Cf. Allison (1990: 61).

our knowledge of freedom is based in our knowledge of the moral law—I will discuss this shift in view in §II).[10]

The fourth use of the term 'freedom' has no unproblematic name in Kant's texts. Nor is it unambiguously explained in any of them. Instead it underlies much of Kant's thinking about freedom without being sufficiently separated out from other concepts at crucial junctures. I will call it 'rational self-determination' (though it is also tempting to call it simply 'rationality'); Kant calls versions of it 'autonomy' (one of many distinct uses of that term) and 'positive freedom'.

A being that is rationally self-determining operates according to a set of laws distinct from natural laws: laws of reason. To say that laws of reason are distinct from natural laws is to say that there will be no reduction of one set of laws to the other, and so no type–type identity between thoughts or behaviours produced in accordance with one and thoughts or behaviours produced in accordance with the other. This is not to say that any being free in this sense will necessarily be transcendentally free as well; token–token identity may hold, in which case the reasoner will be causally determined in the same way as non-rational things in nature (even if not *qua* reasoner). Such a being would be rationally self-determining but not morally responsible on Kant's view, because the results of his or her reasonings would be causally necessitated by events preceding them in time and so would both have their causal impetus outside the agent and be unavoidable.[11]

Kant distinguishes two ways in which beings like us might be said to be rationally self-determining: as makers of judgements and as willers of actions (alternatively: as theoretical and practical reasoners). The argument Kant makes in the first *Critique* and the *Groundwork* from theoretical spontaneity to practical spontaneity in the case of finite rational beings (which I will discuss in the beginning of §II) relies on the assumption that anything rationally self-determining in thinking is also rationally self-determining in acting, and the fact that Kant gives up this line of argument indicates that he has ceased to believe there is good reason to think that assumption true. The same line of argument also relies on a further assumption: that rational self-determination in its theoretical manifestation entails transcendental freedom. I have said that there is no reason to think it must (in either the theoretical or the practical case), but it is clear that at various points and for various reasons Kant disagrees. (I discuss these reasons in §II and in chapter 2.)

Two sorts of property naturally fall under the rubric of freedom so defined: (1) one had by rational agents at those moments when they are properly functioning (that is, behaving rationally); and (2) one had by rational agents per se, whether

---

[10] This view is distinct from the one advanced by Ameriks (2000c: 191ff.). Ameriks explains the apparent shift in view on the basis of a loss of confidence on Kant's part in a theoretical proof of transcendental freedom he had started out by thinking he had. The main problem (admittedly far from decisive) that I see with that interpretation is that I cannot see why anyone genuinely convinced he had such a proof would go out of his way to insist that no such proof is required.

[11] Sellars (1971: 21ff.) makes a good case for this.

they are properly functioning or not (regardless of whether the malfunction is momentary or protracted, so long as the *capacity* for proper functioning remains). In the first case, freedom is equated with rationality as a type of behaviour;[12] in the second, freedom is equated with rationality as a capacity that persists over variations in type of behaviour. Kant uses the term 'autonomy' to refer to both these properties, without drawing a clear distinction between them.[13] (This has been a cause of some confusion; I will return to it in the next chapter.)

What does it mean to say that rational self-determination is a form of *self-determination*? A number of quite distinct interpretations have been proposed, ranging from constructivist readings, on which rational beings create the laws that govern their activity by engaging in that very activity,[14] to realist readings, on which rational beings apprehend laws of reason that exist independently of their activity,[15] to combined readings on which the authority of such laws is explained by the assent of the rational being to be bound by them, but their content is explained by considerations independent of the fact that the agent has consented to be bound by them.[16] Nothing I say here (and in particular, nothing I argue for in chapter 2) rests on taking one or the other of these readings to be the correct one. The problems with the link Kant tries to forge between transcendental freedom and rational self-determination are similar on each of these readings.

In *Groundwork* III, Kant argues that we can see what he calls 'negative' and 'positive' conceptions of freedom as two aspects of the same capacity. Freedom negatively defined is 'that property of [the causality of living beings insofar as they are rational] that it can be efficient independently of alien causes *determining* it, just as *natural necessity* is the property of the causality of all non-rational beings to be determined to activity by the influence of alien causes' (4: 446). The distinction appears to be one between causes whose action is necessitated by other, external causes (non-rational beings; middle links in a causal chain) and causes whose action is not so necessitated (rational beings; first links in a causal chain). The move from the negative to the positive definition is in this passage:

Since the concept of a causality brings with it that of laws in accordance with which, by something that we call a cause, something else, namely an effect, must be posited, so freedom, although it is not a property of the will in accordance with natural laws, is not for that reason lawless but must instead be a causality in accordance with immutable laws but of a special kind; for otherwise a free will would be an absurdity. Natural necessity was a heteronomy of efficient causes, since every effect was possible only in accordance with the law that something else determines the efficient cause to causality; what, then, can freedom

---

[12] In one sense of 'rational' an agent is rational only when it makes the right decision, and in one sense of 'self-determining' an agent who fails to behave rationally is failing to determine itself: other less remote operating causes have intervened (inclination has taken over), and in one quite ordinary sense of freedom, the individual is not acting freely.

[13] Engstrom (1988) distinguishes between a broader and narrower notion of autonomy (and parallel notions of heteronomy) along these lines.

[14] Cf., e.g., Rawls (1999), Korsgaard (1996a, 1996b, 2003), and O'Neill (1989).

[15] Cf., e.g., Ameriks (2003) and Wood (1999).   [16] Cf. Reath (1994).

of the will be other than autonomy, that is, the will's property of being a law to itself? (*GMS* 4: 446–7)

The transition Kant describes here is problematic, in so far as it seems to rely on an equation of (1) action in accordance with a law that does not *specify* the causal dependence of actions on events preceding them in time (as all 'laws of nature' in fact do), and (2) action in accordance with a law that is in some sense self-imposed. The aspect of the law of nature that made it unfeasible as a law of freedom was not that *it* (i.e., the law itself) originated in something outside of the will, but instead that according to it the *causal determination* of the action of a finite will must have its origin outside the will (from other events preceding the action in time). In other words, the problem with natural causal laws (as discussed both in the definition of 'negative freedom' and elsewhere) is not that the law itself has the wrong sort of origin but that it attributes the wrong sort of origin to the causal impetus of actions.

The transition from negative to positive freedom here looks to be a transition from transcendental spontaneity to rational self-determination, a claim to the effect that everything transcendentally free must, as a condition of possibility of transcendental freedom, operate according to a set of laws that is its own. (I will discuss this connection, and this passage, at greater length in the next section.) Together with the claim that rational self-determination is impossible without transcendental spontaneity, it constitutes what Allison has called Kant's 'reciprocity thesis'—the thesis that rational self-determination and transcendental freedom entail one another.

Determinism within appearances

2. The natural world is a mechanistically deterministic system, one in which events are causally dependent on preceding events and could not be different from how they in fact are.

Only the first of the four senses of freedom I have discussed—transcendental freedom—is immediately at issue in the freedom-determinism problem. Each of the other senses is indirectly bound up with it, because Kant introduces each attached to a specific relation to transcendental freedom: comparative freedom entails its denial, and both practical freedom and rational self-determination (on Kant's mature view of these) entail its affirmation.

Kant believed the world as we experience it must be a fully deterministic system. He justifies this view primarily in the second analogy.[17] The argument

---

[17] The discussions of Kant's argument in the second analogy which informed the view I present here are those of Allison (1983: 216–34; 1996: 80–91), Strawson (1966: 133–46), Bennett (1966: 219–29), Harper and Meerbote (1984), and Friedman (1992). The introductory essay of Harper and Meerbote (1984) provides an illuminating (though now outdated) survey of interpretations of the second analogy.

there is roughly as follows: being able to distinguish between objective and subjective occurrences (the distinction between objective temporal order and subjective temporal order) requires being able to distinguish between sequences of representations that could be reversed and sequences of representations that could not be reversed.

> If we enquire what new character *relation to an object* confers upon our representations, what dignity they thereby acquire, we find that it results only in subjecting the representations to a rule, and so in necessitating us to connect them in some one specific manner; and conversely, that only in so far as our representations are necessitated in a certain order as regards their time-relations do they acquire objective meaning. (*KrV* A197/ B242–3)

We can make this sort of distinction (between reversible and irreversible series of representations) only on the basis of beliefs about a necessary causal order of events. Subjective sequences are contingent; objective sequences are causally necessary. This rule, by which we determine something according to succession of time, is, that the condition under which an event invariably and necessarily follows is to be found in what precedes the event. The principle of sufficient reason is thus the ground of possible experience, that is, of objective knowledge of appearances in respect of their relation in the succession of time. (*KrV* A200–1/B246)

There are two ways of taking 'causally necessary order of events' in this context. According to a more modest reading, Kant aims to show merely that every event has some cause that precedes it in time and renders it inevitable. According to a more robust reading, Kant claims to show in addition that like events have like causes, that there are lawlike regularities linking cause and event types.[18] On both interpretations, however, the argument in the second analogy precludes freedom in the libertarian sense. If all events are necessitated by preceding causes, and actions are events, then actions are necessitated by preceding causes. But this is all that is required for conflict with the requirement that actions have their causal ground in agents rather than in preceding events. What matters for Kant is less the lawlikeness of causation in accordance with natural laws than the necessitation of the caused event by the causing event.[19]

Incompatibilism

3. Claims (1) and (2) would be contradictory were transcendental realism true (that is: were the natural world of (2) to be taken to be the world as it is in itself).

Though it is now a commonplace among commentators and contemporary Kantians that Kant's moral commitments taken on their own leave the soft

---

[18] Strawson (1966: 138) attributes the more robust view to Kant. Bennett (1974: 225ff.), Allison (1983: 222–34) and Beck (1978) defend the more modest reading.

[19] On a view like the one suggested by Beck (1960: 191ff.), wherein the second analogy should be read as a (clumsy) statement of the view of causality as a regulative but not constitutive principle, the problem is avoided.

determinist option open,[20] Kant himself was unmistakably an incompatibilist according to the ordinary meaning of the term. The reasons he offers for thinking free agency inconsistent with determinism are the standard ones. If every event is determined by preceding events and the laws of nature, then all actions, *qua* events, are necessitated. 'Obviously, if all causality in the sensible world were mere nature, every event would be determined by another in time, in accordance with necessary laws. Appearances, in determining the will, would have in the actions of the will their natural effects, and would render the actions necessary' (*KrV* A534/B562). The ultimate determinants of an agent's behaviour, being in the past, would thus be beyond the agent's control, and the act would be unavoidable:

For from the [necessity in causal relations] it follows that every event, and consequently every action that takes place at a point in time, is necessary under the condition of what was in the preceding time. Now, since time past is no longer within my control, every action that I perform must be necessary by determining grounds *that are not within my control*, that is, I am never free at the point of time in which I act. (*KpV* 5: 94)

Both conditions on libertarian freedom stated above would be violated. The freedom involved in moral agency presupposes that the causal origin of an action lie within the agent and that agents could sometimes do otherwise than they in fact do; it:

presupposes that although something has not happened, it *ought* to have happened, and that its cause, [as found] in the [field of] appearance, is not therefore so determining that it excludes a causality of our will—a causality which, independently of those natural causes, and even contrary to their force and influence, can produce something that is determined in the time-order in accordance with empirical laws, and which can therefore begin a series of events *entirely of itself.* (*KrV* A534/B562)

Together with his account of moral grounds (and corresponding denial that there can be any theoretical grounds) for belief in God, Kant's incompatibilism was one of the two most controversial features of his practical philosophy in its initial reception.[21] The philosophical landscape of his day was dominated by two

---

[20] Cf., e.g., Ameriks (2000b: 19ff. and 31ff.; 2000c: 226), Korsgaard (1996a: *passim*, but especially the discussion of Kant's 'practical compatibilism' at 209ff.), Meerbote, in Harper and Meerbote (1984: 138–63), and Wood (1999: 173–4 and 177ff.). O'Neill comments critically on the willingness of contemporary Kantians to conjoin Kant's moral theory with the empiricist approach dominant in contemporary moral psychology: 'Many contemporary proponents of "Kantian" ethics want the nicer bits of his ethical conclusions without the metaphysical troubles. They hope to base a "Kantian" account of justice and rights on broadly empiricist conceptions of self, freedom and action' (O'Neill 1989: p. ix). O'Neill's own reading of Kant in *Constructions of Reason* is an instance of the 'primacy of the practical' approach (whose first prominent proponent was Fichte). See O'Neill (1989: 59ff.). The same combination of broadly Kantian ethical theory with a compatibilist (in the modern sense) approach to freedom emerged in the 1890s and informed the views developed by the early Schelling and Hegel. Cf., e.g., Hoffbauer (1798: especially the discussion of freedom at 135–6 and 1799: especially 192).

[21] Kant was not only writing for a clearly compatibilist audience of Leibniz-Wolffians (including Schwab, Feder, Rehberg, and (somewhat later) Jenisch and Hoffbauer); one of their chief complaints about him concerned his incompatibilist position—cf., e.g., Feder (1788: 217ff.), Jenisch (1796: 383ff.), Rehberg's review of the *Critique of Practical Reason* in Bittner and Cramer (1975: 179–96, esp. 191ff.) and Schulz (1975: 230–56, esp. 246ff.).

schools, both compatibilist (empiricists and Leibniz-Wolffians). It is against these that he directs the extended attack on compatibilism in the *Critique of Practical Reason*, calling their 'comparative' concept of freedom (discussed above) a 'wretched subterfuge' by which 'some still let themselves be put off . . . so think they have solved, with a little quibbling about words, that difficult problem on the solution of which millennia have worked in vain' (*KpV* 5: 96). The comparative conception of freedom, as I have said, is one according to which free and unfree acts are distinguished by the different sorts of (naturalistic and deterministic) causes that produced them. Free acts are caused by desires (internal causes, to use the language Kant there employs); unfree acts are caused by external compulsion. What distinguishes such views from his own, Kant tells us, is that they deny that an act's having been done freely entails that it could have been omitted or performed differently. Since standard compatibilist accounts either deny the 'could have done otherwise' condition on moral responsibility[22] or at least interpret it in such a way as to eliminate the conflict with deterministic causality,[23] the text cannot be read as allowing a compatibilist position in anything like the contemporary sense.

Transcendental idealism

4. Transcendental idealism is true, however, which makes (1) and (2) compatible after all, since freedom and causal determination are parts of different total descriptions of things, and so need not come into conflict.

In the first edition of the *Critique of Pure Reason*, Kant described transcendental idealism as the doctrine that 'appearances are to be regarded as being, one and all, representations only, not things in themselves, and that time and space are therefore only sensible forms of our intuition, not determinations given as existing by themselves, nor conditions of objects viewed as things in themselves' (*KrV* A369). Space and time, as the form of our intuitions, are properties only of our intuitions of things, not of things as they are in themselves.[24] The schematized categories (the ones that incorporate spatio-temporal determinations) are applicable to things only as objects of possible intuitions, not to things as they are apart from any intuitions we might have of them. The notion of cause at issue in the second analogy is such a schematized category, and so the argument there applies only to phenomena. Of things as they are in themselves, causal determinism cannot be predicated, simply because the schematized concept of causality (the one involved in the determinism thesis: that every event is necessitated by a cause

---

[22] Cf. Frankfurt (1969).   [23] Cf. Moore (1912: chapter 6).

[24] I will use the terms 'noumenal', 'intelligible', and 'in itself' (or 'in themselves')—interchangeably, because nothing I have to say relies on any differences in Kant's usage of the three terms—to refer to however it is that things are in abstraction from the conditions of possible experience, and the substantives of these terms 'noumenal realm', 'intelligible realm', 'things in themselves' to refer to the totality of things so conceived.

preceding it in time) can apply only to things in time—but that means, only to things as appearances.

Although we cannot apply schematized categories to things in themselves, Kant thought, we can apply non-schematized categories to them (e.g., ground/consequent). The application of non-schematized categories does not allow us to make any theoretically justified claims about how things in themselves are (because the only theoretically justified claims we can make are empirical: they require intuitions, which are always at least temporal). It does, however, allow us to formulate coherent *thoughts* about things in themselves, about how they might (or might not) be. Such thoughts are subject to logical criteria (of coherence) and may even have non-theoretical sources of justification. (The paradigmatic such source is practical reason: the practical postulates of the existence of God and the immortality of the soul are practically justified but theoretically unjustifiable (though also unfalsifiable) statements about how things are in themselves. I will discuss this idea further in §II.)

Like everything else, we are noumena as well as phenomena—or rather, there is a noumenal ground of human agency as well as the (deterministic) phenomenal grounds—though we can claim no knowledge of anything that might be called 'the noumenal self'. In fact we have no theoretical grounds even for asserting a one-to-one correspondence between individual human beings and distinct noumenal entities. There might, for all we know, be one world-soul that is the noumenal basis for all phenomenal human agency. (Kant seems to have believed he had an argument for rejecting this possibility; I will discuss it in §III.) But, for all we know, it might be the case that there is some such correspondence, and that the noumenal ground of human agency possesses the absolute spontaneity required by moral responsibility. In that case, human causality would have a double aspect: mechanistically determined as phenomenon, and absolutely spontaneous as noumenon.

The concept of causality as *natural necessity*, as distinguished from the concept of causality as *freedom*, concerns only the existence of things insofar as it is *determinable in time* and hence as appearances, as opposed to their causality as things in themselves. Now, if one takes the determinations of the existence of things in time for determinations of things in themselves (which is the most usual way of representing them), then the necessity in causal relations can in no way be united with freedom; instead they are opposed to each other as contradictory. . . . Consequently, if one still wants to save [freedom], no other path remains than to ascribe the existence of a thing so far as it is determinable in time, and so too its causality in accordance with the law of *natural necessity, only to appearance, and to ascribe freedom to the same being as a thing in itself.* (*KpV* 5: 94)

Kant goes on to describe how this doctrine makes it possible to hold, at one and the same time, that the actions of agents as empirical beings are, in principle, as predictable as a lunar or solar eclipse, and nonetheless that, as things in themselves, they are absolutely spontaneous (*KpV* 5: 99). That is, 'the same action which, as belonging to the sensible world, is always sensibly conditioned—that is, mechanically necessary—can at the same time, as belonging to the causality of an acting being so far as it belongs to the intelligible world, have as its basis a sensibly unconditioned causality and so be thought as free' (*KpV* 5: 104). Transcendental idealism forbids taking determinations of the existence of things in time to be determinations of things in themselves, and so eliminates the *prima facie* conflict pointed out by the incompatibilist.[25] Kant thought it was the only possibility for eliminating this conflict:

The union of causality as freedom with causality as natural mechanism, the first of which is established by the moral law, the second by the law of nature, and indeed in one and the same subject, the human being, is impossible without representing him with regard to the first as a being in itself but with regard to the second as an appearance, the former in *pure*, the latter in *empirical* consciousness. Otherwise the contradiction of reason with itself is unavoidable. (*KpV* 5: 6n)

Of course transcendental idealism alone entails only that transcendental freedom *can* be thought—that the notion of free causality does not result in a contradiction when applied to things in themselves, in the way that it does when applied to natural items—not that it ought to be thought, or indeed that we have any reason whatever for thinking it. Transcendental idealism is not supposed to entail that we actually have transcendental freedom. Nor does it give us any concrete ways of thinking about how such causality might operate, so the 'possibility' at issue here is mere non-contradiction (not what Kant would call 'real possibility'). Finally, it does not offer much in the way of guidance on the question of how the two sorts of causality (natural and spontaneous) are supposed to fit together (and to be predicated of the same entity: the human agent in its phenomenal and noumenal aspects). This was a major source of concern among contemporary critics in their treatments of Kant's view of freedom. I will fill out these two parts of the story in the next two sections.

II. KANT'S TWO STRATEGIES FOR DEMONSTRATING THE REALITY OF TRANSCENDENTAL FREEDOM

Kant thought not only that we might have transcendental freedom; he thought that we actually do have it, and that this could be demonstrated. The nature of the defence of this view that he gave, however, changed over the course of the 1780s; the main works of the critical period contain quite different accounts. His original

---

[25] This part of the story remains the same over the course of the critical period. The quotations I have given in the main text are from the second *Critique*; exactly similar remarks can be found in the *Groundwork* (at 4: 457) and the first *Critique* (at A536–7/B564–5, A541/B569, and Bxxv–xxix). The similarity in these formulations is significant, especially given the differences that emerged over time in some other aspects of the doctrine of freedom.

strategy was to proceed from the spontaneity of theoretical reason, and to argue that if reason is also practical, an analogous spontaneity must be operative in its practical application. Traces of this strategy are visible in the first *Critique* and the *Groundwork*. The problem of showing pure reason to be in fact practical remained, however, and so Kant adopted a different line of argument, arguing for freedom based on immediate awareness of moral duty (or, in terms introduced in the *Groundwork*, our *interest* in morality), together with some version of the principle 'ought implies can'. This strategy is also discernible in the *Groundwork*, and is dominant in the second *Critique*.

Kant was convinced over the whole course of this development that transcendental freedom and the bindingness of the moral law upon those transcendentally free stand in a relation of mutual entailment (what Allison has called the 'reciprocity thesis'). What changed was his opinion as to which could be established independently, about which should come first epistemically. (I will look more closely at the nature of this connection in the next chapter.)

Transcendental freedom derived from the spontaneity of reason in its theoretical employment

In Kant's early strategy, the one visible in parts of the first *Critique* and *Groundwork* III discussions, transcendental freedom was to be independently established, and the bindingness of the moral law would be derived from that.[26] This strategy, as employed in the first *Critique*, was based on two assumptions: (1) Reason in its theoretical employment requires absolute spontaneity; and (2) Reason has a practical employment (i.e., rational beings are also rational *agents*, possessing rational wills).

In the third antinomy, for instance, Kant not only argues that transcendental idealism leaves open the conceptual possibility of spontaneous causality in the intelligible realm; he also argues that we have grounds for thinking such causality exists (those given in the thesis)[27] and for thinking that finite rational agents have such causality. These grounds are not empirical, clearly, but empirical knowledge is not the only self-knowledge available to us. 'Man, . . . who knows all the rest of nature solely through the senses, knows himself also through pure apperception; and this, indeed, in acts and inner determinations which he cannot regard as impressions of the senses' (*KrV* A546/B574). We know ourselves not only as objects of experience, but also as knowers, and more particularly as (active) reasoners (as opposed to mere passive recipients of sensory input). Reason is to be understood as activity for Kant; the self is the unity of its thoughts, but this unity is its own production. And this means, Kant here claims, that we have to assume

---

[26] For discussions of this development cf. Henrich (1960; 1975) and Ameriks (2000c: 189–227).

[27] In this context the fact that in the third and fourth antinomies both thesis and antithesis are supposed to be *true* is significant.

transcendental freedom to make sense even of theoretical reasoning.[28] In the discussion of the thesis and later, in the discussion of the compatibility of freedom and natural necessity, he is even willing to suggest that our subjective conviction that we act freely might give us some reason to conclude that we do in fact act freely, in the same way that our conviction that our reason is spontaneous suffices to establish that we reason spontaneously.[29]

An exactly similar line of argument appears in *Groundwork* III. Kant asks why we ought to take individual agents to have free causality (*GMS* 4: 451) and replies as follows: we must not only assume an intelligible ground corresponding to the phenomenal presentation of the self (the one accessible through inner and outer sense); we are justified in attributing to that intelligible ground understanding and reason (these being 'part of what there may be of pure activity in [the self] (what reaches consciousness immediately and not through affection of the senses)' (*GMS* 4: 451)). But reason, at least, is pure self-activity, and a theoretical reasoner is obliged to regard her judgements as issuing from rational principles and so (*qua* rational judgements) as *not* causally dependent on preceding events: '[O]ne cannot possibly think of a reason that would consciously receive direction from any other quarter with respect to its judgements, since the subject would then attribute the determination of his judgement not to his reason but to an impulse' (*GMS* 4: 448). In other words, we cannot give causal explanations of the judgements of theoretical reason. From this, together with the idea (that follows from transcendental idealism) that we are obliged to view ourselves as 'members of two worlds' (empirical and intelligible), Kant concludes that we must regard ourselves as subject only to the laws of reason, not at all to the laws of natural causation, insofar as we are members of the latter.[30]

---

[28] Henrich (1960) has shown that in his early critical period Kant wanted to deduce transcendental freedom, and with it the basis of morality, from theoretical reason. The most unambiguous statement of this goal he offers is that in Reflexion 5441: 'Our actions and those of all other beings are necessitated; only the understanding, and the will in so far as it can be determined by the understanding, is free and pure self-activity, which is determined through nothing other than itself' (Henrich 1960: 108). Later Henrich (1975) applies this result to the argument in *Groundwork* III, showing it to contain a mixture of ideas originating in this earlier view with those belonging to the view dominant in the second *Critique*.

[29] '[W]hen we consider . . . actions in their relation to reason—I do not mean speculative reason, by which we endeavour *to explain* their coming into being, but reason in so far as it is itself the cause *producing* them—if, that is to say, we compare them with [the standards of] reason in its *practical* bearing, we find a rule and order altogether different from the order of nature. For it may be that all that *has happened* in the course of nature, and in accordance with its empirical grounds must inevitably have happened, *ought not to have happened*. Sometimes, however, we find, or at least believe that we find, that the ideas of reason have in actual fact proved their causality in respect of the actions of men, as appearances; and that these actions have taken place, not because they were determined by empirical causes, but because they were determined by grounds of reason.' (*KrV* A550/B579)

[30] 'Now, a human being really finds in himself a capacity by which he distinguishes himself from all other things, even from himself insofar as he is affected by objects, and that is *reason*. . . . [R]eason . . . shows in what we call "ideas" a spontaneity so pure that it thereby goes far beyond any-thing that sensibility can ever afford it. . . . Because of this a rational being must regard himself *as intelligence* (hence not from the side of his lower powers) as belonging not to the world of sense but to the world of understanding. . . . As a rational being, and thus as a being belonging to the intelligible world, the human being can never think of the causality of his own will otherwise than under the idea of freedom.' (*GMS* 4: 452)

The argument in *Groundwork* III is an effort to show that the categorical imperative has objective validity in fact. The idea is that proving the objective validity of the moral law will depend on the (independently demonstrated) necessity of ascribing transcendental freedom to individuals. This, together with the claim (argued for in *Groundwork* I and II) that if there is practical spontaneity it must have a law, and that law must be the moral law, would amount to a demonstration that the categorical imperative is objectively valid.

It proceeds in four steps. (1) We know from the fact that our own theoretical spontaneity is inexplicable in empirical terms that we ourselves must, for some purposes, be viewed as intelligible objects. (2) Since we cannot think of the operation of reason as sensibly determined, we cannot think whatever intelligible *causality* inheres in rational beings to be sensibly determined. In other words, an intelligible reasoner cannot think of the causality of its own will except under the idea of freedom (defined negatively as 'independence from the determining causes of the world of sense').[31] (3) Since freedom has been connected with the moral law, as a cause to its law of operation (at *GMS* 4: 447),[32] it follows that (4) when we view ourselves from the intelligible perspective we must view ourselves as subject to the moral law: 'With the idea of freedom the concept of *autonomy* is now inseparably combined, and with the concept of autonomy the universal principle of morality' (*GMS* 4: 452).

One gap in the argument is between steps (1) and (2), as Henrich and many others following him have pointed out.[33] Granted that we know ourselves to be reasoners, and granted even that being a reasoner entails being transcendentally free, still the fact that we are *practical* reasoners, have rational *wills*, does not follow from this. We could be spontaneous in our thinking while lacking practical freedom entirely, being entirely unable to abstract from immediate desires in forming intentions.[34]

---

[31] Compare 4: 448: 'Reason must regard itself as the author of its principles independently of alien influences; consequently, as practical reason or as the will of a rational being it must be regarded of itself as free, that is, the will of such a being cannot be a will of his own except under the idea of freedom, and such a will must in a practical respect thus be attributed to every rational being' (*GMS* 4: 448).

[32] 'Natural necessity was a heteronomy of efficient causes . . . what, then, can freedom of the will be other than autonomy, that is, the will's property of being a law unto itself? But the proposition, that the will is in all its actions a law to itself, indicates only the principle, to act on no other maxim than that which can also have as object itself as a universal law. This, however, is precisely the formula of the categorical imperative and is the principle of morality; hence a free will and a will under moral laws are one and the same' (*GMS* 4: 447).

[33] The spontaneity of reason, Henrich argues, is compatible with a fatalistic position according to which 'in pure thought as such I am free even if I cannot choose the circumstances about which I think, and even if I am in the position neither to sufficiently motivate myself to think nor to cause my insight to influence my action in any way' (Henrich 1975: 66). Cf. also Henrich (1960), Allison (1990: 221–6), and Ameriks (2000c: 224ff.).

[34] Allison attributes the problem with the *Groundwork* III argument to an ambiguity in the notion of an 'intelligible world', claiming that Kant slides from 'intelligible world' as that which is non-sensible ('merely intelligible'), in which he can legitimately locate the spontaneity at issue in the third antinomy, to 'intelligible world' as it had been described previously in the *Groundwork*, as a

Another problem with the argument lies in its first step, with the idea that theoretical reasoning entails absolute spontaneity in the first place. Kant's claims to the effect that theoretical reasoning requires absolute spontaneity occur, in fact, primarily in contexts in which the ultimate aim is to demonstrate the spontaneity of the rational *will*. In other contexts Kant's position looks agnostic,[35] and there are good reasons for thinking that Kant's own argument in the Paralogisms against the substantiality of the self applies just as well to this supposition of its transcendental freedom.[36] Henrich cites Reflexion 5442 as proof of this: 'Transcendental freedom is the total accidentalness of actions. There is logical freedom in acts of reasoning, but not transcendental.'[37]

To the first of these complaints Kant has a response, though one unique to the *Groundwork* III discussion (and dropped immediately thereafter): at least for practical purposes, the presumption of absolute spontaneity is unavoidable. No rational agent is able to *act as if* he were an *automaton spirituale*—there could be nothing that would count as acting that way—and this is enough to secure practical freedom (which, in turn, is all that is required for the moral law to be binding on us). 'Every being that cannot act otherwise than under the idea of freedom is just because of that really free in a practical respect, that is, all laws that are inseparably bound up with freedom hold for him just as if his will had been validly pronounced free also in itself and in theoretical philosophy' (*GMS* 4: 448). This is not intended as a proof of transcendental freedom; instead it is intended to replace such a proof, which Kant claims to be anyway redundant from a practical point of view:

I follow this route—that of assuming freedom, sufficiently for our purpose, only as laid down by rational beings merely *in idea* as a ground for their actions—so that I need not be bound to prove freedom in its theoretical respect as well. For even if the latter is left unsettled, still the same law holds for a being that cannot act otherwise than under the idea of its own freedom as would bind a being that was actually free. Thus we can escape here from the burden that weighs upon theory. (*GMS* 4: 448n)

'kingdom of ends', or totality of rational beings as things in themselves. In the latter, but not the former, reason *must* be conceived as having practical efficacy. 'Consequently, the attempt to establish the necessity of presupposing the kind of freedom that is both necessary and sufficient for morality (transcendental freedom) on the basis of a non-moral premise about our rationality is doomed to failure' (Allison 1990: 228).

[35] Sellars points to Kant's reference to the theoretical subject at *KrV* A346/B404 as 'this I or he or it (the thing) which thinks' and argues that it is a sign that Kant was willing to admit the possibility that a theoretical reasoner might fail to be an agent (cf. Sellars 1971: 21ff.). It is at least conceivable that theoretical spontaneity is only relatively spontaneous—has a spontaneity analogous to that of a computer which processes data in accordance with a certain fixed program. The functioning of theoretical reason might, for all we know, be 'a spontaneity "set in motion" by "foreign causes".' (23) 'Even if "turned on" and humming with readiness, it still does nothing unless a problem is "fed in."' Furthermore, once this happens, it moves along in accordance with its logical disposition.' (23) The theoretical subject might, for all Kant thinks we can conclude about its activity, be a mere '*automaton spirituale* or *cogitans*, a thinking mechanism' (24–5).   [36] Cf. Henrich (1960: 110).

[37] Cited at Henrich (1960: 110).

The objective validity of the categorical imperative can be preserved even in the absence of an independent proof that we have transcendental freedom if we cannot act except as if we did (and so cannot act except as if the categorical imperative had objective validity). Many of Kant's commentators accept the *Groundwork* argument so construed,[38] but Kant himself ultimately did not. All post-*Groundwork* discussions claim that we must be (in fact) transcendentally free if we are to be (in fact) subject to moral demands. That we have to assume freedom for practical purposes—in 'action mode', as it were—is not sufficient to show that we stand under any law whatsoever.

Transcendental freedom derived from our awareness of moral requirements

It is important to distinguish between what Kant says at *GMS* 4: 448 and another point that he makes later in the same discussion (at *GMS* 4: 459–61). There the relation of dependence between morality and freedom is apparently reversed, and an appeal is made to the *interest* which we take in morality. This point is the expression of a wholly different strategy for demonstrating transcendental freedom, and one that is dominant in the *Critique of Practical Reason*. The argument in that work begins from the moral law as a fact of reason and some version of the principle 'ought implies can' (though exactly what this principle amounts to is not perfectly clear, and Kant seems to interpret it in different ways in different contexts). This second strategy still relies on the reciprocity thesis (i.e., the view that 'freedom and unconditional practical law reciprocally imply each another' (*KpV* 5: 29)). But this double hypothetical first gains a hold on our convictions through the law, not the cause, in question.

[O]ur cognition of the unconditionally practical . . . cannot start from freedom, for we can neither be immediately conscious of this, since the first concept of it is negative, nor can we conclude to it from experience, since experience lets us cognize only the law of appearances and hence the mechanism of nature, the direct opposite of freedom. It is therefore the *moral law*, of which we become immediately conscious (as soon as we draw up maxims of the will for ourselves) that *first* offers itself to us and, inasmuch as reason presents it as a determining ground not to be outweighed by any sensible conditions and indeed quite independent of them, leads directly to the concept of freedom. (*KpV* 5: 29–30)

This moral law, Kant now says, is not susceptible of a deduction (for if it were, this would be on the basis of freedom, which we are now prohibited from assuming as a premiss). Nor can one say how it is possible that such a law can be the determining ground of the will (*KpV* 5: 72). The claim is that, as rational agents, we simply

---

[38] They point, that is, to the deliberative irrelevance of determinism (cf. chapter 2 of Bok (1998)), and argue that the moral law holds for all creatures for whom practical reasoning is indispensable (cf., e.g., Korsgaard (1996a: 160ff.) and Wood (1999: 175ff.)).

do know the moral law, and likewise simply do take an interest in its requirements. We are aware of the moral law as we are aware of the laws of theoretical reasoning; there is no longer a relation of epistemic dependence between these two (instead they are parallel).

We can become aware of pure practical laws just as we are aware of pure theoretical principles, by attending to the necessity with which reason prescribes them to us and to the setting aside of all empirical conditions to which reason directs us. The concept of a pure will arises from the first, as consciousness of a pure understanding arises from the latter. (*KpV* 5: 30)

Kant calls this awareness a 'fact of reason', a non-derivative awareness of being under the moral law:

Consciousness of this fundamental law may be called a fact of reason because one cannot reason it out from antecedent data of reason, for example from consciousness of freedom (since this is not antecedently given to us) and because it instead forces itself upon us of itself as a synthetic a priori proposition that is not based on any intuition, either pure or empirical. . . . However in order to avoid misinterpretation in regarding this law as *given*, it must be noted carefully that it is not an empirical fact but the sole fact of pure reason which, by it, announces itself as originally lawgiving. (*KpV* 5: 31)

On the basis of this claim, Kant argues as follows. (1) Laws and causes are inseparable (no law without a cause it governs; no cause without a law that governs it). This principle is absolutely central; were it given up, the claim that freedom and the moral law reciprocally imply one another would likewise have to be given up, and there would be *no* argument for the reality of freedom.[39] (2) The concept 'cause' is objectively valid; as a deliverance of the understanding it acquires an objective necessity, and this objective necessity allows us to apply it to intelligible objects wherever we have a justification for doing so.[40] Theoretical reason gives us no justification to apply it to the intelligible world, but practical reason does give us such a justification, by giving us a *practical law* that applies to the intelligible world:

[T]he moral law, even though it gives no *prospect*, nevertheless provides a fact absolutely inexplicable from any data of the sensible world and from the whole compass of our theoretical use of reason, a fact that points to a pure world of the understanding and, indeed, even *determines* it *positively* and lets us cognize something of it, namely a law. (*KpV* 5: 43)

[39] The application of the principle to the practical sphere is also remarkably unsupported. Kant says, in fact, very little about it, although he presupposes it throughout. I will discuss this assumption further in the next chapter.

[40] Cf. *KpV* 5: 55: 'Now the concept of a being that has a free will is the concept of a *causa noumenon*; and one is already assured that this concept does not contradict itself since the concept of a cause, as having arisen wholly from the pure understanding, also has its objective reality with respect to objects in general assured by the [transcendental] deduction in as much as, being in its origin independent of all sensible conditions and so of itself not restricted to phenomena (unless one should want to make a determinate theoretical use of it), the concept could certainly be applied to things as beings of the pure understanding.'

The result is that (3) we are allowed to infer the intelligible existence of a cause that is governed by this law: the free causality of the intelligible self. This is the inference to freedom as a practical postulate, which is a claim to *knowledge had practically* (rather than theoretically).[41]

Because the moral law is a deliverance of practical but not theoretical reason, the freedom we derive from it is known from a practical rather than a theoretical point of view. But it is, Kant insists, *known* (*erkannt*): 'But is our cognition really extended in this way by pure practical reason, and is what was *transcendent* for speculative reason *immanent* in practical reason? Certainly, but only *for practical purposes*' (*KpV* 5: 133). We cannot even say (from a theoretical standpoint) how a *causa noumenon* is possible in any sense but that of mere non-contradiction, because we cannot say (from that standpoint) how the ground-consequent relation could be differently schematized. Practical reason makes this possibility concrete by providing a practical schematism (as it were) by filling 'this vacant place with a determinate law of causality in an intelligible world (with freedom), namely the moral law' (*KpV* 5: 49). Practical reason determines the nature of the supersensible: '[S]ince the laws by which the existence of things depends on cognition are practical, supersensible nature, so far as we can make for ourselves a concept of it, is nothing other than *a nature under the autonomy of pure practical reason*' (*KpV* 5: 43).

The outcome of this second strategy is a dependence of our knowledge of our freedom on practical reason's demand that we be able to do what we are obliged to do.

[O]f all the intelligible absolutely nothing [is cognized] except freedom (by means of the moral law), and even this only insofar as it is a presupposition inseparable from the law; . . . moreover, all intelligible objects to which reason might lead us under the guidance of that law have in turn no reality for us except on behalf of that law and of the use of pure practical reason. (*KpV* 5: 70)

Note well what sort of freedom this is. It is not the (originally) morally indeterminate freedom that is concluded from the spontaneity of theoretical reason in the first *Critique* or from the phenomenology of deliberation in the *Groundwork*. It is

---

[41] The notion of a practical postulate is a difficult one, and many (including the early Schelling) have thought that Kant's account of the practical postulates is hopelessly flawed. Kant's arguments, Schelling claimed, show that we have a practical need for a belief in freedom, but they are not in themselves sufficient to justify such a belief, because such a belief is not supported by any of the theoretical justifications that we generally find to be required for belief. Schelling makes this point in the first of his *Philosophical Letters on Dogmatism and Criticism* (1795): to say that something is a practical postulate is to say that it is something I need for *action*, not to say that I have any grounds for believing it. No matter how strongly practical reason demands the postulates, as long as theoretical reason remains what it is I cannot hold them to be true (I: 287). Kant himself sees this as an objection (acknowledging it at *KpV* 5: 143n), and this is why he devotes so many pages to the notion of a 'practical postulate'—both distinguishing between the status of these and that of the deliverances of theoretical reason, and insisting that it is not simply a sort of wishful thinking but a real *a priori* demand of reason that is involved in them and a real knowledge (*Erkenntnis*) that they consist in.

morally determinate from the ground up: we have to see ourselves as intelligible *moral* causes since we can see ourselves as free only in virtue of seeing ourselves as bound by the moral law. This epistemic subordination of freedom to the moral law will have interesting consequences for what Kant is able to say about moral evil. (I will discuss these in chapter 2.)

III. UNIFYING THE CLAIMS OF THEORETICAL AND PRACTICAL REASON

Kant's approach to the traditional problem of freedom and determinism has been criticized on a number of counts; in fact on the whole it has found a very unenthusiastic reception. This is due primarily to dissatisfaction with the transcendental idealist programme upon which it relies. But even putting its reliance on that programme aside, there are additional, unique problems that it poses for a theory of agency. In particular, it seems to commit Kant to one theory of agency too many. The self has to be seen, on the one hand, as an absolutely spontaneous noumenal entity and, on the other, as a mechanistically determined object of experience.[42] We can attribute freedom—even in our own case—only to selves as unknowable things-in-themselves, not to selves as objects of experience or theoretical cognition. For, according to all that we experience or can know theoretically about human behaviour, it is as determined as a lunar or solar eclipse (*KpV* 5: 99). How can these two descriptions be descriptions of one and the same moral agent?

Early critics were concerned by this apparent split of the self into empirical and intelligible selves of which radically different things were true, and asked what the relation between noumenal and phenomenal selves is supposed to be.[43] Kant often speaks of noumena and phenomena as if they were different worlds standing in some sort of causal relationship (the first the causal ground, in some non-schematized sense, of the second).[44] There are unfortunate suggestions that

---

[42] The empirical/intelligible character distinction is introduced at *KrV* A539/B567: 'Every efficient cause must have a *character*, that is, a law of its causality, without which it would not be a cause. On the above supposition, we should, therefore, in a subject belonging to the sensible world have, first, an *empirical character*, whereby its actions, as appearances, stand in thoroughgoing connection with other appearances in accordance with unvarying laws of nature. And since these actions can be derived from the other appearances, they constitute together with them a single series in the order of nature. Secondly, we should also have to allow the subject an *intelligible character*, by which it is indeed the cause of those same actions [in their quality] as appearances, but which does not itself stand under any conditions of sensibility, and is not itself appearance. We can entitle the former the character of the thing in the [field of] appearance, and the latter its character as thing in itself.'

[43] Cf., e.g., Schwab (1792). Cf. also Garve (1798), who complains (at 361ff.) that Kant's account cannot solve any problems of freedom we actually have, since these (whatever they are) must be problems that arise within experience. Beiser discusses criticisms along these lines by Feder, Tittel and Selle at Beiser (1987: 171, 185 and *passim*).

[44] For example, at *KrV* A546/B574, A551/B579, *GMS* 4: 451–5 *passim*; *GMS* 4: 460; *KpV* 5: 43, 5: 47, 5: 145, 5: 176, among many others.

empirical and intelligible character might be distinct entities in some sort of causal relationship.[45] Sympathetic commentators from Bernhardi[46] to Beck[47] and Allison[48] have argued that Kant's view loses all coherence when looked at in this way. Noumena and phenomena should be seen not as distinct sets of objects but rather as distinct aspects of (or ways of looking at) the very same objects[49]— and indeed Kant just as often describes empirical character as the 'appearance' (*KrV* A541/B569) or 'sensible schema' (*KpV* A553/B581) of intelligible character, or as its 'determining ground' in some sense that does not suggest separate existence.[50]

However, although there is no genuine problem about the coexistence of two distinct *selves*—since there are not these, but only two ways of looking at the same self—there is indeed a problem about the coexistence of these two ways of *looking* on Kant's view. The problem of the unity of theoretical and practical reason was a highly motivating one for Kant's immediate successors, and overcoming the apparent lack of systematicity in his work was one of the central tasks they set themselves.[51] They worried about the relation between the sets of laws that govern the practical and the theoretical points of view. Kant himself, it seems, found the issue less pressing, though he did offer two suggestions for thinking about this problem.

The first is the second *Critique*'s suggestion that the theoretical standpoint should be taken to be subordinate to the practical. '[I]n the union of pure speculative with pure practical reason in one cognition the latter has primacy . . . For without this subordination a conflict of reason with itself would arise' (*KpV* 5: 121). The interests of theoretical reason (in not overstepping the bounds it sets for itself) are subordinated to the interests of practical reason (in postulating some things of the intelligible world) because 'all interest is ultimately practical and even

---

[45] One of the more worrisome includes the comment at *KpV* 5: 87 describing the 'subjection' of the self-as-appearance to the self-as-noumenon: 'The person as belonging to the sensible world is subjected to its own personality, in so far as this belongs at the same time to the intelligible world.' Discussion of how the 'two selves' are supposed to relate can be seen in Kant's early sympathetic commentators as well as his early critics (cf., e.g., Abicht (1789: 71ff.) and Schwab (1792)).   [46] Cf. Bernhardi (1796: 244).

[47] Cf. Beck (1960: 192ff.).

[48] Cf. Allison (1990: 29ff., 43ff.). Allison's argument against Irwin (1984, at 43–4) is exactly right: if we had to see empirical character as *being* (as opposed to *appearing*, in the technical Kantian sense) causally determined, there would be no way of saving Kant's view.

[49] As Nelkin points out, there are two distinct views here, since commentators like Korsgaard and Hill seem to hold a view distinct from the two-aspects view. For a criticism of these 'two standpoints' construals, cf. Nelkin (2000).

[50] Cf., e.g., *KrV* 5: 97–8: '[E]very action [of the person as phenomenon], and in general every determination of its existence varying in accordance with inner sense, indeed even the whole succession of its existence as a sensible being, is to be seen in consciousness only as the result of its intelligible existence, never as the determining ground of its causality as *noumenon*.'

[51] For discussions of this issue cf. Ameriks (2000b: 66–77, 112–36, 172–85, 219–233; 2000d), Guyer (2000a), Franks (2000), Beiser (1987: 226–65; 2002: 223–39, 273–306, 491–528), Horstmann (1991), Hutter (1995), Pinkard (2002: 66–79, 96–130, 172–183), Pippin (1997: 129–53), and Tuschling (1991).

that of speculative reason is only conditional and is complete in practical use alone' (*KpV* 5: 121).[52] This is the path Fichte takes.[53]

The second is the path taken by Schelling and, after him, Hegel. It builds on a suggestion in first *Critique* (at *KrV* A317–18/B374) that is developed quite substantially in the *Critique of the Power of Judgement*. The suggestion is that even theoretical reason might have need of a fundamentally practical notion—the notion of purpose—to make sense of the unity and systematicity theoretical inquiry expects to find in the natural world. It is not enough, Kant writes in the second introduction, that practical reason demands to produce effects in appearance; there must be some independent conceptual ground that allows us to think how that might work. In other words, it is not enough that we be obliged to think that moral demands can inform our actions as empirical agents: we have to be able to make sense of it as well. The passage is the following:

> Now although there is an incalculable gulf fixed between the domain of the concept of nature, as the sensible, and the domain of the concept of freedom, as the supersensible, so that from the former to the latter (thus by means of the theoretical use of reason) no transition is possible, just as if there were so many different worlds, the first of which can have no influence on the second: yet the latter **should** have an influence on the former, namely the concept of freedom should make the end that is imposed by its laws real in the sensible world; and nature must consequently also be able to be conceived in such a way that the lawfulness of its form is at least in agreement with the possibility of the ends that are to be realized in it in accordance with the laws of freedom.—Thus there must still be a ground of the **unity** of the supersensible that grounds nature with that which the concept of freedom contains practically, the concept of which [ground of unity], even if it does not suffice for cognition of it either theoretically or practically, and thus has no proper domain of its own, nevertheless makes possible the transition from the manner of thinking in accordance with the principles of the one to that in accordance with the principles of the other. (*KU* 5: 175–6)

Bridging this gulf might be achievable, he suggests, by means of a critique of the power of judgement (*KU* 5: 176).

The nature of this unification is indicated in the solution to the antinomy of teleological judgement in §§76–7, where Kant asks us to note a peculiarity of the sort of cognition available to human beings. Theoretical cognition has its source in two quite different faculties, the understanding and sensibility, and the deliverances of the latter are for us entirely contingent. While we can legislate the universal *a priori*, we cannot legislate the particular *a priori*. We need a third faculty—the power of judgement, 'the faculty for thinking of the particular as contained under the universal' (*KU* 5: 179)—to unite these two sources of cognition. Kant thinks the capacity takes two forms: determining judgement,

---

[52] O'Neill's attempt at a unified reading of Kantian reason is along these lines. Cf. O'Neill (1989: especially introduction and chapter 3).

[53] For discussions of Fichte's treatment of the problem cf. Ameriks (2000b: 172–85, 219–33; 2000d), Beiser (2002: 273–306), Neuhouser (1990: *passim*), Pinkard (2002: 105–30), Wood (2000).

which puts a given particular under a 'rule, principle, law' of which we are already
in possession, and reflecting judgement, which extracts a universal from a group
of given particulars. He points out that in our empirical inquiries we make a
number of large assumptions about the capacities of this power of judgement. We
assume, for instance, that reflective judgement will produce a manageable number
of comprehensible laws of nature—that the laws of nature will not turn out to be
simply too complex or numerous for us to grasp. We cannot dispense with this
assumption that our power of judgement is somehow suited to the set of particulars it has to deal with—despite the fact that these are contingent for us. We must
assume, as Kant says, that nature and our power of judgement are in a certain sort
of harmony. Not doing so would amount to expecting that empirical science
might well turn out to be a waste of time.

Kant then asks us to imagine an understanding that, unlike ours, would be able
to legislate both universal and particular. It would have an entirely active (spontaneous) intuition; in its cognition no unification of the manifold would be necessary, and so nothing at all would be contingent for it. We are led, he claims, to
imagine such an understanding as a regulative idea underlying the possibility of
a harmony of the diversity of nature with the universal such that particulars can
be subsumed under universals to begin with.[54] We can imagine this harmony,
contingent for us, being necessary for such an intuitive understanding.

Our understanding, namely, has the property that in its cognition, e.g., of the cause of a
product, it must go from the *analytical universal* (of concepts) to the particular (of the
given empirical intuition); in which it determines nothing with regard to the manifoldness
of the latter, but must expect this determination for the power of judgement from the
subsumption of the empirical intuition (when the object is a product of nature) under the
concept. Now, however, we can also conceive of an understanding which, since it is not
discursive like ours but is intuitive, goes from the *synthetically universal* (of the intuition of
a whole as such) to the particular, i.e., from the whole to the parts, in which, therefore, and
in whose representation of the whole, there is no *contingency* in the combination of the
parts. (*KU* 5: 407)

What Kant is asking us to imagine is an understanding for which the parts could
be seen as dependent upon and determined by the whole, rather than (simply) the
other way around. There would be no distinction between actual and possible for
such an intellect (*KU* 5: 402); nor would there be a distinction between what
should be and what is (*KU* 5: 403–4).

This understanding would in turn be regarded as something like the *cause* of
the whole, the whole being the product of its presentation on the part of this understanding. '[B]ut the product of a cause whose determining ground is merely the
representation of its effect is called an end' (*KU* 5: 408), so that the whole of nature

---

[54] Exactly why and to what extent Kant thinks such an idea to be *required* for us to think we can
unify nature under empirical laws, and what the status of such an idea would be, is a question that
merits more attention than it has so far received. Cf., e.g., Tuschling (1990; 1991), Horstmann
(1991: 191–219), and Pippin (1997: 129–53).

could be viewed as the end of this higher understanding. The mechanism which presents itself in experience continues to be viewed as such, while the 'agreement and unity of the particular law and the corresponding forms' can be viewed as a teleological system, 'and the material world would thus be judged in accordance with two kinds of principles, without the mechanical mode of explanation being excluded by the teleological mode, as if they contradicted each other' (*KU* 5: 409). Mechanism would be seen 'as if it were the tool of an intentionally acting cause' (*KU* 5: 422).

Our cognition of nature as a whole does not work like this, but we do have experience of (what feels like) the subordination of mechanistic causality to ends-based causality when we carry out purposes of our own. Further, we have two models for employing something like this form of cognition to things we have not ourselves created: aesthetic appreciation and understanding of organisms as teleological systems. Both of the latter are cases in which we understand the character of the various parts (of an object or organism) as being necessitated by the character of the whole, rather than (merely) the other way around. The case of organisms is particularly salient here, for Kant thinks that without the regulative ideal of purposiveness as a guide we cannot hope to engage in productive study of the organic world. '[N]o human reason (or even any finite reason that is similar to ours in quality, no matter how much it exceeds it in degree) can ever hope to understand the generation of even a little blade of grass from merely mechanical causes' (*KU* 5: 409). For Kant the idea that we might achieve such a unified view of nature as a whole remains regulative, but for Schelling and Hegel it will become constitutive of properly philosophical knowledge.

This solution is intended to mediate the first two critiques by describing an understanding that can be viewed both as the substrate of the world of appearances of the first *Critique* and at the same time the moral author of the world of the second *Critique*. What it does, primarily, is give us a further way in which we are obliged to think about the intelligible world from a theoretical point of view. It provides a way of thinking about the intelligible realm which unites end-oriented thinking and mechanistic causality in a sort of harmony wherein mechanism is subordinated to teleology. The regulative principle requiring that we think about organisms in teleological terms while thinking that they are nonetheless mechanistically determined provides a concrete example of how such a reconciliation is possible—though the details of the reconciliation cannot be grasped by us, but only by the posited intuiting intellect. This suggests the possibility that we can view mechanism as subordinated to another type of teleology as well, namely that involved in practical agency. We can view nature as a system that is not antithetical to—and perhaps even furthers—moral purposes. We have been given a way of thinking about how the realm of practical reasons and the realm of natural causes can coincide, with the latter subordinated to the former.

What does this say about the problem of moral spontaneity? Apparently something like this: transcendental idealism means, among other things, that the mechanistic principle of causality, according to which a subject must view the events of nature as being determined, is, in some rather strong sense, of his own making. One brings the principle of causality oneself to bear in the unification of the manifold, which, per se, contains no such principle. Why then worry about the spontaneity of one's actions when the principle of causality is at bottom itself the result of one's own spontaneous (theoretical) activity? A good reason to worry might be that the only way one's (theoretical) reason allows one to understand the world is precisely a way that forces one to view one's own empirical acts as part of a deterministic causal series. In other words, theoretical understanding sits quite uncomfortably alongside practical reason and its demand that we be free in a sense incompatible with determinism—even though practical reason is supposed to produce effects in the very same world that the understanding is supposed to grasp in concepts. This is troubling. But what if, even to grasp the world of experience fully in a theoretical manner, one needed to use the same sorts of thinking that one uses in practical reasoning? What if teleology could not be ruled out even from the purely theoretical perspective, and if one needed, as a regulative idea, in order to understand a phenomenon as simple as a blade of grass, the idea of an intuiting intellect that subordinates mechanism to a global teleology? If the world can only ultimately be understood in terms that unite the theoretical and the practical in this way, then the disturbing problem that reason seems split into two competing faculties does indeed appear solved.

This solution, however, leaves a further question unanswered (and in fact makes it all the more pressing). It cannot do without the idea of a higher intellect that intuits the whole as whole and for which each particular as well as the totality of particulars is *necessary*. The necessity at issue is not mechanistic causal necessity, but rather teleological necessity: the necessity that the parts be as they must be if the whole is to be as it is (or to fulfil the function it fulfils). How is the spontaneity of individuals *qua* individuals supposed to be compatible with the necessity of the intuition of this higher intellect? So long as the totality remains a totality of rational ends *to be pursued*, perfectly well. But if the solution is to be a unification of practical and theoretical reason, it must be also a theoretical, not solely a practical ideal—it must in some important sense be an 'is' (something we expect to uncover piece by piece in empirical science), rather than merely an 'ought'. But supposing this means supposing that although there might in fact be differences in the degree of rationality manifested by the participants in this totality, these differences cannot in any genuine sense be up to them—at least, not in the robust sense Kant elsewhere insists on. In other words, the only freedom that is preserved for individuals in this moral world order is that of rational self-determination. Their freedom in this sense—their participation in this rational order as the large-scale instantiation of their own essence as rational beings—is, in fact, guaranteed. What has been lost is their transcendental freedom in the sense defined in the first two critiques, a sense of freedom that was bound up with the contingency of individual choice.

This is a conclusion Kant seems at places to accept, and it is the conclusion characteristic of his idealist successors. Schelling claims to have brought it to its logical conclusion in his early systematic work.[55] But if one is free only in virtue of being a rationally self-determining participant in this moral world order, then it follows that the immoral individual is not free. There is no place for moral evil as an imputable failure to abide by the moral law. This is not a conclusion Kant was entirely happy with. But his account of moral evil has difficulties quite independent of those raised by the third *Critique*, and it is to these that I will now turn.

[55] There is evidence that Kant agreed with Schelling's claim; cf. Tuschling (1991: especially 120–2).

2

Kant on Autonomy and Moral Evil

The central difficulty, for my purposes here, with Kant's account of freedom is that of the possibility of moral evil on his account. That moral evil be conceivable as a fully free choice is hardly considered to be a firm requirement of any plausible theory of moral agency. Socrates surely found the consequence that on it no one can knowingly choose the worse over the better to be a *positive* feature of his view. Medieval and early modern treatments of evil as a cosmological problem had produced a number of conceptions that fit well with this moral psychological commitment. One could call these, collectively, 'negative' conceptions of moral evil: evil as the mere absence of (maximal amounts of) goodness, or evil as the inevitable result of various limitations in human nature. This route seems open to Kant as well. If practical reason is the source of moral goodness, for Kant, then it seems moral evil can be dealt with quickly: it is a failure to achieve maximal practical rationality due to some cognitive or voluntative limitations of finite agents, never a genuinely free choice. This is just how a number of contemporary interpreters present his view.[1]

Kant himself was not wholly content with this result; he struggled with the issue for years. In *Religion within the Boundaries of Mere Reason* of 1793 he comes down quite strongly against the adequacy of any negative conception of evil. There he claims that 'nothing is... morally (i.e. imputably) evil but that which is our own deed' (*R* 6: 31), and the force of this requirement seems to be a demand for an alternative to the Platonic view. The ground of evil cannot be found in the mere fact that human beings are sensible as well as rational; evil must, to be imputable, proceed from the individual's own choice (*Willkür*) (*R* 6: 34–5). 'Evil can have originated only from moral evil (not just from the limitations of our nature)' (*R* 6: 43). It is therefore not a weakness, explained by 'the power of the incentives of sensibility, on the one hand, and the impotence of the incentive of reason (respect for the law), on the other', though this is 'a very common presupposition of moral philosophy' (*R* 6: 59n). Neither is it a lack, the mere absence of good; it is instead a positive counter-force working against the force of good: '[T]he lack of the agreement of the power of choice (*Willkür*) with [the moral law] is possible only as a consequence of a real and opposite determination of the power

---

[1] Many contemporary Kantians take this path; cf., e.g., Korsgaard (1996a: 159–87), Wood (1984, 1999: 172ff.) (both discussed below), and Timmons (1994).

of choice, i.e. of a *resistance* on its part... or again, it is only possible through an evil power of choice (*eine böse Willkür*)' (*R* 6: 22n). Nor, finally, is evil *mere* irrationality. Kant chides the Stoics for mistaking their enemy: the morally good is opposed not to *folly* but to *malice* (*R* 6: 57). Here we have a conception of evil according to which it is the imputable choice of a free will, rather than mere weakness, lack or confusion—what Kant calls a *positive* conception of moral evil.

This was not always his view, however. Various notes from the late 1760s indicate that Kant did not want to claim that evil can be freely chosen—for instance, the following:

Can one also determine oneself to evil through a free resolution? No! one can be determined to [evil] only passively or not at all, for the pure will [*Wille*] indeed always remains and so cannot be bound, but it does not always exercise its activity. (3856)[2]

No one considers freedom as the capacity to desire that which is detestable (evil)... The possibility of consciously willing what is disapproved of by reason is the weak will (*Wille*); the proficiency at willing evil is the evil will. (3867)

Freedom is the capacity to actively will that which is known to be good and is in our power; but to [freedom] does not necessarily belong the capacity to will that which is known to be evil and whose avoidance is in our power. This [latter] is not actually a capacity, but rather the possibility of a passivity. Evil actions stand, indeed, under freedom, but do not occur through freedom. (3868)

In his *Lectures on Philosophical Theology* (from the 1780s),[3] Kant offered a classic negative account, portraying evil as a sort of uncultivatedness, an incompleteness in the development of the seed of goodness: 'Evil has *no special* germ; for it is *mere negation*, and consists only in the *limitation of the good*. It is nothing beyond this, other than incompleteness in the development of the germ to the good out of uncultivatedness' (28: 1078). He also attributed it directly to the strength of human sensuous inclinations, coupled with foolishness:

This predisposition to good, which God has placed in the human being, must be developed by the human being himself before the good can make its appearance. But since at the same time the human being has many instincts belonging to animality, and since he has to have them if he is to continue being human, the strength of his instincts will beguile him and he will abandon himself to them, and *thus arises evil*, or rather, when the human being begins to use his reason, he falls into foolishness. (28: 1078)

The notes and the theology lectures predate *Religion* (by about fifteen years in the first case, eight in the second). But they cannot be dismissed as evidence of an early, perhaps less well-considered, view that was defunct by 1792. For they bear a remarkable resemblance to things Kant has to say as late as 1797—in the introduction to the *Metaphysics of Morals*, where he states that 'freedom can never be

---

    [2] This citation and the following two, from the *handschriftliche Nachlass*, are taken from Bittner and Cramer (1975: 36). Translations are mine.
    [3] These probably date to the early–mid 1780s. Cf. editors' introduction to the *Lectures on the Philosophical Doctrine of Religion*, Kant (1996: 337–8).

located in a rational subject's being able to choose in opposition to his (lawgiving) reason' (*MS* 6: 226), and 'Only freedom in relation to the internal lawgiving of reason is really an ability; the possibility of deviating from it is an inability' (*MS* 6: 227).

The positive conception of evil spelled out in *Religion* thus has a peculiar status, sandwiched as it is between what can only be seen as expressions of a *negative* conception of evil: evil as some combination of sensuousness, folly, and the passivity of the will, not a capacity but rather a limitation on a capacity. Even the later Kant, though he wants to say that evil is imputable, nevertheless does not want to say human beings have a *capacity* for evil (in the way that they have a capacity for good); nor does he want to say that freedom can be defined in terms of the ability to choose *between* good and evil. The picture, then, is not so simple: Kant is willing neither to give a negative account, nor to accept some apparently indispensable features of a positive account, of moral evil. The account in *Religion* is not simply a natural outgrowth of everything else Kant had to say about freedom. It is, instead, an effort to deal with a specific problem, one that had been pointed out by both critics and sympathetic readers and which Kant as a result felt obliged to address.[4] The problem was not so easily soluble, however, since it arose directly from the account of the authority of the moral law Kant had given in his central works of practical philosophy.

In §I, I will discuss that problem, which arises from the idea that subjection to an unconditional practical law is deducible from the notion of a free will—that being governed by such a law is partially constitutive of acting. The difficulty is that there appears to be no way for Kant to construe the 'governed by' relation such that both (1) the moral law is a categorical imperative and (2) imputable moral evil is possible. In §II, I will look at Kant's effort to redress the problem in *Religion*, and his reasons for ultimately repudiating that effort, in the *Metaphysics of Morals*. Kant—like Fichte, the early Schelling, and Hegel after him—was in the end more committed to freedom as rational self-determination than he was to the transcendental freedom whose possibility he had defended in the first *Critique*.

I. CAUSES AND LAWS

In the first chapter of the Analytic of the *Critique of Practical Reason*, Kant claims that 'freedom and unconditional practical law reciprocally imply each other' (*KpV* 5: 29). That is, one can deduce the moral law from the notion of a free will, and one can deduce the freedom of the will from the notion of subjection to an unconditional practical law. The step that leads to freedom from the moral law is some version of the principle 'ought implies can' (cf. *KpV* 5: 30, 5: 94–7; *GMS* 4: 450, 4: 455; *R* 6: 41, 6: 45, 6: 47, 6: 49n, 6: 50). Here,

---

[4] Cf. Lichtenberger (1993) and Prauss (1983: 91ff.).

Kant seems to take it that the step to the moral law from freedom is similarly short:

[I]f one had insight into the possibility of freedom of an efficient cause, one would also have insight into not merely the possibility but even the necessity of the moral law as the supreme practical law of rational beings, to whom one attributes freedom of the causality of their will; for, the two concepts are so inseparably connected that one could even define practical freedom through independence of the will from anything other than the moral law alone. (*KpV* 5: 93–4)

Still, it is not quite clear what the step consists in. The argument for such a step first given in *Groundwork* III—from the premiss that rational beings must take themselves to have free wills (and so a sort of non-natural causality), at least from a practical point of view, to the conclusion that they must take themselves to stand under (in a sense to be discussed) a moral law (in fact, a law of the specific form Kant had outlined earlier in the *Groundwork*)—is open to two interpretations. The first, though both straightforward and suggested by the text, is clearly inadequate. The second requires interpolation (which a number of commentators have been willing to provide) but has some, at least apparent, plausibility.[5] Both are subject to the same difficulty, though the second hides it better than the first.

The moral law as descriptive of agency

The first interpretation links freedom and the moral law through a more general principle, one which Kant suggests applies in theoretical and moral contexts equally, according to which there can be no such thing as a cause without a law that governs it, and no such thing as a law without a cause it governs. We are evidently supposed to take this as a conceptual truth; when Kant mentions it he says things like: 'the concept of causality brings with it that of laws' (*GMS* 4: 446); and 'the concept of causality always contains reference to a law' (*KpV* 5: 89); and 'the thought of a cause operating without any law at all . . . is a contradiction' (*R* 6: 35).

Intuitively, there are two types of cause-law connection, and two senses of 'govern' or 'stand under' that accompany them. In one sense, laws are statements that describe how causes do operate; in a second, laws are imperatives that prescribe how causes (here agents) *should* operate. In the law-cause relationship at work in the second analogy, laws are statements that describe the operation of causes, and to call something a cause is to say that it operates according to a *rule* (with 'rule' designating a way in which it always does in fact act). In calling the free will a cause, Kant cannot be employing 'cause' in precisely the sense at work in the second analogy, as free wills are not appearances and so not in time. But is

---

⁵ Cf., e.g., Korsgaard (1989; 1996a: 159–87), and O'Neill (1989: 51–65). Neither of these allows Kant an escape from the difficulty I will discuss. Wood (1999) offers a partial reconstruction; he denies (correctly, in my opinion) that the *Groundwork* III argument goes through.

there any sense in which the second analogy discussion should apply to free wills? It seems absurd to suggest that Kant wants to employ in the moral context that part of the second analogy notion of cause that links causes with laws as *descriptions* of their modes of operation. Surely the moral law is a law of the second sort, not the first—one that prescribes, not one that describes.

In the second *Critique*, however, he does suggest a very close parallel between natural laws and moral laws as making possible systematic frameworks of sensible nature and supersensible nature, respectively: 'The moral law is, in fact, a law of causality through freedom and hence a law of the possibility of a supersensible nature, just as the metaphysical law of events in the sensible world was a law of the causality of sensible nature' (*KpV* 5: 47). The moral law is the condition of possibility of a supersensible nature analogous in status to the principle of causality which constitutes the condition of possibility of a sensible nature. If we are to take this parallel seriously, it is difficult to avoid taking the moral law as a descriptive one.

Kant also—very often—speaks as though the moral law were a law that governs rational agents in the sense of describing the operation of their causality. The most univocal such passages are those describing what he calls a 'holy will'. Such a will 'stands under' an unconditional practical law, but such a law is not an imperative, not an 'ought' for it. It is instead a *description* of the character of a holy will's volition. This passage is from the *Groundwork*:

A perfectly good will would, therefore, equally stand under objective laws (of the good), but it could not on this account be represented as necessitated to actions in conformity with the law since of itself, by its subjective constitution, it can be determined only through the representation of the good. Hence no imperatives hold for the divine will and in general for a holy will: the 'ought' is out of place here, because volition is of itself necessarily in accord with the law. (*GMS* 4: 414)

Remarks along the same lines can be found in both the second *Critique* (at 5: 52) and *Religion* (in the note at 6: 50). So in the case of the holy will, at least, the moral law is a description, not a prescription.

Kant often speaks as if this were the case with finite rational wills as well, in so far as they are regarded as intelligible. One such passage is in the *Groundwork* at 4: 454–5, where Kant remarks that even morally evil individuals must regard themselves as possessing effectively holy wills when they view themselves as intelligible beings.[6] Another occurs in the second *Critique*, where Kant describes agents like ourselves as subject to two sets of laws (belonging to two points of view):

The sensible nature of rational beings in general is their existence under empirically conditioned laws and is thus, for reason, *heteronomy*. The supersensible nature of these same beings, on the other hand, is their existence in accordance with laws that are

---

[6] Even in the case of the immoral willer, 'The moral "*ought*" is then his own necessary "*will*" as a member of the intelligible world, and is thought by him as "ought" only insofar as he regards himself at the same time as a member of the world of sense' (*GMS* 4: 455).

independent of any empirical condition and thus belong to the *autonomy* of pure reason. (*KpV* 5: 43)

Kant's way of expressing himself here suggests that the self viewed as intelligible object must be seen as perfectly moral. That, combined with the idea that the intelligible world should be taken, for practical purposes, to determine appearances in the phenomenal world—that intelligible character must be taken as the ground of phenomenal character and that the former cannot in its turn be necessitated by any sensible motives inhering in the latter—seems to require us, when viewing ourselves from a practical point of view, to view ourselves as holy wills.[7]

When he goes about trying to show that the free will necessarily stands under the moral law in *Groundwork* III, Kant employs an analogy between natural and free causes (natural causes have laws; free causes must have them too) which would be entirely inapt were the law governing free wills a prescriptive rather than a descriptive one. The analogy is important: Kant uses it to move from the negative to the positive sense of freedom, which in turn allows him to connect freedom of the will with the categorical imperative, in the opening paragraphs of *Groundwork* III:

[T]here flows from [the negative definition] a *positive* concept of freedom, which is so much the richer and more fruitful. Since the concept of causality brings with it that of laws in accordance with which, by something that we call a cause, something else, namely an effect, must be posited, so freedom, although it is not a property of the will in accordance with natural laws, is not for that reason lawless but must instead be a causality in accordance with immutable laws but of a special kind; for otherwise a free will would be an absurdity. Natural necessity was a heteronomy of the efficient causes, since every effect was

---

[7] A slightly different formulation appears in the *Prolegomena*, where Kant insists that his solution preserves the conformability to constant laws of all behaviour *because every action not determined by laws of reason is determined by laws of nature*. 'Now I may say without contradiction: that all the actions of rational beings, so far as they are appearances (occurring in any experience), are subject to the necessity of nature; but the same actions, as regards merely the rational subject and its faculty of acting according to mere reason, are free. For what is required for the necessity of nature? Nothing more than the determinability of every event in the world of sense according to constant laws, that is, a reference to cause in the appearance; in this process the thing in itself at its foundation and its causality remain unknown. But I say, that the law of nature remains, whether the rational being is the cause of the effects in the sensuous world from reason, that is, through freedom, or whether it does not determine them on grounds of reason. For, if the former is the case, the action is performed according to maxims, the effect of which as appearance is always conformable to constant laws; if the latter is the case, and the action not performed on principles of reason, it is subjected to the empirical laws of the sensibility, and in both cases the effects are connected according to constant laws; more than this we do not require or know concerning natural necessity. But in the former case reason is the cause of these laws of nature, and therefore free; in the latter the effects follow according to mere natural laws of sensibility, because reason does not influence it; but reason itself is not determined on that account by the sensibility, and is therefore free in this case too. Freedom is therefore no hindrance to natural law in appearance, neither does this law abrogate the freedom of the practical use of reason, which is connected with things in themselves, as determining grounds' (*GMS* 4: 345–6). This passage is especially puzzling, since it seems to conflate immoral action with amoral (because unfree) action according to Kant's own view.

possible only in accordance with the law that something else determines the efficient cause to causality; what, then, can freedom of the will be other than autonomy, that is, the will's property of being a law to itself? But the proposition, the will in all its actions is a law to itself, indicates only the principle, to act on no other maxim than that which can also have as object itself as a universal law. This, however, is precisely the formula of the categorical imperative and is the principle of morality; hence a free will and a will under moral laws are one and the same. (*GMS* 4: 446–7)

If the moral law is a prescriptive rather than a descriptive law, the parallel drawn in this passage is utterly misleading, for between the relation of descriptive laws to their causes and the relation of prescriptive laws to their causes there can be no such analogy. But Kant does draw the parallel; in fact it is an ineliminable step in the argument. The suggestion, then, is that the moral law is a descriptive one for rational beings, although one that describes only their operation under ideal circumstances (the frictionless plane of intelligible agency).[8]

Taking the parallel literally gives rise to an obvious problem, for if the causality of transcendental freedom is indistinguishable from that form of rational self-determination that characterizes rational agents at those moments when they are properly functioning, then improperly functioning agents fail, as such, to manifest transcendental freedom—from which it follows analytically (given Kant's views about the connection between transcendental freedom and imputation) that only moral actions are imputable, and that immoral actions are not.

Schmid's 'intelligible fatalism'

Still, this interpretation seemed unavoidable to many of Kant's contemporaries. It got its most influential formulation from Carl Christian Erhard Schmid, in his attempt at a systematic ethics in a Kantian spirit (*Versuch einer Moralphilosophie*, 1790). He called the view of freedom presented there 'intelligible fatalism' because of the character of the only answer he could glean from Kant's work (up to and including the second *Critique*) to the question, 'Why is not the same rational activity, the same morality, evident in all actions?' (249).[9] Schmid argues, on the basis of Kant's apparent denial of the possibility of a *contingent* intelligible causality—that is, his apparent insistence that the moral law is a certain sort of descriptive law applying to noumenal agency— that his only option for conceptualizing the intelligible ground of an immoral action is to assume some *second* sort of intelligible causality, distinct from that of reason and sometimes hindering it.[10]

---

[8] Gass (1994) notes the peculiar role of the notion of 'cause' in this passage in the *Groundwork*.

[9] I have cited Schmid according to the selections in Bittner and Cramer (1975); page numbers refer to that volume. Reprinted there are selections of the first edition, published in 1790, which Kant owned (cf. Warda (1922: 55)). All four editions are reprinted in the Aetas Kantiana series.

[10] This is to deny the possibility of an explanation like the one given in the *Prolegomena* passage cited in note 7 above.

We must think that there is something present which, together with the presence of reason, determines [the latter's] effectiveness upon appearances, and the determinate degree of this effectiveness in each case. This something is clearly not itself an appearance, for an appearance cannot determine a thing in itself. But from the fact that sensibility, as it is sensibly represented and known, cannot determine and limit reason in itself, it does not follow that that which *in-itself grounds sensibility* and all its appearances is incapable of limiting *the effects of reason in appearance*. And if we want to avoid groundlessness—that is, theoretical irrationality—in the explanation of immorality, then we must think this problematic idea assertorically. (249)

There are limits to the rationality of action on the part of finite rational beings, and although these limits cannot be defined by sensible inclinations per se (this would be the empirical determining the intelligible), there nevertheless must be something that sets these limits. Since this something is not determined by prac- tical reason (for practical reason always commands us to be moral), one either infers some intelligible limits external to the rational will, or assumes contingency in the action of the intelligible will. Since Kant explicitly forbids the second, Schmid concludes that we must imagine an external limit on the activity of reason in the noumenal realm: 'Reason is, then, free and uninfluenced in respect of everything that it actually does, just as is the case with all of its judgments, in respect of their form. But it is dependent and limited in respect of that which it does not do. It *could not be effective* in these cases' (249–50). Of course, such limits must completely transcend our capacity for knowledge, for they can be neither practical (as they do not follow from the moral law) nor within the scope of theoretical reason (as they pertain to things in themselves). What follows, however, from positing the presence (if not the knowability) of such limits, is:

The necessity of all actions—moral or immoral—by virtue of whatever thinkable, if not always knowable, grounds, lying within or outside of the sensible world, within or outside of the sensible rational being, and therefore the unavoidable necessity of sometimes acting immorally—if there are immoral actions, and if reason tolerates no accident, then no rational being can deny, or even rationally doubt, such necessity. (251)

Schmid bases this conclusion on the first two *Critiques* taken together; but its similarity to the conclusion which Kant himself suggests in the third *Critique* is striking. If practical and theoretical reason are to be thought together, they must be thought as the determination of the whole of temporal existence through an intelligible cause acting outside of time, subordinating phenomenal mechanism to intelligible ends. But from this idea follows directly the conclusion that all actions, moral or not, are intelligibly determined according to an overarching plan. An intelligible determinism (Schmid called it 'intelligible fatalism') emerges to take the place of the determinism that was eliminated by the transcendental reality of space and time.

Schmid claims that this conclusion is incompatible with ethics, and that if it is true, 'then a rational being must either take ethics to be a chimera or, for the sake of ethics—and thus *on rational grounds* (for we are supposed to be ethical by virtue of being rational)—*wholly renounce reason*, its principles and its use. An irrational reason!' (251). Schelling—who was surely familiar with Schmid's 'intelligible fatalism'[11]—would eventually come up with a similar-sounding, and similarly motivated, thesis. Kant was also aware of Schmid's conclusion,[12] and cannot have been content with it—as the discussion in *Religion*, published two years later, suggests.

The moral law as prescriptive, and the problem of its authority

Schmid's view looks like a *reductio* of the descriptive law interpretation, given Kant's efforts on behalf of transcendental freedom in the third Antinomy.[13] The second interpretation I mentioned above has the moral law as a prescription for, not a description of, the volition of free agents in so far as they are free. According to it, Kant's argument should be taken to be something like this:[14] Begin from the standpoint of a rational being that takes itself to have a will that is free (in the transcendental sense).[15] Such an agent cannot act without first choosing a law or

[11] Schmid was a professor at Jena and one of Kant's foremost interpreters. He was the author of a widely read *Wörterbuch zum leichteren Gebrauch der Kantischen Schriften* (this came out in four editions, each longer than the last, in 1786, 1788, 1795 and 1798); his *Versuch* also came out in four separate editions over the course of twelve years (1790–1802, Schelling's formative years, philosophically), and a number of comments on 'critical' or 'Kantian' ethics in the literature of the time are actually comments on Schmid (all of Schwab's in the *Philosophisches Archiv*, for example—cf. Schwab (1792, 1794a, 1794b).

[12] He owned Schmid's *Critik der reinen Vernunft im Grundrisse* (which also contained the first edition of his *Wörterbuch zum leichteren Gebrauch der Kantischen Schriften*), as well as the first two editions (1790 and 1792) of his *Versuch einer Moralphilosophie* (cf. Warda (1922: 53–4)).

[13] Schmid's is the logical conclusion of the descriptive-law interpretation. This is why I am unconvinced by approaches like Wood's (cf. 1999: 172ff.) that try to solve the problem by pointing out that reasons can be causes, and that normative laws can therefore have some descriptive value. Note, though, that there is at least one contemporary defender of the descriptive-law type view (cf. Timmermann 2000).

[14] The following reconstruction is based on Korsgaard (1996a: 159–83). Korsgaard claims that the two-worlds view, which she rejects, underlies the apparent impossibility of evil on Kant's account. Denying the ontological independence of intelligible selves relieves one of any obligation to say how such selves are to be described, she thinks, and so eliminates the apparent inevitability of describing them as necessarily following the moral law. I disagree, and will explain why an analogous problem arises for the two-aspect theory in what follows.

[15] The assumption that the will is transcendentally free is a departure from Korsgaard (1996a), who takes as her starting point instead the impossibility of acting except under the idea of freedom, as Kant appears to in *Groundwork* III. I have already said why I take Kant to have changed his mind on this issue. The fact that he changed his mind, though, does not require—as Korsgaard seems to think (1996: 161)—that he abandon the remainder of the *Groundwork* III argument from freedom to the moral law. For when he remarks (at 5: 47) that the objective validity of the moral law cannot be proved through a deduction, he immediately explains that this is not because the moral law cannot be shown to follow from freedom, but merely because freedom cannot be assumed as a premiss, since we have no independent grounds upon which to assert that we are free. Such a deduction could not be known to be sound, in other words, but it would not be invalid, as Korsgaard suggests.

principle on which to act.[16] Since any principle incorporating reference to the desires the agent has as a sensible being would amount to a sort of voluntary enslavement (a subjection to determining grounds outside the will), the only option consistent with remaining free is for the agent to take the form of law as such as the principle of her will's operation.[17] But the form of law as such just is the moral law (as Kant had described it earlier in the *Groundwork*).[18] So the moral law is not a descriptive law governing the free will's operation,[19] but rather a prescriptive law telling the free will what to do in order to remain (maximally) free. Such a law would be a categorical imperative because it would be a law binding on free wills just in so far as they are free (*GMS* 4: 441).[20]

This, briefly, is the way the story is supposed to go. There are a number of variations in the literature. In the case of none of them, though, is it easy to give a coherent formulation of what it means to say that taking the moral law as one's principle is the only option consistent with one's ineliminable interest in one's free agency. Take two formulations that have been proposed: (1) in acting immorally, the free will is acting as if it had no freedom at all;[21] (2) in acting immorally, the free will is undermining the condition of possibility of its own effectiveness, of its own freedom.[22]

---

[16] Korsgaard (1996a: 166). The crux, of course, is the 'cannot'—why we cannot is far from obvious, as Nagel points out: 'A neo-Humean regularity theory of causation seems an inappropriate model for free self-determination' (Korsgaard 1996b: 202).   [17] Korsgaard (1996a: 166–7).

[18] Wood follows Korsgaard up to the step before this one, but denies that the Formula of the Universal Law can be such a principle. Cf. Wood (1990: chapter 9; 1999: part one, especially 97–107).

[19] Korsgaard's reconstruction is intended to rebut conclusions like Schmid's (though she doesn't appear to have Schmid himself in mind). She claims, plausibly, that such interpretations mistakenly couch the whole question in theoretical terms (i.e., ask how moral evil is possible, as a theoretical question) instead of looking at it from the exclusively practical perspective that Kant intended. This issue was raised by Schmid's early reviewers, for instance in Jakob's review of *Versuch einer Moralphilosophie* (Jakob 1796). Jakob attributes the same mistake to Forberg and Reinhold as well. Eberhard, on the other hand, defended Schmid's extension of the principle of sufficient reason to the intelligible realm as a move to which Kant himself should have been sympathetic. Cf. Eberhard (1792). I will try to show that the problem of moral evil remains even when this mistake—if it is a mistake—is avoided.

[20] '[W]hat it is necessary to do merely for achieving a discretionary purpose [i.e., a hypothetical imperative] can be regarded as in itself contingent and we can always be released from the precept if we give up the purpose; on the contrary, the unconditional command leaves the will (*Wille*) no discretion with respect to the opposite, so that it alone brings with it that necessity which we require of a law' (4: 420).

[21] For examples of this view, see O'Neill (1989: chapter 3), Korsgaard (1996a: 168–73), Silber (1960: p. xc), and Hill (1985).

[22] There are two versions of this view in the literature. According to one version, the agent destroys its freedom in the act itself. Immoral action is a sort of indirect suicide of the will. Cf., e.g., Carnois (1987: 101ff.): 'The possibility of choosing a maxim which may either conform to or oppose the moral law evidences a weakness of freedom, insofar as it is incapable of determining itself solely in respect to the representation of the good' (101); 'By choosing evil, freedom freely consigns itself to heteronomy. In a way, it annihilates itself' (103). Is the suicide permanent, or does the will spring back to life in time for the next decision? According to another version, the evil action merely undermines the agent's *future* freedom. Cf., e.g., Guyer (1998: 34ff.): 'Both good and evil actions are free actions, the former expressing the free decision to preserve and promote further opportunities for free action, the latter expressing an equally free decision to destroy or damage further opportunities. On

Although the first is true, according to Kant, it does not in any obvious way show what it would need to show. Acting as I would were I not a free agent (whatever that amounts to) need not make me any less a free agent—no more than acting as if I were ill need have any impact on the state of my health. This formulation gains what apparent plausibility it has by running together seeming unfree and being unfree.[23] The second formulation suggests a material threat to freedom from immorality, but it brings its own difficulties. If the claim is taken to be that the evil will is somehow ineffectual, it entails that moral evil (an imputable choice of immoral action) is a literal impossibility.[24] If, on the other hand, it is taken to be that the immoral will genuinely acts and thereafter becomes ineffectual (a difficult view to formulate given Kant's position on the atemporality of intelligible freedom), would this then mean that it thereafter becomes pathologically determined? This would make moral reform impossible— a peculiar result and one Kant does not (where he discusses the issue) ever seem to accept.[25]

All such reconstructions face the same dilemma: either they fail to provide a compelling explanation for why any rational agent, *qua* agent, *must* take the moral law as its principle, or they succeed by making morality partially constitutive of

this account, it should be clear that there is no logical puzzle how an evil act can be both free and yet undermine freedom—it's just a matter of one token of freedom affecting other tokens' (35). Every immoral action leads to an incremental loss of freedom, and successive acts are incrementally less free. (This interprepation requires that moral responsibility admit of degrees, on Kant's account.) Guyer (2000b: 54ff.) expresses the wish that Kant should have the very logical problem Guyer (1998) claims Kant avoids: it is a *weakness* in Kant's *Groundwork* III argument, he writes there, that 'a free will is not *logically* or analytically compelled to act only on moral rather than material considerations, but rather must do so only if it is to *maintain* or *preserve* its freedom' (56). A better argument, in other words, would have shown immoral action to be logically impossible.

[23] Gass (1994) points out this error.

[24] Wood offers an interpretation like this in Wood (1984: 81–2) and gives an example that exposes the difficulty of this position: 'Consider a parallel case. An indifferent swimmer may have the power to save himself if he falls into deep water. But he has no power, only a possibility, of drowning in the same eventuality. Although he has the power to swim, he may drown if he does not exercise that power effectively, due (say) to confusion or panic. In the latter case, his possibility of drowning is due to a kind of weakness or lack of power, though not to a lack of the power to swim.' The problem with Wood's example is with the claim that such a failure can be called free in the morally relevant sense. We would not feel comfortable attributing the swimmer's drowning to his free choice. But if the case really is parallel, why should we feel any more comfortable attributing evil to an agent's free choice? Silber's formulation of this point is a good one, and is intended to point out the difficulty of Kant's position: 'The will escapes the law only in the sense that a prisoner who is shot to death as he goes over the wall of a prison can be said to have escaped. The categorical imperative is inescapable because its violation, according to Kant, destroys the personality of the violator. Since freedom is a power whose fulfillment depends upon the structure of rationality, its irrational misuse results in impotence' (Silber 1960: p. cxxv). Silber explains Kant's difficulty with moral evil by saying it is the result of a misleading analogy between theoretical and practical reason. Kant, he believes, concluded from the fact that irrationality is theoretically impotent the (false) claim that irrationality is practically impotent (Silber 1960: p. cxxx).

[25] Cf., e.g., 6: 47. Note, though, that Kant's position on the atemporality of intelligible freedom itself makes trouble for his account of moral reform.

action. The prescriptive law interpretation succeeds, then, only if it also encounters the very problem the descriptive law interpretation does.[26]

It is important to notice that this is not simply a problem having to do with a certain class of backward-looking assessment of conduct (though my way of putting it up until now—in terms of imputability—has surely suggested that). It is a problem with the forward-looking, deliberative perspective as well. Anyone convinced that the very possibility of acting relied on using one's agency according to the moral law would have to attribute any potential failure on her part to act in accordance with that law to factors outside her control, or to limitations in the effectiveness of her rational agency. (In fact this is just the view of moral failure Kant himself suggests in the second *Critique*.)[27] It makes no sense for an agent holding such a view to subject her motives to intense scrutiny (since if her behaviour follows from the wrong ones—what is it to *her*?). Striving to be a morally better person amounts, on such a view, to striving to act (rather than merely behaving) more often—perhaps something we should want to do,[28] but surely not identical to striving towards moral improvement. Such a view, in short, is both false to the phenomenology of agency and perniciously morally optimistic. So, at least, thought Kant's critics. That Kant thought so as well is evidenced, I argue in §II, by the project in *Religion*.

Reinhold's complaint

As Kant was at work on *Religion*, his effort to clarify his position on moral evil, Reinhold was working on the same problem simultaneously.[29] He came up with a

---

[26] Note that the distinction between *Wille* and *Willkür*—which Kant evidently introduced in order to rebut the contention that he had equated the will's transcendental freedom with its capacity for rational self-determination—in fact does nothing to remedy the problem. *Wille* is practical reason; it legislates the moral law. *Willkür* is the power of choice which forms the maxims that guide action. The distinction between these capacities cannot solve the problem unless one can conceive of a relation between them that allows both that the legislation of *Wille* determine *Willkür*'s maxims *and* that *Willkür* be capable of forming maxims that prioritize the incentives of the agent's sensible nature over the moral law's demands. If one denies the first, one thereby denies that the legislation of *Wille* is *Willkür*'s *own* law; if one denies the second, one denies that evil is possible as a free choice. Despite these considerations, some commentators have thought that some response to the problem of the imputability of evil can be made out on the basis of the *Wille/Willkür* distinction. Cf., e.g., Beck (1960: 176–208) and Hudson (1991).

[27] 'Recognition of the moral law is . . . consciousness of an activity of practical reason from objective grounds, which fails to express its effect in actions only because subjective (pathological) causes hinder it' (5: 79). The explanation of the possibility of such hindrance is the same as the explanation of why obedience to the moral law is a duty and not a fact: because of the limitations of humans as finite rational beings. 'All three concepts, however—that of an *incentive*, of an *interest* and of a *maxim*—can be applied only to finite beings. For they all presuppose a limitation of the nature of a being, in that the subjective constitution of its choice (*Willkür*) does not of itself accord with the objective law of a practical reason' (5:79). Fischer (1988: 32) points out, commenting on this section of the *Critique*, that 'Kant simply dodged the second part of the task of his appraisal of what is good and evil in itself.'

[28] Cf. Velleman (1996).

[29] According to Prauss (1983: 84), also independently.

response instructively different from Kant's, and published it in the second volume of his *Briefe über die kantische Philosophie*.[30] Kant's view in the second *Critique*, he charges, comes too close to the Leibniz-Wolffian compatibilist view which defines freedom as reason-determined action in opposition to drive-determined action (264).[31] Reinhold worries that this amounts to freeing the will from the passions by enslaving it to the intellect.

All those who have tried to unite the necessity of moral action with the freedom of it have found no means to do this other than taking freedom to consist in a particular type of necessity, a necessity peculiar to the moral law—in *moral necessity*. The knew no other way to rescue the will from enslavement to instinct than to make it the slave of the intellect. (294)[32]

He points out that this entails the unfreedom of all immoral conduct: 'Out of the conflation of the action of practical reason—which only gives the law and which is indeed self-active but by no means free—with the action of the will ... must follow nothing less than the impossibility of freedom for all *immoral* action' (267). Freedom ought instead to be taken to consist:

neither in the mere independence of the will from compulsion by instinct ... nor in the mere independence of practical reason from everything apart from itself, nor again *only* in these two types of independence taken together, but rather also *in the independence of the person from necessitation by practical reason itself*. In the *negative* sense [freedom] comprises these three types of independence, and in the *positive* sense it is, in addition, the capacity for self-determination through free choice for or against the practical law. (272)

The alternative view Reinhold proposes, though, is based on a fundamental disagreement with the second *Critique's* account of how we know we are free. He thought that we are directly aware of our own freedom (instead of indirectly, through awareness of the moral law), and that this awareness cannot be mistaken,

---

[30] Reinhold (1790–2, vol. 2). Page numbers in this discussion refer to the original edition. Cf. Ameriks (2000b: 81–162), Beiser (1987: 226–65), Pinkard (2002: 96–104), and Frank (1997: 152–285), for discussions of the importance of Reinhold, and especially his *Briefe*, for the dissemination of Kant's philosophy.

[31] 'Some', he writes (267), explicitly interpret Kant this way, taking Kant to mean by 'freedom' only practical *reason's* independence of determination by desire. The 'some' involved clearly include Schmid; Reinhold cites Schmid's *Wörterbuch zum leichteren Gebrauch der Kantischen Schriften*, which had by this time already come out in a second edition (269). They may also include Brastberger, who explicitly equated transcendental freedom with rational (moral) willing (cf. Brastberger 1792: 61). They may include Abicht as well, who discusses a Reinhold-style 'moral necessitation' complaint and offers a response based on the familiar distinction between outer and inner (moral) necessitation. Unlike the former, Abicht argues, the latter is not a sort of passivity, because what it consists in is '*self-* necessitation (better, self-determination)'—and since this just *amounts* to a thing's activity, it cannot hinder or constrain a thing's activity (cf. Abicht 1789: especially 67ff.).

[32] He goes on to point out (300) that a view like Schmid's cannot ultimately distinguish between moral and natural necessity, because the effectiveness of practical reason depends on the absence of intervening external forces, that is, ultimately, on something other than itself (of course, Schmid had admitted almost as much). He compares (303) these new Kantians to the Leibnizians: the latter sacrificed freedom to theoretical reason; the former to practical reason.

any more than our awareness that we are rational beings could be mistaken (352). Freedom is incomprehensible in this sense only: just like other faculties, it must be known through its effects, and its source must be a mystery (315).

> I know just as well that I have a will, and that it is free, as I know that I have sensibility, understanding and reason. I also *know* what these faculties consist in through their effects. But in the case of none of them do I know *whence* and *through what* they arise, because they are basic faculties. (284)[33]

Of course, this view was unavailable to Kant, as I have already indicated. Kant was concerned about the status of immoral actions for reasons similar to Reinhold's, and was working on his own attempt to address the problem of moral evil in his moral psychology at the same time Reinhold was working on his *Briefe*. But this disagreement with Reinhold on the status of our knowledge of our freedom is one of the reasons for the ultimate failure of that effort.

II. KANT'S VIEW IN *RELIGION WITHIN THE BOUNDARIES OF MERE REASON* (AND ITS PARTIAL RETRACTION)

It seems as though Kant gave the account of moral evil that he gave in *Religion* precisely because it appeared impossible for him to give such an account. That is what people were saying in print, and it looked like a *reductio* of his view of freedom. If the first two books of *Religion* are to be read as the solution to a problem—the problem of how evil can be a positive choice—then we should begin by assuming the positive conception of evil outlined in the passages from *Religion* I quoted at the beginning of the chapter, and try to answer two questions. In what does moral evil consist? How does Kant revise or develop his account of moral personality in *Religion* in order to make sense of the possibility of a choice of evil so construed?

Moral evil in *Religion*

The problem of evil Kant discusses is not that of how there can be actions that are contrary to the moral law, but rather that of how an individual can be fundamentally disposed to produce non-moral actions when placed in appropriate circumstances. Kant held that an agent's moral character is fundamentally unitary. Actions are informed by maxims (i.e., subjective principles of conduct) and lower-order maxims are informed by higher-order maxims, all arrayed under a single (posited) highest-order maxim, the individual's fundamental moral disposition. The question about evil is, then, a question about the basic constitution of the agent's character rather than a question about the moral quality of individual

---

[33] Jakob, like Reinhold, took freedom to be a *Grundvermögen* or basic faculty (cf. Jakob 1794: 47).

actions. Kant approaches the issue in this way for a number of reasons, two of which are relevant for the following discussion.

The first is that the assumption of a system of maxims explains the sort of continuity of character that moral agency seems to require. That actions are governed by guiding principles is what makes them attributable as actions. Kant sometimes says that an agent's basic moral disposition can be inferred from the individual's conduct, or could be if we had all the relevant psychological information (cf. A549/B577). He sometimes says the opposite: that moral character is inscrutable, even to the agent himself (cf. A551n/B579n and 6: 51). But in either case moral character is assumed to have a high degree of continuity—for good or ill—over time. This in itself is not psychological determinism; it is continuity of character. Kant's second reason, though, was in fact his eagerness to accommodate the thesis of psychological (as well as mechanistic) determinism for agents viewed as phenomena. The unity of character thesis allows a tidy explanation for the psychological predictability that he wants to ascribe to empirical characters—for instance the fact that a bad character can be foreseen even in an individual's childhood (cf. *KrV* A554/B582, *KpV* 5: 99–100, *R* 6: 25).[34]

There are three ways, Kant says, in which a character can be morally evil. The first is frailty. In this case, although the will's maxim is good (in conformity with the moral law), when the time for action comes the maxim turns out to be a weaker incentive than inclination. The individual acts according to inclination, as it were in spite of himself. The second is impurity of motive. In this case the maxim is in conformity with the moral law, but is adopted not purely out of respect for that law. Rather, other incentives determine the will to act in accordance with duty (e.g., those of the shopkeeper who refrains from cheating the child out of fear of losing the

---

[34] There are serious difficulties with this aspect of Kant's position. Chief among them is the problem of moral reform. Granted that the empirical character an individual has is based upon his intelligible character, and hence free, nevertheless, for the confirmed sinner the question must arise, how could I do otherwise *now*? Moral imputation demands that reform be possible. 'If a man is, however, corrupt in the very ground of his maxims, how can he possibly bring about this revolution through his own powers, and of himself become a good man? And yet duty bids us do this, and duty demands nothing of us which we cannot do' (*R* 6: 47). Kant replies to the problem by claiming that a radical change of heart is always possible, and that reform, if it occurs, is not gradual but revolutionary: 'This can be effected only through a *revolution* in the character of the person ... and he can become a new man only by a kind of rebirth, as through a new creation ..., and a change of heart' (*R* 6: 47). In response to the question of whether this change of heart would not create a disturbing discontinuity in someone's empirical character, which after all is supposed to be predictable on the basis of empirical psychological principles, Kant responds that such a revolution would *not* in fact produce a sudden break in the continuity of behaviour. Even in the presence of a change of heart, of a morally good will, empirical virtue requires long practice: 'Virtue in this sense is won little by little, and, for some men, requires long practice ... during which the individual passes from a tendency to vice, through gradual reformation of his conduct and strengthening of his maxims, to an opposite tendency' (*R* 6: 47). Of course it is hard to see what the good is, morally speaking, of a change of heart following which *none* of the agent's actions would be different from the actions the agent would have performed in the absence of the change of heart. But to admit that they might be different seems to run squarely against the very problem that Kant is trying to defend against, namely the threat of unpredictability of empirical action.

parents' business). The third case Kant calls variously depravity, or the corruption or perversity of the will. In this case the will's maxim subordinates the moral law to non-moral incentives. The law is followed only when it does not conflict with these incentives (*R* 6: 29–30). In each case, the relevant maxim informing action can be traced back through a series of higher-level maxims to a posited highest maxim, or governing moral disposition, which, as it appears from the three options, could have one of three forms: (1) act in accordance with the moral law, regardless of whether it is in my interest to do so (and the weak-willed individual must be presumed to have this maxim, though inclination often has the upper hand when it is transformed into lower-level maxims informing actions); (2) act in accordance with the moral law, since it is on the whole in my best interest to do so (only certain interests can obtain here—Kant mentions ambition, self-love and sympathy—for if one endorsed interests not reconcilable with the legality of one's actions, one would fall into either the first or the third category); and (3) act in accordance with inclination, regardless of the dictates of the moral law (the genuinely evil will).

There are a couple of things worth noting about Kant's account of the third type of case. (It is with this third case that I will be concerned, though similar considerations apply in the other two.) First, Kant believes that the content of the evil individual's highest maxim cannot be: 'act in opposition to the moral law in every circumstance'. Were this the case, the will would be not (humanly) evil, but rather diabolical (*R* 6: 5). Immorality for its own sake—i.e., the express programme of thwarting the moral law in every instance—is not, according to Kant, a humanly possible motivation: 'The human being (even the worst) does not repudiate the moral law, whatever his maxims, in rebellious attitude (by revoking obedience to it). The law rather imposes itself on him irresistibly, because of his moral predisposition' (*R* 6: 36). For this reason, Kant says, the viciousness (*Bösartigkeit*) of human nature is not malice (*Bosheit*) 'if we take this word in the strict sense, namely as a disposition (a subjective *principle* of maxims) to incorporate the evil *qua evil* into one's maxim' (*R* 6: 37). It is, rather, a 'perversity of the heart' which is only to be called evil because of its effects (*R* 6: 37). This view is based on Kant's belief that the conditions of moral accountability presuppose a rational nature (and that a rational nature is one that cannot be moved to act irrationally just for the sake of acting irrationally).[35] Except in the case of holy wills, they also presuppose an

---

[35] Wood (1978: 210–15) defends this claim by pointing out that it is not a psychological one, but rather one that follows directly from the conditions of moral obligation as Kant defines them. In order to be morally accountable, we must recognize that the moral law applies to us, and this recognition must give rise to a respect for the law which provides a motivation to follow it. A being incapable of recognizing the validity of the moral law would not be capable of good and evil in the first place. Wood's is not an entirely adequate defence, however, for it seems that one could quite easily recognize that the law applies to one, and thwart it for that very reason. This seems to be what Augustine describes in *Confessions*, 2: 4, when he says that what he sought was 'to be gratuitously evil', and that there was no cause of his evilness other than the evilness itself. 'I loved to stray—not that toward which I strayed, but I loved the straying itself.' This idea of evil as motivated by pride or defiance is one of the main differences between Schelling's (late) view of moral evil and Kant's.

inclination to take desires as sufficient grounds for action. Kant here insists (in contrast to the second *Critique* discussion) that this is a tendency of the will (i.e., something imputable to the will), not a tendency of the sensuous nature to over-ride the will (i.e., something attributable to the sensuous nature or to an external limitation on the activity of the will) (cf. *R* 6: 34–5). Finally, the difference between a good and an evil will cannot, for Kant, be that the first simply chooses the moral law and the second simply chooses the principle of self-love. Rather, the evil will results from a 'perverse' ordering of the two main motivations, whereby the moral law is subordinated to the principle of self-love, with obedience to the first conditional on its compatibility with the second. The good will is a result of the proper ordering of motivations, such that the principle of self-love is subordin-ated to the moral law.

When Kant approaches the question of how the moral law can come to be subordinated to the inclinations in a person's disposition, he relies on a new distinction between two capacities—the will (*Wille*) and the power of choice (*Willkür*)—of the will as a general faculty (also *Wille*). He introduces this distinc-tion most explicitly only in the introduction to the *Metaphysics of Morals*, but he uses it centrally in *Religion*. The moral law is the product of the legislation of the *Wille*, which is equivalent to practical reason; this legislation is binding upon the *Willkür*, which is that part of the will responsible for the formation of maxims. Here is Kant's formulation of the distinction from the *Metaphysics of Morals*:

> Laws proceed from the will (*Wille*), maxims from choice (*Willkür*). In man the latter is a free choice (*eine freie Willkür*); the will, which is directed to nothing beyond the law itself, cannot be called either free or unfree, since it is not directed to actions but immediately to giving laws for the maxims of actions (and is, therefore, practical reason itself). Hence the will directs with absolute necessity and is itself *subject to* no necessitation. Only *choice* can therefore be called *free*. (*R* 6: 226)

Incentives become grounds of action, according to Kant in *Religion*, only through being freely incorporated, by *Willkür*, into its maxims.

> [F]reedom of the power of choice has the characteristic, entirely peculiar to it, that it cannot be determined to action through any incentive except so far as the human being has incorporated it into his maxim . . . ; only in this way can an incentive, whatever it may be, coexist with the absolute spontaneity of the power of choice (of freedom). (*R* 6: 23–4)

Since maxims form a system, with lower-order maxims subsumed under higher-order maxims of increasing degrees of generality, the subordination of the moral law to the principle of self-love at issue is that occurring in the fundamental moral disposition, the ultimate maxim, of an individual. The adoption of this maxim, which determines moral character, must itself, Kant claims, 'always be a deed of freedom (for otherwise the use or abuse of the human being's power of choice with respect to the moral law could not be imputed to him, nor could the good or evil in him be called "moral")' (*R* 6: 21; see also 6: 31 and 6: 44). One of Kant's aims in *Religion*—one I will not discuss—is to show how the propensity towards moral evil can be both the result of a free choice and universal among human beings.[36] This is why he refers to moral disposition as an 'innate characteristic' in this passage, whose main thrust is nevertheless that one's fundamental moral disposition is chosen rather than given:

> Moreover, to have one or the other disposition by nature as an innate characteristic does not mean here that the disposition has not been earned in the human being who harbours it, i.e. that he is not its author, but means rather that it has not been earned in time (that he has been one way or the other *always, from his youth on*). The disposition, i.e. the first subjective ground of the adoption of the maxims, can only be a single one, and it applies to the entire use of freedom universally. This disposition too, however, must be adopted through the free power of choice, for otherwise it could not be imputed. (*R* 6: 25)

A posited highest maxim, or governing moral disposition, provides a subjective justificatory reference point for lower-order maxims without having such a subjective reference point itself. This is not to say that there is nothing with reference to which it could be justified. Rather, according to Kant, it requires an objective and not a subjective justification. It is objectively self-justifying if it dictates conformity with the moral law, unjustifiable if it dictates non-conformity.

That is, although a good disposition has a reason for being what it is (the moral law), an evil disposition is what it is *without* any reason. We can give neither an empirical nor a subjective explanation of how such a maxim is chosen. If we could give a causal explanation, the choice would not be free, as it must be if we are to hold an agent responsible for his moral disposition as a whole (*R* 6: 39–40). If we could give another subjective reason, we would have to posit a still higher-order maxim; the posited highest maxim would then not be the highest after all, and a regress would begin.[37] Finally, such a maxim is not, by hypothesis, grounded in practical reason.

The incomprehensibility of evil

Kant remarks at several points in the *Religion* discussion that to be grounded in freedom, such a choice of disposition must be 'contingent' (e.g., at 6: 32, where he says evil maxims must be viewed as 'accidental', and at 6: 40, where he equates 'freedom' and 'contingency' of the moral disposition). But these remarks occur right alongside remarks to the effect that a free being cannot see itself as not being

---

[36] For discussions of this issue, cf. Allison (1990: 152–7), Rossi and Wreen (1991: 54–76), Wood (1970: 208–48; 1999: 283–320).

[37] 'That the first subjective ground of the adoption of moral maxims is inscrutable can be seen provisionally from this: Since the adoption is free, its ground (e.g. why I have adopted an evil maxim and not a good one instead) must not be sought in any incentive of nature, but always again in a maxim; and since any such maxim must have its ground as well, yet apart from a maxim no *determining ground* of the free power of choice (*der freien Willkür*) ought to, or can, be adduced, we are endlessly referred back in the series of subjective determining grounds, without ever being able to come to the first ground' (*R* 6: 21n).

subject to laws because it is impossible to conceive of a lawless cause, for instance at 6: 35: 'To think of oneself as a freely acting being, yet as exempted from the one law commensurate to such a being (the moral law), would amount to the thought of a cause operating without any law at all (for the determination according to natural law is abolished on account of freedom): and this is a contradiction.' This apparent conflict is surely Kant's reason for holding that moral evil is incomprehensible: 'the original predisposition (which none other than the human being himself could have corrupted, if this corruption is to be imputed to him) is a predisposition to good; there is no conceivable ground for us, therefore, from which moral evil could first have come in us' (*R* 6: 43); 'The rational origin . . . of this disharmony in our power of choice with respect to the way it incorporates lower incentives in its maxims and makes them supreme, i.e. this propensity to evil, remains inexplicable to us . . .' (*R* 6: 43).

Moral evil is incomprehensible because it must be the work of a lawless cause, and lawless causes are incomprehensible. But if moral evil is incomprehensible, how can we know there is any, according to Kant? What grounds can there be for asserting that this incomprehensible choice is in fact possible? This is a difficult question for Kant to answer (though he never acknowledges this difficulty in the text of *Religion*). There are two possible sources of such knowledge: what we are allowed or required to infer from the fact of reason about our noumenal causality, and what we can say on the basis of empirical moral psychology (that is, on the basis of introspection and of observation of other agents).

We get no such knowledge from the first source. There is nothing about the concept of freedom in general that entails a capacity for evil as well as good.[38] And the freedom that we know ourselves to have is revealed to us exclusively by the moral law; we infer from this law, for practical purposes, a cause that can act in accordance with it. The moral law, however, contains no provision that we be capable of acting against it as well as in accordance with it, and so in the absence of some further grounds, we cannot conclude, for practical purposes, the existence of freedom to transgress or reject the law. This is true on either of the two interpretations of 'law' given in §I above. We cannot conclude on the basis of what we know through practical reason that evil is possible, for this would amount, on the first interpretation, to conceiving a cause as acting independently of the law that allowed us to posit the existence of the cause in the first place, or, on the second, to conceiving of the moral law as one whose thwarting agency would survive.

That leaves the empirical option, and this is the one Kant takes, both in *Religion* and in the *Metaphysics of Morals*. We are allowed to think that we are capable of

---

[38] The concept of freedom does not contain the notion of a capacity for good *and* evil, Kant tells us in a discussion of God's freedom (made in an addition for the second (1794) edition to the footnote at 6: 49): 'There is no difficulty in reconciling the concept of *freedom* with the idea of God as a *necessary* being, for freedom does not consist in the contingency of an action (in its not being determined through any ground at all), i.e. not in indeterminism ([the thesis] that God must be equally capable of doing good or evil, if his action is to be called free) but in absolute spontaneity' (*R* 6: 49n). Human beings are capable of both good and evil, but not, or at least not solely, in virtue of being free—for God is free without being capable of anything but good.

evil because moral evil is *empirically* given: '. . . the existence of this propensity to evil in human nature can be established through experiential demonstrations of the actual resistance in time of the human power of choice against the law . . .' (*R* 6: 35). The placement of this claim in the discussion in *Religion* (in the paragraph following the claim that it is contradictory to conceive of a cause operating without a law) is exactly right: because we cannot conceive of such a cause *a priori*, we can infer its operation only from experience. Kant grants that there is an '*a priori* concept' of moral evil (*R* 6: 35); but the nature of his discussion of it is hypothetical: we know *a priori* that if there *were* moral evil, it would consist in the subordination of the moral law to sensible inclinations. It is upon this *a priori* concept that Kant bases his description of the evil will, as well as his claim that rebelliousness for its own sake is impossible. But the possibility of moral evil as an act of will is deduced not from the will's freedom but instead from the actual moral evil encountered in experience.

The claim that evil is given empirically (and only empirically) is reiterated throughout *Religion*. Kant first makes it in the opening discussion: the proponents of an optimistic view of human moral progress, he remarks, 'surely, if the issue is *moral* good or evil (not just growth in civilization), . . . have not drawn this view from experience, if they mean the *morally* good or evil (as opposed to civilization), for the history of all times attests far too powerfully against it' (*R* 6: 20). Of the claim that there is an inherent propensity to evil rooted in human nature, he says: 'We can spare ourselves a formal proof that there must be such a corrupt propensity rooted in the human being, in view of the multitude of woeful examples that the experience of human *deeds* parades before us' (*R* 6: 32–3). He then goes on to cite examples. The peculiarity of this procedure is striking.[39] That there is moral evil is something that can be known only through empirical observation—the same empirical observation that, according to Kant, must see human behaviour as both causally and psychologically determined, and does not allow us to see the true nature of our own or any one else's (noumenal) moral character—'for the depths of [an individual's] heart (the subjective first ground of his maxims) are to him inscrutable' (*R* 6: 51; see also *KrV* A551n/B579n).[40]

---

[39] This problem was not overlooked by critics (cf., e.g., Eberhard 1794: especially 40).

[40] Interestingly, Kant, at the same time as he sets down the position that evil is unintelligible (even if empirically given), also takes that position that, according to Kierkegaard, goes hand in hand with it: (1) Evil is a *universal* human propensity, so deeply rooted in the will that 'we must say that it is found in the human being by nature' (*R* 6: 35), 'as natural propensity, . . . not to be *extirpated* through human forces' (*R* 6: 37), which corrupts the ground of all maxims (*R* 6: 37). It is evil we see empirically, but what we conclude on this basis is not a capacity of the *Willkür* but an incapacity, a universal *deficiency* in man's nature, one that (2) human beings can never wholly overcome. For the human individual with such a propensity can never wholly measure up to the demands of morality. The most an individual can hope for is 'constant *progress* from bad to better' (*R* 6: 48). But this progress can never amount to justification, for having started from evil (as everyone does) leaves 'a debt which is impossible for him to wipe out' (*R* 6: 72). 'He cannot regard the fact that, after his change of heart, he has not incurred new debts as equivalent to his having paid off the old ones. Nor can he produce, in the future conduct of a good life, a surplus over and above what he is under obligation to perform each time; for his duty at each instant is to do all the good in his power' (*R* 6: 72).

Yet this is the only way Kant can proceed: In the *Metaphysics of Morals*, he explains why more explicitly:

[F]reedom of choice (*Willkür*) cannot be defined—as some have tried to define it—as the ability to make a choice for or against the law (*libertas indifferentiae*),[41] even though choice as a *phenomenon* provides frequent examples of this in experience. For we know freedom (as it first becomes manifest to us through the moral law) only as a *negative* property in us, namely that of not being *necessitated* to act through any sensible determining grounds. But we cannot present *theoretically* freedom as a *noumenon*, that is, freedom regarded as the ability of the human being merely as an intelligence, and show how it can *exercise constraint* upon his sensible choice; we cannot therefore present freedom as a positive property. But we can indeed see that, although experience shows that the human being as a *sensible being* is able to choose *in opposition to* as well as *in conformity with* the law, his freedom as an *intelligible being* cannot be *defined* by this, since appearances cannot make any supersensible object (such as free choice) understandable. We can also see that freedom can never be located in a rational subject's being able to choose in opposition to his (lawgiving) reason, even though experience proves often enough that this happens (though we still cannot comprehend how this is possible). (*MS* 6: 226)

Kant concludes this discussion with the observation: 'Only freedom in relation to the internal lawgiving of reason is really an ability; the possibility of deviating from it is an inability' (*MS* 6: 227). The point is this: although we see empirically that not every action is moral, we cannot attach any (independently derived) noumenal ground to this phenomenal observation. For neither negative freedom (independence from determination by sensible inclinations) nor positive freedom (determinability by pure practical reason) is or entails freedom for morally evil actions.[42]

Reinhold's reaction to the remarks in the Introduction to the *Metaphysics of Morals* is easy to anticipate.[43] How is it possible, he asks, that the Kant who, in *Religion*, denies that evil arises directly out of sensible impulses, and affirms that moral evil is possible only through our own act, that the *a priori* concept of evil must involve the free resistance of the power of choice to the moral law, can write,

---

[41] Kant is wrong to identify the view that the freedom of choice is a capacity to act for or against the law at will with the indifference view of freedom, for the latter is generally seen as implying either a balance among competing motives or an ability to ignore motives altogether, but the former need imply neither of these. Reinhold points this out. Nevertheless, it is not the idea of indifference that Kant is really objecting to. It is, rather, the idea of a *capacity* of the will to choose against the moral law.

[42] Note the continuity of formulation: the formulation in the *Metaphysics of Morals* is identical to those in the *Groundwork* (at 4: 446) and the second *Critique* (at 5: 33): '*Freedom* of choice is this independence from being *determined* by sensible impulses; this is the negative concept of freedom. The positive concept of freedom is that of the ability of pure reason to be of itself practical. But this is not possible except by the subjection of the maxim of every action to the condition of its qualifying as universal law' (6: 213–14). Kant's gestures in the direction of a positive conception of evil in *Religion* have brought about no change in his definition of freedom.

[43] The following remarks were published in Reinhold (1796–7). I quote them as reproduced in Bittner and Cramer (1975), and the page numbers below refer to that volume. Translations are mine.

in the introduction to the *Metaphysics of Morals*, that the freedom of choice cannot be defined as the freedom to choose for or against the moral law? (310–11). 'If the moral law announces to us no other freedom than that which consists in the self-activity of reason, then the capacity to act *immorally* is not only an *incapacity*, but is simply *impossible*' (323–4).

[The categorical imperative] *is valid* only in those cases in which it is followed, and can therefore never be transgressed. Its *not having been followed* cannot be a *transgression*. It is, rather, a necessary result of the circumstance that *human choice*, in certain cases, has *no negative freedom*, no independence of sensible incentives—is no *human choice*—and that *positive freedom* in these cases is not effective, *practical* reason is *not practical*. (314–15)

He accuses Kant of accepting Schmid's position: 'I can answer these questions on the basis of the Kantian doctrine either not at all, or at best through the principles of *intelligible fatalism*' (318).

Of course, Reinhold's characterization of Kant's view is more univocal than that view itself. Kant had good reasons for wanting, in some sense, to say that moral evil *is* a free choice of the will, and that freedom is not exclusively a capacity to adopt maxims in accordance with the moral law. These reasons are, ultimately, the same as Reinhold's. Where he differs from Reinhold is in also having good reasons for denying just this claim. For he wants neither to make transcendent claims about human freedom nor to undermine the notion that the moral law is binding on the free will in virtue of being the only possible principle of such a will's operation (i.e., the 'freedom entails an unconditional practical imperative' direction of the reciprocity thesis)—both things Reinhold's *Briefe* account ended up doing. So what Kant does, most evidently in *Religion* but to some extent throughout his moral-philosophical works, is to try to steer a path 0between acknowledging a freedom that has no law corresponding to it, in any ordinary sense, and denying that there can be such a capacity. But no such path exists. The end result is a situation in which the notion of autonomy and that of moral responsibility that Kant had intended to join together in fact stand in tension with one another. Kant's successors would have to decide which of the two to preserve.

3

Idealism and Autonomy in Schelling's Early Systems

Schelling, like many in his generation, began his career concerned with a task that might best be described as systematizing Kant. Since he accepted, along with his contemporaries, a substantial distinction between the spirit and the letter of the critical philosophy, his results contained stark disagreements with the actual Kant from very early on. Still, central Kantian problems were his main concern. How to think human freedom together with a systematically comprehensible natural world? How to reconcile the demands of theoretical and practical reason?

Fichte had embraced the strategy, suggested in the second *Critique*, of answering both questions with the same move by subordinating theoretical reason to practical. Schelling thought the Fichtean solution resulted in the impossibility of seeing nature as independent of us, seeing natural science as constituting an autonomous sphere and making autonomous knowledge claims. Instead he (like Hegel after him) followed the suggestion Kant had made in the *Critique of Judgment*: that the tension between theoretical and moral standpoints might be resolvable through the regulative idea of an overall teleology of nature. Schelling's early philosophy of nature (expounded in a series of works during the period between 1797 and 1806) was an attempt to show how a version of Kant's principle of teleology could have the status (to use Kant's terminology) of an objectively and not merely subjectively valid principle, and how its application could be extended to inorganic as well as to organic nature. In this he took himself to be following Kant's own lead, or at least heading in a direction that Kant, for consistency's sake, would also have been obliged to take.[1] His philosophy of spirit, developed over the same period, applied the general framework to epistemology, ethics (including the problem of individual freedom) and the philosophy of history.

This chapter traces the development of Schelling's thinking about freedom, system, autonomy and evil through 1806. I show how the general unification of theoretical and practical reason Schelling had offered by the end of his early period shared not only the virtue of Kant's suggested solution (making it possible to see how natural beings *qua* natural beings can nevertheless be rationally self-determining), but also its vice (making it impossible to see how moral and immoral action can be

---

[1] Cf. Horstmann (1991: 131ff.).

the result of free choice in the broadly libertarian sense Kant had originally endorsed). The chapter that follows this one will examine the reorientation of Schelling's thinking beginning with his 1809 essay *On the Essence of Human Freedom*. I will argue there that this reorientation was inspired by an appreciation of the incompatibility of an autonomist account of the source of normativity with the possibility of moral evil, and that the revised conception of freedom Schelling develops underlies the other differences between his earlier and later works.

In this chapter my goal, then, is to answer two questions. First, how does Schelling propose to achieve the 'unity' of theoretical and practical reason that he and his contemporaries sought? Second, what conception of freedom is at issue in this attempt?[2] I will begin, then, with a brief examination of Schelling's conception of philosophical system (in §I) and continue with an examination of his freedom conception (in §II). My discussion will emphasize the continuity underlying the often surprising revisions undergone by both aspects of the view over the course of the twelve-year period (1794–1806) at issue. *The System of Transcendental Idealism* (1800) will be given disproportionate weight, because of its relative transparency and its status as one of the most widely read works (in the decades immediately following its publication) of Schelling's early period. The early works on *Naturphilosophie* will not figure as centrally. I will discuss only the conception of natural causality at work in them, as it is central to Schelling's vision of the unity of nature and freedom. But how Schelling thought his approach would contribute to the theory and practice of natural science, though a topic that deserves more attention than it has so far received, is tangential to my purposes here.[3]

I. THE EARLY SYSTEMATIC PROJECT

The constraints of systematicity

In the background of Schelling's attempt at systematizing the Kantian critical philosophy stood a conception of philosophical system influenced by Reinhold and the early Fichte and characterized by (what seem today excessively) strong

---

[2] There is one disclaimer I ought to make at this point. Schelling's systematic ambitions were grand. How anyone could have envisaged doing what he set out to do is the topic of a book in and of itself—and it has already been the topic of many. The variety of interpretations testifies to the obscurity of Schelling's view (about which he himself changed his mind several times in the course of a very few years). In the following discussion I propose to examine only what Schelling set out to do (and why); I will not offer a judgement on what he succeeded in doing (and how). Helpful discussions of Schelling's larger project, its justification and its development, can be found in Beiser (2002: section IV), Frank (1985), Fischer (1872), Horstmann (1991: chapters IIB and IIIB), Horstmann (2000), Marquet (1973), Pinkard (2002: chapter 7), Tilliette (1970), White (1983b) and Wieland (1967).

[3] An excellent discussion of the motives informing Schelling's philosophy of nature can be found in Wieland (1967). Other helpful discussions include Beiser (2002: 483–550), chapters by Wolfgang Förster and Hans Heinz Holz in Sandkühler (1984), Heuser-Kessler (1989), Koeller (1989), and Küppers (1992).

constraints of unity and certainty. Let me say something about these constraints before explaining how they inform Schelling's approach to the 'unity of reason' problem he found in Kant.

First, Schelling accepted the project of articulating a body of philosophical knowledge that would be immune from sceptical attack of the kind advanced by early critics of Kant and Reinhold (especially those enunciated by Schulze and Maimon).[4] Second, he thought that such a project could be realized only as a system of propositions arrayed in a hierarchy of justification with each ultimately deducible from indubitable first principles. Finally, he thought that there could be no more than one such first principle, and that the result of accepting more than one would be the introduction of an unpalatable distinction between different kinds of knowledge and different kinds of truth. A paradigmatic discussion of his constraints on philosophical system can be found in the opening section of the *System of Transcendental Idealism*, where Schelling argues that philosophical knowledge must begin with a single highest principle, known with certainty, which allows all and only true propositions to be deduced from it. The ensuing discussion is focused on the nature and motivation of these constraints.

In the most minimal sense, to claim that knowledge must be systematic is to claim that propositions are not known in isolation from other propositions. One cannot know something unless one has appropriate reasons for believing it to be true, and these reasons must also be known to be true if they are to count as reasons—that is, they also must be systematically linked with other propositions. But Schelling introduced two stronger conditions as well.[5] First, he thought that relations of justification must be hierarchically ordered, with lower-level propositions deriving epistemic warrant from higher-level ones, but not the converse. Since he thought that all properly philosophical propositions should be known with certainty, this meant there had to be some one or several highest-level proposition(s) which would be self-justifying or indubitable (Schelling did not distinguish between these two), from which all other propositions would derive their certainty. He thought of the relationship between the first principle(s) and the lower-level propositions as one of entailment. Second, Schelling argued that only one such hierarchical system of knowledge could be sensibly postulated. His main target, in insisting on this point, is the idea that there might exist two or more distinct bodies of knowledge (for instance, one system of practical knowledge and

---

[4] Cf. Beiser (2002: 223–59), Franks (2000), Horstmann (1991: chapters II and IIIA) and Neuhouser (1990: chapters 2 and 3) for discussions of the importance of the view that Kant's epistemology leaves him open to sceptical objections for Schelling's and Fichte's early development.

[5] Hegel would reject the first but accept the second of the two conditions I am about to outline. He agreed with Schelling's objections to theoretical/practical dualism, but he disagreed with Schelling's foundationalism, arguing that the systematicity constraint can be met with a coherentist approach to justification. He devotes much of the preface of the *Phenomenology of Spirit* (Hegel 1977) to making this point. This means he also rejected Schelling's desire to find a 'first principle' of philosophy. One point on which the two agreed was with the claim that all preliminary discussions of the nature of knowledge must remain hypothetical. No argument that we have philosophical knowledge can be shorter than a fully worked-out philosophical system.

another system of theoretical knowledge). Why be dissatisfied with such a possibility? Were one to admit of two (or more) such systems, Schelling argues, one would have to posit not one type of truth, but two (or more). So he writes in the *System of Transcendental Idealism*:

[A]ll truth is absolutely uniform. There may well be degrees of probability, but truth has only one degree; what is true, is just true.—But that the truth of all the propositions of knowledge be absolutely uniform would be impossible, if they owed their truth to different principles . . . , and therefore there must be only one (mediating) principle in all knowledge. (*StI* III: 354)

Putting aside for the moment the claim that there must be one *principle* to which all truths 'owe their truth', let us look at the claim that *truth* must be unitary and that the acceptance of a plurality of systems of knowledge would make that requirement impossible to fulfil.

At issue here are Kant's set of claims about knowledge of freedom, God and immortality in the second *Critique*—in particular the idea that these are objects of cognition (*Erkenntnis*) had practically but not theoretically (that is, justified on practical but not theoretical grounds and so employable for practical but not theoretical purposes). The younger Schelling was not as concerned with immortality as the older Schelling would be; and as a happy pantheist, he certainly was not concerned with the possibility of knowledge of a transcendent God. But as a naturalist (even if of a peculiar stripe) who was as inspired by Rousseauian ideas as Kant himself had been, Schelling *was* deeply concerned with the status of human freedom and our knowledge of it, and so with the question: how can objects of theoretical explanation be at the same time objects of praise and blame?

Kant's view that moral and theoretical judgements attach to different aspects of the human person suggests that the two sorts of judgement can never come into direct conflict. But Schelling was not convinced, and it is easy to see why that might be so. Once one admits the possibility of responsibility-negating immaturity, psychopathology, or coercive external conditions, difficulties arise with the Kantian view. Kant denied that there are cases in which an agent is *externally* coerced to such a degree as to be no longer morally responsible for what he does. (This is the point of the gallows example at *KpV* 5: 30.) But he did admit that children who have not yet matured into the full use of their rational capacities are not to be held (fully) responsible for their actions. The same would have to be true of at least some cases of mental incapacity. But whether factors such as these are present is certainly an empirical question. So it seems that something we can know about the agent viewed purely as an object of experience can tell us something about whether that agent is to be held responsible. This looks like a direct conflict of the sort from which the two-aspects view was supposed to relieve us.

One way to reply is to say that we have no strictly moral interest in making such judgements of praise- or blameworthiness about other people (although we might have a political or legal interest in it), just as we have no strictly moral interest in being able to pass moral judgement on others (or even on ourselves).[6] We need only know that we can do what we ought—for in the context of moral deliberation questions like 'Am I mature (or sane) enough to be bound by this obligation?' do not arise. This reply seems to me to be inadequate to address the difficulty, though, since some moral deliberation clearly regards whether we really can do something we know we ought to do *if* we can.[7] It seems clear that it cannot be satisfactory from a Kantian perspective, for it relies on the idea that the only freedom one needs in order to see oneself as bound by moral laws is the freedom implicit in the situation of deliberation—the freedom-from-a-practical-point-of-view of *Groundwork* III— and Kant, as we have seen, himself repudiated this idea in the second *Critique.*

Schelling had a further reason for being unhappy with the idea of two systems of knowledge, this one clearly shared with Kant. Schelling thought that to say there are two types of cognition is to say that there are two faculties of reason which govern their pursuit. We have seen (in chapter 1) that Kant himself, though he was willing to endorse knowledge of a purely practical nature, was not happy with the bifurcation of the faculty of reason which his view suggested. But if one resists the conclusion that there are two distinct faculties at work, one is forced to the conclusion that the same faculty of reason is the source *both* of the demand for a systematic grasp of nature (and, for Kant, the claim that the principle of causality has an unlimited scope in the phenomenal world) *and* of morality (and the presupposition of a freedom incompatible with deterministic necessity). There is clearly a conflict of some sort between these demands, and now it looks like a conflict of reason with itself. What is needed is an explanation of why what are apparently two systems of knowledge are at bottom the same—either because they are two parts of the same system unified under some higher (set of) principle(s), or because they are two manifestations of the same structure applied to different spheres (in such a way that their conclusions never conflict).[8]

Schelling's articulation of a first principle of philosophy

Schelling gives no (to my mind) satisfactory account of why the foundation of a unitary system must be a *single* principle (that is, why there might not be several

---

[6] In the discussion of the malicious lie in the *Critique of Pure Reason* (at A551n/B579n), Kant claims that the real moral character of one's actions is not knowable, even to oneself. In his discussion of moral reform in *Religion* (at 6: 51), the point is reiterated: 'The human being cannot, however, attain naturally to assurance concerning [such a revolution], either by immediate consciousness or through the evidence furnished by the life which he has hitherto led; for the depths of the heart (the subjective first ground of his maxims) are inscrutable to him' (*R* 6: 51). In neither of these discussions, however, is there any indication that this inscrutability of character poses a problem for moral deliberation or moral striving. In the *Religion* discussion, Kant insists that just the opposite is the case.

[7] This is true not only in the obvious case of imperfect duties but also in the case of some perfect duties, like promise-keeping. Genuine questions can arise about whether one is physically capable of fulfilling some promises (for instance, whether an injury is serious enough to require going immediately to the hospital rather than to an important meeting).

[8] These are what Neuhouser, in his discussion of Fichte, labels the 'systematic unity of reason' and the 'structural identity of theoretical and practical reason' (respectively) approaches to the unity-of-reason problem. Cf. Neuhouser (1990: 12).

equally indubitable first principles which jointly provide warrant to the rest of the propositions in a single system, in the way the axioms of an axiomatic system do, but having the status of certainties rather than posits). On its face this is the most implausible of Schelling's requirements. It is also, for a different reason, the one that makes his systematic ambitions seem most precarious. Why think the multiplicity of claims in various areas of philosophy are such as to be even *conceivably* derivable from a single first principle?

A purely historical answer is this: a major early line of criticism raised against Kant focused on the apparent weakness of his defence of the categories (and on the apparent arbitrariness of the list of categories he endorsed). His metaphysical and transcendental deductions were no deductions at all, in any strict sense—and if they were meant to be, they failed miserably. So argued Reinhold.[9] A derivation of whatever categories are required for philosophical thinking from a single principle would escape the appearance of arbitrariness; if that principle were indubitable as well, the defence of the categories would be solid. So the early Schelling, like the early Fichte, accepted the major components of the Reinholdian first-principle foundationalist model of philosophy.[10]

An admittedly partial philosophical answer begins with the fact that Schelling's major concern was with answering the question: how should the relation between mind and world be conceptualized at the most basic level? This is one question, and it seems to demand one answer. A first principle should enunciate this relationship in a maximally simple, but also maximally fruitful way. So, at any rate, Schelling seems to have thought. He says of his first principle that it must contain a 'unification' of subject and object and that this unification must be 'immediate'. What do these considerations mean, and what do they require? Schelling held a correspondence conception of truth, and so of knowledge: 'All knowledge is founded on the conformity of something objective with something subjective.— For one *knows* only the true; truth, though, rests in general on the conformity of a representation with its object' (*StI* III: 340). Knowledge, then is the correspondence or 'unity' of (subjective) representation and (objective) state of affairs. What grounds this unity (and justifies the knowledge claim)? Normally, one knowledge claim is justified by another knowledge claim (which also, if genuine, expresses or contains a unification of subject and object). If a regress is to be avoided, Schelling thought, a principle is required which would unite representation and object in some immediate and self-evident way—immediate to stop the regress, self-evident to satisfy the sceptic.

---

[9] Henrich has argued that the relevant use of 'deduction' in the *Critique of Pure Reason* was intended by Kant to be taken in a legal, not a logical sense. Cf. Henrich (1989). The answer to the question of why, if this sense of deduction was available at the time, no one (not even his contemporaries) thought of attributing it to Kant can be explained by what Pinkard calls Reinhold's 'Jesuit, Austrian background' in which 'a "deduction" meant a logical derivation from unshakeable first premises,' together with his early prominence as an interpreter of Kant. Cf. Pinkard (2002: 101).

[10] Discussions of the Reinholdian conception of philosophical system, and contemporary criticisms of it, can be found in Ameriks (2000b: part II), Beiser (1987: chapter 8, especially 8.5 and 8.6), Frank (1997: part II), Franks (2000), Neuhouser (1990: 68ff.), and Pinkard (2002: 96–104).

Fichte had thought the sort of principle required was one wherein the thinker and the object of thought coincided (i.e., some sort of self-knowledge). Schelling took this idea as his starting point in the *System of Transcendental Idealism*, whose first principle was a modification of Fichte's idea of an absolute subject as the posited transcendental ground both of empirical individuals and of the world that is the object of their (theoretical) knowledge and the medium for their (practical) activity. Schelling added a historical dimension, with the idea of a spirit that objectifies itself in order to become an object of knowledge to itself (one that leaves its state of immediate, pre-reflective self-consciousness, loses itself in a world of its own creation, and eventually comes to know itself again).

The prototype for our knowledge of the resulting history is the *intellectus archetypus* Kant had described in the third *Critique*. Schelling knew, and admitted,[11] that Kant had denied that beings with cognitive capacities like ours possess intellectual intuition. But he thought this denial was illegitimate. Although he was not perfectly consistent on this issue, he tended to think that beings with our cognitive powers are capable of constructing (quasi-geometrically; see III: 349–50) the general features of the natural and spiritual world *a priori*. Although we cannot intuit the full range of particulars, and must rely on observation and experimentation to know them, these activities are themselves guided by the constructive method, which presupposes the possession of the sort of intuiting intellect (for which the particulars follow from the universal) that Kant denied we possess. Schelling thought he was supported in his view by the fact that Kant himself (apparently) relied on intellectual intuition in explaining the transcendental unity of apperception in the first *Critique*. He accepted Fichte's claim that self-consciousness is possible only on the basis of something like intellectual intuition. Also following Fichte, he thought that since we have a concrete experience of how intellectual intuition works (in self-consciousness), we can at least argue by analogy from ourselves to the absolute cause of the world as a whole, which, predictably, he has begun by characterizing as an 'absolute I'. Schelling never holds the view that I (as *empirical* subject) intellectually intuit the world (as if creating it as I represent it). Rather, he thinks that I can conclude (from the conditions on knowledge just outlined), that if knowledge is possible then I must (as *absolute* subject) be able to do so.

Causation in Schelling's *Naturphilosophie*

There is another modification of Fichte's view that is worth noting here, and that is that Schelling presents the *System of Transcendental Idealism* as but one part of a two-part system. The other part consists of the philosophy of nature, and aims to rebut what Schelling saw as the most serious criticism of Fichte's view: that it deprived nature of any autonomous status. Nature in Fichtean idealism is the

---

[11] Cf., e.g., *Vom Ich als Prinzip der Philosophie* (1795).

'mere not-I', posited only in order that the I may have an object (to reflect its subjectivity and permit it to become self-conscious). Schelling wanted a philosophy which would acknowledge the dignity of nature as an independent realm governed by its own laws. He also wanted to place intelligence within that realm, and to explain mental phenomena as products of those natural laws (see III: 339–41), so his philosophy of nature aimed at what we would now call a physicalist explanation of mental phenomena. It was supposed to show how not only organic life in general, but also the spiritual and moral life of human beings arises out of natural processes.

Central to the project of Schelling's *Naturphilosophie* is a revision of the notion of natural causation inherited from Kant. Kant's third *Critique* suggestion employed two quite different accounts of causation—mechanistic and teleological. This seemed (to Kant and others) to be one account of causation too many; a further story was required to show that they are consistent with one another and that neither is redundant.[12] Kant told two such stories, one that dealt with the issues at the epistemic level and another that dealt with the issues at the metaphysical level. The first used the distinction between constitutive and regulative ideas to subordinate one conception of causality to the other in our knowledge. Kant saw mechanistic causality as being ineliminable from our understanding of the natural world, 'constitutive' of experience. Teleology, on the other hand, is something we must simply assume in order to make sense of the unity of the natural world as a totality (and so the possibility of unity of experience of the natural world) as well as to make sense of specific (organic) parts of that world. Its status is that of a 'regulative' idea: not an ultimate source of explanation, but instead merely a heuristic guide to experimentation and systematization. The constitutive/regulative distinction allows these two principles of causality to coexist, but it also accords the latter a subordinate epistemic status.

Now, this resolution of the problem of how these two models of causation coexist in our knowledge leaves open the question of how the two models are supposed to apply to one and the same world. Here Kant's suggestion is of a system in which the relationship of subordination is reversed. This is the second story, dealing with the issues at the metaphysical level—explaining how we can conceptualize a world in which both sorts of causality are in play. We are invited to think of an overall purpose of nature—the realization of human autonomy—in whose achievement mechanistic causation is subordinated to teleological. Nature can be seen as mechanistically determined and at the same time oriented to furthering moral ends if the mechanism is viewed as a tool in the hand of a purposive creator, if the determination has been guided by some divine purpose.

12 The constitutive/regulative interpretation I refer to is not universally accepted; many accept a regulative/regulative interpretation (one according to which the view in the third *Critique* implies a revocation of the constitutive status accorded to mechanistic causality in the first *Critique*). Discussions of the problem and how it is to be solved can be found in Werner Pluhar's introduction to his translation of the *Critique of Judgment* (Kant 1987), and in McFarland (1970).

Schelling replaces the mechanistic notion of causation at work in natural scientific explanation with a conception of causality inspired by work on the phenomena of electromagnetism. The fundamental causal relation is 'Wechselwirkung' (reciprocal action) rather than (linear) cause-and-effect. The most basic constituents of the natural world are forces (not matter). Force exists (and acts) only together with counter-force in a relationship of dynamic interaction. The two primal forces produce a ramified system of derivative force-pairs which constitute the world—producing inorganic nature, organisms, and ultimately moral agents. The system does have something like a *telos*—maximal ramification, the development of a complete system of nature with humanity as its highest product—but appeal to this final cause is supplemented at each step by an explanation in terms of reciprocal action of causes which is not mechanistic but dynamic (not a causal chain, but a causal web). Schelling's claim is that there is no even *prima facie* conflict of ideas of causality, because the dynamic of forces that explains nature has a certain 'directedness' built in.

Schelling was convinced that the apparent conflict between natural causation and moral agency that Kant acknowledged was (at least in part) the result of the false mechanistic view of causality that Kant had endorsed. The problem with seeing human actions as natural events arose because this required seeing them as effects of preceding causes, and because on the Kantian view effects are *passive products* of their causes. In Schelling's conception of causality no sense can be made of the idea of an effect as a passive product, and he seems to have thought this a solution to the problem of freedom and determinism.[13] Much more can be said about how Schelling justifies his conception of causality, but its role in the reconciliation of accounts of nature and spirit is what will be at issue in the discussion of Schelling's account of freedom in the second section of this chapter.

The evolution of the two-part system and the genesis of the *Identitätsphilosophie*

Schelling called his position 'real-idealism' to distinguish it from the 'one-sided idealism' of Fichte. The peculiar result of endorsing such a two-part system was that the project of overcoming the subject/object (mind/world) split had to be accomplished twice: once from the perspective of the subject, and once from the perspective of the object. The philosopher's task, then, is a double one: to show (1) given the objective, that the subjective follows from it; and (2) given the subjective, that the objective follows from it. These are accomplished in: (1) a philosophy of nature which begins from the natural world (the objective) and demonstrates that the development of its basic principles leads inevitably to an

---

[13] Schelling was not the first, and would not be the last, to say that the freedom–determinism problem arises only as a result of a false conception of causality wherein effects are passive products of active causes. For an influential twentieth-century statement of this view, cf. Ayer (1954).

intelligence (the subjective) that knows it; and (2) a philosophy of the subject, which begins from the I and shows that from its principles its object can be derived.

Note that this double-task model is not at all the same as the two-system model Schelling rejected. First of all, the systems at issue in the rejected model were those of practical and theoretical philosophy, both of which belong in the 'ideal' part of the two-part system as Schelling conceives it (at least the first and part of the second do, depending on where the line is drawn between epistemology and foundations of natural science). Second, Schelling is committed to an account of the unification of the two parts (although he did have some difficulty providing such an account).

Schelling's conception of how this double task should be carried out changed over the course of the early period. He saw two options for 'developing' spirit from nature and nature from spirit. Either nature could develop towards spirit because it is itself already implicitly spirit, or it could be caused to develop towards spirit by some further principle. The same alternative he thought to hold of the opposite movement, from spirit to nature. These two options map out the split between Schelling's first system (consisting of the writings on the philosophy of nature up to 1800, together with the *System of Transcendental Idealism*), and his second system (the so-called *Identitätssystem*, presented in the *Darstellung* (1801) and *Fernere Darstellungen* (1802), together with the 1804 *System* which Schelling did not publish).

The first system follows the first option—the systematic principle is not one out of which the subjective and the objective can both be shown to arise; rather it is a principle which *is* somehow both subjective and objective. The principles of nature and those of intellect are not two different sets of principles; the purpose of the two-part system is to show how they could appear, to the naive understanding, to be two separate principles, while in fact being identical. The second option informs the strategy of the second system, which proceeds from a highest principle which is neither subject nor object, but some third thing: the original 'indifference' of the subjective and objective somehow (nevertheless) originally differentiated such that it contains the origins of both.

Schelling's movement from the first to the second sort of system seems to have been motivated by a difficulty in showing that the two parts of the original system really were two parts of the same system. One question that must arise for this sort of system is: how can I know that the real and ideal halves of the system correspond? This looks like a question that can be answered only in the ideal part of the system (since it looks like a knowledge-question, not a nature-question). But if that is the case, the two parts of the system are not equals, and the view is an idealist one after all, not a real-idealist one. (Taking the question to be a nature-question and answering it on that basis would be committing oneself to a naturalistic reduction, which would again have the result that the system is unified only by a move that undermines its double character.)

Schelling tried to maintain the equal partnership of perspectives while answering the question of unity by positing an absolute above the subjective and objective aspects, above the real-ideal distinction, and so neither real nor ideal. There were two main problems with this. First, it is not clear what model we have for thinking this sort of absolute. Schelling called it 'absolute indifference' of subject and object (what Hegel derides as the 'night in which . . . all cows are black'; 'cognition naively reduced to vacuity').[14] What sort of thing is that, and how does it give rise to subjects and objects? Second, once the first principle becomes the 'absolute indifference' of subject and object, it is unclear why we should continue to think that any analogy with self-consciousness holds such as would underwrite the assertion that we intellectually intuit such a thing. Schelling leaves the Fichtean model entirely behind and takes Kant's second prototype, namely our ability to estimate on the one hand nature and on the other works of art, to fill the gap. Through the early system's many permutations, it is always organism in the philosophy of nature and art in the philosophy of spirit that provide the ultimate cognitive models for our understanding of the world as a whole, by providing an example of our ability to grasp something as if the product of an intuiting intellect (as if cognition of the object and creation of the object coincide).

II. FATE AS FREEDOM

There are two substantial treatments of freedom in Schelling's early systematic work: in the *System of Transcendental Idealism* (1800) and in the *System der gesamten Philosophie und der Naturphilosophie insbesondere* (written in 1804 but unpublished in Schelling's lifetime). (Schelling produced a series of dialogic works simultaneously with the systematic works of the early period, but these often contradict what he says in the systematic works, and certainly embody a quite different spirit. I believe it is better to view them as precursors to the shift in outlook that became final with the 1809 *Freiheitsschrift* than to try to integrate them into an understanding of the early systematic works.) The accounts in these two works reflect a trajectory in Schelling's thinking from a form of compatibilism best known in its Hegelian version to a form of fatalism modelled more or less explicitly on Spinoza. I will discuss the two end-points of this trajectory in turn.

Freedom in the *System of Transcendental Idealism*

I have said that the *System of Transcendental Idealism* is in part an elaboration upon an idea of Fichte's—the idea that the absolute I posits the fundamental features of both the empirical I and its object (the external world) in a free but unconscious act. This act of positing is principled, not arbitrary, and its principle is essentially

---

[14] Cf. *Phenomenology of Spirit* ¶16 (Hegel 1977: 9).

practical: the object it posits is a world of experience in which it is possible for agents to realize their moral ends. This world has a history characterized by the gradual coming to self-knowledge of this absolute in the increasing knowledge (of themselves, their history and the nature of the physical world) on the part of empirical individuals.

The conception of freedom at work in the *System of Transcendental Idealism* has several layers.[15] The first layer arises from the account of natural causality that I described above: mechanistic causality is no longer a threat to freedom, because mechanism has been eliminated from the philosophy of nature. The second layer has its source in the account of the origin of nature given in the *System of Transcendental Idealism*: nature is the self-externalization of the absolute I and so itself a product of subjectivity. A third layer consists of an organicized descendant of Kant's notion of rational self-determination. For Schelling, autonomy is development in accordance with one's own rational nature, but 'rational nature' is given a broader interpretation than it had in Kant. Every natural product has a rational nature in this broad sense, and so one's rational nature is now also one's *natural* nature (if I may put it that way). This is not to say that Schelling views human agents in exactly the same way he views plants, but he does see a strong analogy between them: both are self-governing systems which cause themselves to develop in accordance with dynamically conceived essences. The result is that rational self-determination no longer requires as a postulate the ability of the agent to separate himself from nature as it did in Kant. The law one gives oneself is just another law of nature. (This might seem to trivialize rational self-determination. What is it that I have that my dog (or my geranium) does not? The answer will be: a higher degree of self-consciousness and reflection in my pursuit of my natural ends. It is in this, the self-consciousness of their rational activity, that human beings are unique in nature, and the unique natural product capable of realizing, in their knowledge, the self-knowledge of the absolute.) When both moral and natural laws are rooted in the absolute I as the ground of both, and when, further, the two sets of laws are perfectly analogous and tend in the same direction, moral aims and natural processes need no longer be separated. The conception of self-determination operative for human beings is continuous with the innate developmental tendencies of organisms as natural ends. So freedom for the early Schelling was freedom *in* nature, never freedom *from* nature.

The view is a fundamentally compatibilist one. The determinism with which freedom is compatible on this view is dynamic/teleological rather than mechanistic, but it is the same as mechanistic determinism in this respect: it entails the inability of agents to do otherwise than they in fact do. The world in which the empirical subject acts is governed by the necessity imposed upon that world by itself viewed as absolute subject (which is the same across individuals).

---

[15] A good comparison (though not one with which I agree on all points) of the freedom conception in Schelling's early work with that of Kant can be found in Gerhardt (1989).

(The necessity of the way in which the object is posited is motivated by the threat of the solipsism that would result if the idea of an absolute I were abandoned in favour of a subjective idealism in which each individual knower were seen as creating its own world in its own way.) This necessity applies to actions as well. The spontaneity of the individual in the *System of Transcendental Idealism* is its freedom *qua* absolute subject to create a world which functions according to principles which are intelligible, because its own creation, but unchangeable: 'We act freely, and the world comes to exist independently of us' (*StI* III: 567). The creation of a world in absolute freedom, a world functioning according to the laws of its own nature, exhausts the subject's spontaneity. Nothing in the world of experience can happen except according to natural laws (*StI* III: 570).

An appeal to pre-established harmony accounts for the problems arising from one remaining phenomenological fact, namely the conviction an empirical agent may have that she could have done otherwise, by bringing the agent's apparently arbitrary choice and the objective determination of her action together. Schelling's most evocative description of this view is contained in the following passage:[16]

If we think of history as a drama, in which everyone who takes part plays his role entirely freely and according to his pleasure, then we can conceive of a rational development of this confused play only if we think that a single spirit speaks in everyone, and that the playwright, whose fragments (*disjecti membra poëtae*) are the individual actors, has already harmonized the objective outcome of the whole with the free play of each individual, in such a way that in the end a rational outcome must actually emerge from it. Now, if the playwright actually *were* independent of his drama, then we would be mere actors who speak the lines he has written. If he *is* not independent of us, but rather reveals and discloses himself only successively through the play of our freedom itself, such that without this freedom he himself would not *be*, then we are co-authors of the whole, and creators of the particular roles that we play. . . . The absolute acts through each individual intelligence. That is, their action is *itself* absolute, and to that extent neither free nor unfree, but rather both together—*absolutely* free, and for this very reason also necessary. (*StI* III: 602)

The harmony at work here is a harmony among the empirical intuitions of a plurality of individuals and between the intuitions of some and the apparently arbitrary actions of others; it is supposed to have its basis in the identical structure of the absolute subject in each of them. This is what Schelling means when he says that the author of this drama is not separate from the individual actors in it. God is nothing more than this 'progressive, gradually self-disclosing revelation of the absolute' (*StI* III: 603).

This harmony is merely postulated. The self-disclosing of the totality of things as God can never be completed within history. If it were, the condition of history would vanish, since that condition is the appearance of freedom, which itself

---

[16] This passage is the one paraphrased by Kierkegaard in *Either/Or* II and characterized as 'the summit of the esthetic'. I discuss it in chapter 5, §I.

would vanish if an empirical intuition of the whole (as whole) were possible and we could have an experience of the unity of action and intuition.

But now if this absolute that can everywhere only *reveal* itself, had actually and fully revealed itself in history, or were ever to do so, it would at once put an end to the appearance of freedom. . . . [I]f the absolute synthesis were ever completely developed, we would see that everything that has come about through freedom in the course of history was lawlike in this whole, and that all actions, though they seemed to be free, were in fact necessary, precisely in order to bring forth this whole. The opposition between conscious and unconscious activity is necessarily an infinite one, for were it ever cancelled the appearance of freedom, which rests entirely upon it, would be cancelled as well. (*StI* III: 601–2)

The appearance of an arbitrary choice on the part of an empirical individual is mere appearance; it rests on our inability to experience empirically the necessity of each particular detail.

Schelling thought a conception of history like this is possible only if the absolute is conceived as an agent acting according to ends which are continuous with the ends of empirical subjects (because that agent is in some sense they themselves). That it is impossible if the absolute is conceived as material acting according to mechanical laws of motion Schelling had claimed already in 1795, in his *Vom Ich als Prinzip der Philosophie*:

If, however, such a system is inconsistent enough to claim both a thing in itself on the one hand and transcendental freedom on the other, then it will never, not even through pre-established harmony, be able to render comprehensible the coincidence of natural causality and causality through freedom. *For even pre-established harmony cannot unite two simply opposed absolutes*, which would have to be the case, as it would assume on the one hand an absolute not-I, on the other an empirical I, which itself is incomprehensible without an absolute [I]. (I: 239–40, my emphasis)

An immanent pre-established harmony is possible in the *System of Transcendental Idealism* because the objective is grounded in the absolute subject, and because the absolute is the same for all individual subjects and a part of them all. This means that there is a sense in which individuals can be said to have causal ultimacy despite lacking alternate possibilities—though they have it not *qua* individuals, but instead *qua* empirical manifestations of absolute subjectivity. So the compatibilism of the *System of Transcendental Idealism* is neither the compatibilism of the Leibniz-Wolffians nor that of contemporary philosophers, but a compatibilism peculiar to German idealism, made possible by its peculiar brand of panpsychist metaphysics.

The space left for transcendental freedom by the resolution of the third antinomy has been filled, on this view, by the claim that the absolute subject unites moral and theoretical reason by creating/intuiting a purposive world according to necessary laws—just as the suggestion in Kant's third *Critique* seemed to entail. The law of the will's causality—the moral law—has been transformed from an 'ought' to an 'is'. Though one can make sense of a certain sort of contingency on this view, in the form of the possibility that some things might fail to actualize their natural potential, one cannot make sense of a capacity on the part of any natural product to *choose* not to fulfil its natural end. And since natural ends are not chosen by empirical individuals, the idea that an agent might choose to fulfil a different set of ends makes no sense.

Freedom in the 1804 *System der gesamten Philosophie*

Schelling came to doubt the viability of this pre-established harmony account, and began to think his system required a single absolute over and above the unconscious activity of a plurality of individuals. This was part of the move from the early two-part system to the *Identitätssystem*. The results of this shift for Schelling's thinking about human freedom are most clearly visible in the 1804 *System*, which Schelling described as an attempt to rewrite Spinoza's *Ethics* from a post-Kantian perspective.

The 1804 *System* is not a work Schelling ever published, and this is reason enough to think that he himself was dissatisfied with its results. There are, however, good reasons to include it in an exposition of his early view of freedom. First among them is the fact that he deals with the issues of freedom and the ethical life at such length and in such detail (in the early *systematic* work) only here and in the *System of Transcendental Idealism*. Second, the 1804 *System* is important as an indication of the direction in which Schelling's systematic efforts were taking him: it shows his early tendency taken to the extreme. The subjectivized absolute of the early transcendental standpoint (from *Vom Ich als Prinzip der Philosophie* to the *System des transzendentalen Idealismus*) became the absolute as unity in indifference of subject and object in the 1804 *System*, and the results for practical philosophy are significant. In 1800, Schelling had written that the absolute '*is* not independent of us, but rather reveals and discloses himself only successively through the play of our freedom itself, such that without this freedom he himself would not *be*, [with the result that] we are co-authors of the whole, and creators of the particular roles that we play' (*StI* III: 602). In the 1804 *System* the relationship of dependence between parts and whole is reversed, and Schelling finds himself writing that it is not we who act at all, but rather divine substance that acts in us: 'In the soul as such there is no freedom; rather, only the divine is truly free, and the essence of the soul, insofar as it is divine. (But in this sense there is no individual.)' (*SgP* VI: 541).

The 1804 *System* is built up from the idea of an absolute having two sorts of manifestation—the 'ideal' and the 'real'—which are distinct manifestations of the same underlying substance. The real is made up of the physical world (things, events and states of affairs, including empirical actions); the ideal is made up of the mental (representations, including knowledge). This is a (familiar) way of dissolving the problem of the interaction of mind and world: the real and the ideal are not two separate realms and so cannot (and need not) interact. Rather, every state or change in state of the one corresponds to a state or change in state of the other. This requires a redefinition of both 'willing' and 'knowing', since both these concepts seem to involve the idea of causal interaction between the mental and the physical. I will not discuss Schelling's treatment of knowledge in the 1804 *System*; what concerns me here is his treatment of the will.

Willings are mental (ideal) in the sense that they are representations; they correspond to physical (real) events not because they cause them, but rather because representations and events are 'aspects' of the same substance (*SgP* VI: 500–1, 548–9). The correspondence relation is a 'being the representation of' (or as Schelling sometimes says, 'being the concept of') relation: my willings are the representations of the movements of my body. (What guarantees that the correspondence will be one-to-one? Ultimately, the fact that individuals are not independent entities but rather aspects of an underlying absolute substance.) There is no such thing as a *faculty* of the will, then, if this is understood as a capacity of the mind to produce effects in the world, for there are no such effects. The notion of a faculty of the will, Schelling explains, is only the reification of an abstraction from individual willings.

Only those physical movements count as cases of acting (*Handeln*) which correspond with (*not* 'are caused by') adequate ideas in the ideal realm (VI: 537–8). Any bodily movement corresponding to an inadequate idea is a case of being-acted-upon (*Leiden*). So the things that happen with the body which can be called 'free actions' are all and only those that correspond to adequate ideas, while bodily happenings corresponding with inadequate ideas are cases of being acted upon. Since willings are just the ideas of things going on with the body, there are, then, willings which contain adequate and willings which contain inadequate ideas. What is it for a willing to contain an adequate idea? It is for it to flow from the essence of the willer. So actions are bodily happenings that arise out of oneself; cases of being acted upon have their source outside. But arising 'out of oneself' in the relevant sense means flowing from one's essence, not being the result of one's free choice. Adequate ideas are not freely chosen—they are determined by the nature of the agent: 'A free cause can only be that which acts according to the law of identity, according to the necessity of its essence, with no other determination' (*SgP* VI: 538). Only those who are necessitated (in this sense) to action are really acting, in the same way that only those who reach the conclusions they do of necessity are properly reasoning. *Willkür* is not freedom; those who think they are acting as they like (*willkürlich*—'arbitrarily') are really being acted upon by outside forces.

Schelling allows as a consequence of this view that individuals cannot ultimately be viewed as *self*-determining. Actions flow from an individual's essence, but the essences of individuals are (more or less perfect) manifestations of the essence of absolute substance: 'Free self-determination [on the part of finite beings] is therefore a contradiction' (*SgP* VI: 539). Only God is *self*-determining. It is also incorrect to call individuals free in any sense that involves thinking of them as the causal sources of the way they are. 'In the soul as such there is no freedom; rather, only the divine is truly free, and the essence of the soul, insofar as it is divine. (But in this sense there is no individual)' (*SgP* VI: 541). It is not we who act, but rather divine substance that acts in us, for this is the only way a harmony between soul and body can be explained (*SgP* VI: 550). If only substance acts, how is it that particular actions can be attributed to particular individuals? 'That an action is *my* action means only this: that what acts in me and what knows in me are one in the same' (*SgP* VI: 550). This sameness is a function of a correspondence in location on the soul/body 'map' of absolute substance. 'Only the idea that that which acts in us is different from that which knows led to the idea that there can be freedom independent of necessity' (*SgP* VI: 541). So in this later version of the system, the absolute is the single locus of causal force operating through many individuals, and it is incorrect (even incoherent) to call those individuals free (in the sense of Kant's transcendental spontaneity) *or even* self-determining (since they are ultimately determined not by themselves but by their position within the absolute).

Far from being a total departure from Schelling's earlier thinking, these ideas are consistent with a certain tendency already present from the very beginning. For instance, from 'On the I as Principle of Philosophy' onwards, Schelling's description of morality has it consisting not in the highest exercise of personality, but rather in an overcoming of personality. In that early essay, the highest law of morality (for the empirical subject) is to become like the absolute I—'Be absolute—be identical with yourself' (read as: 'contain nothing accidental, only your own nature'). For empirical individuals, that translates into the imperative to overcome one's particularity (equivalently: to overcome one's individual personality):

> In the finite I is the unity of consciousness, that is, personality. The infinite I however knows no object, therefore no consciousness and no unity of consciousness, no personality. Thus the last goal of all striving can be represented as the widening of personality to universality, that is, as the negation of personality. The final aim of the finite I as well as the not-I, that is, the final aim of the world, is its *negation as* world, as the essence of finitude. (*VI* I: 201)

'Existence' and 'actuality' are distinguished from 'being' in the terminology of the essay as limited being or being-in-a-certain-way from being *simpliciter*. 'He knows nothing of the absolute I who can say that *it is actual. Being (Sein)* expresses *absolute* being-posited *(Gesetztsein), existence (Dasein)* however expresses *in general* a *limited* being-posited, *actuality (Wirklichkeit)* a being-posited in *a certain manner*, through a *determinate* limitation' (*VI* I: 209–10). The task of the empirical self is to overcome its actuality—its determinateness, in other words—and strive towards the absolute being of the absolute I: 'The striving of the moral I cannot be represented as a striving toward *actuality*, precisely because it strives to posit all reality *within itself*. Rather it strives to elevate all actuality to *pure being*, and to elevate itself out of the sphere of existence into which it, limited by the not-I, has fallen' (*VI* I: 209n). Since the self is not, in its empirical state, identical with itself, the fulfilment of this moral law becomes the object of an endless striving, one that can never be completed.

What is interesting in this view is the direction of the empirical individual's moral striving: it is a striving to lose oneself, one's individual personality, through a sort of immersion in a larger order of things, in the absolute. There is something peculiar in this conception of moral striving. It appears to involve, as part of the moral imperative itself, the elimination of the locus of moral responsibility to which the imperative is directed. The imperative of morality is to render *itself* otiose.[17] If finite individuality exists only to strive to annul its existence *qua* finite individuality, however, then the nature of the moral imperative that applies to the individual is radically different from that described by Kant. He would, in fact, be unable to recognize this as a *moral* imperative at all. For one should not, on this view, strive to *act* rightly; one should not aspire to any sort of agency at all. Rather, one should strive to be a passive vessel, to allow the absolute to act through one. But this means that the essential aspect of moral consciousness—that *I* have duties, that it matters what *I* do—is not merely explained away on theoretical grounds, but is even denied on moral grounds.

I point out this characteristic here in part because it will come up again, both in the discussion of Schelling's *Freiheitsschrift* (though in a different form) and in the discussion of Kierkegaard's religiousness A. But it also helps us understand the other (for my purposes) salient feature of the 1804 *System's* approach to freedom and the ethical life: in that work, the individual as locus of responsibility *has* been eliminated (though not by its own striving, but rather by metaphysical fiat), and the result is a world in which moral good and evil do not exist. I would like to pay particular attention to the treatment of moral evil in the 1804 *System*— specifically, to its elimination—which proceeds in several steps over the course of the final pages of the essay.

In the first step, moral evil is described as inevitable. Freedom is necessity, the necessity of seeing things in the right way—but even seeing things in the wrong way is not a cause for blame, as it is in its own way just as necessary. That there are various degrees of correctness individuals can achieve is inevitable. In the second step, evil is described as mere *privation*. But privation is not something real. All privation is a fiction of the imagination, Schelling writes, for we see privation only when we compare things with one another, not when we observe them in themselves. '[N]othing regarded in itself is finite' (*SgP* VI: 542–4); privation, finitude in general, arises only from the imagination's 'regarding things in relation'.

---

[17] One might think this is a general feature of moral imperatives: once they are perfectly carried out, they cease to exist. There is nothing left that ought to be done because everything has already been done, morally speaking. But the moral imperative of self-negation that Schelling here entertains is different. Here, there is nothing left that ought to be done because there is no one left who ought to do it. The agent, rather than the task, has been negated.

To the essence of the blind man as such, for example, belongs just as essentially his blindness as does sight to the essence of the sighted man. Only in comparing him with other men (most of whom are sighted) do we come up with the idea that he is somehow deprived. Likewise with evil: from a conception of evil as mere privation it is a short step to the claim that evil is non-existent, that there are only varying degrees of good (which emerge when we compare actions with one another). Every action, looked at in itself, is perfect (*SgP* VI: 544).

Schelling then goes on to propound an error theory of moral evil. He takes as an example the desire and intention to harm others, which is generally regarded as evil. When this desire is looked at absolutely in itself (not in comparison with other possible ways of behaving) it must be seen as something positive, 'for [it] belongs . . . necessarily to the nature of this person' (*SgP* VI: 544). If we compare the man who acts on these desires and intentions with other men, whom we see as good, we think his actions contain a lower degree of reality than theirs. But if we compare him with animals, whose power and wildness we admire and find a perfection, he looks better (*SgP* VI: 545). If we regard him in himself, though, we can see that he is perfect just as he is, in so far as his actions follow directly from his essence, which, like everything else, though in its own way, does ultimately express the reality of the absolute.

How does the fallacy that evil is a (real) privation come about? It has to do with the nature of human knowledge. We create concepts, 'universals', as abstractions from sets of individuals, and we add into the universals (e.g., 'man') what we find positive (i.e., desirable to us) in human beings. Our concepts are always coloured by what is useful for us. When we apply these concepts to particulars (in this instance particular human beings), we often find that they come up short. From the perspective of the absolute (the divine intellect that intuits particulars as particulars and is in no need of concepts), finite beings are perfect, even if they do not contain the highest degree of reality, because perfection for them consists in their being just what they are (*SgP* VI: 546). Moral good and evil are thus, from the divine perspective, non-existent. The only genuine distinction among finite individuals is in the degree of reality they embody, but the instantiation of each instantiated degree of reality is as necessary as that of any other degree to the perfection of the world (*SgP* VI: 547).

Now, if all that is perfect is determined to be so by the absolute (with individuals merely the passive vessels through which it comes to be), then there can be no individual responsibility for individual variation in degrees of reality. If good and evil are figments of the human imagination, there can be no responsibility for these either. And if individuals are not morally responsible, then it appears that no moral imperatives can apply to them. This is just what Schelling concludes: from all of the above it follows that 'there is no absolute ethical life (*Sittlichkeit*) in the sense that can be thought of as an accomplishment or as a work of human freedom' (*SgP* VI: 560), because an individual is virtuous (with 'virtue' again the product of flawed human cognition) not through *Willkür*, but through the necessity of his nature, if at all. The identity of freedom and necessity need not even be brought about; it just is (*SgP* VI: 555). Viewed absolutely, the actions and fates of human beings are neither free nor necessary, but expressions of the absolute identity of freedom and necessity (*SgP* VI: 568).

This view of evil is not a departure from, but rather a continuation of, a line of thought present in Schelling's earlier work, in which evil, where it is addressed at all, is treated as privation of good. This is thus an extreme version of the 'negative conception of evil' that Schelling will explicitly reject in the *Freiheitsschrift*.

While it reads like a distinctly un-Kantian revival of rationalist metaphysics, the view here is really not that far from what the proposal sketched in the third *Critique* would have to entail, and the treatment of self-determination and its relation to *Willkür* is not very far from the implications drawn by Reinhold and Schmid. This is not a problem unique to Schelling's effort, but one that arises out of Kant's suggested solution itself. The idea of an intuiting intellect determining the world in all its particulars with a sort of teleological necessity, though it makes sense of the compatibility of human freedom and an order of nature where freedom is viewed as rational self-determination, actually sharpens the problem of the compatibility of human freedom with a systematic structure of the world when the freedom at issue is transcendental spontaneity. For the intelligible space left in the first *Critique* for the spontaneous causality of individual agents is filled up by the strict necessity (however non-mechanistic this necessity may be) attributed to the presentation/creation of the world on the part of the absolute. Schelling followed Kant's suggestion to its natural conclusion, and his development shows clearly what Reinhold and Schmid foresaw: that this strategy for reconciling moral and theoretical objectivity must lead to a denial of the conditions of moral responsibility that made the reconciliation seem both necessary and desirable to begin with. But in his early work Schelling did not simply overlook it. He explicitly denied that it was a problem. (Indeed, in his *Abhandlung zur Erläuterung des Idealismus der Wissenschaftslehre* he goes so far as to quote the passage from the introduction to the *Metaphysics of Morals* where Kant denies that freedom can be freedom to choose for or against the moral law at will (I: 434).)

What about the idea that morality consists in overcoming individual personality? While this sounds like a radical departure from Kant's moral psychology, in fact it is implicit in the Kantian idea that the will's causality and its rationality are linked—in the reciprocity thesis, that is. In *Der Formalismus in der Ethik und die materiale Wertethik*, Max Scheler gave a forceful articulation of this problem with what he called 'formalistic' ethics: though it seems, in contrast to broadly utilitarian theories, to be able to accommodate the idea that the person has a value that is beyond price, in fact it threatens (though in its own way) the status of the person as uniquely valuable: 'by virtue of its subordination of the person to an impersonal *nomos* under whose domination he can become a person only through obedience'.[18]

---

[18] Scheler (1973: 370).

Formalist theories are inclined to define the person (insofar as it is a source of moral worth) as a placeholder, not a concrete individual but a mere outlet, as it were, of universal reason. In fact, Scheler echoes Reinhold in his complaint that 'The person could not even be "obedient" to the moral law if, as its executor, he were created, as it were, by this law.'[19] For this reason, he writes:

If one fixes his attention on the above erroneous definition (Kant, fortunately, did not do so) the result is an ethics that leads to anything but the so-called *autonomy* or dignity of the person qua person. What must follow from this definition is not autonomy (a term in which *auto-* is supposed to point to the independence of the person) but *logonomy* and at the same time extreme *heteronomy* of the person. This consequence has been drawn from the Kantian concept of the person by J. G. Fichte and to a greater extent by Hegel. For with both Fichte and Hegel the person becomes in the end an indifferent thoroughfare for impersonal rational activity.[20]

Scheler acknowledges (in the parenthetical caveat) that Kant fails to instantiate perfectly the characteristic failure of ethical formalism, since he is torn between a view of human freedom wherein the causality of the will is independent of practical rationality, and one wherein that causality is governed by the moral law in the sense of being described by it. He notes that the ambiguity is eliminated in Kant's idealist successors.

His failure to mention Schelling in this context is odd, given the historical significance of the early Schelling's treatment of freedom and of the unity-of-reason problem. Hegel developed a descendant of the idea behind Schelling's *Identitätsphilosophie* into the system that would come to dominate the German philosophy from the 1820s to the 1840s. He developed most of the view far beyond its beginnings in Schelling's rudimentary sketch, adding much to Schelling's very rudimentary conception of political liberty, and developing the ideas of self-determination and of freedom as reasoned reconciliation with one's place in a larger social and historical order beyond anything Schelling would, or probably could, have done. But the core conception of human freedom—together with the account of the compatibility of freedom and the systematic order of nature and history—remained the same. And it shared with Schelling's account the characteristic that in it 'the person becomes . . . an indifferent thoroughfare for impersonal rational activity'.

Schelling's achievement, in contrast with Hegel and the later Fichte, is to have recognized that this position becomes absurd when taken to its logical conclusion—to have realized that the Kantian conception of freedom is not preserved in this form of absolute idealism, and to have shown that this view is no different, in its moral consequences, from Spinoza's. Schelling knew, probably even as he wrote the 1804 *System*—for *Philosophie und Religion* was, after all, written at roughly the same time—that a major rethinking of the problem of human freedom was in order. This is what, in the *Freiheitsschrift*, he went on to produce.

---

[19] Scheler (1973: 372).   [20] Scheler (1973: 372).

4

Freedom against Reason: Schelling's *Freiheitsschrift* and Later Work

Schelling's early work was characterized, as we have seen, by a commitment to a very ambitious project of 'constructing' nature and history and showing them to follow from an underlying rational principle and to be, at least in outline, rational and necessary. By the mid-1830s Schelling had given up this ambition. In a set of lectures given in Munich in 1832–3 he embraces what looks to be just the opposite view of the relation between reason and reality:

The first impression (and this is decisive not only in life, but also in knowledge) of this thing, on the whole and in the particulars so *highly contingent*, that we call the world—this cannot possibly be the impression of something that has arisen out of *rational necessity*, that is, through a mere *logical emanation*. The world resembles nothing less than it resembles a product of pure reason. It contains a *preponderant* mass of *unreason*, such that one could almost say that the rational is merely the *accidens*. (*GpP* 99–100)[1]

We should give first impressions their due, Schelling says here, because in philosophy as in life they often disclose the ultimate truth. The world does not merely look chaotic and irrational to the philosophically naive observer; it really is chaotic and irrational. Philosophy will not discover any underlying rational principle that explains the diversity of phenomena, because there is no such principle to be discovered.

What happened to Schelling between 1804 and 1833?

His early programme had already begun to lose momentum in 1804. His pace of publication slowed, and his focus broadened. He published a few small works whose goals seemed orthogonal to those of the early system. Then in 1809 he came out with an essay, titled *Philosophical Investigations into the Essence of Human Freedom and Related Matters*, that marked the end of his adherence to the idealism of the early period. That essay posed two questions. What would human freedom need to be like in order to be freedom *for good and evil*? What consequences for the systematic project would the attribution of that sort of freedom to human beings have?

---

[1] '*GpP*' refers to Schelling (1972), Munich lectures WS 1832–3, and SS 1833. Fuhrmans includes passages from the collected works where they elucidate or complement (or are basically identical to) the manuscript, and in such cases I will cite the standard pagination.

The question of how human beings would need to be in order to be capable of good and evil had long since been supplanted in the mainstream of German philosophy by the question of how they would need to be in order to be capable of rational self-determination. The question about moral responsibility in the traditional sense (what causal and rational powers must we attribute to human beings if we are to see them as morally responsible agents?) had been replaced by a new question about autonomy (what causal and rational powers must we attribute to human beings if we are to see them as self-determining agents?). These questions are similar and can even look the same. We have seen that Kant was often tempted to equate them, and that the idealist programme relied on doing so systematically. But morally responsible agents are capable of good *and* evil, and accounts of freedom that reduce freedom to rational self-determination cannot account for this. By 1809, Schelling had come to the conclusion that the investigation into the conditions of possibility of rational self-determination could shed no further light on the question of the conditions of possibility of moral agency in a more general sense, because it could shed no light at all on the possibility of moral evil. He gave the sketch of a new theory of moral agency in the *Freiheitsschrift*; I will give as clear a summary as I can of that difficult discussion in §I of this chapter.

The systematic ambitions of German idealism—in particular the goal of unifying practical and theoretical reason in a single system wherein the real and the rational (with 'rational' meaning both 'humanly comprehensible' and 'morally endorseable') coincide—relied on the reduction of human freedom to rational self-determination. To the second question, then, the answer was that there would be no way of preserving the sort of systematic project that the young Schelling had proposed if one adopted an account of moral agency of the sort outlined in the *Freiheitsschrift*. This was not obvious from the beginning—not even to Schelling himself, and certainly not to those of his contemporaries who were working out successor versions of his early systematic efforts. Schelling's attempts at a sketch of a new system in the *Freiheitsschrift* are a failure, and his publication of the *Freiheitsschrift* was followed by a long silence, during which he began to work on what he hoped would be a new way of doing systematic philosophy.

Schelling spent the rest of his career working out, in one way or another, the consequences of the shift in view that began with the *Freiheitsschrift*. The development of the late system began with the *Weltalter* fragments of 1810–15 and continued, in revisions to his lectures on positive philosophy, throughout the 1830s and 1840s. The result was what Schelling called his 'positive' philosophy, essentially a systematic history of religion (the philosophy of mythology and revelation) underwritten by a methodological programme which he called 'philosophical empiricism'.

This new system was distinguished from the early one by three main characteristics: (1) a view of the nature of human freedom and the nature of agency arising from the *Freiheitsschrift*; (2) a radical theological voluntarism in ethical theory (inspired by (1)); and (3) an anti-idealist insistence on (to put it in terms common to Schelling and Kierkegaard) 'the priority of being to thought'. I will discuss these (in reverse order) in §II. The third of these is the most prominent claim of the late system and the one that has received the most attention from commentators. Schelling's enunciation of this claim, and his arguments for it, were pivotal in the anti-Hegelian turn of mid-nineteenth-century German philosophy. It is of central significance for both Kierkegaard and Marx[2] (though for quite different reasons). The epistemological aspect of Kierkegaard's critique of Hegelian metaphysics has its source here. The object of less attention, but equally important for the mid-nineteenth-century movement of which Kierkegaard was a part was the theological voluntarism (and accompanying anti-rationalist moral epistemology) that Schelling championed. Schelling tailored the meta-ethical view of the late work to the account of moral agency (together with its characteristic constraint: that human beings be free for both good and evil) outlined in the *Freiheitsschrift*. The rationalistic, inward-looking character of the idealist approach to moral knowledge was replaced by a view according to which the individual looks outward towards a source of moral value that is revealed (though in a peculiar way) in experience. Revelation replaced reason as the source of moral norms. This view, like the view of agency arising from the *Freiheitsschrift*, received a less detailed treatment in Schelling's lectures, and most Schelling commentary has overlooked it. But Schelling's intellectual biography tells us that considerations about the nature of human agency were central, and provided the motivation for the new system and therefore of the new view of the relation of thought and being. I will argue for this reading of the late Schelling in §II of this chapter.

Schelling's later systematic efforts never fully satisfied him. Although he did make arrangements with his son to have certain of his lecture notes published posthumously, he was never willing to publish the new system himself. Instead he presented it as an evolving three-part lecture series to students in Erlangen, Munich and Berlin, over the course of about twenty years. His efforts were not completely satisfying to his students, either, but the call he made for a new approach motivated by the questions posed in the *Freiheitsschrift* received a broad response. While first Hegel and then the young Hegelians were gaining ascendancy in the German academy, a small but distinguished anti-Hegelian movement was organizing itself around Schelling's few published works after 1809 as well as *Nachschriften* and published summaries of (and surely also rumours about) his lectures circulated by his students. I will discuss this circle, led by Christian Weiße and Immanuel Hermann Fichte (J. G. Fichte's son), in the excursus that follows this chapter.

---

[2] Frank (1992) is the definitive treatment of this topic and its importance (especially for Marx), but cf. also Bowie (1993) and White (1983b).

I. 'FREEDOM FOR GOOD *AND* EVIL': FREEDOM AND SYSTEM IN THE *FREIHEITSSCHRIFT*

In the preface to the *Freiheitsschrift*, Schelling remarks that in his previous work he did not solve, or even address, the real system/freedom problem, which he characterizes as that posed by the apparent opposition of freedom and necessity. He writes that this problem is to be addressed in the 'ideal' portion of the system and that the ideal portion of the system has not yet been presented, except provisionally and in an insufficiently clear manner in the 1804 piece *Philosophie und Religion* (which in fact has very little to say about the problem). He makes no mention of other early efforts to construct the 'ideal' portion of the system and effect a reconciliation of freedom and necessity—although the 1804 *System* and the *System of Transcendental Idealism* at least purport to contain solutions to this problem. Schelling does not tell the reader he has changed his mind about the adequacy of those solutions. In the case of the 1804 *System* this is understandable: since it remained unpublished in his lifetime, it was unavailable to his readers in 1809. Those same readers might also have expected the account in the *System of Transcendental Idealism* to have been abandoned when Schelling abandoned his early two-part system in favour of the *Identitätssystem*. So Schelling's claim that he had so far had nothing to say about how the problem of the apparent opposition of freedom and necessity can be addressed within his current systematic framework is literally true. Still there is something disingenuous about Schelling's pronouncement here: it is apparent that he has changed his mind about human freedom in a quite fundamental way.

Why exactly he changed his mind has had as many different interpretations as the content of the *Freiheitsschrift* itself has had—and that is quite a few.[3]

---

[3] One is that Schelling did not change his mind about anything, and that the *Freiheitsschrift* is simply an investigation into the cosmological problem of evil. This interpretation (cf. Schulz 1975) ignores the fact that the 1804 *System* presents a perfectly consistent (if ethically unsatisfying) solution to the cosmological problem of evil. For other interpreters (Fuhrmans (1940: especially 15–56) chief among them) the *Freiheitsschrift* is the beginning of a turn away from pantheism and towards theism, which turn resulted from Schelling's encounter with Baader and theosophy. It is primarily a rejection of his early system as inconsistent with Christianity in general and Christian ethics in particular. The main problem with this interpretation is Schelling's own insistence throughout the essay that the problem of freedom can and must be solved within the confines of a philosophical system, a system basically like the one presented in his early works. On still another interpretation (this one from Theunissen (1965)) Schelling has conceived an interest in the ethical standpoint of the existing individual, has had an anthropological turn, so to speak. But, according to Theunissen, the *Freiheitsschrift* is unique in Schelling's work—the anthropological way was quickly given up in favour of a different system. There is something to each of these views. Although I find Theunissen's to be the most convincing, the discussion in the second part of this chapter will make it clear that I disagree with Theunissen's claim that the *Freiheitsschrift* is an anomaly, and hold instead that Schelling's motivations remained constant across the second half of his career. Further helpful discussions of the *Freiheitsschrift* and the turn in Schelling's thinking can be found in Marquet (1973, 1974), Marx (1977), Peetz (1995), the essay on Schelling in Rivelaygue (1990), Tilliette (1970, 1975), and Snow (2000). Baumgarten (2000) compares Schelling's conception of moral evil in the *Freiheitsschrift* with Kant's.

The plurality of interpretations is due almost certainly to the essay itself, whose different parts seem to work at cross purposes. It seems to me that Schelling is motivated by two main goals in the work, and that these are difficult, probably impossible, to reconcile. First, he wants to add a more traditional libertarian model of freedom to the self-determination model of freedom as it had been developed after Kant. He finds the roots of this libertarian conception in Kant as well, primarily in Kant's discussion of an intelligible choice of fundamental moral disposition in *Religion within the Boundaries of Mere Reason*. But, and this is the second of Schelling's main goals in the essay, he wants, in making this incorporation, to pull off the reconciliation that Kant could not: to show the *compatibility* of such an account of radical choice of moral character with a philosophical system along the lines mapped out in the third *Critique*. If what I have said in the foregoing discussion of Kant is correct, what Schelling has set himself in the *Freiheitsschrift* is an impossible task. This impossibility would suggest a fundamental incoherence in the essay itself, which in turn would explain the difficulties in its interpretation.

Moral evil and moral responsibility

Schelling's motivation in adding the more traditional libertarian model to the classical idealist conception of freedom as self-determination is, as I have said, straightforward. He has come to think that an adequate account of freedom must show how it can be a 'capacity for good and for evil' (*FS* VII: 352). In fact the main preoccupation of the essay is the problem of evil, which Schelling approaches from a cosmological as well as a moral-psychological perspective.

In his long opening discussion of the tasks of the essay, Schelling explains that what is at issue is not a negative conception of moral evil (of the sort we found at work in the earlier treatments), wherein evil is weakness, finitude, privation of (maximal amounts of) good, or indeed entirely absent (*FS* VII: 352–5). What one needs is a positive conception of evil, one wherein morally wrong choices are genuine choices and evil has genuine effects in the world. Evil needs to be seen as a positive opposite of good, since 'all other explanations leave both the understanding and ethical conscience dissatisfied' (*FS* VII: 367). The mere consideration that moral evil arises only in human beings, the most highly developed natural forms, should have discredited the view that the ground of evil lies in 'defect or privation' (*FS* VII: 368). 'Imperfection in the general metaphysical sense is not the ordinary character of evil—for it often shows itself united with a superiority in individual powers that far more seldom accompanies the good' (*FS* VII: 368–9).

Schelling thinks that the accounts of evil available in idealistic systems before 1809 lack this positive character, and he suggests two reasons for this to be so. First, it seems that idealistic systems (like other pantheistic systems) can allow only a negative conception of evil for cosmological reasons (*FS* VII: 352). Since these are monistic systems, they face the classical problem of being unable to account for a positive counter-principle to their (divine or quasi-divine) organizing principle. Second, this systematic assumption has been accompanied by an excessive optimism about human nature. Contemporary philosophy, he writes, '[carries its] philanthropism to the point of denying evil' (*FS* VII: 371).

According to [the notions of our age], the only ground of evil lies in sensibility, or in animality, or the earthly principle, in that they oppose heaven not to hell, as they ought, but rather to earth. This idea is a natural consequence of the doctrine according to which freedom consists only in the domination of the sensual desires and inclinations by the intelligent principle, and that good comes from pure reason—from which it follows of course that there is no freedom for evil (since here the sensual inclinations dominate); or rather, to speak more correctly, evil is entirely cancelled. For while the weakness or inefficacy of the intelligent principle can be a ground for deficiency in good and virtuous actions, it cannot be a ground for positively evil actions and those contrary to virtue. (*FS* VII: 371)

Schelling objects to this excessive 'philanthropism' by pointing out that it is false to moral experience, since it makes evil incomprehensible from a practical perspective: no one who embraces this sort of view can see him or herself as capable of evil. This is what he means, I take it, when he says that evil can have no *subjective meaning* on such a view:

If one assumes, however, that sensibility or the passive attitude toward external impressions produces evil actions with a sort of necessity, then the human being himself would have to be passive in them [viz. evil actions],—i.e. evil would have no meaning with respect to the person, that is, subjectively—and since what follows from a natural determination also cannot be evil, [evil] would have no meaning at all. (*FS* VII: 371–2)

He links this optimism to the rationalism of contemporary moral psychology, in particular to the inclination in Kant and post-Kantian idealism to link freedom with (the capacity to) reason. The Kantian view makes comprehensible only one determination of the will—will to the good. 'There is therefore according to this explanation only one will . . . not a double one' (*FS* VII: 372).[4] He goes on to claim that there are only two ways in which one might try to explain evil in a generally Kantian context, neither of which is acceptable. The first, that the sensuous inclinations simply overcome the intellectual principle, leads to the result that evil is pure passivity. The second, that the intellectual principle permits the sensuous impulses to take precedence, has the result that evil is unintelligible, 'For why does [the intellectual principle] not exercise its power?' (*FS* VII: 372). Schelling also links the post-Kantian idealist view to what he calls the 'Platonic' view (presumably, the view that virtue is knowledge), though he does not pursue the comparison, in this discussion or elsewhere in the essay.

---

[4] Schelling makes the same critique in his 1812 polemic against Jacobi. To say that man's freedom is only a capacity for good is to retain only the word freedom, having deprived it of its meaning. 'Natural feeling, as well as understanding, tells us that when there is no free will for that which is called evil, then this evil cannot be a true evil' (VIII: 92–3). This is the exact opposite of the position he had taken in the 1797 *Abhandlung*.

Schelling objects to the idea that the source of an individual's capacity for moral responsibility lies solely in his capacity to reason, for 'no matter how highly we may esteem reason, we still do not, for instance, believe that someone can be virtuous, or a hero, or a great man at all, by means of pure reason' (*FS* VII: 413). But he does not accuse Kant and post-Kantian idealism of being *unequivocally* committed to this reduction. For he finds within that tradition another way of thinking about freedom, upon which he intends to found his view. He acknowledges this debt explicitly. Idealism, he writes, produced the first perfect *formal* concept of freedom (*FS* VII: 351). What he means by 'perfect formal concept of freedom' is transcendental spontaneity in the Kantian sense (and its successor notion in Fichte).

Schelling singles out two aspects of that notion as salient to his problem. First, such spontaneity is transcendental. It is not attributed to the self viewed as an empirical item, object of experience and natural scientific explanation. Instead it is attributed to the intelligible ground of the empirical self. Kant thought that such a view is compatible with empirical determinism, and Schelling here agrees (although again, determinism for him is not conceived in terms of Newtonian mechanics as it was for Kant). He explicitly rejects the option of attributing spontaneous causality to *empirical* individuals. This is probably due to his acceptance of a point about empirical indeterminism made by Hume (and others); at least, he discusses this objection at the relevant point in the text.

Both empirical determinism and empirical indeterminism, he writes, make freedom incomprehensible (*FS* VII: 383), the former by making actions inevitable, the latter by making them non-imputable. Determinism would be a threat to freedom, were the empirical perspective on agents the only one available. But empirical *in*determinism would not help to secure freedom, because at the empirical level the absence of determinism can only introduce chance. 'Accident, however, is impossible and conflicts with reason as well as with the necessary unity of the whole; and if freedom is to be saved only by the complete accidentalness of actions, then it cannot be saved at all' (*FS* VII: 383). The idea here seems to be that the only empirical source of determination available (the only way to explain actions seen as natural phenomena) is causal determination. This sort of causal determination, if it were the whole story about actions, would rob them of their spontaneity. But mere lack of empirical causal determination does not help, because undetermined actions must be seen (again, from the empirical scientific perspective) as random, and random events cannot be imputed to agents as their actions.

Schelling admits that, given the assumption that the standpoint of scientific explanation is the only one available, freedom is impossible.[5] But one is not forced

---

[5] 'The usual concept of freedom—according to which it is placed in an entirely undetermined capacity purely and simply to will one or the other of two contradictory opposites, without any determining grounds—has, indeed, the original indecision of human essence in the idea to its credit, but applied to individual actions it leads to the greatest absurdities. To be able to decide without any motivating grounds for A or ⁓ A would, to tell the truth, be but the prerogative to act entirely irrationally' (*FS* VII: 382).

to choose between naturally caused and non-imputable actions. The actions of empirical agents are imputable to them because they are the empirical manifestations of the choices of those same agents viewed non-empirically (viewed as intelligible objects). Such agents are not determined in a freedom-threatening sense, since they stand outside of time and natural causation-relations (*FS* VII: 383). Nor are their actions random and hence inexplicable, however. Their actions flow from their intelligible agency and are (morally, not natural-scientifically) explicable as the manifestations of the fundamental character of that agency.

So an agent's transcendental spontaneity determines that agent's fundamental moral character, as that character is manifested in empirical actions. So far this is a clearly Kantian view. Schelling goes further than Kant, though, in two ways. First, not only the agent's actions, he claims, but *everything* about the empirical agent (including 'even the nature of his embodiment' (*FS* VII: 387)) is determined by that agent viewed as intelligible object. What one's transcendental spontaneity determines is not only one's moral character, but everything about one. Second, this first aspect of transcendental freedom is attributed to *all of nature*. The essence of each natural item is determined not in time via causal interactions with other things, but instead by its place in an atemporal conceptual order of things:

The intelligible essence of each thing, and especially of human beings, is [according to idealism] outside of all causal relations, just as it is outside of or above all time. It can therefore never be determined by something that precedes it, since it itself rather precedes everything else that is or comes to be in it, [precedes it] not according to time, but rather according to the concept, as an absolute unity that must always already exist whole and perfect if individual actions or determinations in it are to be possible. (*FS* VII: 383)

The nature of all being, not just human being, is determined conceptually rather than mechanistically, and this determination is in some sense a *self*-determination. 'There is in the last and highest instance no being other than will. Will is primordial being' (*FS* VII: 350). Schelling criticizes Kant for not having acknowledged that freedom is the positive characteristic of the in-itself as such, in this passage:

It will always remain curious that Kant, after he had first distinguished things-in-themselves from appearances only negatively through their independence of time, and thereafter (in the metaphysical pronouncements of his *Critique of Practical* Reason) had actually treated independence of time and freedom as correlate concepts, did not progress to the thought of extending this latter, the only possible concept of the in-itself, to things. (*FS* VII: 351–2)

So 'free action' in this formal sense of freedom means, in part, action that arises from (and perhaps expresses) what one essentially is. Note, though, that this part of the specification of the formal concept of freedom Schelling attributes to idealism is still that applicable to all of nature: the magnet or the plant is as free in this sense as the human being.

Everything is self-determining in accordance with its essence, and so human beings are as well. But we have not yet learned about anything *specific* to human freedom. Nor have we, by Schelling's own admission, heard anything that differs materially from the freedom conception in the early system. This is where the second salient aspect of Kant's transcendental freedom comes in. In *Religion*, Kant had developed the idea of a non-temporal choice of fundamental moral disposition. Intelligible character was not merely that which determined empirical character (providing a sense in which empirical character is self-chosen). It was itself the result of a radical choice (a choice to subordinate the moral to sensible incentives, or the converse; a choice of a morally evil basic disposition or a morally good one). This aspect of Kant's view had been absent in Schelling's earlier account (even the account in the *System of Transcendental Idealism*). There, the intelligible character of individuals (their character as transcendental egos) was determined by their place in the moral world order. An individual's actions cohered with the actions of other empirical individuals to form an ordered whole because the moral ordering principle was not individual but rather universal: it was world spirit, constituted by the set of transcendental egos and constraining the possibilities open to each of them. Again, humans shared the fundamental characteristic of self-determination in this sense with all other natural products. It is this part of the view Schelling proposes to change.

One can understand what is at stake here by putting the matter in terms of the two classical libertarian criteria for free will: causal ultimacy and alternate possibilities. The self on Schelling's earliest view (in the *System of Transcendental Idealism*) had a sort of causal ultimacy, but it did not have alternate possibilities. It had causal ultimacy in virtue of being self-positing (something whose nature could not be understood except in terms of its own activity). But it did not have alternate possibilities, because it was not capable of having a nature different from the one it in fact had. The absence of alternate possibilities was required in order to preserve the rational (moral) world order. (Of course, this applies only to the view presented in the *System of Transcendental Idealism*, since not even causal ultimacy was had by the individual in the 1804 *System*.) Schelling's innovation in the *Freiheitsschrift* consists in adding the alternate possibilities to the causal ultimacy criterion and attributing both to the individual self viewed as intelligible object—just as Kant had done in *Religion*, and for the same reason. This forms the basis of the distinction between the freedom of human beings and the freedom of magnets or plants, according to the *Freiheitsschrift* conception: every natural product, viewed essentially, has causal ultimacy; only human beings have alternate possibilities. Schelling's formulation echoes Kant:

The human being's essence is essentially *his own act*.... In the original creation, the human being is an undecided being ... only he can decide himself. But this decision cannot happen in time; it happens outside of all time and therefore together with the first creation (though as an act different from it).... The act through which his life in time is determined does not itself belong to time, but rather to eternity: nor does it precede life temporally, but goes through time (untouched by it) as an act that is by nature eternal. (*FS* VII: 385–6)

Man is placed on a pinnacle, where he has the source of self-movement toward good and evil equally within himself. . . . He stands at the point of decision—what he chooses will be his act. (*FS* VII: 374)

Schelling echoes Kant in claiming that the view explains why an individual can seem to have been fundamentally good or evil from childhood on, and why he can both feel a certain inevitability in his actions and feel responsibility for being the way he is (*FS* VII: 386). In fact, Schelling appears to hold even more consistently than Kant to the consequences of this view. For instance, to the objection that it eliminates the possibility of moral reform, Schelling replies by denying the possibility of genuine conversion from evil to good or vice versa (*FS* VII: 389). The 'formal essence' of freedom, then, is independence of determination by anything outside oneself, coupled with determination by one's own essential character, where such essential character is defined by an arbitrary choice for good or evil.

In reintroducing the alternate-possibilities criterion of the libertarian view Schelling seems to leave his view open to another criticism, namely that this amounts to reintroducing the indifference conception of freedom eliminated at the empirical level to the choices of agents viewed as things in themselves. In fact he does not have a satisfactory answer to this criticism. He does gesture towards an answer that might help if he could wholeheartedly embrace it. This is the view of the self as radically self-constituting, which would allow him to say that the agent, even viewed intelligibly, does not choose among options, since it does not pre-exist its radical choice of character—for this would amount to pre-existing its own activity of self-constitution, and that is incoherent. If one cannot make sense of the agent viewed intelligibly standing before (conceptually speaking) its options and picking one or the other of them, one need not imagine such an agent standing before such choices with nothing to determine it one way or the other. Or so the story would go.

Schelling does gesture towards such a story in the essay (at *FS* VII: 384–5), but he cannot wholly embrace this solution because of another, ineliminable aspect of his view. The human self is a creature, according to the story in the *Freiheitsschrift*, and as something created it cannot be self-positing in the right way. It must pre-exist its choice of essence, must be 'originally undecided' in whatever sense that is possible for a timeless being—as Schelling says in the passages quoted above—because its existence as locus of moral responsibility cannot be its own doing.[6] Created things can be responsible to some extent for how they are, but

---

[6] Note that 'existence as locus of moral responsibility' or 'existence as agent' need not mean existence *simpliciter*: Fichte could hold that selfhood is self-constituting in the sense of being absent whenever a certain sort of self-relating activity is absent, *without* holding that human individuals create their bodies (or whatever the material substratum of that self-relating activity is) through their own mental acts. Schelling's point here is also not in the first instance about embodiment (despite his strange claims about embodiment mentioned above): his claim is that the *agent-hood* of individuals cannot be the result of their self-relating activity exclusively.

they cannot be responsible for the fact *that* they are without ceasing to be created things. The same thing goes for created agents: they can be responsible for how they use their agency, but they cannot be responsible for the fact that they are agents to begin with without ceasing to be created agents.

This captures a part of the phenomenology of agency as Kierkegaard and later figures in the so-called 'existentialist' tradition experienced it and which distinguished them from Fichte and even Kant. Agency did not seem to them to be self-starting. Human beings are agents whether they choose to be or not. They receive their agency as a gift or have it imposed on them as a task; they do not self-constitute as agents.

Schelling's philosophical motivation in insisting on the created status of individuals is not directly phenomenological. Instead, it is primarily systematic. This feature of created things is just what Schelling needs in order to rescue the individual person from the threat of being swallowed up in the *nomos* (to use Scheler's language). It opens up the possibility of an account of the origin and willing capacity of individuals within the system which transcends their place in the moral world order. Individuals need not be, *qua* causally efficacious, mere conduits for the causal efficacy of a rational principle that transcends them. This eliminates the worry that they somehow cease to be proper objects of moral imputation as soon as they fail to will rationally.

This commitment is ineliminable, then, because it is the basis for Schelling's answer to the main question of the essay: how is a positive conception of moral evil possible? Schelling's answer in the essay is long, metaphysically involved, and highly obscure. The motive behind it, however, is clear: he is concerned that the account of the willing capacity of individuals not be made incoherent by cases of non-law-abiding willing. For this reason he is concerned that the agency of individuals not be seen as *constituted* by their rational activity, or indeed *any* specifiable sort of activity they may engage in. But this means that the broadly Fichtean strategy of defining subjectivity (that is, the type of being had by moral agents) solely in terms of a self-constituting activity is simply not open to Schelling—for that is to define agency in terms of a specifiable sort of activity. This seems (or seemed to Schelling) to leave open only the option of incorporating into his conception of agency elements of a more traditional view, wherein an agent is a substantial something with a peculiar capacity to engage in morally appraisable action in virtue of some characteristic(s) it has. This account is what he will provide to fill out the Kantian placeholder self-*qua*-noumenon.

But Schelling cannot stop with the notion of transcendental spontaneity coupled with the Kantian individual choice of basic character taken from *Religion within the Boundaries of Mere Reason*. A positive definition of human freedom of the sort required would contain not only an account of why human beings have the causal powers they do; it would also contain an account of the moral options available to agents, and a story about what choosing these would amount to. That is why Schelling says that the 'merely formal' idealist conception is 'insufficient for demonstrating the specific difference, i.e., the distinctness of human freedom'. (*FS* VII: 352). He cannot take over that part of Kant's view that links the content of the moral will (the moral law) with the will's freedom. But this eliminates the possibility of taking over the Kantian account of what morality consists in. It also blocks one path for saying why whatever it is that morality consists in is normative. He cannot give an account according to which one's own constitution as an agent provides an answer to the question of what one is to do and why one should want to do that, for such an account was the source of the problem with moral evil to begin with.

So Schelling needs to provide such a positive story of his own. It seems that a minimum requirement for such a story will be at least the outline of an ethical theory. How, after all, can he explain how human freedom can be freedom for good and evil if he does not tell us what good and evil are? At the point in the essay at which he seems to be obliged to turn to ethics, however, Schelling turns instead to cosmology. What I shall try to do in the next few paragraphs is extract a comprehensible view from that discussion, which is far from fully comprehensible.

Cosmology and moral epistemology

Schelling begins with an account of the constitution of things (including persons) in terms of two fundamental principles—a 'real' principle (which Schelling also calls the principle of the *ground*), and an 'ideal' principle (which Schelling also calls the principle of the understanding, or the intellectual principle).[7] Schelling portrays these two principles in terms of various oppositions in the course of the essay, the most important among them being gravity/light; chaos/order; non-understanding/understanding; and creaturely self-will/universal will. The most enlightening opposition, oddly enough, turns out to be the first, which Schelling takes from his philosophy of nature. The gravity/light opposition is one of *contraction* versus *expansion*, and it is in light of this opposition that the other pairs of opposed terms are best understood. The principle of contraction is one that separates things off from one another, allowing them to exist as distinct individuals. The principle of expansion brings these distinct individuals into connection with one another.

Schelling generally refers to the first principle as the 'ground'. The second has no fixed appellation—he calls it light, understanding, the universal will, and sometimes God (although this last term is somewhat deceptive given the claim, made elsewhere in the essay, that God, like finite personalities, is a synthesis of the two principles). Each principle is an instantiation of will, now the basic ontological category, but the wills of the two principles are distinguished both according to content and according to character. In terms of content, the will of the ground

---

[7] The claim that there must be *some* two basic principles (united in a synthesis of some kind) rests on a staple of Schelling's philosophy of nature: only in (synthesized) opposition is there life. For a particularly eloquent presentation of this idea, cf. *WA* II 27–32 in Schelling (1946).

is a sort of egoism, while the will of the understanding is to the subordination of egoistic self-will within a larger order (*FS* VII: 381). In terms of character, the will of the ground is unconscious or semi-conscious, 'blind craving and desire' (*FS* VII: 372), while that of the second principle is fully conscious.

Schelling had already brought the notion of a tension between two opposed principles to his construction of organic nature. Life, he claims here as elsewhere, is possible only as a struggle (*FS* VII: 400). He had already used the notion of the resistance of a contracting force to the work of an ideal, expansive force to explain nature as a history, and more basically to explain the fact that things come to be in time, rather than already being what they are from eternity. However, in the previous works nature had presented a spectrum of instantiations of the synthesis of ideal and real, with the ideal element clearly dominant in spiritual (human) nature, the real element dominant in inorganic nature, and organic nature somewhere in between. All of these syntheses were fixed in a determinate developmental progression guided by a final cause: the production of that synthesis in which the ideal element most thoroughly dominates the real element, or, the production of the most perfect spiritual life.

In the *Freiheitsschrift*, the idea that the multiplicity of natural products as well as the temporal character of their manifestation arises out of a tension between fundamental forces remains, but the outcome of this struggle is no longer determined in all cases by a natural end. The cases in which it is not so determined are cases of *personality*. This category applies, in nature, only to human beings. Since personality is an instance of life, it makes sense only in the context of a view that posits two opposed principles. Schelling thinks this is true to the empirical notion of personality in particular, because, on the one hand, the universalism of the understanding cannot account for individuality, while, on the other hand, the separateness of the ground cannot account for consciousness, which is always characterized, according to Schelling, by some form of understanding. As is the case with natural forms, personality is not simply the conjunction of these two elements, but rather their synthesis in some concrete unity. What distinguishes the 'personality' of the *Freiheitsschrift* from the 'spiritual nature' in the earlier works is that this unity need not be one in which the ideal principle thoroughly subordinates the real principle, in which the light subordinates the ground. Rather, two sorts of synthesis are possible, one in which the ground is subordinated to the understanding, and one in which the understanding is subordinated to the ground—good and evil.

Conscious human willing is always general or universal in form. That is, being conscious, it always has in view the totality of the cosmos and its place there. But sometimes it wills to place itself (its particular needs or desires) at the centre of things. What this amounts to is elevating the ground (its being-as-distinct) to the status of an end in itself, subordinating the universal to the status of a means. 'Will that ... [strives] to make itself, as general will, at the same time particular and creaturely, strives to reverse the relation of the principles, to elevate the ground . . . from which disturbance both within and outside of it follows' (*FS* VII: 365). This is moral evil. 'The general possibility of evil consists . . . in the fact that the human being can, instead of making his selfhood a basis, an organ, instead strive to elevate it to [the status of] ruling and general will, while striving to make the spiritual in him into a means' (*FS* VII: 389).

So far it is of course far from clear why good and evil should consist in these two options of the self so construed. These do not look like moral categories at all, and several further elements of the discussion seem to confirm this impression. Schelling's comparison of evil to physical illness (*FS* VII: 366)—construed as the rebellion of a part (an organ or system) against the order in which it belongs (the body)—seems to involve both a questionable way of looking at illness and a peculiarly naturalistic conception of moral evil.[8] Schelling also construes evil in terms of disharmony, pointing out that disharmony is not a mere lack of harmony, which would be equivalent to the separation of the forces, but rather a false union (*FS* VII: 371). In fact what he is trying to get across in both of these metaphors is the idea of a positive opposition of an individual, which belongs to an overarching order (the body, the piece of music) where it has a proper part to play, instead rebelling against that order in a way that distorts both itself and the whole. This emphasis on rebellion or defiance fits well with his insistence on a positive conception of moral evil. So does his denial that the ground is the causal source of evil, or the understanding the causal source of good. The cause of both good and evil is, instead, personality, which is always a synthesis of the two: '[J]ust as it is by no means the intelligent or light principle in itself, but rather this combined with selfhood (i.e., raised to spirit), which is effective in the good, so evil does not follow from the principle of finitude taken on its own, but rather from the dark or selfish principle brought into intimacy with the centre' (*FS* VII: 372).

The question Schelling raised (in criticizing the Kantian account) about the incomprehensibility of the failure of the will in evil ('For why does it not exercise its power?') has, he thinks, been answered: the will *does* exercise its power in evil, by organizing itself around that principle within it that makes its existence as an individual will possible. This link of the possibility of independent personality with the principle of the ground allows for an interpretation of evil as defiance. Evil is rebellion against one's place in the cosmic order. It is a striving to make oneself, as particular creature, the centre of the universe—the 'insolence of wanting to be everything' (*FS* VII: 391). Being a self is *itself* a temptation, and a nearly overwhelming one. In describing the human capacity to create its essence on its own, independent of the divine order, Schelling uses an analogy that Kierkegaard will later take up: that of dizziness, and a concept that will become central to Kierkegaard's view: anxiety. The very fact of its independence 'awakens within it the desire for the creaturely, like the one who, on a high and peak [surrounded by

---

[8] It is this tendency, I believe, that leads Kierkegaard to criticize Schelling for portraying evil as akin to illness in *The Concept of Anxiety*—despite the fact that Kierkegaard ultimately comes back to the same formulation himself, in *The Sickness unto Death*.

precipitous drops], is gripped by dizziness and seems to hear a secret voice calling to him to fall' (*FS* VII: 381). '[T]he merging of the universal will with a particular will in the human being appears to be a contradiction, the union of these difficult if not impossible. The anxiety of life [i.e., of synthesis] itself drives the human being out of the centre' (*FS* VII: 381).

What, then, is the part human beings are *meant* to play in the cosmic order of the *Freiheitsschrift*? There are two sorts of answer to this question to be found in the essay. Parts of the discussion suggest that the part they play remains the same as in the early system: they are the vehicles for the self-disclosing of the absolute. But parts suggest a quite different role: they are creatures whose moral role consists in obedience to a central authority, their moral obligations essentially religious ones. This slide between two conceptions of the human vocation in the essay marks a slide between two conceptions of religion at work there: the pantheism of the early works and the theism of the later works. This transition from early to later views is motivated at least in part by the difficulty of mapping out a moral task for human beings within the framework of Schelling's early system. What ought a vehicle for the self-disclosing of the absolute *to do*? 'Gain knowledge' seems the right, the only, answer to this question. But this seems to reduce the sphere of action to that of contemplation (as Kierkegaard will argue in *Either/Or* and *Concluding Unscientific Postscript*). Still, the second sort of account is no more satisfying from the perspective of philosophical (as opposed to theological) ethics. The fact that Schelling tries to combine the two by suggesting that the failure of human beings at fulfilling their task viewed in the second way is a (covert) route to succeeding in their moral task viewed in the first—at *FS* VII: 402, where Schelling suggests that evil comes into being so that God can have a reason to reveal himself—does not make the picture any more appealing. Indeed it looks as though Schelling repudiates the entire project of giving a philosophical ethics. In the process of telling us a more convincing story about why we can sometimes do other than we ought, he has rendered himself incapable of telling us what we ought to do and why.

The meta-ethics of the *Freiheitsschrift* is tied up with this absence of a substantive normative ethics there. Its most characteristic claim is that in order to be free for good and evil, human beings must find the source of the norms to which they are subject outside themselves. The centre, the moral absolute, is not immanent to the will of the creature, in the sense of being the principle of its operation or the law governing its efficacy. In saying this, Schelling is rejecting the available Kantian and post-Kantian accounts. Agents cannot look to their reason or to some other aspect of their intrinsic nature as a source of norms. Nor do they create norms themselves through their own activity, rational or otherwise. The deed that is the basis of the fundamental moral disposition of an individual is one of orienting itself towards or away from some source of norms that is outside of it. And so it is no surprise that Schelling cannot specify what the norms we should live by are. For the model of moral knowledge that he began with was the

Kantian and post-Kantian rationalist one, and this has become unusable. But his conception of philosophical knowledge has not yet been modified to accommodate a different model. In particular, it does not allow for the sort of broadly empirical inquiry that would be required in this essentially religious form of moral realism.

Schelling will go on, in his later works, to modify his epistemology to accommodate a new account of the source of norms. He has additional motivations for this change in epistemology as well, arising from another result of his inquiry into moral evil in the *Freiheitsschrift*. As we have seen, Schelling has modified the account of transcendental spontaneity taken over from Kant and Fichte by adding a layer of indeterminacy in the constitution of moral character. This modification does not require Schelling to countenance anything like disruptions of the laws of nature brought about by the actions of empirical individuals. The idea that this character is fixed by a non-temporal act of contingent self-determination which is compatible with the inevitability of each empirical action given events preceding it in time is linked not only to Kant's *Religion*, but also to Schelling's own earlier account of the relation between the absolute I and the empirical I from the *Ich-Schrift* through the *System of Transcendental Idealism*. Schelling reiterates that theme in the *Freiheitsschrift*: 'In consciousness, insofar as this is self-comprehending and merely idealistic, this free act, which becomes necessity, cannot be seen, since it precedes and *constitutes* consciousness as it precedes [and constitutes] essence' (*FS* VII: 386). The pre-conscious nature of the free character-determining act was one of the mainstays of the *System of Transcendental Idealism*, invoked (as it had been by Fichte) as a way of reconciling the claim that the self constitutes itself in complete freedom with common sense's claim that the self finds itself already existing in, and already constrained by, an empirical world and empirical personal characteristics. This portion of the earlier view persists through the *Freiheitsschrift* and into the *Weltalter* period (of the 1810–15) as well.[9]

So Schelling's modification does not entail any lawbreaking capacities of empirical individuals or the complete lawlessness of nature as it is experienced. Still, it seems that this layer of indeterminacy—if it really is efficacious in the actions of individuals—must be sufficient to disrupt the clarity of the manifestation of reason that the early Schelling had thought he saw in nature and human history. If the world is determined in terms of final causes in the sense in which the third *Critique* suggests that it might be, evil looks like the disruption of that determination by the thwarting of those ends. Leaving room for evil, then, requires giving

---

[9] It can be found, for instance, at *WA* II: 138–9: 'And so that primordial deed, which precedes all particular actions and through which a man is genuinely what he is, once accomplished, in exuberant freedom, immediately sinks into the night of unconsciousness. It is not a deed that could occur and then stop, but rather a permanent and never-ending deed, and can for this reason never again be brought to consciousness.'

up the claim that the order, the rational determination, is total; it requires introducing some degree of chaos.

Indeed, we find this is the case. In the context of a discussion of the cosmological place of evil Schelling makes the point that we can see the effects of evil not only in human conduct, but also in a certain accidentalness in the determination of nature: 'There are accidental determinations in nature which are only explicable by appeal to an excitement of the irrational or dark principle of the creature—activated selfhood—in the first creation' (*FS* VII: 376). This accidentalness is not evil per se, but instead its natural result: 'The irrational and the accidental, which shows itself to be bound to the necessary in the formation of beings, especially organic ones, proves that it is not a mere geometrical necessity that was at work here, but instead that freedom, spirit and self-will were in play' (*FS* VII: 376). The irrational and accidental are 'bound' to the necessary in the sense of being *mixed* with the necessary in the world as it is experienced. '[N]owhere does it appear as though order and form are original, instead it seems as if something originally ruleless had been brought to order. This is the ungraspable basis of reality in things, the indivisible remainder, that which cannot be analyzed by the understanding even with the greatest exertion' (*FS* VII: 359–60).

The idea that the exercise of human freedom is actually responsible for the introduction of chaos into the order of things, prefigured in *Philosophie und Religion* (1804), is a staple of Schelling's late view—but it becomes dominant only with the *Weltalter* drafts, and coexists in the *Freiheitsschrift* alongside remnants of Schelling's earlier view. According to this later view, the existing world, the world of experience, is the fallen world, and as such incorporates an element of chaos: a reflection in nature of evil in man. The existing world is distinct from the ideal world which, as idealized blueprint of 'world' in general, *is* rationally constructible (the construction being the work of what Schelling will later call 'negative' philosophy), and it is in comparing the actual world to this idealized blueprint that we can know that the actual world is fallen.

Schelling runs up against the difficulty this idea poses for a philosophical system built according to the monistic first-principle model in his discussion of the unity of the two principles (ground and intelligence) in the essay. He tries to unify these along the lines of the earlier system. The claim is that the two are unified because the principle of understanding itself develops out of the ground (*FS* VII: 359). The ground is prior to the understanding in the sense of being the real basis of the understanding—that in virtue of which it has being. The understanding is then in turn the ideal basis of the ground— that in virtue of which it can be thought. While the ground produces the understanding in the sense of bringing it into being, the understanding produces the ground in the sense of making it thinkable. This set of claims is at once consistent with similar claims made in the earlier works—this is just the relation that the real principle and the ideal principle had had to one another from the beginning of Schelling's systematic thought—and a radical departure from them.[10] It is a departure because of the characterization Schelling here gives of the real principle, namely as something chaotic and positively opposed to intelligibility. The basic statement of real-idealism as it is made here entails not only that understanding in fact arises out of the unintelligible as its real basis, as Schelling admits (*FS* VII: 360), but also that the understanding itself produces the unintelligible as its explanation of its own real source. Note that 'unintelligible' here means not merely pre-conceptual but non-conceptualizable (or resistant to conceptualization). Compare this passage from the Munich lectures of the 1830s:

Nothing is more comprehensible than the concept, and whoever makes this into the object of his development has chosen for himself the most flexible material. The true concept is only an act of thought. The ungraspable begins only with that which is *opposed* to the concept. . . . Nothing is easier than to transport oneself to the realm of pure thought, but it is not so easy to get out of it again. The world does not consist of mere categories or pure concepts; it does not consist of concrete *concepts* but of concrete and contingent things, and the real question concerns that other, that which is *not* the concept but its opposite, and which accepts the concept only unwillingly. Here philosophy must pass its test. (*GpP*: 225)

Important here is the idea, prefigured but not wholly embraced in the *Freiheitsschrift*, that the task of philosophy is to grasp (somehow) in concepts 'that which accepts the concept only unwillingly'—to grasp a nature that presents itself as, at least in part, a manifestation of unreason.

This, then, is the other motivation for a new account of knowledge. The idealist account tells us how we can come to know the idealized blueprint, but not how we can come to know the actual world. If we are to be able to know irrationality to be at work, to know that the actual world is distinct from the rational blueprint of 'world' as such, it seems that Schelling is obliged to give us some alternative account of how we can know this. An alternative account of philosophical knowledge is required, one according to which we have at least some irreducibly empirical knowledge. There is no such account in the essay; giving one will be a major task of Schelling's later work.

---

[10] Schelling had gone from claiming, in his first systematic efforts, that this reciprocal grounding of real and ideal can be understood on its own, to claiming, in the *Identitätssystem*, that a single principle above these two is necessary to conceptualize their integration. In the *Freiheitsschrift*, as in the *Identitätssystem*, this principle is called 'indifference', and Schelling comes to a discussion of this principle late in the essay. Unfortunately, his characterization of indifference in the *Freiheitsschrift* is not much more informative than those earlier characterizations famously criticized by Hegel in the preface to the *Phenomenology*. Here he calls it the 'original ground' or 'unground' (*Urgrund* or *Ungrund*) of the two principles, containing both implicitly. In indifference the principles are neither opposed to one another nor brought to identity, but indifferent to one another, as possible predicates of an in-itself predicateless indifference. This indifference is the 'absolute regarded in itself' (*FS* VII: 408).

II. A NEW SYSTEM: SCHELLING'S 'POSITIVE PHILOSOPHY' OF THE 1830s AND 1840s

Schelling began his second lecture in Berlin[11] by announcing that the 'relation of philosophy to actuality' would be his theme (*Paulus* 98),[12] and Kierkegaard wrote in his journal:

I am so happy to have heard Schelling's second lecture—indescribably.... The embryonic child of thought leapt for joy within me as in Elizabeth, when he mentioned the word 'actuality' in connection with the relation of philosophy to actuality. I remember almost every word he said after that.[13]

What is it that he remembered? Schelling began his lecture series that year by summarizing the line he had taken on idealistic philosophy for roughly the preceding fifteen years. The various idealist systems are accounts, according to this line, of 'the relations which things take on in pure thought' rather than an account of '*existence*, what *actually exists*' (*GnP* X: 125); Idealism knows nothing of actual things; it knows only possible things (*Paulus* 119); '[R]eason, so long as it takes itself as its principle, is capable of *no actual knowledge*' (*Paulus* 152).

If idealism provides knowledge only of an idealized blueprint, and if what philosophy ought to provide (and what the later Schelling aims to provide) is knowledge of the actual world, there are two questions he needs to answer that fall under the rubric 'the relation of thought to actuality': (1) what is the relation of the idealized blueprint to the actual world?; and (2) how do we come to know that part of what is true of the actual world that we do not know simply by knowing the idealized blueprint? The answer to the first question is complicated by Schelling's aim of preserving as much as possible of the claims of the idealist systems (viz. his own early work and its Hegelian successor) within the later system—and by his changing estimation of how much of it can be preserved. The answer to the second is unsurprising, though there are some complications here as well. I will discuss these two answers in turn.

---

[11] Schelling's new system consisted of a systematic history of religion (two one-year lecture courses on mythology and on revealed religion, respectively) preceded by a methodological introduction (generally also a year-long course of lectures) which included a history of recent philosophy and an account of the motivations for the new historical/empiricist orientation. Schelling normally gave the whole course over three years, but the first course of lectures he gave in Berlin—the course attended by Kierkegaard—was uncharacteristic. He began with a very compressed version of the methodological introduction and, after a very brief discussion of mythology, proceeded directly to the philosophy of revelation.

[12] 'Paulus' refers to the Paulus edition of a set of notes from Schelling's first set of lectures in Berlin (1841–2), published by Frank under the title *Philosophie der Offenbarung* (Schelling 1977). Pagination refers to that volume.

[13] Kierkegaard (1909–78: III A 179); Kierkegaard (1997–, vol. 19: 235 Notesbog 8: 33). Translation from Kierkegaard (1967–78).

The limits of negative philosophy and the contributions of positive philosophy

Schelling did not want, in this later period, to entirely reject his own earlier work. He wanted to incorporate it into a larger system as the 'negative' counterpart to a new, 'positive' philosophy. The 'negative' philosophy is essentially Schelling's earlier idealist position (an *a priori* construction of the natural and spiritual world which leaves no space for any significant degree of contingency), whereas the 'positive' philosophy is from the outset an account of history (focused on the history of religion: Schelling's three-year lecture series consisted of one year each of lectures on philosophy of mythology and revelation, following a year-long methodological introduction) whose premiss was that history is radically contingent, reflecting the exercise of divine freedom and human freedom (a radically free creation and the destruction of the original order of that creation by the fall of man). Interpretive problems arise from the claim that these two philosophies are supposed to form parts of a single system; their relative place in Schelling's thought is the crux of the debate about the true nature of his later work, and amounts, ultimately, to the question of whether that work is to be viewed as a completion or a rejection of the idealist project.[14]

The question about the relation between idealism and positive philosophy receives a number of answers in the late lectures—not all jointly consistent— ranging from conservative (retaining most of Schelling's early view) to radical (rejecting most if not all of it).[15] In the first series of Berlin lectures—the ones Kierkegaard heard—Schelling describes the idealist conception of philosophy

---

[14] Landmarks in this debate are Schulz (1975), who presents the late Schelling's work as a completion of the idealist project, and Fuhrmans (1940), who presents it as a rejection of idealism in favour of a proto-existentialist Christian view. Further helpful discussion can be found in Hutter (1996), who sees Schelling's late work as a return to and an extension of the Kantian critical project, and Frank (1992), who shows how it prefigures mid-century materialism. Cf. also Courtine (1990) and Tilliette (1970).

[15] The tensions I point to here are not the ones due to revisions Schelling made in his lectures over the course of time, since my discussion here focuses on the first instantiation of the mid-1830s together with the first lecture course in Berlin, and mostly disregards the revisions of the mid- and late-1840s. The reason for this is that the propagation of Schelling's views through the circle of late idealists surrounding I. H. Fichte and Christian Weiße was overwhelmingly based upon the Munich work of the late 1820s and 1830s, and it is largely through them that Kierkegaard learned what he knew about Schelling. Not much depends upon this orientation to the 'earlier' late work. The Munich introduction (read, under the title 'Grundlegung der positiven Philosophie', in either one or two semesters over the course of Schelling's stay in Munich) was completed by 1827 and remained basically unchanged until just before his move to Berlin in 1841. (Cf. Fuhrmans introduction to Schelling (1972: 7)). The later version of this introduction—the one published by Schelling's son as SW XIII: 1–174—differs from the earlier version in spending less time on the history of philosophy, more time on the working out of the foundations of the negative, as opposed to the positive, philosophy, and in being slightly less aggressive in its critique of Hegel. Much, however, remained unchanged, and the argument presented here does not depend upon taking the Munich *Grundlegung* as definitive, as it clearly was not. I supplement the argument with passages taken from both earlier and later works, where they are consistent (as they generally are) with the view presented.

(what in these lectures he calls 'pure rational philosophy' or 'negative philosophy')
as the task of constructing 'the content of all of being', and criticizes Hegel for
assuming that this content can be identified with actual being:

> I am in complete agreement with the *Hegelian definition of philosophy: it is the science of
> reason, insofar as this latter becomes aware of itself as all of being.* . . . In it, reason becomes
> aware of itself as all of being—*assuming that by 'being' one does not understand also actual
> being [daß unter dem Sein nicht auch das wirkliche, aktuelle verstanden wird]* but rather that
> in rational science reason appears as all of being according to its content. *That in philosophy
> reason becomes aware of its own content as the content of all of being—this is the explanation of
> pure rational science.* But we must not fail to make this distinction! (*Paulus* 122)

What does Schelling hope to achieve by making this distinction? His formulation
here leaves important questions open. Is what 'pure rational philosophy' constructs
the totality of possible worlds? If so, is the actual world the only possible one? The
idealists (including the early Schelling) seemed committed to an affirmative
answer to both questions. The ramified totality of contents of thought is the
ramified totality of characteristics of the actual world, because the actual world is
the only possible world and so is in all its characteristics necessary.[16] This does
leave a gap between 'philosophy' and 'actuality', since the only possible world
might fail to be instantiated. And Schelling's most conservative statement of the
gap between the conceptual totality reason can construct and the actuality it
purports to describe is his well-known reiteration of Leibniz's question: '[I]f I
want to proceed to the limits of all thought, then I must also admit that it is possible that there be nothing at all. The last question is always, why is there anything
at all, why is there not nothing?' (*PO* XIII: 242). If reason cannot answer that
question, then it lacks the resources to show that its contents must be instantiated.
The later Schelling maintains (plausibly, if without argument) that it cannot.

I call this statement 'conservative' because it does not provide the basis for a
particularly deep criticism of the idealist project. What Schelling does here is
take exception to Hegel's claim that reason (the Hegelian 'concept') is inherently
self-actualizing. (The early Schelling seems also to have been committed to a
version of this idea, though he denies this in the late lectures.) But putting Hegel's
system on a hypothetical footing ('if there were to be reality, it would have to be
rational and indeed to have the content outlined in the Hegelian system'), though
certainly at odds with Hegel's view of his results, does not do much to discredit
those aspects of the system with which the later Schelling ought to have his most
serious complaints. If there is only one possible world, governed in its outlines and
its development by rational necessity, pointing out that it is a contingent fact that
this world is instantiated does not amount to making space for the sort of freedom

---

[16] Both the early Schelling and Hegel allowed space for contingency in the details, but neither
allowed for contingency in the fundamental structure, of reality. (Part of what this meant is that the
contingency in the details was confined there: it could not ramify (causally) to affect the fundamental
structure.)

that the later Schelling can be expected to require. Since we know that there is something rather than nothing—our own existence being a presupposition of our posing this question—this criticism seems weak.[17]

In a discussion of the status of the construction of the potencies in the *Identitätssystem* given in Munich (at *GpP* 222ff.), Schelling offers a criticism of the idealist systems that goes one step further. There he makes a distinction between the content of the early system (which was correct) and its account of how it arrived at that content (which was in error). In the early work the claim had been that when we think being, we *must* think of it as something that produces its own self-consciousness in the form of self-conscious human beings. The construction of the potencies and their relation was an *a priori* exercise that described the natural and spiritual worlds according to their necessity; the claim was that it was impossible to conceive of being without understanding that it must give rise to reason. Now, Schelling tells us, he has come to realize that it is a *contingent* fact that the world is such as to produce rational beings. 'One can always go on to ask, why *is* there reason, why not unreason?' (*DpE* X: 252) The construction of the potencies is to be maintained, but it is to be demoted from the status of a set of necessary truths to that of a set of contingent ones—contingent on the existence of reasoning beings. Since we are reasoning beings, we know these exist, and therefore know that the construction is correct (of our world). But there are possible worlds containing no reasoning beings, and of those the account of nature in the early work is incorrect, even in its fundamentals. What Schelling's early systematic philosophy provided, he now tells us, was something like a deduction of the conditions of possibility of rationality in nature.[18]

This criticism of idealism also does not go far enough to accommodate the freedom conception of the *Freiheitsschrift*, since it maintains that there is but one possible state of things consistent with the existence of rational beings. But at other points the later Schelling does say things that go that far, denying that the actual world corresponds wholly, even according to content, to the idealized blueprint that is the result of negative philosophy.

One such place is in the discussion of the history of modern philosophy in the Munich lectures. There, Schelling chastises modern philosophy for its narrow conception of properly philosophical knowledge—its emphasis on *a prioricity* and use of mathematics as a model—and calls for an approach (one he finds in

---

[17] Hegel's refusal to accept such an *a posteriori* presupposition of his system does get a lot of attention in Kierkegaard, who says at one point that Hegel's whole undertaking would be reasonable if only he admitted its conditional status. White (1983a; 1983b) takes this to be the crux of the later Schelling's criticism of Hegel, and actually tries to rebut it on Hegel's behalf.

[18] As a further clarification of Schelling's line of thought it might be helpful to note that he remarks, throughout, that even if we could make sense of reason's being primary, we would thereby close off not only the possibility of an extra-rational world (*GpP* 227), but also the possibility of introducing any irrationality or contingency—for we could never derive unreason from reason. Schelling says Hegel goes in just this direction, claiming that everywhere there *is* only sense (*GpP* 222), which entails that nonsense, irrationality, is literally impossible.

pre-modern conceptions of philosophy) that embraces knowledge of contingent truths as properly philosophical.[19] In this discussion (as elsewhere in the later work) Schelling equates philosophical necessity in the sense operative in rationalism and idealism with tautology, and complains that tautologies cannot tell us anything we did not know before—though they might make explicit some things we knew implicitly (cf. *GpP* 100). He also equates these two with *a prioricity* and, rejecting (as always) Kant's distinction between synthetic and analytic *a priori* as well as his account of mathematical knowledge, claims that mathematics is the model for negative philosophy and that *history* should be the model for positive philosophy. Only knowledge of contingent truths is knowledge in the proper sense of the term—'Where a *knowing* knowledge is claimed, there must be something at hand whose opposite is also possible' (*GpP* 96)—and knowledge of such contingent truths is had through experience—'*Knowledge in the proper sense I call only that which is concluded not through pure thought alone, but through actuality*' (*GpP* 97).[20] One is obliged to conclude that his own early system—as the culmination of 'modern' philosophy and the paradigm of 'negative' philosophy—is now to be considered at best a partial description of the philosophically interesting characteristics of the world.

In later iterations of the positive philosophy one finds similar claims: negative philosophy is an abstract scaffold upon which a concrete description of the actual world must rest—but not itself a (sufficiently) concrete description. 'We live in this determinate world, not in an abstract or universal world, as we so enjoy convincing ourselves by holding only to the *universal* properties of things without penetrating to their real relationships.... The coherence of the world is not so simple as some pretend; the current state of things in the world is an infinitely determinate one' (XIV: 332). Together with Schelling's statement that negative philosophy is a science of the 'knowable' (*Paulus* 118), an examination of the general characteristics of objects of 'possible experience' (*Paulus* 116), not a full science of things as they actually, concretely are, this suggests a view according to which the actual world is not the only possible one. On the most straightforward reading, the role of the negative philosophy is to outline the necessary as opposed to the contingent features of that world; the role of the positive philosophy to add an account of some (philosophically significant) contingent features.

Note that—so far—the claim is merely that we should look beyond the *a priori* in doing philosophy. That some philosophically interesting features of reality are not necessary need not mean that whatever necessity is admitted is not a real

---

[19] Hutter (1996: 77–105) has a nice discussion of Schelling's motivations in these passages.

[20] In this discussion Schelling writes that the common error of all philosophical systems since Descartes has been their 'merely logical' character (*GpP* 74–5). He distinguishes between what he calls '*unwissendes Wissen*' and '*wissendes Wissen*'—the latter being the positive knowledge that negative philosophy ignores. 'Where a *knowing* knowledge is claimed, there must be something at hand whose opposite is also possible' (*GpP* 96). This means that only where doubt is possible is knowledge also possible. '*Certainty is nothing other than the positive opposite of doubt*. But there is not doubt where there are not at least two possibilities' (*GpP* 97).

necessity in the nature of things. What is 'concluded through pure thought alone' may perfectly well be true of actuality, even if it need not be discovered empirically. Schelling appears to confirm this reading at various points—for instance, at *Paulus* 99 ff., where he insists that negative philosophy does grasp the actuality of things, just not the *complete* actuality.

But there are also clear statements in the late works of a more radical view. Schelling often seems to be saying that the necessity inhering in the constructions of negative philosophy is one governing only the way we must think the world— as opposed to the way that world really must be. The metaphysically necessary and the *a priori* need not coincide. There may be metaphysical necessities that are knowable only *a posteriori* (this is one way of understanding Schelling's complaint about the ontological argument),[21] and there may equally be cases of *a priori* claims to which no metaphysical necessities (or even contingent truths) correspond.

This distinction between what-we-must-think and how-things-actually-are has two possible scopes: the former term can refer to only a subset of experience, or it can refer to all of experience. The former option would make Schelling a quasi-Kantian: some aspects of experience have the veneer of necessity, but that is due only to the existence of some invariant rules in our way of apprehending the world and corresponds to no necessity (indeed no specifiable characteristic at all) in things as they are in themselves. The latter option would make Schelling's position a subjective-idealistic version of Hegelianism: everything about the way we think about the world has the veneer of necessity, but that corresponds to no necessity in the way things actually are. On either of these readings, the only necessity we can know there to be governs how we think, and far from governing reality, thought does not even track it, except (perhaps) via the senses (if and to the extent that we can escape the necessity of thinking of things in a certain way—the apparent commitment to this possibility being the reason to refrain from calling the late Schelling a *genuine* Kantian).

There are problems with the subjective idealist Hegelian option—the idea that the world looks like a necessary totality, and must so look to the thinker or to 'thought', but this is just how it has to *look*, not how it has actually to *be*. One is that if it is true, it precludes our having any evidence for its truth. How could one know that this way-that-we-have-to-think-the-world-as-necessary-totality is really just an appearance? Hegel's arguments pointing to the difficulty of positing a Kantian 'thing in itself' (that if we are not allowed to say anything determinate about it, we should also not be allowed to say that it is potentially distinct in character from the object of experience or that it is the cause of that experience) are sharpened in a view that differs from Kant's in allowing no apparent contingency in experience. Apparent contingency is what clues us in to the receptive component of our cognition, and receptivity is what leads us to posit an external root of experience (viz. a thing in itself which affects us). If there were no contingency, there would be no clue, no reason to think there might be anything beyond (and causing) our experience. How in this case would it be possible to take seriously the proposition that the totality whose rational necessity presents itself to cognition is really just an appearance? Although this might be a possibility that could not be ruled out, it certainly cannot be a position for which any positive argument could be made. A second problem is that Schelling both needs (for his account of agency) and admits (in the passages I have quoted, among others) contingency *in* experience.

There are problems with the Kantian option as well, since it is inconsistent with the claims Schelling (even in his late work) wants to make on behalf of his own early system. Still, the late Schelling often seems committed to some such view. He makes three sorts of claim that seem to commit him to it. First, he often puts his criticism of the idealist account of knowledge in terms that seem to force this reading. The only way one could in principle claim to know that how things really are *must* be such as to correspond to the concept of being constructed in thought would be to deny that there is being except in thought. He characterizes this as the idealist assumption which he now rejects.

We can produce everything that appears in our experience *a priori*, in thought alone, but in this way it is just that, *only in* thought. If we want to change this into an objective positing—to say that everything is in itself also only in thought—then we must return to the standpoint of a Fichtean idealism.[22] If we want to think of anything that is outside of thought, we must begin from a being that is absolutely independent of all thought, that precedes all thought. (*PO* XIII: 164)

The result of beginning not from the contents of thought but from the 'being that precedes all thought' (what Schelling calls *das unvordenkliche Sein*, which is meant to form the ontological foundation of the later system)[23] is that the correspondence of being to thought cannot be grounded in thought. This means that the conceptual constraints on thought cannot be known to apply to anything in nature. Second, at various points Schelling portrays nature as in fact fundamentally lawless and devoid of any necessary characteristics whatsoever (e.g., at *GpP* 90, where he remarks: 'We are here beginning to grasp that *the so-called eternal truths* are nothing other than propositions abstracted from the present state of things. There are no *eternal* truths in this sense.'). But if there is no necessity in nature, the logical constraints on negative philosophy can at most be constraints on thinking, not constraints on how things are. Third, Schelling's criticism of the ontological argument for the existence of God, which occupies a prominent place in the late lectures, seems to rely on a distinction between thought-necessity and real necessity.

---

22 Schelling thinks Fichte's position, taken this way, is, at the very least, subject to a vicious regress whose beginning is indicated by the question: 'What about thought itself? Is its being only in thought?'—so, at least, Frank (1992: 66–7) argues, and this argument has been widely accepted.

23 Discussions of this point can be found in Frank (1992: 151–204), Bowie (1993: 127–77) (who essentially follows Frank), White (1983b: 146–86), and Schulz (1975: 61–83).

What sense is to be made of this range of options for the interpretation of the relation of negative to positive philosophy in the late Schelling? One conclusion to draw is that Schelling himself was not certain of what conclusions he was actually forced to by the commitment to human freedom as contingency-producing, and how those conclusions could be compatible with the preservation of some non-illusory species of necessity in the philosophical grasp of reality.

A slightly different conclusion, which I prefer, is that the set of statements about the relation of negative to positive philosophy is somehow deceptive, or not the best place to look to get a good sense of Schelling's view of the nature and limits of (metaphysical and causal) necessity. The idea would be that where he explicitly addresses the issue of the relation of idealism to the positive philosophy, he is moved by two competing extra-theoretical motivations: that of elevating the status of his own early efforts, and that of denigrating those of his rival Hegel. This is a difficult combination of goals, because there is simply not enough difference between his early view and Hegel's on the points that matter, and that difficulty distorts his estimation of the relation. So although these discussions are critical to an understanding of the late system, no unified reading can be constructed whose evidence is drawn wholly or even primarily from them.[24]

More clarity is to be found, I believe, in those places where Schelling discusses the nature of God, creation, and human moral and religious knowledge. These show a view comprised of four main points. (1) Although some features of the actual world are necessarily thought (their negation seems *prima facie* incoherent to us), this necessity is not absolute. Rather, both these features and our reason are the result of a decision to create a world with these features (including human beings with reason which grasps these features) on the part of a transcendent creator. (2) Some but not all events are causally necessary. (3) The causal necessity of even those events is not a metaphysical necessity even in the sense described in (1). (4) The basic factual and moral outlines of the world and human experience are, to some extent at least, empirically knowable (again, as a result of a divine intention that this be so). In order to elucidate this view (and especially the fourth point) I turn to a discussion of the theology of the positive philosophy.

Divine freedom and positive theology

Schelling intended the late system as an extended empirical argument for God's existence, and his insistence on the contingency of the structure of the world and of reason itself is of a piece with his conception of God. The conceptualization of

---

[24] Many of these irreconcilable options, and confusions, are reproduced in the *Concluding Unscientific Postscript* discussion of the relation of 'thought' to 'actuality', but I will not discuss every correspondence when I come to address that work—in part because, with these options laid out here as they have been, it is fairly easy to see how they map on to the various, and often conflicting, statements on that topic in the *Postscript*, but mainly because like Schelling, Kierkegaard can hold, and is obliged by his other commitments to hold, only a fairly small subset of them.

the role of God in human moral life and of the nature of human epistemic access to God were both fundamental for the mid-nineteenth-century anti-idealist reaction (which, of course, included Kierkegaard)—at least as important as the explicit criticisms of idealist metaphysics and epistemology just discussed.

Schelling conceives of God as being radically self-creating in a manner that is perhaps most easily conveyed by saying that God's existence precedes his essence, and that this essence is a result of God's own contingent acts of will. God is what he wills to be, and the world he creates is what he wills it to be, with no prior constraints (moral or metaphysical) on its existence or character (VIII: 168; *GpP* 241, 286, 298, *et passim*). Schelling's endorsement of theological voluntarism about ethical content is one part of his view that remained stable over the whole later period. It is best expressed in this passage:

It belongs to the familiar, popular rationalist ideas that God, absolutely and by nature, could *only* do good, and by 'good' one understands that which is in accordance with the moral law. But God is outside of and above all law, for he himself is the law. God is the master *jure absolute positivo*... There is no good before or outside of him that he must will—there is good only after him and as a consequence of him. The good is only *what* he wills and it is good *because* he wills it (not in itself). If he did not will it, it would not be good. (*GnP* X: 58)

Schelling makes this point in the context of a discussion of Leibniz, in which he claims that the latter's distinction between moral necessity and metaphysical necessity is, in the cosmological context, a distinction without a difference:

Leibniz tries only to soften this necessity by presenting it as a *moral* one. but if the moral necessity to choose the good—and, under given circumstances, the best—belongs to the *nature*, to the *essence* of God, as Leibniz claims, then this is only an effort to mediate and make understandable the necessity according to which, as Spinoza says, everything flows from the essence of God, not to cancel it. (*GnP* X: 58)

The problem with Spinoza's emanation doctrine, according to Schelling, is that it subjects 'God' to the necessity of 'creating' by claiming that the finite forms follow necessarily from absolute substance, both in respect of the fact that there are finite forms to begin with and in respect of what these finite forms are. So Schelling's voluntarism about the moral goes hand in hand with his voluntarism about the basic characteristics of reality. Both commitments follow from his commitment to perfect divine freedom, together with his new conception of what that freedom consists in.

What perfect freedom means in the divine case in the later work stands in sharp contrast to that in the earlier work. Schelling explicitly repudiates that earlier conception of freedom as unimpeded development in accordance with one's own essence. This is the main distinction he points to between the early system and the late system:

[In the early system,] the [absolute] subject is indeed determined by nothing *outside* of it and to this extent free; but on the other hand this movement is in a certain sense *inescapable* for it, because only *in this movement* does it become a true life. We attribute *perfect* freedom only to that cause, however, for which the action is *fully indifferent* relative to itself. And so to this extent we cannot call that subject [viz. the absolute as conceived in the early system] a *truly* free cause. (*GpP* 214)

Note that it is internal teleology that Schelling now finds to be incompatible with full freedom; he even goes so far as to say that pure and full freedom is present only 'when it is *totally indifferent* (*völlig gleighgültig*) *to me* which of two opposites I do or do not do' (*GpP* 212).[25] Such must be the freedom of a free creator: it must be wholly 'indifferent' to him whether he creates a world or not, and whether he creates it in one way rather than another. This does not mean (as Schelling's language suggests) that God is unfree to the extent that he cares whether and how the world is or takes an interest (in the everyday sense) in what he does. What Schelling means is that God's causal power must be independent of the content of the action undertaken: 'If the cause is supposed not to have an interest in the action, that which is posited by the action must be such that it neither adds something to the being of the cause, nor takes something away from it, if it is *not* posited' (*GpP* 214). What he means is that God does not gain or lose anything with respect to his self-sufficient being or causal efficacy in creating a world separate from himself and in creating it in one way rather than another.[26] This is just the opposite of the view Schelling had earlier endorsed, according to which one's nature determines one's activity in the sense that only those deeds that follow from one's nature can be called (genuinely) instances of activity and those that do not are seen as the product of outside forces (and therefore instances of passivity, not actions in the genuine sense at all). The divorce of causal power from content of action that Schelling endorses here is an extension of the freedom conception first suggested in the *Freiheitsschrift*.

Not surprisingly, this discussion follows upon a discussion of the positivity of evil couched in terms that are, if anything, even more uncompromising than those of the *Freiheitsschrift*. Leibniz's *Theodicy*, Schelling writes, 'was concerned with an object upon which the rationalist cast of thought must necessarily run aground' (*GpP* 155n)—namely the origin of evil in the world. Schelling attacks both Leibniz and Spinoza for portraying evil as mere limitation in the capacity for good, and cites the question about the origin of evil in the world as one that already presupposes a free relation of God to the world—for if the world were mere emanation, there could be neither the truly evil nor even the truly bad (*GnP* X: 55). Leibniz, he says, could explain only banal evil (*das gemein Böse*) but not evil 'in its great manifestations in world history, where it shows itself to be combined with the highest energy and exceptionality—not merely of the spiritual, but even of the moral powers' (*GnP* X: 57). So at least part of what is important about

[25] Cf. *WA* II: 45: 'This already is free will: to be able to be something, and to be able not to be it.'

[26] This is the descendant of the idea that God, like every personality, must have a (relatively independent) ground of being that was mentioned in the discussion of the *Freiheitsschrift*. Cf. also *Denkmal der Schrift von den göttlichen Dingen* (VIII: 69).

positing God as 'prior to all thought' (and so to reason, both practical and theoretical) is that this makes sense of the situation of *human* agency—that human beings be capable of both good and evil.

I have said that Schelling intended his late system to be read as an empirical argument for God's existence. His view that God's essence is to some significant extent self-chosen (and that to be genuinely self-chosen it must be contingent) means that we cannot have *a priori* knowledge of that essence, and he is right to think that this precludes the possibility of a meaningful *a priori* argument for the existence of God. Arguments of an ontological form, even if they could be convincing, could prove at best the actual existence of whatever has necessary existence. But this placeholder cannot be replaced by 'God' without some non-*a priori* account of God's essence. The objection to the cosmological argument he offers is both familiar and in the same spirit: such an argument demonstrates at most the existence of a first cause, and cannot (taken on its own) connect any of the qualities one might want to attribute to God to this cause. Schelling's own argument for God's existence is not *a priori* but empirical. We know God through experience— not through direct (sensible or non-sensible) intuition (*GpP* 240),[27] but instead through an inference (from direct, sensible intuition) like that we make whenever we infer the existence of an agent, a set of intentions and a unified personality underlying a set of phenomena. Like all free personalities, God is known through his deeds (*PO* XIII: 113) and can be grasped in a positive sense only because he is self-manifesting (*GpP* 108, 245; *PO* XIII: 249; see also *GpP* 252: '*With a personal being I must stand in an empirical relationship*. Such an empirical relationship is, however, forbidden to reason, as is, in general, all that is personal.').[28] Schelling compares this understanding to the understanding we have of the content of a book, as opposed to the direct perception we have of the inscription on the page (*GpP* 272).[29] Coming to a satisfactory understanding, Schelling thinks, is a process of trial and error. The history of human consciousness (and especially the variety of forms of religious consciousness) is the history of failed attempts at

[27] Schelling does accept that it might in principle be possible to intuit God directly in the way the Theosophists claimed to have done. Their premiss, he says, is not in itself implausible (*GpP* 263). But he denies that such knowledge could have any *general* human significance. For, relying as it does on being in a special (not mundane) state, it is by definition not available to all. There can be no communication to others of whatever is intuited in such an ecstatic state—for to those who do not 'have it', such communication will seem incomprehensible, while to those who do, no communication is necessary (*GpP* 263).

[28] Theunissen (1964–5) argues that this 'revelation' of God is to be seen not as an unambiguous manifestation, but rather as a dialectic of revelation and concealment—a central link between Schelling and Kierkegaard. To say that God is a self-manifesting being is to say that he is not immediately evident, and Schelling's claim that a further inference is required and that making this inference is the result of a certain sort of trial and error indicates that God is as much concealed as revealed by history. The main difference between Schelling and Kierkegaard on this particular point is as to the extent to which God is concealed from human consciousness.

[29] It is thus similar—and perhaps related—to the hermeneutic approach to history Schleiermacher envisioned, one involving a sort of sympathetic identification with the desires, intentions, and hence also the world views, of agents in substantially different historical situations.

a unified interpretation. Schelling calls the succession of philosophical systems a 'school of experience' (*GpP* 273); this explains the centrality of an account of the history of philosophy in the introduction to his late system, and the fact that the bulk of the system consisted of a history of forms of religious consciousness (the lectures on mythology and revelation).

Schelling took care to distinguish the argument for God's existence he offered from the argument from design, to which it is quite close in character. He offers two objections to the design argument. First, natural purposiveness alone does not point to the existence of a free creator, according to Schelling. The entire point of his *Naturphilosophie* had been to show how we can see nature as the purposive creator *of itself*. In the later work he still claims to have been successful in that endeavour: 'For as I find in nature completely blind forces, even as I perceive actions within it that, relative to its ends, are just as purposive as the most superior creations of man, so no one can be denied the right to view nature as a great living thing, which takes on purposive forms blindly and instinctively' (*GpP* 113). This is why the evidence-base for Schelling's argument goes beyond nature to the history of human religious thought.

The second objection has to do with the fact that the argument from design proceeds not just from the empirically given to the existence of God, but rather from the empirically given to the *attributes* of God, as from the effects to the cause (i.e., from the nature of the effects to the nature of the cause). This seems a peculiar characteristic to object to. If the character of God cannot be known *a priori*, but also cannot be inferred from experience of his manifestation (as from effect to cause), how can it be known at all? What Schelling seems to have in mind is this: while we verify (or fail to verify) the existence of God by means of the success or failure of our interpretation of the world and history (the sort of interpretation Schelling aims to give in his lectures on mythology and revelation), we arrive independently at our *conception* of the God whose existence we aim to verify. But doesn't this just push the conceptualization of God back into the *a priori*? The answer, surprisingly, is no. The conceptualization of God does begin with an analysis of the concept 'God', but it is not exhausted by it (and so does not amount, for example, to a spelling out of the notion of 'perfection'). Instead the attributes we take God to have depend on a particular existential quandary in which human beings find themselves. We need for there to be an intelligent designer of the world who is also the author of the moral value in it and who orders it providentially (see, e.g., *PO* XIII: 202–3, *GpP* 85–7 and 108–9), because we find that the practical perspective makes no sense without these assumptions. The conception of God arises in part from a human ethical need and in part from conceptual constraints on the sort of being able to fulfil that need.

Schelling's claim is that 'moral author', 'providential orderer', etc., are not necessary characteristics of anything that could be the causal author of the world. These attributes are not contained conceptually in some overarching notion (e.g., 'maximally perfect being'). Nor are they attributes of an intelligent designer which can be extracted from a consideration of nature (say, as a condition of theoretical explanation of the items found there). Instead these characteristics arise out of a set of (primarily practical) human needs. They are the set of things we *want* when we want there to be a God.

The task is to become aware of what we actually want, when we want the *perfect* being... this whole process takes place in thought, and consists in a progression to a concept that is *adequate* to our desire. The approval of the concept that has been found consists, then, not in its correspondence with something objective, but rather in its correspondence with our own idea. (*GpP* 108)

Perhaps there is no such being (*GpP* 109). But knowing how to answer the question of whether there is (i.e., knowing what to look for) requires first getting clear on what we want in wanting there to be a God. The set of needs is like the set of specifications in a want-ad. The task of the systematic history of religion Schelling presents in the late lectures is to uncover evidence for the existence of a plausible candidate.

The process is complicated by the fact that the entity sought is two steps removed from the phenomena to which we have empirical access. First, as this God would have to be a free personality, the required qualities could not be surface phenomena. Agency is always (in some sense) hidden behind behaviour. Second, as this divine personality would not be an empirical individual, there are potential individuation problems. Schelling himself does not countenance the possibility that there may literally be more than one God (or that God might be a committee), though he thinks that the mythological consciousness concluded that there must be more than one precisely because of the way it put the pieces of the picture together. Or one might suspect that it is not a person at all that one is faced with. Schelling does not countenance this possibility either, though he thinks the rationalists made something like this mistake. But the reason Schelling does not countenance these possibilities is not that they do not, empirically, fit into place (although as a matter of fact he does not think they do). It is that they are inconsistent with what (Schelling thinks) we want in wanting there to be a God.

To Schelling's auditors his claims on behalf of the late system often seemed extremely ambitious,[30] but this must have been largely a product of his tone, since the actual claims made are very modest. What Schelling claims to have shown is that what we are faced with in experience can *plausibly* be construed as the manifestation of God. He does not claim to be able to demonstrate this conclusion—at least not according to the usual standards of philosophical demonstration, since the demonstration can be complete only once the world turns out to have been providentially ordered, and since history is not over, the evidence is not all in (*PO* XIII: 131). The end of philosophy is still the end of history (*GpP* 119), but the end has not been reached. The closed system of the early work has become an open system, a system continually progressing towards completion but

---

[30] See the reactions reprinted in Schelling (1977).

never finally complete (cf. *PO* XIII: 133). So what Schelling calls his 'positive proof' for God's existence is not a proof in the ordinary sense; it is only a schema for making human access to a God conceived as radically prior (and inaccessible) to reason conceivable.[31]

Religion and ethics in the positive philosophy

So what is it that we want, according to Schelling, in wanting there to be a God? In particular, why is a God who is 'prior to all thought' the sort of God we ought to want? This requirement has seemed to some to arise straightforwardly out of a desire for consistency with the Judaeo-Christian religious tradition.[32] But the demands of that tradition hardly explain the insistence; in fact Schelling's strongly voluntaristic view occupies a fringe position within the tradition. I think it is clear that the major motivation for Schelling's theology is the set of considerations about the nature of agency first addressed in the *Freiheitsschrift*. It is true that Schelling does not often discuss *human* agency in the later lectures. But where he does, what he says clearly supports this interpretation. The interests that inform the concept of God are, he says, interests in freedom and in the objective presence of a providential world order, the need to make sense of history as something other than a deterministic process. He describes a feeling of freedom which revolts against the clockwork vision of nature and wants to see causal necessity in nature as a contingent rather than an absolute necessity (*GpP* 85–6). He also describes a desire for a transcendent God, belief in whom would underwrite belief in a partial transcendence of nature on the part of humanity.

True philosophy wants to overcome the world; but we can overcome it only by grasping something that is outside of or *above* it. The demand is to be free against the world. This we

---

[31] One might wonder, if the proof is completed only at the end of human history, what one is to do in the interim. The answer, according to Schelling, is: belief. He takes care at this point to distinguish his view of the relation between knowledge and belief from the most prominent competitor, Jacobi's (both in the late lectures and, in print, in his *Denkmal der Schrift von den göttlichen Dingen* (1812) at VIII: 19–136). Jacobi's position (to put it extremely briefly) was that reason has all the answers—that the rationalist view is consistent and indeed the only rational account, and that Spinoza's conclusions follow directly from it—but that one can nevertheless believe in what reason demonstrates to be impossible, e.g., in a personal God and human freedom. Against this, Schelling counters that one cannot hold as a 'belief' something that directly contradicts what one knows with certainty. It would be impossible to believe in a free creator if one in any sense accepted the rationalist premiss that everything follows with logical necessity from the essence of God (cf. *GpP* 80). In other words, only where doubt is possible (e.g., in the case of contingent propositions) is belief also possible; and so only where reason finds no answers is belief in order. This is also the space occupied by positive knowledge. 'There is a knowledge . . . [of the sort that] Jacobi would not recognize: a *knowledge* that has belief *even formally* essentially within itself' (*GpP* 259). Belief is opposed to immediate knowledge, Schelling claims, to perception. But it forms an inseparable part of mediated knowledge, which the knowledge of free personalities must be. Belief involves 'will and act' (*GpP* 260)—though it is not only a question of will—as we see in Schelling's accusation that Jacobi refuses to subject his 'faith' to possible falsifiability (VIII: 84–5). In 1812, Schelling outlines his task as that of showing how it is possible turn *mere* belief into genuine knowledge (VIII: 55).

[32] Fuhrmans (1940) is the chief example here.

can be only if we see the world not as eternal, when we can instead say: there was a time when it was *not*. (*GpP* 87)

The most complete discussion of the interests that inform the concept of God is in a posthumously published manuscript that goes by the name '24th lecture' of the *Philosophische Einleitung in die Philosophie der Mythologie oder Darstellung der reinrationalen Philosophie*.[33] Here Schelling quite dramatically presents what one can only call 'existential' considerations as motivation for the theological view he favours. The passage is concerned with the transition from negative to positive philosophy, the object of the positive philosophy, and its method. Many discussions in the later work cover the same ground, but this discussion is unique in presenting a set of practical rather than theoretical considerations as the motive for the transition, and reads like a comment by Schelling upon his own philosophical biography. The primary motivation is characterized as the despair of the individual agent who requires a personal God to make sense of his existential situation. Positive philosophy arises out of 'a will that demands with inner necessity that God not be a mere idea' (*EPM* XI: 565).[34]

The discussion begins with a consideration of the dissatisfactions of the individual vis-à-vis the 'universal'. This universal is the law—not merely the law as an imposition of the state,[35] but primarily the inner law of ethical conduct: the rational moral law. The individual suffers under the moral law because, being impersonal, it can only be alienating: 'Even *being commanded* would not be so irritating to the I if it only proceeded from a person. But to be subordinated to an impersonal power is unbearable. He who wants to be *himself* is asked to see himself as subordinated to the universal' (*EPM* XI: 554). No amount of struggle to subordinate itself to the law will enable the individual to obey it with a glad heart, because the law does not present the individual with a heart 'like its own'.[36] In a footnote to this passage we find a criticism of Kant's failure to see the importance of this shortcoming in his own moral philosophy. Schelling sums up his complaint by saying that although reason (in the form of the moral law) can impose a certain order on the practical sphere, reason cannot render it '*selig*' (happy, blessed). The unhappiness of action (*die Unseligkeit des Handelns*) is a problem that the individual cannot solve on his own. Nor is it something that can

---

[33] This lecture series probably dates from between 1847 and 1852. The twenty-fourth lecture was not composed by Schelling as a unit. It consists of notes from scattered pages, compiled by Schelling's son in accordance with his father's instructions to form a transition between the *Darstellung* and the *Abhandlung über die Quellen der ewigen Wahrheiten*. Cf. editor's note at XI: 553.

[34] 'This will is not accidental; it is a will of spirit which, because of inner necessity and in longing for its own liberation, cannot stop with that which is contained in thought' (*EPM* XI: 569).

[35] Schelling's meditations on the necessarily coercive character of the political state in a fallen world are, however, interesting in their own right. For an excellent discussion of this, cf. Habermas (1971).

[36] 'For as universal and impersonal, it cannot be other than hard,—as a power of reason that knows so little of personality that it does not slacken one iota for the sake of the person, and even when its demands are *entirely* fulfilled is not grateful' (XI: 554).

be solved within a community of moral agents guided by the rational moral law.[37] Finally, it is not something that can ultimately be solved by a rejection of the practical sphere altogether (i.e., a renunciation of activity and a turn to contemplation).

Interestingly, Schelling now characterizes the standpoint of idealism as an attempt to carry out this last strategy: to abandon the practical standpoint in favour of the contemplative. The turn proceeds in three stages: (1) an act of self-forgetting (attempt at mystical unity with the divine); (2) selfless production (art) in which the ego makes itself similar with the divine; and (3) contemplative science in which the ego contemplates the divine idea. In the third stage philosophy acquires the correct concept of God, 'being-for-itself which is free from being', as its principle, something it can achieve only through designating 'the I as non-principle, subordinated to God' (*EPM* XI: 560). The second and third of these stages certainly look familiar from Schelling's own early works (the *System of Transcendental Idealism* and the 1804 *System*, respectively). Schelling gives a theological criticism of those views: that 'contemplative science leads only to the God who is *end* and therefore not the real [God]—to that which is God according to its essence, but not to the actual [God]' (*EPM* XI: 559)—but this *prima facie* theological point turns out to have a practical motivation. Although a relationship to God-as-idea is the most that the human mind can achieve on its own (*EPM* XI: 558), and although this would be adequate were a purely contemplative life possible, in fact '[t]he renunciation of action cannot be carried out; one *must* act' (*EPM* XI: 560), and as soon as one tries to act, the relation to an ideal God proves inadequate, 'and the previous despair returns' (*EPM* XI: 560). What the individual needs is to see himself in a relationship with a personal God to replace reason as the source of the set of norms by which the agent is to be governed. The individual seeks a God who is 'outside of and above reason, for whom that is possible which is impossible for reason', namely to make it free from the law, which is reason itself (*EPM* XI: 567).

Schelling distinguishes God as the object of this sort of need from God as practical postulate in the Kantian sense: 'Just as this demand cannot proceed from thought, neither is it a postulate of practical reason. Not this [i.e., practical reason], as Kant will have it, but only the individual leads to God. For it is not the universal in human beings that craves bliss, but the individual' (*EPM* XI: 569). There are two distinctions between this view and Kant's view of God as a postulate of practical reason that should be pointed out. First, while the need for a God with these characteristics arises out of the standpoint of agency, confidence in the existence of such a God is something that can be had only through theoretical inquiry, according to Schelling. This is why he offers an empirical demonstration of the existence of God in the late system: the practical need does not suffice for belief. Second, the positive philosophy presents a philosophical religion, but not a

---

[37] Cf. Habermas (1954).

rational religion, not a 'religion within the limits of reason alone' (*EPM* XI: 568).[38] This is as it should be, given the role God is expected to have in providing normative content to practical deliberation.

The remarkable similarity of these claims to the ones Kierkegaard will later make is hard to miss. Needless to say, even if the content of this passage had been heard in the lecture hall precisely as it stands in the collected works, it was not heard by Kierkegaard. But it does throw a very significant light on the content of Schelling's late work, showing that Schelling himself, at least at some points, took the *Freiheitsschrift* issues to lead to conclusions very close to those Kierkegaard would draw.[39] *Very* schematically: The universalist (Kantian/autonomous) ethical standpoint is one of despair. It must be subordinated to some sort of religious standpoint. This standpoint cannot, however, be the religion of contemplation, with God as a necessary idea and in some strong sense continuous with a rational world order of which the human being is also a part (religiousness A). It must be a religious standpoint whereby the individual acquires a personal relationship with a transcendent personal God, a relationship which is not that of rational cognition (religiousness B). We must hold that such a religiousness, such a relationship, is possible, because anything short of it is, from the practical standpoint, despair.

The several aspects of Schelling's later work I have explored in this chapter—(1) the conception of freedom taken from the *Freiheitsschrift* (human freedom as a positive capacity for evil as well as good, and the idea that this requires orientation to an agency-external standard of value), the commitment to theological voluntarism in (2) morality and (3) the nature of reality (i.e., the being-prior-to-thought thesis, properly construed)—go hand in hand. This is of course not to say that anyone holding one of these views must be committed to the other two. Indeed it is far from clear, on the basis of the texts we are left with from Schelling's late period, what the relations of conceptual priority between them are even in Schelling's own mind. In the following chapters I will show that these components were taken and arranged by Kierkegaard into what has long looked like a radical departure from the concerns and approach of the German idealists, but which—as the identity of the components illustrates—in fact was not. Before I do that, though, I need to say something purely historical about the route of transmission of these Schellingian ideas to Kierkegaard.

---

[38] Schelling always emphasizes that though the revelation he is interested in is not simply the biblical one (*GpP* 83), neither is it something contained within reason alone. If it were, it would be redundant (*Paulus* 98). If the only defensible religion were religion within the limits of reason alone 'boredom would empty the churches' (*GpP* 82).

[39] Fuhrmans (1940) takes it as part of the foundation of any 'existentialist' reading of the late Schelling. Even Schulz (1975: 145 ff.), whose argument is compromised by this lecture more than by anything else, expresses no doubt as to its legitimacy.

Excursus: Late Idealism and Schelling's Influence

The standard view of Kierkegaard's relation to Schelling (if there can be said to be a 'standard view' of this issue) is that there was nothing in Schelling's late philosophy beyond his critique of Hegel that could have held any positive interest for Kierkegaard.[1] Kierkegaard's critique of Hegel does, indeed, owe both its general form and many of its particular tactics to the critique Schelling presented in Munich and Berlin in the thirties and forties. But this is not the end of the story. Nor does its continuation have Kierkegaard taking from Schelling, in addition to the critique of Hegel, only a conviction that Schelling's metaphysics should stand as a negative model for subsequent philosophy, or that the failure of Schelling's project demonstrated the necessity of abandoning systematic philosophy entirely in favour of some other approach.[2] The generally accepted view tends to rely

---

[1] According to Thulstrup (1972), for example, the story of Kierkegaard's attendance of and reaction to Schelling's lectures in Berlin is best explained as one of superficial infatuation and immediate disappointment. The positive content of Schelling's philosophy is inconsequential, and even the details of Schelling's critique of Hegel are redundant in terms of the development of Kierkegaard's thought. On this interpretation, Kierkegaard looked to Schelling for two things: (1) legitimation of his own objections to Hegel; and (2) a solution to the problem of the ethical task of the concrete individual (the topic he had begun to address in earnest with *Either/Or*, which he had begun very shortly before his departure for Berlin and worked on fairly continuously while there). According to Thulstrup, he was satisfied regarding the first, but disappointed regarding the second, and so stopped taking notes after Schelling finished with the critique of Hegel and began to lecture about the system of positive philosophy, and left before the course was finished—because he could not reconcile Schelling's positive philosophy with his own work in progress, but instead 'found only a new attempt at system building, for which he had no reasonable use' (228). (The claim about Kierkegaard's note-taking is incorrect: the critique of Hegel was read in December, but Kierkegaard continued to take notes until the beginning of February, and continued attending for several weeks after that, until the end of the winter semester.) Dempf (1957) tells a similar story.

[2] White (1983b), for example, argues that 'Schelling's strongest influence was negative' (188), in the somewhat broader sense that Schelling not only convinced his listeners that Hegel's path could not be followed, but also convinced them that his own path could not be followed, thus setting the stage for the radical break that is, in White's view, the post-idealist movement. Schelling's failure resulted, according to White, in the abandonment, after Schelling, of systematic philosophy in general: 'Kierkegaard and Marx, having abandoned metaphysics, attempt to establish in its place distinct forms of philosophical anthropologies. . . . Both of these turns to anthropology were, again, mediated by positive philosophy in three ways: both Kierkegaard and Marx accept the general demands on philosophy articulated by Schelling in his opening lectures; both accept Schelling's critique of Hegel, at least in its main outlines; and both take positive philosophy as a disastrous failure, one that teaches us only that Schelling's metaphysical empiricism is impossible' (189). The importance of Schelling's positive philosophy consisted, according to this interpretation, in its (inadvertent) demonstration of the inviability of what seemed to be the only remaining option for systematic philosophy—after Hegel—that had any chance of success. But even if we could accept (or even make concrete sense of)

rather heavily upon two pieces of historical evidence. I do not believe these will bear the weight that is usually placed on them, and it is my aim in this excursus to explain why.

Kierkegaard's letters

The first piece of evidence is that of Kierkegaard's letters from Berlin. Kierkegaard went to Berlin for the winter semester of 1841–2 in order to hear Schelling's first course of lectures there, and his expectations were very high. What he apparently expected was a definitive (negative) assessment of Hegel, and a sketch of a new, acceptable post-Hegelian direction. He had written, the previous year, 'The view that Hegel is a parenthesis in Schelling seems to be more and more manifest; we are only waiting for the parenthesis to be closed.'[3] His expectations were in line with those of other students of his generation, as well as with Schelling's Prussian employers. Schelling had been called to Berlin to fight the 'dragon-seed of Hegelian pantheism',[4] and he seemed the right person for the task because, far from having pursued his philosophical education in an atmosphere in which Hegelianism was the dominant philosophical position, he was in fact the source of many of its more influential ideas. If he had now turned against it, he was the one who could be expected to present the most authoritative critique.[5]

Kierkegaard's initial reaction to the lectures was enthusiastic:

I am so happy to have heard Schelling's second lecture—indescribably. I have been pining and thinking mournful thoughts long enough. The embryonic child of thought leapt for joy within me as in Elizabeth, when he mentioned the word 'actuality' in connection with the relation of philosophy to actuality. I remember almost every word he said after that. Here, perhaps, clarity can be achieved. . . . Now I have put all my hope in Schelling.[6]

the thesis that some final option in metaphysics was exhausted by Schelling's late work, it would not be clear why this should leave philosophical anthropology as the only path to pursue. In fact we know from Frank (1992—but note that the first edition of this book was published in 1975, so well before White's) that what was most important for Feuerbach and Marx was a point in Schelling's metaphysics (namely, the being-prior-to-thought thesis). There is an analogous argument to be made for a positive debt in Kierkegaard's case as well—one I make in the next two chapters. (It should be said that White's main concern is with defending Hegel against Schelling's criticisms rather than estimating Schelling's positive contribution. But as Bowie (1993: 141ff.) points out, he has also missed the main point behind these, elucidated by Frank in 1975.)

[3] Cf. Kierkegaard (1909–78: III A 34; 1997–, vol. 19: 185, Notesbog 5: 8). Translation from Kierkegaard (1967–78, vol. 2: 214, entry #1589).

[4] Cf. Frank's introduction to Schelling (1977) for historical background on Schelling's call to Berlin.

[5] That is, he could not be counted among the mass of 'those who have gone beyond Hegel'. 'Those who have gone beyond Hegel are like country people who must always give their address *via* a larger city; thus the addresses in this case read—John Doe *via* Hegel.' Kierkegaard (1909–78: III A 260). Translation from Kierkegaard (1967–78, vol. 2: 207, entry #1572).

[6] Kierkegaard (1909–78 III: A 179; 1997–, vol. 19: 235, Notesbog 8: 33). Translation from Kierkegaard (1967–78, vol. 5: 181, entry #5535).

But soon he became disappointed, and his letters from Berlin in February express nothing but dissatisfaction. On 6 February, he writes: '[A]s soon as Schelling is finished I am coming home . . . Please say that the reason for my return is that I am extremely dissatisfied with Schelling, which by the way is only all too true.'[7] And on 27 February: 'Schelling talks endless nonsense both in an extensive and an intensive sense.'[8] He had originally planned to stay a year and a half in Berlin;[9] in the end he left after only one semester. Although he returned twice in the years to follow, he never heard Schelling again.

But was Kierkegaard really finished with Schelling in February 1842? Even if one read no further than the auction catalogue of Kierkegaard's library, it would have to be clear that there is something missing from this picture of early fascination and immediate disappointment, since Kierkegaard acquired works by[10] and about[11] Schelling published *after* this purported break. More important evidence comes from two works published in June 1844—*The Concept of Anxiety* and *Philosophical Fragments*—which show that Kierkegaard spend a substantial amount of time thinking through Schelling's *Freiheitsschrift* and his late system *after* the return from Berlin.

The importance of the *Freiheitsschrift* for *The Concept of Anxiety* has been well documented in the German-language secondary literature[12] (though it has as often as not been overlooked in the English-language secondary literature).[13] The textual connections between the two works are impossible to miss. Most striking is *The Concept of Anxiety*'s description of anxiety as the 'dizziness of freedom' which echoes a similar passage in which both anxiety and dizziness are employed to describe the phenomenology of freedom in the *Freiheitsschrift*.[14] Kierkegaard refers to Schelling by name more often in this work than any other. These references are usually critical—they include, for instance, a footnote

---

[7] Letter #68, 6 February 1842, to Emil Boesen. Translation from Kierkegaard (1967–78, vol. 5: 199, entry #5551).

[8] Letter #69, 27 February 1842, to Emil Boesen. Translation from Kierkegaard (1967–78, vol. 5: 201, entry #5552).   [9] Hannay (2001: 159).

[10] The second edition of Schelling's *Bruno* (1842).

[11] Rosenkranz, *Schelling Vorlesungen* (1843).

[12] Cf., e.g., Figal (1980) and Hennigfeld (1987).

[13] Quinn (1990), for example, correctly diagnoses the importance of Kant and Schleiermacher for interpreting *The Concept of Anxiety*, but overlooks the third critical figure, Schelling. But cf., e.g., McCarthy (1985).

[14] The passage in *The Concept of Anxiety*: 'Anxiety may be compared with dizziness . . . anxiety is the dizziness of freedom, which emerges when the spirit wants to posit the synthesis and freedom looks down into its own possibility, laying hold of finiteness to support itself. Freedom succumbs in this dizziness. . . . In that very moment everything is changed, and freedom, when it again rises, sees that it is guilty. Between these two moments lies the leap' (*BA* IV: 331; 4: 365–6). The passage in the *Freiheitsschrift*: 'For this reason it [the will of the ground] reacts against freedom as supercreaturely and awakens within it the desire for the creaturely, like the one who, on a high peak, is seized by dizziness and seems to hear a hidden voice calling to him, telling him to fall . . . In itself the merging of the universal will with the particular will in the human being appears to be a contradiction, the union of the two difficult, if not impossible. The anxiety of life itself drives the human being out of the center . . . Hence the general necessity of sin and death' (*FS* VII: 381).

taking qualified exception to one aspect of the position in the *Freiheitsschrift* (at *BA* IV: 329n; 4: 363n) and another claiming ignorance about the meaning Schelling attached to the term 'positive philosophy' (at *BA* IV: 293n; 4: 328n). But Kierkegaard was never one to scatter praise in his footnotes, and the second claim is falsified by the fact that Kierkegaard is himself in the midst of drawing a distinction (at *BA* IV: 288–96; 4: 323–31) between 'first' and 'second' philosophy (also referred to as 'first' and 'second' ethics), which is closely related to the one made in Schelling's Berlin lectures (*Paulus* 97–110), and is used in exactly the same way. (First philosophy is idealism; second philosophy is a philosophy of revelation, having dogmatics as its basis. The essence of the first is 'immanence' (*BA* IV: 293; 4: 329) in the sense that its content is internal to reason (*Paulus* 107); the essence of the second 'transcendence' (*BA*, IV: 293; 4: 329) in the sense that its content is 'external to reason' (*Paulus* 110).)[15] And in any case, very central elements of the book (including the theory of agency presented there) take their inspiration from Schelling (as I will show in the chapters that follow).

Philosophical Fragments has not seemed to commentators to bear the stamp of an encounter with Schelling's later work, although it also contains several clear references. For example, in the context of a discussion of proofs of the existence of God, Kierkegaard summarizes Kant's and Schelling's versions of a critique of the ontological argument and concludes the summary with the remark: 'Whether one wants to call existence an *accessorium* or the eternal *prius*, it can never be demonstrated' (*PS* IV: 207; 4: 245). '*Accessorium*' refers to Kant's discussion of the argument; 'eternal *prius*' to Schelling's.[16] The same discussion contains a parallel to Schelling's discussion (from the *Weltalter* period) of the need to leave

---

[15] Theunissen (1964–5: 141–2) explains this reference as a statement of the position Schelling and Kierkegaard held in common against Hegel on the one hand, and Kant and Jacobi on the other. Like Hegel, he explains, they argue against the latter for a non-subjective concept of God; in opposition to Hegel, they deny that God is fully graspable by reason. Whereas for Hegel, God is world-spirit, fully revealed in world history, for Schelling and Kierkegaard, God is both revealed and concealed—his revelation is really a dialectic of revelation and concealment. Further, his claim that God is fully revealed is the source of both Schelling's and Kierkegaard's claims that Hegel robs Christianity of its own character, that his Christianity is indistinguishable from paganism—for Schelling corresponding to the mythical framework, for Kierkegaard to religiousness A. Kierkegaard's claim that revelation is unreasonable (the absurd) is directed at Hegel's view. Schelling does not go so far, Theunissen notes—revelation is supra-rational (something that goes beyond reason). Unlike Hegel, these two both think that reason is not the addressee of revelation. I agree with Theunissen's account of this point—it is an excellent discussion of an important aspect of Kierkegaard's and Schelling's relationship—but an account of *why* Kierkegaard and Schelling hold this theological position requires a rather longer explanation. I argue that the position relies upon their common account of freedom—something with which Theunissen seems not to agree—and that the latter is the more central concern. Cf. Theunissen (1964–5).

[16] This is clear from the context even though neither figure is mentioned by name. The Kant reference has been picked up by a number of commentators; the Schelling reference was missed even by the commentator for the most recent edition of Kierkegaard's works (cf. Kierkegaard 1997– *Kommentarbind* 4: 240).

behind demonstrations of God's existence in order to become aware of God's existence (although since this view was not unique to Schelling, it is of interest but not conclusive).[17]

The Concept of Anxiety was begun in late 1843 and *Philosophical Fragments* in early 1844—more than a year and a half after the return from Berlin. The sheer number of textual parallels in these works alone give the lie to the story told by the letters. It is impossible to believe that Kierkegaard was finished with Schelling in February of 1842.

Schelling's publication record

Schelling's virtual silence in print after 1812 is the second piece of historical evidence cited for denying that Kierkegaard was responding in any significant way to Schelling's late work.[18] Kierkegaard did own the only publication in which Schelling presented anything in print about the late system (before his publication of his opening Berlin lecture in 1841). This was a German translation of Victor Cousin's *Fragments Philosophiques* (1834), which contained a preface by Schelling. (It was the only work by Cousin that Kierkegaard owned, and so we may safely

---

[17] The passage in *Philosophical Fragments*: 'And how does the existence of the god emerge from the demonstration? Does it happen straight away? Is it not here as it is with the Cartesian dolls? As soon as I let go of the doll, it stands on its head. . . . So also with the demonstration—so long as I am holding on to the demonstration . . . the existence does not emerge, if for no other reason than that I am in the process of demonstrating it, but when I let go of the demonstration, the existence is there. Yet this letting go . . . is, after all, *meine Zuthat.*' (*PS* IV: 210; 4: 247–8). The passage in the *Weltalter*: 'But philosophy is not a demonstrative science—philosophy is, to say it briefly, a *free act of the spirit*. Its first step is not a knowing, but rather explicitly a non-knowing, a giving up of all knowledge for human beings. . . . When [the philosopher] says: I, as I, cannot know, I do not *want* to know—when he renounces knowledge—he makes room for that which is knowledge, i.e. for the absolute subject, of which it is shown that it is knowledge itself' (*Erlanger Vorträge* IX: 228–9).

[18] It is cited, for instance, by Koktanek (1962), in which it is argued that Kierkegaard *could* have learned something important from Schelling, had he known Schelling better, or known the right works by Schelling—but that in fact he did not. Koktanek's account of the correspondence in views between the two includes the claim that Hegel's philosophy seems to overlook actuality, human freedom, the reality of evil and suffering, and the loneliness of existence (20); the view of God as a living personality rather than absolute world-spirit, and of human beings, the creations of this personal God, as suffering creatures with immortal souls rather than neutral carriers of the world-soul (31); the importance of Christ as mediator between God and the world and the claim that Hegel failed to understand the significance of Christianity (35). Koktanek argues, however, on the basis of the publication history of Schelling's work, that the catalogue of correspondences between Kierkegaard's views and Schelling's has to be largely *accidental*. Kierkegaard left Berlin too soon to understand most of what Schelling was trying to say, and Schelling's actual influence on his development was meagre: 'Kierkegaard attended forty-one lectures, but left, disappointed and disgusted, in the middle of the philosophy of mythology, and so did not hear the presentation of the philosophy of revelation, which would actually have been important for him. *Thus he had no direct experience of decisive positions of Schelling's late thought, and apparently never came to know them.* . . . There was no encounter [between them] in the actual common space of [their] interest. In terms of content, Kierkegaard must have been left empty by Schelling; formally, however, in the already evident tendency of his thought toward reality, freedom and existence, he must have felt strengthened' (Koktanek 1962: 68—my emphasis).

assume that, like many others, he acquired it only in order to read Schelling's preface—the first piece of work that had been published by Schelling in over twenty years.)[19] This preface contained a sketch of the project in the positive philosophy (alongside a not very complimentary assessment of how Cousin's work measured up to recent German philosophy), but the sketch was no more detailed than what Kierkegaard would later encounter in the Berlin lectures. Kierkegaard also owned volume 1 of Schelling's *Philosophische Schriften* (1809), containing the *Freiheitsschrift* along with several earlier works,[20] and he owned re-editions of two of Schelling's early works.[21] He also had several reference works on Schelling,[22] and a published copy of Schelling's first lecture in Berlin[23] (i.e., the one he himself attended in 1841).[24] I take the fact that Kierkegaard owned nearly everything published by Schelling post-1809 to be significant, but since most of the substance of the late philosophy was not published in Schelling's lifetime (or Kierkegaard's—Schelling's collected works having appeared beginning in 1856), a large gap does seem to remain.

It might appear, then, that the main exposure that Kierkegaard could have had to Schelling (apart from the early published works and the *Freiheitsschrift*) was through the lectures he attended in Berlin. But these lectures gave an extremely condensed account of the methodological introduction of the positive philosophy—what in past courses had been a year's worth of lectures was condensed into half a semester during Schelling's first year in Berlin. So Kierkegaard heard very little of what I explained in the second half of chapter 4

[19] Note also the presence of I. H. Fichte's reply to Schelling's preface, *Ueber die Bedingung eines spekulativen Theismus* (1835), in Kierkegaard's library.

[20] *Vom Ich als Prinzip der Philosophie* (*Of the I as Principle of Philosophy*), *Philosophische Briefe über Dogmatismus und Critizismus* (*Philosophical Letters on Dogmatism and Criticism*), *Abhandlung zur Erläuterung des Idealismus der* Wissenschaftslehre (*Treatise Explicatory of the Idealism of the* Wissenschaftslehre), and *Ueber das Verhältnis der bildenden Künste zu der Natur* (*On the Relation of Fine Art to Nature*).

[21] The third edition of the *Vorlesungen über die Methode des akademischen Studiums* (*Lectures on the Method of University Study*) (1830) and the second edition of *Bruno* (1842).

[22] *Schelling Vorlesungen* given by Karl Rosenkranz in Königsberg in 1842 (1843a), the second edition of I. H. Fichte's *Beiträge zur Charakteristik der neueren deutschen Philosophie* (1841) (which contained a large segment on Schelling), and possibly also Rosenkranz's *Ueber Schelling und Hegel* (1843b). (Hirsch, in his commentary on *The Concept of Anxiety*, argues that Kierkegaard used this work, although it was not part of his library when it was auctioned. Hirsch bases this conclusion on the fact that Kierkegaard's reference to Schelling's dispute with Eschenmayer in *The Concept of Anxiety* is probably second hand, and Rosenkranz is the most likely source. Cf. Kierkegaard (1953–64 vol. 11/12: translator's footnote #56, p. 246). It is true that the absence of this work from the auction catalogue does not mean Kierkegaard did not own it, since he was in financial straits in the last years of his life and sold off older books to buy new ones (cf. introduction to Rohde (1967)). But there were other places to learn about the Eschenmayer Briefwechsel, notably the many mentions of it in the pages of the *Zeitschrift für Philosophie und spekulative Theologie*, whose significance I am about to discuss.)

[23] *Schellings Erste Vorlesung in Berlin* (1841).

[24] He also owned a copy of Steffens's *Nachgelassene Schriften*, prefaced by Schelling (1846). But this was published too late to be of significance, and Kierkegaard had an independent interest in Steffens, so we are not allowed to conclude that Schelling's preface was any part of the reason Kierkegaard acquired this work.

in the Berlin lecture hall. (Just how little can be found out by perusing Kierkegaard's[25] or Paulus's[26] notes to those lectures.) So if it were true that Kierkegaard's main exposure to Schelling was through the lectures, there would indeed be a large gap between what Kierkegaard would have found of interest in the later Schelling and what he could actually have encountered.

But this appearance is misleading. It is a common misconception that Schelling's ideas were as little known in his own time as they have become today. In fact, his lectures over the course of two decades had attracted a large follow-ing,[27] and the most detailed *published* discussion of his position is actually to be found in his students' writings, not his own. The school of thought which Leese (1929) called 'late idealism' (whose main proponents included Christian Weiße, Immanuel Hermann Fichte, Hubert Beckers, and Friedrich Stahl) was inspired by Schelling's positive philosophy. What concerned the members of that circle (and what attracted them to Schelling) was primarily the sense that the notions of personality (both human and divine) and of freedom (in the sense they thought required for moral responsibility: freedom for good and evil) had been given an inadequate treatment in idealism.[28] These individuals had access to Schelling's ideas not only through the last published writings, but also and even primarily through the lectures in Munich on which I have based the greater part of the discussion in the preceding chapter.

Much of the content of these lectures was first made public by Stahl in his 1830 work, *Die Philosophie des Rechts nach geschichtlicher Ansicht* (*The Philosophy of Right from a Historical Point of View*). This work was, as its title suggests, primarily a work of political philosophy—but, like Hegel's work on the same topic, it included a lengthy treatment of the will, freedom, and the foundations of ethics. Stahl presented his view on these topics as a develop-ment of Schelling's, informed by lectures he had attended in the winter semester of 1827–8. His discussion of Schelling's views on the relevant topics is both extended and for the most part accurate (that is, in agreement with the evidence we have from other sources, including the manuscripts I used in the reconstruction in chapter 4). So, for instance, he characterizes Schelling's peculiarity (even in his early work, as against Fichte and Kant) as his placement

---

[25] These can be found at Kierkegaard (1909–78: III C 27, vol. XIII: 254ff.; 1997–, vol. 19: 305ff., Notesbog 11). They are translated along with *The Concept of Irony* in Kierkegaard (1989a).

[26] These are reprinted in Schelling (1977).

[27] Cf., e.g., Fuhrmans's introduction to Schelling (1969) and Frank's introduction to Schelling (1977).

[28] Fuhrmans (1940) argues that the 'late idealist' conviction that Christianity and idealism are ultimately irreconcilable, and the consequent turn away from idealism and towards the concrete, the problems of actuality and irrationality, constituted Schelling's main significance to the philo-sophical constellation of the late nineteenth and early twentieth centuries. Although Fuhrmans recognizes that the main impulse behind Schelling's late work, as behind the *Freiheitsschrift*, was the issue of freedom and the inadequacy of idealist theology and Kantian moral philosophy to take account of it, he nonetheless sees a deep divide between Schelling's and Kierkegaard's approaches.

of God (the 'absolute') rather than man at the centre of the system (I: 251), but points out that for the early Schelling (as for Hegel) this God was not a 'person' but a 'principle'. This was the problem with the idealistic/pantheistic systems, in his estimation: the fact that in them God has no self-consciousness distinct from that of his creatures (I: 258). Since there can be no individual personality in such systems either, the freedom of individuals also becomes a problem (I: 255–6). He characterizes the *Freiheitsschrift* as the beginning of a 'new epoch', but points out the precursors to the change of view in, e.g., Schelling's letter to Eschenmayer (I: 254–6). He explains Schelling's connection of freedom with personality and creation and paraphrases him as follows:

Deed is freedom and freedom is the inner essence of personality. Each deed is, according to its concept, a creation, and creation is only thinkable as a free deed. For through it a self-conscious will gains determinations which in no way previously belonged to his essence, determinations which are therefore something outside of him—a product. In this way, the world is outside of God. (I: 334)

Note the importance attributed to a person's gaining *new* determinations through the act of willing. Stahl opposes this conception, which he calls a 'positive conception' of freedom as creative arbitrary choice (II: 25), to what he calls a 'negative' conception of freedom as determination by one's own nature rather than some external force (II: 20). On a 'negative' conception, no new determinations are possible. One is self-determined in the sense that one's essence determines one, not in the sense that one's determinations are the result of one's choices. (This is a recognizably Schellingian distinction, since these are very like the freedom conceptions inherent in 'negative' and 'positive' philosophy, respectively.) Stahl lists 'Spinoza's absolute substance', 'Kant's reason' and 'Hegel's dialectical law' as all examples of the same 'negative' conception of freedom and denies any significant difference between them (II: 23). Freedom in this sense is not distinguished from necessity, and even that which operates necessarily according to mechanical laws can be free in this negative sense (II: 20). No sense can be made of a choice between good and evil on such an account, and this is why such otherwise diverse thinkers as Kant and Spinoza posit freedom as the overcoming of evil (II: 24, 70).

Stahl defines positive freedom in general as choice—not the choice between good and evil, since God does not have this choice, but is free, but instead simply 'infinite, creative' choice (II: 25). God does not have the choice between good and evil because these arise only from his will; Stahl is a theological voluntarist about morality. Moral imperatives are the sort of things that must be imposed by a higher authority; they cannot be imposed by one's own nature: 'One's own nature is never the source of an ought—only the command of someone higher can impose it' (II: 58). True law must be revealed law (II: 78). God has no moral imperatives because none is higher than him; man has them from God (II: 58).

'All more recent ethical theories are for this reason instead theories of unethicalness; for they all aim to find a norm by means of which man can find the ethical without God, and prescribe for him as a goal a way of acting in which he has no need of God' (II: 60).

Stahl's view of the origin of moral evil and sin is not exactly Schelling's, but it is close and its divergences are interesting in their own right. He attributes to God two sorts of demands on human beings: that man become godlike (morality) and that man 'keep his will in god's' (religiousness) (II: 59). Original sin, he claims, consisted not in immorality, but in irreligiosity. It was not a breaking of any laws, but a fall from grace. Immorality came only after this. (Rationalism has this backwards, according to Stahl, since on the rationalist account morality comes first and out of morality come duties regarding God (religiosity). Original sin is not a breach of religiosity but a breach of morality (II: 67).) Sin makes apparent what we recognize to be the specific character of human freedom: choice between good and evil. This is a peculiarity of human freedom, rather than part of the essence of freedom itself, since God does not have this choice (II: 68).

In summary, on the topics of freedom, the origins of moral norms and the relationship between God and creation, Stahl's line is very close to the late Schelling's, and Stahl makes this debt explicit in the work. Now, there is no reason to think Kierkegaard read Stahl's *Philosophie des Rechts* (at least, we do not find it in the auction catalogue, and we find no clear references to it in the published works or journals). But he would not have needed to. Through Stahl's work (and others like it),[29] the details of Schelling's late system became common knowledge in the German academy by the early 1830s. This is clear from the works of the members of the late idealist circle. And there is overwhelming evidence that Kierkegaard (like other Danish theology students of his generation) followed the work of the members of this circle fairly closely, especially in the middle to late 1830s.

He owned, for instance, the two main early documents of the movement—Christian Weiße's *Die Idee der Gottheit* (*The Idea of the Divine*) of 1833 and Immanuel Hermann Fichte's *Die Idee der Persönlichkeit und der individuellen Fortdauer* (*The Idea of Personality and of Individual Immortality*) of 1834. Both works take Stahl's account of Schelling's Munich lectures, Schelling's *Freiheitsschrift* and his 1812 polemic against Jacobi as their major points of reference. In *Die Idee der Persönlichkeit* (which we know Kierkegaard read in February 1837)[30] Fichte diagnoses the shortcoming of Hegelianism as its total inability to answer, or even raise, questions involving the concepts of 'personality' and 'freedom'—questions which he prescribes as the central occupations for post-Hegelian

---

[29] I. H. Fichte mentions, in the second volume of the *Zeitschrift*, that Beckers also gave 'them' the specifics of the late Schelling's system. Cf. Fichte (1838: 25).

[30] Cf. Kierkegaard (1909–78): II A 31; 1997– , vol. 17: 41ff., AA: 22).

philosophy (8–9). (For Hegel, on Fichte's reading, the individual is a 'moment' in the universal about which—since it has no individual subsistence to begin with— no questions of individual *per*sistence (of immortality, that is) can arise (22).) Fichte reiterates Schelling's view that a conception of God as a personal creator cannot be found at the 'end' of the system but must be placed at the 'beginning', that the actual must be the result of a free deed and must be known by experience or revelation, in which *a priori* knowledge has a limited, subordinate place (11), that logic (on the Hegelian conception, as general ontology) is only 'propaedeutic' to philosophy and that a grasp of the 'primordial forms' of being and thought does not constitute a grasp of reality (39–40). Although his explication of what these claims amount to is no more precise than Schelling's had been (and indeed reproduces some of Schelling's ambiguous formulations), Fichte does clearly explicate the idea of an empirical but indirect intuition of God as personality which Schelling uses as the basis of his 'proof' (89–90).

Kierkegaard owned several other works by Fichte. One example is the second edition of Fichte's *Beiträge zur Charakteristik der neueren Philosophie* (*Contributions to a Characterization of Recent Philosophy*), published in 1841. (Martensen had recommended the first edition, alongside Fichte's *Ueber Gegensatz, Wendepunkt und Ziel heutiger Philosophie* (1832), as reference works for students taking his course on the history of modern philosophy.)[31] In the *Beiträge* Fichte emphasized the significance of the *Freiheitsschrift* for post-Hegelian philosophy, noting the distinction between the freedom conception there and that of idealism (732), and commenting on the historical impact of the last sentences of the essay—the call for a speculative recognition of revelation in the 'concrete' sense (i.e., the idea of a progressive unfolding of revelation in all of nature and human history, as opposed to taking revelation 'rationalistically' or 'symbolically') (741). This, call, he claimed, led to a new era in the philosophy of religion and was far more influential than the actual metaphysics of the essay. Fichte also characterized Schelling's late system in general terms, covering the topics of the divine as personality rather than abstract organizing principle (742–3), the elimination of the fatalism that had characterized the early system (759), the 'positivity' of creation (i.e., its status as the contingent result of free divine act) (759), the idea that 'one cannot get to actuality with the *purely rational (a priori)*' (759), the rejection of pantheism and the rehabilitation of traditional ideas of individual will and personality (769), as well as a characterization of what Fichte saw as the 'methodological inadequacy' of Schelling's late system (that it can never be finished (771), and that it is a hypothetical construction which must find its confirmation or disconfirmation outside itself (773–6)). (One might have thought this was precisely a methodological virtue, given the rejection of *a priorism* that Fichte also endorses.)

---

[31] Cf. Kierkegaard (1909–78: II C 25, vol. XII: 281). Fichte's *Beiträge* is in fact still one of the better philosophical histories of the post-Kantian period.

Also in Kierkegaard's library was Fichte's response to Schelling's preface to the Cousin volume, published in 1835 under the title *Ueber die Bedingung eines spekulativen Theismus (On the Requirement of a Speculative Theism)*. As I have said, Kierkegaard also owned the Cousin volume, whose preface was Schelling's first philosophical publication since 1812. In that preface Schelling had given a sketch of an account of the later system, including an account of his reassessment of his own early system and its relation to Hegel. He had also offered a critique of Hegel there, along the lines of what he would later present in Berlin: that the Hegelian system takes account of the universal and necessary (that which cannot not be thought), but not of actuality (*VC* X: 213–14), but that philosophy has a legitimate interest in providing a positive explication of actuality (*VC* X: 214–15). Fichte's discussion expands on these brief remarks. He characterizes Schelling's main distinction from other critics (and followers) of Hegel as his inclination to press on the transition from logic to philosophy of nature (wherein the 'idea' 'actualizes itself' but the actualization is still an *a priori* philosophical content) as the real weak spot in the system—rather than taking issue with the beginning of the logic (the problem of a 'beginning' of the system having been a major preoccupation of Hegel's defenders and critics) (13). Fichte characterizes the late Schelling's fundamental claim in this way: 'It is impossible to arrive at actuality by means of the purely rational (the *a priori*). This requires the empirical, the living conception of actuality; so [Schelling calls for] an empiricism transfigured by the speculative idea' (16). He offers what looks like an elaboration of Schelling's 'rereading' of his early system in Munich: that the early system was historical 'in form' but not truly historical because it was just an elaboration at a certain level of abstraction of the idea of the absolute, not an elaboration of the actual progress of history (23–4; cf. Schelling *GpP* 203–16). He points out Schelling's difficulty in spelling out the relation between negative and positive philosophy (37), but expresses hope that Schelling will offer an answer to 'the riddle of the age' and anticipation of Schelling's 'reappearance' (41—presumably, his reappearance in print is what is intended). In other respects, the points he highlights about the later Schelling's system—the personality of God, the positivity of creation, the concreteness of revelation, the nature of human freedom—echo those highlighted in the *Beiträge* (both editions of which were published later) and *Die Idee der Persönlichkeit* (published one year earlier).

Kierkegaard owned other book-length publications by members of the late-idealist school.[32] But even more important than these monographs was the philosophical journal edited by Fichte, in close collaboration with Weiße

---

[32] Among those by I. H. Fichte are *Sätze zur Vorschule der Theologie* (1826), his *Grundzüge zum Systeme der Philosophie* (1833–6), and his *De principiorum contradictionis, identitatis, exclusi tertii in logicis dignitate et ordine* (1840a).

and looser collaboration with a long list of co-editors: the *Zeitschrift für Philosophie und spekulative Theologie* (*Journal of Philosophy and Speculative Theology*), of which Kierkegaard owned every number from its inception in 1837 until 1848 (and, after a break, from 1853 to 1855). Kierkegaard clearly read the *Zeitschrift*; it is mentioned several times in the journals. Many articles from it were also published in Danish translation in the *Tidskrift for udenlandsk theologisk Litteratur* (the *Journal for Foreign Theological Literature* published in Copenhagen by Reitzel beginning in 1833), to which Kierkegaard also refers often. All the major problems with post-Kantian idealism were raised and discussed in its pages. Through it, Schelling's late position was widely disseminated and became part of the philosophical dialogue of the immediate post-Hegelian period.

It is from this source that Kierkegaard had his main exposure to Christian Weiße's work,[33] which, together with Fichte's, dominated the *Zeitschrift*'s offerings. In the first volume of the journal Weiße offered his estimation of the state of the field (in an article titled 'The Three Fundamental Questions of Contemporary Philosophy'—and on that estimation Schelling is the main point of reference for a younger generation trying to go 'beyond Hegel' (73). Weiße goes on to offer an interpretation of the relation of negative to positive philosophy in Schelling's system, one whereon negative knowledge is a system of 'conditions of possibility' of things being as they are but not a full account of how things are (90). He agrees with Schelling that real being is not that which could not not be, but only that which could have been absent or otherwise (167), and that it is to be conceptualized as the result of a free act of creation (177). On the interpretation of Hegel's system whereon it is true, its results are characterized by a relative but not an absolute necessity. If there is reason, the construction is correct (as a set of conditions of possibility of something that is known to be actual), but there need not have been reason (since whatever is actual is a contingent work of freedom) (95–6). But Weiße seems to be caught in the same ambiguity as the later Schelling, for he also argues against Hegel on the grounds of a difficulty with the place of contingency in the Hegelian system. The necessity inhering in the 'unity of subjective and objective' in Hegel (the principle of knowledge) is at odds with contingency. The result is that someone with Hegel's theory of knowledge is either a wholesale determinist (something Hegel explicitly denied, but a position which his followers—Weiße mentions Göschel—found themselves forced to accept), in which case no sense can be attached to the distinction between logic and nature made *within* the Hegelian system; or else he admits contingency (and the distinction between logic and nature) at the cost of giving up knowledge (103–6). Now, if this sort of contingency is present then the results of negative philosophy do not even possess the

---

[33] *Die Idee der Gottheit* of 1833 was the only monograph by Weiße Kierkegaard owned. He bought it in 1844.

relative necessity Weiße attributes to them (as I have argued in chapter 4), but Weiße claims that contingency is necessary for a proper account of human freedom (164–5), and praises Schelling for endorsing the common-sense notion wherein self-conscious or rational beings have the choice between (equally possibly) doing something or not doing it (without this amounting to a motivational 'equilibrium' with the Buridan-alleged problem) (167–8). He agrees with Schelling that any system that does not want to deny the possibility of evil must take care not to deny the possibility of *Willkür* (and that Hegel does deny it) (175). He also seems to want to praise Schelling's empiricist turn in epistemology (102), and claims that knowledge is only possible with divine assistance (114). (In a later essay, 'On the Historical Development of Philosophy as Science' in volume 5 (1840), Weiße reproduces Schelling's distinction between *'wissendes'* and *'unwissendes' Wissen*, indicating by the former knowledge of contingency and the latter knowledge of tautology, associating the latter with speculation and the former with positive knowledge and, like Schelling, apparently equating necessity and tautology (235).) Again, these commitments leave less room for the validity of the idealist starting point than Weiße seems to start off by assuming—the same problem Schelling encountered when trying to preserve a 'relative' validity for his own early work.

There were many other Schelling-influenced contributors to the *Zeitschrift*. I will offer some more examples from the first few volumes (the most important, since they came out during the time that Kierkegaard was completing his education).

Otto Krabbe also takes up the issue of the inadequacy of the Hegelian account of freedom and sin/evil in his article on the relation of philosophical and Christian ethics ('On the Relation of Philosophical and Christian Ethics to One Another') in the journal's first volume. Krabbe claims that Hegel's own account of sin falls to the criticism he himself had made of Schelling's *Identitätssystem*—that in it there is no room for a distinction between good and evil. Hegel has difficulty keeping the distinction sharp, because on his (pantheistic) account the creature is insufficiently independent of the creator (213). Christian ethics can deal with freedom and moral responsibility in a way that philosophical ethics in the idealist tradition cannot, because it can separate creature from creator in the requisite way (217). This allows it to give a positive account of evil, one whereon evil is qualitatively and not just quantitatively different from the good (i.e., not distinguished from the good as a lesser quantity or degree of the same thing, e.g., reality or perfection) (217). The truth of Christianity, he claims, shows itself primarily in its relation to human nature—in the fact that it manages to fulfil human nature's deepest needs—among them a conception of moral responsibility along these lines (218).

H. M. Chalybäus, in an article on the philosophy of history ('Philosophy of History and History of Philosophy'), also in the first volume, makes a related point about the absence of human freedom and moral responsibility in Hegel's system. The central contradiction in Hegel comes, according to this diagnosis, when we ask whether we can (or should) have a conception of human freedom that introduces accidentalness. Hegel's answer, it seems, has to be no.

Should we hold to [this] proposition, that reason is actually and in truth the all-realizing, the power that presents itself and—no other—in everything, then either everything—also the most individual, even the evil and immoral, indeed even the irrational, if there is any— is also rational and necessary, and that which seems arbitrary, or natural, or individual is only the realization, taken to the most determinate degree, of infinite spirit itself; or else that which seems irrational in fact does not exist *at all*, is only appearance, apparent being. (318)

This, Chalybäus concludes, means that there is not room for an adequate conception of human freedom in Hegel's system: 'If the individual—this is our opinion—cannot be free *against* the idea, rebel *against* universal reason, then it cannot be free' (319). In this he takes himself to agree with Schelling, and he also mentions with approval Schelling's criticism of Hegel on the relation between thought and actuality later in the essay (328).

The most extensive application of Schelling's *Freiheitsschrift* freedom conception is to be found in Carl Philipp Fischer's essay 'On the Speculative Concept of Freedom' in volume 3 (1839b). This is a review of Romang, *Ueber Willensfreiheit und Determinismus* (*On Freedom of Will and Determinism*, 1835). Romang defends determinism (according to Fischer) on an early-Schellingian model of *Naturphilosophie*. Fischer wants to defend a conception of freedom as involving *Willkür* while at the same time showing that it does not entail 'indifference', arguing that this form of indeterminism, like determinism, presupposes the passivity of the agent (presupposes that the subject is 'nothing but the passive unity of intellectual and sensible motives' which result in action on the basis of their relative strength (121)—in other words, presupposes the denial of free will to begin with). He especially criticizes Romang for seeking to eliminate the qualitative difference between good and evil, reducing the difference to a merely quantitative one (evil as a negative or a lesser magnitude of good) (112). The essay also contains criticisms of Hegel for denying the difference between good and evil and an extended discussion of the possibility of freedom for evil which takes up most of the article. (Kierkegaard also owned Fischer's *Die Idee der Gottheit* (*The Idea of Divinity*) of 1839.)

Finally, I. H. Fichte's writing dominates the pages of the *Zeitschrift*, and here again there are numerous accounts of the main themes of the later Schelling. In an article in the second (1838) volume ('On the Relation between the Formal and Real Principles in the Contemporary Philosophical

Systems'), he describes his and Weiße's work as aligned with Schelling's in these terms:

[Unlike Hegel's system, according to which the reality of everything is in the concept, he and Weiße have a system wherein] the essential aspect of things is not merely, indeed not at all, their conceptual necessity, that about them which could not not be or could not be other than it is, but instead what in relation to their concept could also not be or also be otherwise—how each thing develops itself out of its own basic determinacy (i.e., individuality), what it itself does, that which is *free, irrational* according to Schelling's expression, in which the aspect of form and necessity is just as much posited as cancelled. That is why Weiße, with Schelling, calls the new standpoint the system of *freedom*, and why I call it the system of *individuality*. (26n)

In the first instalment (in volume 5, 1840b) of a six-part article ('On Speculative Theology'), Fichte again characterizes Hegel's system as one that leaves no room for personality: not only is his God impersonal; his human individuals are impersonal, and for the same reason. There exist only principles and their expressions; there are no persons. (His discussion here is very like Scheler's as reproduced above.) Schelling was guilty of the same mistake in his early works, but the *Freiheitsschrift* signalled a departure from this configuration (107–10). Here Fichte reiterates the absolute/conditional necessity distinction, and reports that the 'necessity' (of things being as they are) in the system is at most conditional, and that this conditionality points to the existence of a free creator—that is, since the system of essences is not self-actualizing, it needs to have been actualized (172–3). He also remarks that Schelling's idea of a blindly working ground in things (the *Freiheitsschrift's* 'principle of the ground') allows him to introduce personality (in individuals and God) into the system, and to avoid Hegelian pantheism and the hegemony of reason (216–26). More discussion of Schelling's criticism of Hegel and the nature of positive philosophy can be found in Fichte's article 'The Concept of the Negative Absolute and of Negative Philosophy' (published in two parts, in volumes 10 and 11, 1843a and b) and in his 1842 review of *Schellings erste Vorlesung in Berlin* (volume 9, 1842b).

The writings of the late idealists were also well represented in the *Tidskrift for udenlandsk theologisk Litteratur*, to which Kierkegaard also subscribed.[34] The second volume contained, for instance, a translation (under the title 'Religion and Philosophy in their Current Relation to One Another') of a review of Hegel's *Lectures on the Philosophy of Religion* by I. H. Fichte (1834b). A translation of Fichte's 'Speculation and Revelation' appeared in volume 5 (1837). In volume 6 (1838) there were two pieces by Weiße (1838a and b)—'On the Reliability of Evangelical History', a response to Tholuck's comment on

---

[34] The purpose of this journal, published beginning in 1833 by H. N. Clausen and M. H. Hohlenberg—both theology professors at the University of Copenhagen—was to provide Danish translations of articles from foreign-language theology journals.

Strauss's *Leben Jesu*, and a translation of the first volume of Weiße's work on evangelical history, 'Evangelical History treated Critically and Philosophically'. Volume 10 contained a translation of a treatise by Fichte (published in the *Zeitschrift* in 1841) on the difference between the immanent trinity and the revealed trinity ('Some Remarks on the Difference between the Immanent Trinity and the Revealed Trinty, according to Lücke and Nitzsch, and with Reference to Hegel and Strauß', 1842a) and a treatise by Fischer on the idea of immortality also first published in the *Zeitschrift* ('Attempt at a Scientific Explanation of the Idea of Immortality', 1842).

The *Tidskrift* is less important as a source—after all, Kierkegaard had access to most of this work in the original editions—than as an indication of the profile of this group of scholars in Danish-language theology in the 1830s. Kierkegaard was by no means alone in his interest in the late idealists. In fact Poul Martin Møller (clearly one of Kierkegaard's major early influences)[35] himself participated in the debate about the possibility of personal immortality in a Hegelian framework in which Fichte's *Idee der Persönlichkeit* was a landmark.[36] It may have been Møller who first introduced Kierkegaard to this debate and to I. H. Fichte's work.

This is by no means a full account of the presentations of Schelling's late views that were in print and available to Kierkegaard (in his own library, no less) by the late 1830s and early 1840s.[37] But it is already more than enough to prove my point. How important these views actually were for Kierkegaard's position can be shown only through a detailed consideration of the latter's works (to which I am about to turn). But it is clear that Schelling (through his lectures and his followers) had set the agenda for central post-Hegelian discussions in philosophy of religion and moral psychology. Schelling was one of the main figures in relation to which a theology student had to orient himself in the late 1830s—little wonder, then, that Kierkegaard made the journey to Berlin to hear Schelling's lectures first hand. The position of so many commentators that such influence can be ruled out on purely

[35] It is widely agreed upon that Møller was the teacher of whom Kierkegaard was most fond. One of the aspects of Møller's thought that Kierkegaard surely found most sympathetic was his endorsement of what I will call the 'existing-in' test—the idea that an ethical-religious view must pass the test of fit with the first-person perspective of the individual agent for whom it claims validity, and that this is the most important means at our disposal for deciding among competing views of life. Møller also thought he could offer a sort of 'indirect proof' of God's existence based on the impossibility of living without the idea of personal immortality and a personal God—very akin to the ideas of the later Schelling and the late idealists, though not one Kierkegaard himself ultimately endorsed. (For a discussion of this proof, cf. Thielst (2003: 58–9).)

[36] Møller's contribution can be found in an article titled 'Thoughts on the Possibility of Proofs of Human Immortality', in *Maanedskrift for Litteratur* 17 (1837: 1–72, 422–53).

[37] One more example: J. U. Wirth's contribution to volume 11 (1843), 'On the Concept of God as Principle of Philosophy', contains a minutely detailed play-by-play of the development of Schelling's later philosophy, beginning from the 1802 dialogue *Bruno*.

historical grounds is, I take it, definitively refuted by the evidence cited here. There are certainly no grounds for concluding that Kierkegaard could not have known Schelling's position in any detail (even if he could not have known most of the late lecture material *first hand*). Just the opposite is the case: for someone with Kierkegaard's interests in Kierkegaard's generation, the odds of escaping intimate familiarity with Schelling's views were very slim indeed.

5

'Despair' in the Pseudonymous Works, and Kierkegaard's Double Incompatibilism

The complex of problems surrounding the accounts of freedom and autonomy in German idealism seem to me to be utterly central to Kierkegaard's philosophical concerns and to his project in the pseudonymous works. In this chapter and the one that follows, I will present an interpretation of Kierkegaard's theory of agency and of the place of that theory in the wider project in the pseudonyms. The theory, I will argue, is a descendant of Schelling's as presented in the *Freiheitsschrift*—fuller, more coherent, less strange, better psychologically and phenomenologically informed, but a relative of Schelling's nevertheless and informed by his primary concerns. I will also argue that the theory of agency so understood is central to Kierkegaard's project in the pseudonymous works, in two ways.

First, Kierkegaard's characterization of Christianity and what limited defence he offers of a Christianity so characterized is informed, I will argue, by the view of agency. This defence is often thought to take the form of an argument against the plausible alternatives (in particular, the three alternative views of life presented in the pseudonyms: aesthetic, ethical and religiousness A) on the grounds that these are somehow at odds with the situation of existing subjectivity—that each somehow fails to fit once we try it on and seek to understand ourselves in its terms. I agree that this is the basic form of the argument, and that it is a central one in the pseudonymous works. (Note that a defence on these negative grounds hardly constitutes a closed case. I will argue that Kierkegaard not only accepts but in fact embraces this limitation.) Where I disagree with other interpreters is in my estimation of the substance of the criticisms of the aesthetic, ethical and philosophical-religious views of life. My disagreement with the available interpretations is sharpest in my estimation of the complaint against the ethical view—an area in which, I believe, no remotely plausible account has yet been advanced. A plausible account needs to explain both what unites the views that are the target of the criticism and what is wrong with whatever that is. It needs to explain what ties these views together in Kierkegaard's mind, and what about them makes them inadequate to the situation of existing subjectivity. In order not to be question-begging, it needs to do that without presupposing the truth of religious commitments or even the applicability of religious concepts. The ethical view of life needs to fail on its own terms or presuppose a manifestly implausible account of human experience. Otherwise we risk attributing to Kierkegaard the completely uninteresting view that what is wrong with non-religious ethics is that it is non-religious. Kierkegaard's texts have not seemed to offer a clear and plausible criticism of the targets he names. I contend that this is because they are full of argumentative gaps resulting from certain well-known quirks in his style of presentation (chiefly his odd use of philosophical terms, which is as often loose and metaphorical as precise and literal, and his employment of pseudonyms whose views are genuinely jointly inconsistent on some points), and that interpreters have tried to fill those gaps either not at all, or by placing the texts against a background with the wrong pattern. The correct background is the one provided by the discussion of the issue of free choice of immorality (and related themes) in Kant and post-Kantian accounts of freedom.

There is a second way in which the view of agency is central to the project in the pseudonyms, and this is its role in the attack on academic metaphysics and epistemology. Here also I believe the correct general approach is to see the view under attack as being somehow at odds with the situation of existing subjectivity, being such that it fails to fit once we try it on and seek to understand ourselves and our activity in the terms it provides. That is, I do not see Kierkegaard as offering any original theoretical reasons for doubting the possibility of metaphysics in general. Nor do I see him as claiming that we are somehow forbidden by our existential situation to engage in these pursuits (although if we do it as a way of masking the details of that situation from ourselves we are guilty of a form of self-deception). Instead, what Kierkegaard gives us in the pseudonymous works (especially in the Climacus pseudonyms) is an attack on the particular commitments of German idealist metaphysics from the standpoint of his conception of agency. The commitment to rejecting any metaphysics that precludes making sense of one's own activity in doing metaphysics (or anything else) is not new with Kierkegaard—in fact it was fundamental to the idealist project from Kant onwards. Like Kant, then, Kierkegaard asked what our metaphysical views (including our conception of the divine and its relation to the human) must be like in order to be consistent with how we must conceptualize our activity as thinkers and moral agents. But he disagreed with Kant and the idealists on the results, and this disagreement is informed by his refusal to substitute the rational self-determination conception of freedom for the spontaneity conception—the same refusal that characterized the later Schelling's turn away from idealism. So here again, Kierkegaard's view can be got right if we fill in the gaps in his account with the right background picture, and again the central figures in that background picture are Kant and Schelling.

In this chapter I will begin by exploring why Kierkegaard thinks the perspective of agency is at odds with idealist metaphysics (in §I), and then look at why he takes it to be at odds with the idealist ethics of autonomy (in §II). I will attribute to Kierkegaard what today might be called two sorts of incompatibilism, and I will argue that the unified project behind the pseudonymous works consists in part in arguing for that double incompatibilism. In chapter 6, I will go on to explain some central aspects of the positive view with which Kierkegaard would replace the then-prevailing view: his account of the foundations of ethics and of ethico-religious knowledge (§§ I and II), and his positive theory of agency (§III). This order of presentation follows what I take to be the order or argumentation in the pseudonymous works as well: the negative argument formulated in this chapter is not informed by, but instead informs, the positive views outlined in the next.

I have said that Kierkegaard endorses a double incompatibilism about free will. But of course he himself would never have dreamed of putting his position in these terms. What he does instead is give an extended characterization and criticism of various perspectives on existence ('stages' or 'views' of life). In the first section, then, I will interpret the argument for the rejection of the 'aesthetic' view of life in *Either/Or* as an argument for a commitment to the standpoint of agency, and more specifically to free will in an incompatibilist sense, to a descendant of Kant's notion of transcendental spontaneity. In the second section, I will examine the criticism of the 'ethical' view of life and argue that it relies on the argument from evil against the autonomy model of normativity. In the course of that discussion I will show that a related criticism applies to religiousness A. In the process I will look critically at some other available interpretations of what is wrong with the non-Christian life-views and show that these alternatives either presuppose an antecedent commitment to Christianity or are simply unconvincing (or both).

Some of the position outlined in Kierkegaard's pseudonymous works is motivated purely by religious commitment and has no application apart from the project of leading a certain sort of Christian life. However, for the most part, that position's truth was meant to be judged from the standpoint of the reasonably reflective, but uncommitted, agent. This is true, I believe, even of one of the central claims of that position: that Christianity, though irrational and justifiable in neither historical nor philosophical terms, is nevertheless (and perhaps even because of that) peculiarly well suited to the situation of human moral agency—is, as Climacus (who does not consider himself a Christian) puts it, a 'perfect fit' with the situation of existing subjectivity (*AE* VII: 193; 7: 210). This chapter presents the negative part (I will address the positive in the next chapter) of the rationale for that claim: that three other plausible candidate life-views do not fit.

I. THE AESTHETIC VIEW OF LIFE AND
THE FIRST INCOMPATIBILISM

Kierkegaard's pseudonymous authorship begins with a characterization of what he calls the 'aesthetic' view of life (the papers of the aesthete *A* comprising the first volume of *Either/Or*), followed by an extended argument for the rejection of that view (the two letters to *A* from Judge William comprising most of the second volume). The question of what the specifics of the Judge's argument are has got about as many answers as the work has had interpreters. Uncontroversially, the basic claim is that the aesthetic life is despair, and the ethical life (attained by 'choosing oneself') offers an escape from despair. But the meaning of each of the key terms in this statement is far from obvious.

The Judge addresses a number of views in *Either/Or* II, only some of which bear any clear relation to the name 'aesthetic': aesthetic immediacy (the unreflective pursuit of some goal or series of goals—paradigmatically, pleasure in some form), a series of standpoints incorporating progressively greater degrees of reflection (e.g., the pursuit of 'the interesting'—two versions of this are outlined in Crop Rotation and The Seducer's Diary), *A*'s position (which I take to be most closely related to some of the thoughts expressed in Diapsalmata), the views of 'some of the German philosophers', a group which turns out to include the Schelling of the *System of Transcendental Idealism* (whose view might reasonably be called 'aesthetic', since it is the experience of art that is supposed to provide the highest cognitive paradigm in that work), as well as Hegel (a view it is harder to associate with the term 'aesthetic', given that Hegel explicitly distinguished his position from Schelling's in part by criticizing Schelling's emphasis on aesthetic appreciation as a cognitive model, and aesthetic presentation as a communicative model, of philosophical truth).

One can list these views that the Judge groups together under the rubric 'the aesthetic view of life'. What is more difficult is to say what they all have in common—and what exactly is wrong with whatever that is. The Judge tells us that they are all, in one form or another, despair (*Fortvivlelsen*). This is not very helpful, though, if we do not know what 'despair' means. That the word has the everyday meaning is ruled out by two of the Judge's commitments: first, that nearly everyone who has ever lived has done so in despair; and, second, that the vast majority of them have been unaware of that fact. Appealing to the use of the term in some other of Kierkegaard's works also has its problems, at least if one feels any respect for Kierkegaard's injunction to avoid arbitrarily mixing up the views presented by the various pseudonyms. I will argue that there is a quite strong connection between the notion of despair in *Either/Or* and that in later works (in particular, in *The Sickness unto Death*), but that connection has to be established on the basis of a reading of *Either/Or*, not the other way around.

The notion of an ethical view of life also turns out to be problematic, in so far as the Judge uses the expression '*det Ethiske*' to refer to all of the following: (1) the idea that one is a morally responsible agent (such that accepting the ethical standpoint means accepting that one is responsible for what one does); (2) the idea that one is autonomous in a broadly Kantian[1] sense; (3) the normative force of social

---

[1] In fact I think, and have argued (in a forthcoming paper), that the Judge's presentation of the view is closer to Fichte's than to Kant's. But Fichte himself was a Kantian, and the differences between their two views, while interesting and important for the interpretation of *Either/Or*, do not intersect with the issues I will be concerned with here.

and cultural institutions in general; and (4) more specifically, that concrete set of ethical duties that he takes to apply to both himself and *A* in virtue of (2) and (3).

My view is that despair, for the Judge, is the conscious or unconscious assumption of a passive or fatalistic attitude towards one's existence, motivated by a misconstrual of the nature of one's agency. The aesthetic view is despair because it is characterized by the denial of the claims of ethics in sense (1). This is apparently not the most obvious reading, and so I will begin by showing two alternative readings that appear to be more intuitive to be, in fact, unacceptable. I have chosen these because of their currency, but also because their limitations are instructive. The failure of the second will point to an explanation of the link between the philosophical views the Judge discusses and *A*'s view, a link which will be an important step towards understanding the core meaning of 'despair' as it applies to views that the Judge labels 'aesthetic'.

Despair as the risk of failure and the ethical as assurance of success

The Judge's central presentation of the concept of despair (at *EE* II: 163; 3: 175) suggests the first of the alternative readings I have just mentioned. Aesthetic views, he says there, are those that place the highest importance on pleasure, satisfaction or happiness in some (apparently) ordinary sense: '[T]he popular expression [for the aesthetic life-view] heard in all ages and from various stages is this: One must enjoy life' (*EE* II: 163; 3: 175). And the criticism he brings seems to be that enjoyment is a goal whose fulfilment cannot be relied upon: '*But the person who says that he wants to enjoy life always posits a condition that either lies outside the individual or is within the individual in such a way that it is not there by virtue of the individual himself*' (*EE* II: 163; 3: 175—emphasis in original). The individual with an aesthetic life-view takes as his goal or standard something that is not in his power and whose attainment therefore cannot be guaranteed. The argument continues as follows: when things go awry for such an individual, he despairs, in a quite ordinary sense of that term—he feels unhappy, without hope, at a loss. But this, claims the Judge, means that he was in despair *all along*. For anyone who is susceptible to despair in this way is *eo ipso* already in despair. So long as things do not go awry, he is simply in the dark about his despair (*EE* II: 174; 3: 186):

> Let us now see why they despaired. Because they discovered that they had built their lives on something transient? But is that [namely, the discovery] a reason for despair; has an essential change taken place in that on which they built their lives? Is it an essential change in the transitory that it manifests itself as transitory, or is it not rather something accidental and inessential about it that it does not manifest itself this way? Nothing new has supervened that could cause a change. Consequently, when they despair, the basis of it must be that they were in despair beforehand. The difference is only that they did not know it. (*EE* II: 173–4; 3: 186)

The Judge lists a number of goals (hedonistic pleasure, honour, wealth) that depend on conditions 'outside the individual' and one (cultivation of one's talents) that depends on conditions 'within the individual in such a way that [they] are not there by virtue of the individual himself'. Such goals admit of failure—one can fail to achieve them due to impossible circumstances, to bad luck, or to one's own mistakes. But since one cannot be assured of success, the view seems to be, one cannot really enjoy life in the way the aesthetic individual pretends. The possibility of failure casts a pall over the entire project, and this pall is despair in the implicit sense.

This is a quite intuitive interpretation of the Judge's argument: one should be risk-averse with respect to one's main goals in life; aesthetic goals are risk-prone; the ethical individual escapes this risk by choosing a goal that is assured of success.[2] This line of interpretation relies, though, on a reading of 'implicit despair' that we cannot accept. Take the Judge's formulation of the most popular expression of the aesthetic life-view: that one must 'enjoy life'.[3] How is the risk of failure supposed to interfere with this project? There seem to be only two possibilities: (1) one cannot enjoy life (in the everyday sense) in the present because one cannot be certain that one will always do so in the future; or (2) one cannot reckon oneself a success in some sort of whole-life sense unless one knows that no misfortunes will befall one in the future. But (to (1)) extremes of paranoia aside, one can perfectly well enjoy oneself, in the *everyday* sense, knowing that the causes of one's enjoyment are contingent and transitory; and (to (2)) the possibility of future misfortunes affects only one's ability to *know now* whether one will have been a success in this sense, and does not at all affect the question of whether one will in fact have been a success in this sense.

If this is the Judge's argument against taking the aesthetic view of life (here, again, defined as the pursuit of enjoyment or fulfilment in one of the senses outlined), then it is a remarkably weak one, for it fails to answer the obvious question of why assurance of success should be the first criterion for a life-view's acceptability. Further, the criticism so construed has *prima facie* applicability only

---

[2] A version of this reading is endorsed by Poul Lübcke (1991). According to his view, 'despair is a normative concept, referring to a life that has the *possibility* of despair in a *psychological* sense' (99). 'This is probably the central argument in the whole letter—and in Kierkegaard's philosophy too. If you have a goal in your life that can be missed, and if you look upon this goal as an absolute goal, as a *conditio sine qua non* for the fulfilment of your life, then you are living in despair regardless of your being a success or the opposite' (97). The ethical individual, then, escapes despair by choosing a goal (the ethical goal) that is assured of success. This requires that the ethical goal be unmissable, and Lübcke's interpretation of the Judge's ethics is informed by this requirement. He argues, for instance, that ethics for the Judge must be deontological (for the possibility of miscalculation of outcomes threatens to make the ethical goal missable for a consequentialist as well) and that the Judge must be an egalitarian about potentials for ethical success (for if fulfilling ethical demands required a special talent, out-of-the-ordinary strength of character, or anything else that someone might lack, then the ethical life would be despair in the sense that the aesthetic life is). His conclusions are informed by this reading of the argument from despair. Greve (1990) endorses a similar interpretation of the problem with the aesthetic standpoint.

[3] We should probably take living for honour, say, or the cultivation of talents, to be simply less popular ways of living in aesthetic immediacy, as the Judge clearly intends to treat all such cases analogously. The reader may substitute any one of these in the discussion that follows, although in the case of some (e.g., honour) only consideration (2) might be applicable.

to the ways of life unreflectively oriented towards the pursuit of some good or other. The sort of second-order enjoyment of pleasure *and* pain, success *and* failure, practised by Johannes the Seducer and theorized about in Crop Rotation does not seem to be exposed to this sort of risk. In fact, it seems designed precisely to avoid this risk. Although we do hear in Crop Rotation that boredom will eventually catch up with one, and that one has a boredom-induced death to look forward to no matter what—dying of boredom or shooting oneself out of curiosity (cf. *EE* I: 260–1; 2: 278)—the second of these two options looks, at least, like an escape.[4]

This reading of implicit despair is also inconsistent with important aspects of what Kierkegaard has to say in later pseudonymous works. It will suffice to note that if this is what despair is, then the religious individual, who is after all expected to exist in a state of the most extreme insecurity—'over 70,000 fathoms of water'—is surely in despair as well. But the religious life is supposed to be a life of freedom from despair. This tension is a problem not because reading the Judge's position as partially at odds with positions expressed by the other pseudonyms is a problem per se. (It *is* at odds with them, in ways I will explain.) Rather, this specific inconsistency would be a problem, because Kierkegaard's pseudonymous argument against the aesthetic life is made primarily in *Either/Or*. If accepting a religious standpoint meant giving up the Judge's criticisms of the aesthetic life, we would be left with nothing to say against such a life from such a standpoint. On developmental-psychological readings of the stages, this is not a problem; since one will not have arrived at the religious view without passing through the ethical one, it will be too late (as it were) to be tempted by the aesthetic life.[5] But there are difficulties with such readings. The project in the pseudonyms is not purely descriptive; there is a justificatory story being outlined there as well, and appeals to one's own developmental stage do not justify. The justificatory story would be substantially less convincing if the core problem of the aesthetic view of life were invisible from the religious perspective.

Despair as arrested development and the ethical as the full human life

If the problem with the aesthetic view is not the instability of its goals, then perhaps the problem is an intrinsic unsuitability of its goals. That is, perhaps the problem with 'enjoying life' is that it is simply inadequate as a human goal, that the fulfilment of this sort of goal is not a plausible way to seek human satisfaction to begin with. This alternative is suggested in the many places where the aesthetic

---

[4] Hartmut Rosenau (1993: 95) has pointed out the difficulty of these two sections of *Either/Or* I for interpretations that conflate the problem of the aesthetic life-view with the problem of immediacy.

[5] By these I have in mind readings that emphasize Hegel's *Phenomenology* as background to the theory of stages. Cf., e.g., Taylor (1975, 1980) and Westphal (1996).

life is described as 'relating oneself absolutely to relative ends'. It requires a different reading of the Judge's complaint that the aesthetic life 'posits a condition that
either lies outside the individual or is within the individual in such a way that it is
not there by virtue of the individual himself', but there is a plausible alternative
available: what is needed is not a condition that is within one's control, but rather
one that is within one's nature (as it were). There is something in himself, some
intrinsic ethical *telos*, that *A* is thwarting in living as he does. Despair is a dissatisfaction arising not from the risk of failure, but from the inability even of success,
according to aesthetic criteria, to provide genuine satisfaction.

A number of attempts have been made at reconstructing the Judge's argument
in this broadly eudaimonistic manner.[6] This seems a promising strategy, since the
Judge often seems to be relying quite heavily on some behind-the-scenes justification of his account of ethical duties (in which family, professional vocation and
friendship figure prominently), and given the historical context—the hegemony
of Hegelianism and the Hegelian revival of Aristotle's ethics—and given the set of
duties involved, Aristotle and Hegel do look like plausible candidates.[7] But there
are difficulties with reconstructing the Judge's criticism along either Aristotelian
or Hegelian lines.

The list of immediate goals the Judge considers and the order in which he
considers them recalls the list Aristotle considers and rejects as accounts of happiness in the *Nicomachean Ethics* (cf., e.g., I: 5 1095b15–1096a10). This makes it
tempting to think that the Judge is following Aristotle in refusing to separate
morality from happiness or well-being in some fundamentally psychological
sense, while arguing that aesthetic pursuits cannot provide true satisfaction, and
that true satisfaction can be had only through moral virtue. But some aspects of
the Judge's account are puzzling if this sort of redefinition of happiness along
eudaimonistic lines is what he is after. First, he should be unwilling to say of those
immediate individuals for whom nothing had gone awry that 'these people were

---

[6] Among the more current is the view, due to Anthony Rudd, that prerequisite for a meaningful
and fulfilled life is a stable sense of self, and that this requires having roots in a particular set of social
structures, and seeing oneself as subject to the duties and standards that go with these. '[A] stable
personal identity can only be achieved through commitment to social roles and relationships which
carry with them objective standards of assessment. One must become a participant in communities
and the traditions which define them, and must develop the virtues necessary for such participation.
The failure to do this will render one's life quite literally pointless. Without any unifying *telos*, one's
life collapses into a series of disconnected moments, and to live in this way . . . is to live in despair'
(Rudd 2001: 139). Cf. also Rudd (1993). Rudd's main point of reference is Alasdair MacIntyre's
recent revival of Aristotle rather than Hegel's early nineteenth-century revival, but these look similar
enough that the reading is not problematically anachronistic. (As I will explain below, I fully agree
with Rudd's rejection of MacIntyre's Kierkegaard reading.) Mehl (1995) offers a similar reading, also
taking its orientation from MacIntyre and Charles Taylor.

[7] Jörg Disse has argued that the Judge's view is Kantianism shorn of Kant's account of practical
reason. Cf. Disse (1991, 2000). But the sorts of duties the Judge emphasizes are not *moral* duties at all
for Kant. I have argued elsewhere that Fichte is a better candidate than Hegel or even Kant for the
source of the ethical view the Judge presents. On both such reconstructions the eudaimonistic reading
of the critique of the aesthetic view is out of place.

indeed happy'—yet this is precisely what he does say (*EE* II: 173; 3: 186). Those individuals who do succeed according to aesthetic criteria are happy, enjoy themselves, etc.—*and* they are in despair. Second, his claim should be that the lower pleasures of the aesthetic life are replaced in the forefront of the ethical individual's life by the higher satisfactions of the exercise of virtue. Instead we find him arguing at length that what he himself labels 'aesthetic' satisfactions are consistent with and preserved in the life of duty (for instance, in his 'aesthetic defence of marriage').

The reading of the Judge's view as reiteration of Hegel's criticism of the romantic idea of a life oriented to aesthetic goals rather than ethical (*Sittliche*) ones seems likewise promising, especially in light of Kierkegaard's embrace of the Hegelian criticism of romantic irony in *The Concept of Irony*.[8] But there is a serious problem here as well, for in the very middle of the Judge's condemnation of the aesthetic view of life, we see the first appearance of a claim that will be reiterated throughout the pseudonymous works and that should, on this interpretation, come as a surprise: that the position of 'the German philosophers'—and it is clear from the discussion that the German philosophers in question are none other than Hegel and his school—is yet another form of despair (*EE* II: 190; 3: 204). In fact, the Judge explicitly links *A*'s position with that of 'the philosophers'—in the following way:

The polemical conclusion, from which all your paeans over existence resonate, has a strange similarity to modern philosophy's pet theory that the principle of contradiction is cancelled. I am well aware that the position you take is anathema to philosophy, and yet it seems to me that it is itself guilty of the same error; indeed the reason this is not immediately detected is that it is not even as properly situated as you are. You are situated in the area of action, philosophy in the area of contemplation. As soon as it is moved into the area of practice, it must arrive at the same conclusion as you do, even though it does not express it the same way. (*EE* II: 154; 3: 166)

This equation is highly instructive. For it tells us that we should view the problem with speculative philosophy discussed in the second letter as somehow *of a piece* with the problem of *A*'s view. But what is this conclusion that both *A* and 'the philosophers' would have in common, were the latter to address the 'area of practice'?

Aesthetic fatalism and agency

What the Judge says is that for both, 'life comes to a halt' (*EE* II: 155; 3: 167). What he means seems to be this: the justification Hegel thought one could give for the ethical validity of the concrete social structures in place in the early nineteenth century relied on seeing them as the results of a history that is the

---

[8] Westphal (1996) and Taylor (1975, 1980) read the transition to the ethical standpoint in these terms. A similar account can be found in Theunissen (1958).

self-development of world-spirit in human consciousness and its social forms—a development towards a social situation characterized by objective rationality and individual self-determination. But history can be understood in this way only from a unique historical perspective, and only in virtue of being philosophically reconstructible according to its necessity—in the sense at issue in the classic Schellingian appropriation of Kant's third *Critique*. The justification of the ethical view in Hegel's *Philosophy or Right* thus presupposes the same sort of historical determinism that Schelling's early system had pioneered.

In the first letter of *Either/Or* II, the Judge paraphrases a passage from the *System of Transcendental Idealism*,[9] Schelling's account of freedom as subjective assent to and participation in the rationally necessary order of things, and he describes it as expressing 'the highest in aesthetics':

> Here I am at the summit of the aesthetic. And in truth, he who has humility and courage enough to let himself be aesthetically transformed, he who feels himself present as a character in a drama the deity is writing, in which the poet and the prompter are not different persons, in which the individual, as the experienced actor who has lived into his character and his lines is not disturbed by the prompter but feels that he himself wants to say what is being whispered to him, so that it almost becomes a question whether he is putting words in the prompter's mouth or the prompter in his, he who in the most profound sense feels himself creating and created, who in the moment he feels himself creating has the original pathos of the lines, and in the moment he feels himself created has the erotic ear that picks up every sound—he and he alone has brought into actual existence the highest in aesthetics. (*EE* II: 124–5; 3: 136)

The highest in aesthetics: as the Judge puts it earlier in the first letter, the affirmation of the 'unity of freedom and necessity', wherein 'the individual feels drawn by an irresistible power . . . but precisely therein feels his freedom' (*EE* II: 42; 3: 52). The cunning of reason in history has the same function in Hegel that the image of the dramaturge deity has in Schelling's *System of Transcendental Idealism*.

But Kierkegaard rejects this idealist-compatibilist account of freedom, both in *Either/Or* and throughout the pseudonymous works: 'Philosophy', the Judge writes, 'sees history under the category of necessity, not under the category of freedom, for even though the world-historical process is said to be free, this is in the same sense as one speaks of the organizing process in nature' (*EE* II: 158; 3: 170). The fact that philosophy sees history under the category of necessity 'accounts for its incapacity for having a person act, its inclination to let everything come to a standstill, for what it actually demands is that one must act necessarily, which is a contradiction' (*EE* II: 158–9; 3: 171). To choose oneself according to one's necessity is to take the ethical choice 'aesthetically in vain' (*EE* II: 207; 3: 221). Note that the Judge's objection in this passage (*EE* II: 155–9; 3: 167–171) is not to the historical character of Hegelianism

---

[9] I cited the original passage from Schelling above in chapter 3, §II.

per se—though the many quips about the backward-looking philosopher who 'hastens so fast into the past that . . . only his coattails remain in the present' (*EE* II 155; 3: 167) can make it seem to be that. Rather, the objection is that seeing one's activity as part of a deterministic historical process (even if this process is correctly described as the becoming-actual of reason) cannot be reconciled with the forward-looking standpoint of agency which forces deliberation and choice.

This point is argued directly in the words of the Judge, and indirectly in the portrayal of *A* and his situation. *A* is also an incompatibilist—but one who embraces determinism. His situation is that of an individual stymied by his own refusal to believe that anything is up to him. The Judge characterizes *A*'s attempt to see himself as a spectator in life rather than a participant in it (cf. *EE* II: 155; 3: 168: *A* is 'not a participant'; he is 'outside') as the aesthetic attitude made explicit. But this is not simply the Judge's characterization; it is *A*'s self-characterization as well. 'My soul,' *A* writes in Diapsalmata, 'has lost possibility' (*EE* I: 25; 2: 50), as a result not of leading a hedonistic life, but of leading a life ruled by the injunction to see oneself from the standpoint of the necessary order of things—'It is not merely in isolated moments that I, as Spinoza says, view everything *aeterno modo*, but I am continually *aeterno modo*' (*EE* I: 23; 2: 48).[10] The result is that he feels 'as a chessman must feel when the opponent says of it: that piece cannot be moved' (*EE* I: 6; 2: 30). (In fact, *A* uses the word 'freedom' in *Either/Or* I exclusively in the sense of freedom of action, never in the sense of freedom of will.)[11] It is little wonder, then, that *A* finds time senseless (*EE* I: 13–14; 2: 38), existence tedious (*EE* I: 9; 2: 33), and nothing meaningful (*EE* I: 15; 2: 40.)

It is also little wonder that *A*'s maxim is not to begin anything, not to *will* at all (*EE* I: 23; 2: 48). But this is an impossible intention to carry out, as the Judge points out (with the ship's captain analogy at *EE* II: 149; 3: 161); more than that, it is an incoherent intention to have. The Judge's claim is that *A*'s view is self-defeating, because it is a normative stance (one that tells us what to do and to avoid doing, even where its injunctions are merely prudential, as in Crop Rotation) that simultaneously denies that there is any addressee of normative claims. 'The personality is . . . seen . . . within the categories of necessity, and there is left only enough freedom to be able, like a restless dream, to keep the individual half-awake and to lead him astray into the labyrinth of sufferings and vicissitudes, where he sees himself everywhere and yet cannot come to himself' (*EE* II: 215; 3: 228–9). *This* state, rather than some state of (actual or potential)

[10] In *Concluding Unscientific Postscript*, Climacus describes 'the speculative result' in the same way: 'the existing subject, thinking, wants to abstract from his existing and wants to be *sub specie aeterni*' (*AE* VII: 63; 7: 83).

[11] A paradigmatic example is at *EE* I: 268; 2: 286: 'If an individual is many [i.e., is weighted down by wife or friends], he has lost his freedom and cannot order his riding boots when he wishes, cannot knock about according to whim.'

disappointment with one's life project, should be the prime candidate for the psychological aspect of despair as described in *Either/Or*.[12]

The conversion to an ethical standpoint is, in the Judge's characterization, equivalent to the acceptance of choice, the taking up of responsibility. This is, in the Judge's view, itself an exercise of a freedom always possessed by the aesthete but never acknowledged by him, which is why he talks about a 'choice' of the ethical stance. The way in which the Judge characterizes this choice is a source of confusion, though. To choose, writes the Judge, is in the first instance to choose oneself: 'But what is it then, that I choose—is it this or that? No, for I choose absolutely, and I choose absolutely precisely by having chosen not to choose this or that. I choose the absolute, and what is the absolute? It is myself in my eternal validity' (*EE* II: 192; 3: 205). It is easy to take 'choosing oneself' to be opposed to 'choosing something else'—as though what were at issue in the choice between the two views of life were fundamentally a choice between different *ends*. (Taking that choice this way is fundamental to the two interpretations I looked at above.) But the primary meaning of this injunction to choose oneself in one's eternal validity is not: choose a *standard* or *set of goals* that is somehow more secure or more adequate. For look at how the Judge cashes out the notion of choosing oneself (immediately following the above): 'But what is this self of mine? If I were to speak of a first moment, a first expression for it, then my answer is this: It is the most abstract of all, and yet in itself it is also the most concrete of all—it is freedom' (*EE* II: 192; 3: 205). The 'choice of oneself' is in the first instance a choice of oneself as agent, not the choice of a set of characteristically ethical values over a set of more or less hedonistic ones.

Of course the Judge presents not one but two exclusive disjunctions in the second letter of *Either/Or* II, and these are not clearly distinguished. The first is the either/or of incompatibilism in an ordinary sense: either freedom or necessity; either an active, ethical attitude or a passive, contemplative, aesthetic attitude. The second is the either/or of specifically moral choice that appears if one accepts the first term of the first disjunction: either good or evil; either a moral life or an

---

[12] Mark Taylor (1975) also argues that 'the most fundamental characteristic of the aesthetic stage of existence is the absence of decision' (128), but he and I disagree about what exactly Kierkegaard finds wrong with that. According to Taylor, failure to decide results in a lack of *integration* of personality that is equivalent to failure to be a self in Kierkegaard's terms (129). The aesthete is inauthentic (181–2), out of balance (183), 'becomes "multifarious" either as an array of conflicting sensuous desires or as a collection of incompatible possibilities' (184). What, though, is wrong with being multifarious? Why, according to Taylor, should one want to be a self in Kierkegaard's sense? Because to fail to be a self in that sense is to fail to be fully developed—to remain in some sense a child (75). Taylor sees the relation between the different life-views in the pseudonymous authorship largely in developmental-psychological terms (75), with the result that the deficiencies in one stage are visible only from the (more advanced) standpoint of the succeeding stage. Thus, on his view, the aesthete's failure is measurable only against a model of selfhood foreign to the aesthetic point of view. On my view, the aesthetic standpoint is intrinsically unstable, because it requires the aesthete to take a contradictory stance towards his own agency. I see this as a better result—since the Judge clearly intends his criticism to be appreciated by *A* himself.

immoral one. It is easy to mix these two up, such that one takes the Judge to be arguing for a moral life (first term of the second disjunction) over an amoral one (second term of the first). In other words, it is easy to take the second letter as an attempt at an answer to the question, 'Why should one live a moral life?' (and for each specific aspect of the Judge's moral picture, so: 'Why should one get married when bachelorhood is so much more interesting?' etc.), rather than the more modest question, 'Why should one take oneself to be a moral agent, subject to ethical demands?'[13]

The second letter's formulations invite this conflation[14] because we are meant to attribute to the Judge a broadly Kantian commitment to a link between 'the ethical' in the first and second senses I distinguished above (i.e., (1) the idea that one is a morally responsible agent (such that accepting the ethical standpoint means accepting that one is responsible for what one does), and (2) the idea that one is autonomous or capable of autonomy in some sense). We are meant, that is, to attribute to the Judge a commitment to a version of the reciprocity thesis. The Judge believes, with the Kant of *Groundwork* III, that the negative concept of freedom as absence of determination by alien causes gives rise to a positive concept of freedom as self-determination, which in turn gives rise to a law which gives content to the moral life. This aspect of the view is not clearly spelled out, though, because Kierkegaard is relying on a broadly Kantian framework whose details it would have been redundant, in the context, to spell out. Of course, Kierkegaard himself did not endorse this move: in every later work the two notions of freedom are kept separate.

This characterization of the point at issue between *A* and the Judge calls into question what is surely the most popular reading of the position enunciated by Kierkegaard in *Either/Or* as a whole. This is the view according to which Kierkegaard puts before the reader two separate and self-standing ways of life— the aesthetic, characterized by enjoyment, and the ethical, characterized by duty—and asks the reader to choose between them. On this interpretation part of Kierkegaard's point in the work is to show that there are no grounds for choosing one way of life over the other. The choice is an arbitrary one, not informed by any set of values to which the chooser could appeal, but rather positing with it an entire set of values that then gives meaning and coherence to the life thus led. Not

---

[13] In this I agree with Davenport (2001), although I find his effort to cash out this point in terms of Frankfurt-style identification with one's desires and to read being an aesthete as an instance of being a wanton misguided. The Judge purports to be describing not only a single highly reflective individual with a clear set of second-order volitions (as Crop Rotation shows), but also variety of human types into one of which much of humanity falls. Frankfurt's distinction between wantons and persons, by contrast, is meant to cash out the distinction we seem to see between normal adults on the one hand ('persons') and *animals* (and perhaps very young children or the severely mentally damaged) on the other (non-'persons').

[14] Cf., e.g., *EE* II: 196; 3: 209: '[T]he either/or I erected between living esthetically and living ethically is not an unqualified dilemma, because it actually is a matter of only one choice. Through this choice, I actually do not choose between good and evil, but I choose the good, but when I choose the good, I choose *eo ipso* the choice between good and evil.'

only the form of the work, but also several comments made by the Judge himself are taken to support this reading. He does, for instance, place before *A* the choice of two types of life: 'either a person has to live aesthetically, or he has to live ethically' (*EE* II: 152; 3: 164)—and he does seem to sever this choice from any possible value judgement: 'Rather than designating the choice between good and evil, my either/or designates the choice by which one chooses good and evil or rules them out. Hence the question is under what qualifications one will view all existence and personally live' (*EE* II: 153; 3: 165).[15] The characterization I have given of the ethical as the embracing of choice and the aesthetic as denial of choice cannot be made to cohere with this reading, for the simple reason that no sense can be made of a choice *between* fundamental approaches to life, if one of those approaches is defined by the denial of the possibility of choice. The idea of a choice of the aesthetic life is, on the reading I have given, an incoherent one. The Judge is explicit that the commitment to one life or the other is not a matter of choice in the strictest sense. In fact, the presentation of the purported choice between two different sorts of life—'either a person has to live aesthetically, or he has to live ethically'—is followed immediately by just this condition:

Here . . . it is still not a matter of a choice in the stricter sense, for the person who lives aesthetically does not choose, and the person who chooses the aesthetic after the ethical has become manifest to him is not living aesthetically, for he is sinning and is subject to ethical qualifications, even if his life must be termed unethical. You see, this is, so to speak, the *character indelibilis* of the ethical, that the ethical, although it modestly places itself on the same level as the aesthetic, nevertheless is essentially that which makes the choice a choice. (*EE* II: 152–3; 3: 164–5)

The aesthetic and the ethical are not placed on an equal footing—just the opposite—and given this fact it is not at all clear why one should conclude that the reader is asked to choose between them with no grounds for a choice one way or the other.

Aesthetic despair in later works

My discussion so far has focused on *Either/Or*, but I think it is important to notice that the line of criticism of the aesthetic view here reconstructed is found again in later works—most prominently, directed against the character of the present age

---

[15] MacIntyre is the chief proponent of this reading, and has based upon it some equally popular criticisms of *Either/Or* (cf. 1966: 215–17, 1984: 40–1, 2001). One criticism points to the excessively abstract characterization of the chooser—'devoid of desires, goals, and needs prior to the presentation of the two cases'—that would be required by this view: 'But who is this "I" who chooses? And for such a being what can hang in any case upon choosing in one way rather than in another?' (MacIntyre 1966: 217). Another criticism, legitimate given this reading, is that the only life that can be thus led is the aesthetic life, for actually leading an ethical life requires a conviction that the values it embodies are the true ethical values—i.e., that these are precisely *not* based on the arbitrary choice of the individual bound by them (MacIntyre 1984: 42).

in *Two Ages*, and as a characterization of some forms of despair in *The Sickness unto Death*.

The target of Kierkegaard's attack in *Two Ages* is the member of 'the crowd' rather than the 'aesthete', but the discussion there echoes closely the Judge's characterization (especially at *EE* II: 154–9; 3: 166–71) of the pernicious influence of Hegelian philosophy on the contemporary sense of individual responsibility. The present age is characterized as one not of action but of passivity, where contemplation has taken the place of engagement. People transform themselves from participants in historic events to spectators of them, and consider this the highest prudence (*LA* VIII: 69; 8: 71); being a citizen has come to mean being an outsider, a spectator (*LA* VIII: 74; 8: 76). '[L]eveling has its profound importance in the ascendancy of the category "generation" over the category "individuality" ' (*LA* VIII: 79; 8: 81).[16]

There are stronger parallels in the work that presents the most detailed discussion of despair in all its forms, *The Sickness unto Death*—and in that work it is quite clear that what is at issue in despair is not at all the legitimacy of goals or conceptions of satisfaction of the despairing individual so much as the legitimacy of his conception of and attitude towards his agency. In *The Sickness unto Death*, Anti-Climacus describes an 'unconsciously' despairing individual (cf. *EE* II: 173; 3: 186) as one who is ignorant of the fact that he is a self to begin with, and as a sort of innocent: 'one could humanly be tempted almost to say that in a kind of innocence it does not even know that it is despair' (*SD* XI: 154–5). 'The self is bound up in immediacy with the other in desiring, craving, enjoying, etc., yet passively; in its craving, the self is a dative, like the 'me' of a child' (*SD* XI: 163). This state is that of having 'no conception of being spirit' (*SD* XI: 155), in which the self regards itself as 'an indefinable something' and, instead of seeing itself as an individual source of capacities and locus of responsibilities, 'vaguely rests in and merges in some abstract universality (state, nation, etc.)' (*SD* XI: 158). 'The appearance of such words as "self" and "despair" in the language of immediacy is due, if you will, to an innocent abuse of language, a playing with words, like the children's game of playing soldier' (*SD* XI: 163). The generality of Anti-Climacus's pronouncement upon this self is the same as that of the Judge: 'every such existence, whatever it achieves, be it most amazing, whatever it explains, be it the whole of existence, however intensely it enjoys life aesthetically—every such existence is nevertheless despair' (*SD* XI: 158). To the conscious despair of the

---

[16] Compare *LA* VIII: 63; 8: 65: 'It is not uncommon to hear a man who has become confused about what he should do in a particular situation complain about the unique nature of the situation, thinking that he could easily act if the situation were a great event with only one either/or. This is a mistake and a hallucination of the understanding. There is no such situation. The presence of the crucial either/or depends upon the individual's own impassioned desire directed toward acting decisively, upon the individual's own intrinsic competence, and therefore a competent man covets an either/or in every situation because he does not want anything more. But as soon as the individual no longer has essential enthusiasm in his passion but is spoiled by letting his understanding frustrate him every time he is going to act, he never in his life discovers the disjunction.'

immediate individual (cf. *EE* II: 174; 3: 186) corresponds the first form of Anti-Climacus's conscious despair, the sort brought about by some external blow. 'This form of despair is: in despair not to will to be oneself. Or even lower: in despair not to will to be a self. Or lowest of all: in despair to wish to be someone else, to wish for a new self' (*SD* XI: 165). Such despair is possible, Anti-Climacus claims, only if one is both in some sense aware of having a self and nevertheless views this self as an externality that can be changed, 'as easily as one changes clothes' (*SD* XI: 165). To the fatalism *A* expresses when he complains that his soul 'has lost possibility' (*EE* I: 25; 2: 50) likewise corresponds a discussion to the same effect in *The Sickness unto Death*: 'To lack possibility means either that everything has become necessary for a person or that everything has become trivial. The determinist, the fatalist is in despair, and as one in despair has lost his self, because for him everything has become necessity' (*SD* XI: 152). The determinist 'cannot breathe, for it is impossible to breathe necessity exclusively, because that would utterly suffocate a person's self' (*SD* XI: 153). The relevant idea in these, as in all the instances of despair described in *The Sickness unto Death*, is that the person in despair has the wrong conception of himself as agent.

It is because one's conception of oneself is always in some sense voluntary that despair can be described as not *willing* to be a self at all, or not willing to be the self that one is—willing to be more or less than one is as a self. Despair is described as in the first instance an act, not a psychological state. This is the import of the insistence that despair is always a sickness one has brought on oneself, that 'every moment [one] is in despair he *is bringing* it upon himself' (*SD* XI: 130). There is indeed a characteristic psychological state that is associated with despair, but the problem to which the book is addressed is not that of getting out of this state, but rather that of freeing oneself from the false self-conception that gives rise to it.

Despair in the most general sense will turn out to be the unwillingness to accept human agency with all of its particular conditions. There are many ways to do this, and each will be accompanied by a corresponding distortion—a failure of fit. Such a failure becomes visible when, inevitably, one contemplates the future from the agent-perspective—when one tries to exist in the false self-conception. The aesthetic point of view fails the existing-in test in a very fundamental way, because its reflective form is partially constituted by the denial that it makes any sense to contemplate the future from the agent-perspective. Its commitments lead to puzzlement about the possibility of such a perspective. (This is its link to idealist metaphysics, which fails the test for similar reasons.) But Kierkegaard will argue through the pseudonyms that the ethical standpoint fails the existing-in test as well, that it also involves a false and self-defeating conception of agency.

Before I move on to a discussion of that set of arguments, I would like to point out that 'the ethical' in the first of the senses distinguished above—the commitment to the acceptance of moral responsibility—is also a part of both forms of religiousness (A and B). It is this sense of the ethical to which Kierkegaard refers when he says that the ethical and the religious lie 'so close that they continually communicate with each other' (*AE* VII: 134; 7: 150), that the ethical or subjective standpoint 'culminates in immortality, without which the ethical is merely custom and habit' (*AE* VII: 145; 7: 162), in concern for an eternal happiness (*AE* VII: 105; 7: 122), and in the conviction that the issue of an eternal happiness or unhappiness is decided in time (*AE* VII: 74–6; 7: 92–5). That something of infinite importance is at stake is simply the most emphatic expression of the conviction that it matters what one does—that is, that one is a *locus* of moral responsibility. Despite what Kierkegaard himself often says about a tripartite division of stages of existence, there is good reason to think that the most basic division is actually that between views of life that embrace passivity and those that embrace the possibility of action.[17]

Of course there are important differences within this range of views that fall on the ethical side of the aesthetic/ethical divide. These differences concern not only the content of ethical norms but also what the source of conduct-guiding norms is taken to be and how the agent's epistemic access to them is understood. In the ethical view in the second sense distinguished above (the ethics of autonomy), the source is some aspect of the will of the agent himself. In the religious views, the source of norms is God. The two types of religiousness (A and B) differ on how those norms come to be known. In religiousness A, they are known through reason; in religiousness B, they are known through revelation. The deep differences amongst these various views suggest that the criticisms of the first two (the ethics of autonomy and religiousness A) that Kierkegaard offers in the pseudonymous works must be quite distinct. In the next section I will argue that the opposite is the case—and that in fact the criticisms all fall out of the same set of commitments about the nature of agency that informed the criticism of the aesthetic view of life in *Either/Or* II.

II. THE ETHICAL VIEW, RELIGIOUSNESS A, AND THE SECOND INCOMPATIBILISM

Many of Kierkegaard's post-*Either/Or* pseudonyms express criticism of a position that looks like the very position the Judge advocates in *Either/Or* II. This position is called the 'universal ethical' in *Fear and Trembling*, the 'first ethics' in *The Concept of Anxiety*, and the 'immanent ethical' in *Concluding Unscientific Postscript*. I will argue here that the target is the ethics of autonomy, and that the criticism of the ethical standpoint presented in these works is continuous with that of the aesthetic standpoint: it involves a misrepresentation of the nature of agency in the form of a denial of freedom—not of choice in general but of choice

---

[17] Hiroshi Fujino (1994) has also argued that the contemplative orientation of 'the philosophers' should be construed as an 'aesthetic' view, and that the basic division between orientations is dual rather than tripartite.

of good and evil in particular. Again, this is not the most obvious interpretation, and so again I will begin by considering two fairly prominent alternative readings and showing why they are unacceptable. These readings seem to be suggested by Kierkegaard's two earliest statements of the view that there is a higher standpoint than the 'immanent' or 'universal' ethical one, in *Fear and Trembling* and in the introduction to *The Concept of Anxiety*.

Suspension of the ethical in *Fear and Trembling*

A natural reading of *Fear and Trembling*, and one to which many newcomers to the text are drawn, is one on which it is intended to provide an argument, aimed at the inhabitant of the ethical standpoint, to the conclusion that something is fundamentally amiss with that standpoint and that it therefore needs to be 'teleologically suspended' in favour of a religious one.[18] How would such an argument go? The text presents us with a dilemma which might serve as a first premiss: either we give up on Abraham as a paradigm of righteousness or we admit that the ethical standpoint (construed either as the ethics of custom and social duty, or the ethics of universal moral principles) can or must be abandoned in favour of some higher, religious standpoint. This is the way Johannes *de silentio* puts it: either the story of Abraham contains a teleological suspension of the ethical, or Abraham is an ordinary murderer (*FB* III: 115–16; 4: 159); 'either . . . the single individual as the single individual stands in an absolute relation to the absolute, or Abraham is lost' (*FB* III: 165; 4: 207). Now, in order to get from this dilemma to the conclusion that there really is some limitation to the ethical standpoint, we need a further premiss stating that Abraham *is* a paradigm of right-eousness. That looks hard to establish. (In fact, given that the possibility of any *ethical* justification of Abraham is ruled out, it looks trivially impossible to establish to the satisfaction of any inhabitant of the ethical standpoint.) But if it cannot be somehow established, the argument (on this construal) can have no addressee. The text presents us with two possibilities for establishing the second premiss: an appeal to the authority of scriptural revelation, or an appeal to some generalizable features of Abraham's case that we have non-scriptural grounds for finding compelling. On the first, it is the justification of the biblical Abraham we refuse to give up. On the second, we think Abraham serves to define a class any member of which we would find justified, but not *ethically* justified, even in the absence of a direct scriptural endorsement. Unfortunately, though, there is no way to make either argumentative strategy work consistent with the material available in the text.

The first strategy is question-begging. On it, the force of the argument relies on acceptance of a premiss which all on its own entails (and is in fact much stronger

---

[18] Kierkegaard commentators have long opposed this reading; the argument that follows is not aimed primarily at them.

than) the argument's conclusion. Anyone who accepts the authority of Scripture and its description of Abraham's situation has already accepted a religious standpoint. This is because an essential aspect of the story—and an essential presupposition of this strategy of argument—is that Abraham was in fact a knight of faith and was in fact justified in the eyes of God. But no such thing can be evident from the biblical account viewed as a piece of (mere) history.

This is why Kant felt compelled to reject the Abraham story. In *The Conflict of the Faculties*, Kant argued that apparent direct manifestations of the will of God can never be action guiding, because they either tell us to do something in conformity with the moral law (in which case they are redundant, because we are allowed to do whatever is in conformity with the moral law on our own authority anyway), or they tell us to do something in contravention of the moral law (in which case we are obliged to ignore them, because our certainty of the dictates of morality is total, whereas our certainty that something is a divine command can never be).

For if God should really speak to a human being, the latter could still never know that it was God speaking. It is quite impossible for a human being to apprehend the infinite by his senses, distinguish it from sensible beings, and be acquainted with it as such.—But in some cases the human being can be sure that the voice he hears is not God's; for if the voice commands him to do something contrary to the moral law, then no matter how majestic the apparition may be, and no matter how it may seem to surpass the whole of nature, he must consider it an illusion. (7: 63)

In the footnote, Kant cites the 'myth' of Abraham as something we have to reject once we have grasped this point. 'Abraham should have replied to this supposedly divine voice: "That I ought not to kill my son is quite certain. But that you, this apparition, are God—of that I am not certain, and never can be, not even if this voice rings down to me from (visible) heaven"' (7: 63n). Abraham should have taken the content of the command ('sacrifice Isaac') to constitute positive proof that the source of the command was not God. The same point is made in *Religion within the Boundaries of Mere Reason* in the context of a discussion of miracles (at *R* 6: 87); again the reference to Abraham is explicit. Kierkegaard shows us, in taking care to insist that Abraham is certain of the ethical impermissibility of what he is about to do[19] and that he has no means of verifying that the source of the command is God,[20] that he is well aware of Kant's position.

[19] Kierkegaard describes Abraham as, in ethical terms, 'a murderer' at *FB* III: 82, 105, 107, 116, 123; 4: 126, 149, 150, 159, 166. 'In ethical terms, Abraham's relation to Isaac is quite simply this: the father shall love the son more than himself' (*FB* III: 107; 4: 151)—but, 'In the moment he is about to sacrifice Isaac, the ethical expression for what he is doing is: he hates Isaac' (*FB* III: 122; 4: 165).

[20] Cf. *FB* III: 126f.; 4: 169f.: 'The tragic hero is soon finished . . . . The knight of faith, however, is kept in a state of sleeplessness, for he is constantly being tested, and at every moment there is the possibility of his returning penitently to the universal, and this possibility may be a spiritual trial as well as the truth. He cannot get any information on that from any man' and *FB* III: 112f.; 4: 155f.: 'How does the single individual reassure himself that he is legitimate?'

More importantly, Kierkegaard himself accepts that there is no way to understand Abraham's exemplariness solely on the basis of the historical account. While the actions of the knight of faith are visible, his *being* a knight of faith (rather than a lunatic) is not. This means that even having an example of the sort Abraham is supposed to provide requires prior acceptance of a religious view. This may be why Climacus (in *Concluding Unscientific Postscript*) calls *Fear and Trembling's* portrayal of the knight of faith 'only a rash anticipation' and says that 'the beginning was made by ignoring the contradiction—how an observer could become at all *aware* of him in such a way that he could place himself, admiring, outside and admire that there is nothing, nothing whatever, to *notice*' (*AE* VII: 435n; 7: 453n). It is also why *de silentio* has to imaginatively construct a knight of faith in the Preamble instead of finding one he can observe (see *FB* III: 89ff.; 4: 133ff.). His description of the imagined one makes it obvious that even if he had a knight of faith as a next-door neighbour, he could never know it. If the knight of faith is, *qua* knight of faith, invisible, then there can be no way of seeing such a one in any actual example. Climacus concludes from this that the portrayal of a knight of faith in *Fear and Trembling* must be a 'poetic construction'—because only the author's omniscient point of view could bring together both the presupposition that the individual is a knight of faith and the absence of any sign at all that this is the case.

Can a mere poetic construction go any way towards establishing the second premiss of our argument? Perhaps it can. This, at any rate, is how the second strategy would proceed. Abraham would be taken to define a class of cases which cannot be accommodated within the ethical standpoint at issue but which we must nevertheless admit to be justified (in some non-ethical sense). The argument on this reading has a potentially broader audience; it also embodies a quite different complaint: that the ethical point of view does not leave room for a sort of case for which, for some reason or other, we think it ought to leave room. Now, instead of supplying the case, we need to supply (in addition to the dilemma) some general reason for wanting to accommodate cases relevantly similar to Abraham's.

Here, again, there are different possibilities.[21] One is to cite Abraham's depth of commitment and his strength of character as good-making features invisible from the perspective of a morality of *Sitten*, or a morality of universal laws. It encounters the difficulty of sufficiently distinguishing Abraham's depth of commitment or strength of character from that of *de silentio's* contrast cases of Agamemnon, Jephthah and Brutus. A second variant sees Abraham's case as an illustration of the need for personalized duties—duties not following from universal practical principles coupled with non-moral facts about the world and

---

[21] I will cite specific readings below, but two good recent overviews of such efforts to read *Fear and Trembling* as an argument on behalf of a higher standpoint than that of ethics can be found in Lippitt (2003: chapters 4 and 6), and in Green (1998: section III). The characterization I give here is far from exhaustive.

our situation.[22] But the cases about which it is most plausible to say that there is some *ethical* need for individualized duties are those in which we need to adjudicate multiple competing moral demands. Yet Abraham's is a case where a perfect duty (to refrain from murdering his son) encounters no competition *except* from the alleged divine command. The command is the source of the ethical problem, not a solution to any ethical problem Abraham had already. Finally, we are familiar with arguments—made by both atheists and theists—to the effect that no sense can be made of ethics on any but theological voluntarist terms.[23] As I will claim, Kierkegaard makes such an argument *himself* in other pseudonymous works. But there is no trace of such an argument in *Fear and Trembling*—unless, that is, we take the appeal to the example of the biblical Abraham as a premiss in it.[24] Further, this strategy of assimilating the ethical to that which is commanded by God suggests the answer to the question posed by the second Problema ('Is there a teleological suspension of the ethical?') must be 'no'—Abraham's action *is* ethical, on the correct understanding of ethics.[25] It therefore conflicts with *de silentio*'s repeated insistence that there are *no* ethical considerations to which Abraham can appeal (that his conduct is absolutely unethical).[26]

What if one took the complaint to be that the ethical standpoint as described is committed to a substantive point of metaphysics—namely, the non-existence of a God who could (or would) step into human experience and overwrite the ethical—and lacks the resources to justify such a strong metaphysical commitment? Kant's doctrine of God as practical postulate and Hegel's doctrine of the divinity of ethical life both look like live options for the target of such a criticism. But although criticisms of the practical postulate view had been expressed countless times in the writings of Kant's critics, the idea that ethics might be overstepping its bounds in purporting to answer metaphysical questions does not appear in *Fear and Trembling*. Likewise, although Problema II does begin with a reference to Hegel's pantheism and his view of ethical life as the objective expression of *Geist*, and although arguments against Hegelian metaphysics on both metaphysical grounds and ethical grounds are found *elsewhere* in the pseudonymous works,[27] *Fear and Trembling* contains none of these. Instead, Johannes proceeds to point out

---

[22] Adams (1987) takes this idea—that the individual is in danger of being 'morally fragmented, crushed or immobilized' in cases in which general ethical principles plus non-normative facts about my situation fail 'to write my name legibly on any particular task'—as a major concern of Kierkegaard's and a major impetus behind his endorsement of religious as opposed to philosophical ethics. Adams admits, though, that the major instances of overriding religious duties Kierkegaard discusses (Abraham's case, but also the cases of the estranged fiancés) are ones in which 'universalist' ethics has indeed written the individual's name perfectly legibly on the task at issue (to care for one's own son, to keep one's own promises of marriage) and it is the religious that excuses the individual from what would otherwise quite unambiguously be required of him.

[23] The most often cited today are due to Anscombe (1958) and Mackie (1977). Cf. also Mavrodes (1986).

[24] Even if we do that, as Green argues (1998: 267ff.), other necessary theological premisses are lacking.

[25] Donnelly (1981); Evans (1981).   [26] Cf. Green (1998: 264ff.).

[27] I mentioned one such in the discussion of *Either/Or* II above; others will be mentioned in the discussion of *Concluding Unscientific Postscript* in chapter 6.

that 'If this train of thought is sound, if there is nothing incommensurable in a human life . . . then Hegel was right. But he was not right in speaking about faith or permitting Abraham to be regarded as its father' (*FB* III: 117; 4: 160). Instead of the expected criticism, we find only an appeal to Abraham.

It seems to me mistaken to read *Fear and Trembling* as aimed at articulating the shortcomings of the ethical standpoint in a way convincing to an inhabitant of that standpoint. Instead, we should read it as aimed primarily at articulating the constraints imposed by a life of faith, and so presupposing, rather than arguing for, a religious standpoint. A description of faith and the life of faith will include an account of the place in that life of the ethical demands of citizenship and family as well as whatever demands arise out of practical rationality in general. But that the claims of citizenship, family and perhaps practical rationality itself have a scope that is limited by the claims of religious faith, if these turn out to be in conflict, is not argued for but presupposed in *Fear and Trembling*; likewise, that the ethical standpoint is subordinate to the religious figures among the book's presuppositions, not the points it aims to establish. But that sends us back to the drawing board, so far as the *criticism* of the ethical standpoint goes.

Ethical ideality and finitude in *The Concept of Anxiety* and *Concluding Unscientific Postscript*

The second interpretation of the criticism of the ethical point of view that I would like to discuss begins from a natural reading of the introduction to *The Concept of Anxiety*. What Kierkegaard seems to be saying at various points in that introduction is that the ethical standpoint is inadequate because it is defined by a commitment to living up to a set of standards that are in fact impossible to live up to. The central claim of the introduction, that the 'first' ethics (philosophical as opposed to religious ethics) is 'shipwrecked' on sin, looks like a claim to the effect that the necessity or universality of sin undermines the validity of the ethical standpoint. This reading is supported by passages like the following: 'Ethics proposes to bring ideality into actuality. On the other hand, it is not the nature of its movement to raise actuality up into ideality. Ethics points to ideality as a task and assumes that every man possesses the requisite conditions. Thus ethics develops a contradiction, inasmuch as it makes clear both the difficulty and the impossibility' (*BA* IV: 288; 4: 323–4). If the 'requisite conditions' are conditions for success in the ethical project, then failure to possess them entails the inevitability of failing at that project. This seems to be the point of various other comments made in this discussion, for instance: 'all ancient ethics was based on the presupposition that virtue can be realized' (*BA* IV: 292; 4: 326)—the suggestion being that this presupposition is false, and that its falsehood undermines the project.[28]

---

[28] These passages in the introduction echo comments in Problema III of *Fear and Trembling* (also on the topic of sin): 'In sin, the single individual is already higher (in the direction of the demonic paradox) than the universal, because it is a contradiction on the part of the universal to want to

Since we are given no sufficiently concrete specification, either in the introduction or in the main text of *The Concept of Anxiety*, of what this impossibility might consist in, the temptation is to look elsewhere in the pseudonyms. The Judge makes several references to the unavoidability of guilt on his view of the ethical; in fact he claims that choice of the ethical is always a choice of oneself as *already* guilty.[29] In choosing the ethical the individual 'discovers that the self he chooses . . . has a history . . . and this history contains painful things, and yet he is the person he is only through this history' (*EE* II: 193; 3: 207). The ethical task is to appropriate one's history with its (newly recognized) guilt, and 'the expression for this struggle, this acquiring is—repentance' (*EE* II: 194; 3: 207). The Judge motivates this claim by appeal to the idea that what is involved in the ethical must be self-choice rather than self-creation: 'only when I choose myself as guilty do I absolutely choose myself, if I am to choose myself absolutely in such a way that it is not identical with creating myself' (*EE* II: 194; 3: 208). The idea seems to be that the self one takes responsibility for must be the concrete self one is, which comes attached to a set of physical and emotional capacities and proclivities, a social role and its commitments, and also a history. That one never starts any life project from a blank slate is a point that is reiterated elsewhere (e.g., in the main text of *The Concept of Anxiety*; see below). One is supposed to take all this on not for the purpose of leaving it be, but for the purpose of transforming it into something one makes of oneself. Repentance is part of that transformation: '[A] person can choose himself according to his freedom only when he chooses himself ethically, but he can choose himself ethically only by repenting himself, and only by repenting himself does he become concrete, and only as a concrete individual is he a free individual' (*EE* II: 222; 3: 236); '[I]f I cannot repent of the past, then freedom is a dream' (*EE* II: 215; 3: 228).

But guilt arising from one's past is not the only guilt that is necessary, according to the Judge—at least not if we take at face value the message of the Ultimatum. To this third letter to *A* the Judge appends a sermon written by a friend, saying of it that 'In this sermon he has grasped what I have said and what I would have liked to have said to you; he has expressed it better than I am able to' (*EE* II: 304; 3: 318). The topic of the sermon is 'the upbuilding that lies in the thought that before God we are always in the wrong'. The sermon takes the correctness of the thought as a given and examines it only from the standpoint of its potential for

demand itself from a person who lacks the *conditio sine qua non* . . . . An ethics that ignores sin is a completely futile discipline, but if it affirms sin, then it has *eo ipso* exceeded itself' (*FB* III: 146; 4: 188). This claim seems to be that everyone is 'excepted' from the ethical because no one is capable of living up to its demands. This has nothing to do with Abraham, *de silentio* points out: 'As long as I move around in these spheres, everything is easy, but nothing of what has been said here explains Abraham, for Abraham did not become the single individual by way of sin—on the contrary, he was a righteous man, God's chosen one' (*FB* III: 146; 4: 188).

[29] Of course, *he* does not take this as any reason for thinking the ethical standpoint as he presents it uninhabitable—but if there is some shortcoming with that standpoint, it will of necessity be one the Judge overlooks.

edification. For clarification of the thought that one might *always* be guilty, in everything one does, one is tempted once again to turn elsewhere—this time to the long meditation on the existential pathos of guilt in *Concluding Unscientific Postscript*. The point there looks similar, but the discussion is more substantive, presenting at least five reasons to think that guilt is inevitable.

First, no matter when in life we take up the ethical task (and we presumably do not take it up at birth), we have always already done something or other that is ethically prohibited, or failed to do something that is ethically enjoined. In other words, the ethical situation of a human being is always one that contains a past for which he must hold himself responsible despite the fact that it is (now) out of his control. This is simply a reiteration of the Judge's point about repentance. Second, ethical action requires ancillary time expenditures—for deliberation, preparation, some degree of ineliminable inefficiency—which means that there will always be wasted moments (and we are responsible for wasted moments):

> *In abstracto* and on paper, it goes more easily. There one sets forth the task, has the individual be an abstract something that in every way is 'at your service' just as soon as the task is set forth—and then one is finished.
>
> In existence, the individual is a concretion, and time is concrete, and even while the individual deliberates he is ethically responsible for the use of time. Existence is not an abstract rush job but a striving and an unremitting 'in the meantime.' Even at the moment the task is assigned, something is already wasted, because there is an 'in the meantime' and the beginning is not promptly made. (*AE* VII: 459; 7: 478)

We can infer from the nature of this objection that we should take the ethical task to be both urgent and such that it cannot easily be accomplished in the time we have at our disposal. Our finitude, in other words, entails some degree of ethical failure. Third, there is the further problem that acting ethically means transforming the ethical ideal into some concrete set of actions in some concrete set of circumstances, but every expression of the ideal in the concrete is at best an approximation. Most charitably read, this objection states that the fact that we must exercise error-prone determinative judgement in every effort to put an ideal into practice entails inevitable failures.

One would think that these problems are given a sufficient reply with the observation that if all this is the case, then all that can be required of one ethically is that one do one's best. But here a fourth problem enters—that of the impossibility of ever being sure that one *has* done one's best: 'Where, then, is the boundary for the single individual in his concrete existence between what is lack of will and what is lack of ability; what is indolence and earthly selfishness and what is the limitation of finitude? . . . Let all the dialecticians convene—they will not be able to decide this for a particular individual *in concreto*' (*AE* VII: 426; 7: 444). Every translation of duty into action requires a prior judgement as to what we are capable of, and judgements of what we are capable of can be difficult, and are generally impossible to be entirely certain of. The author of the sermon in *Either/Or*'s Ultimatum makes a similar point. A 'wisdom frequently heard' is that

'One does what one can and if one is ever somewhat negligent, God will never forget that we are weak and imperfect creatures.' The author's response to this 'easy, cozy conclusion':

One does what one can? Was it such an easy matter for you, my listener, to determine how much that is: what one can? Were you never in such danger that you almost desperately exerted yourself and yet so infinitely wished to be able to do more, and perhaps someone looked at you with a skeptical and imploring look, whether it was not possible that you could do more? . . . I ask you: Did you find rest in those words, 'one does what one can'? (*EE* II: 310–11; 3: 324–5)

Climacus spends some time on a closely related, fifth problem in the extended discussion of the amusement park at *AE* VII: 430ff.; 7: 448ff. A certain amount of diversion, forgetfulness, relaxation (an occasional trip to the amusement park, in other words) is required if an individual is not to be psychologically crushed under the burden of such overwhelming demands. But since it is impossible to know with certainty how much and when it is necessary (this week? next?), even this diversion ends up adding to the burden of guilt already present (*AE* VII: 468; 7: 487–8). These final two problems have more apparent force. Some consequentialists seem to have the second problem, and even Kantians have the first (though Kant himself did not give it the attention it deserves).

The basic idea behind this interpretation, if it is to explain why the ethical standpoint must be abandoned in favour of a religious one, must be that the religious life offers a solution to these problems. What is that solution supposed to be? There are two alternatives (or, perhaps, two components): forgiveness and grace. For the significance of both one can point to suggestive passages.

As for the first, in the introduction to *The Concept of Anxiety*, we read that 'What is said of the law is also true of ethics: it is a disciplinarian that demands, and by its demands only judges but does not bring forth life' (*BA* IV: 288; 4: 324). One might extrapolate from this comment to something like the position Arendt takes on forgiveness in *The Human Condition*:[30] action is impossible without forgiveness, for guilt is the sort of thing that, in the absence of the possibility of absolution, leads one to despair of the ethical project. The burden of guilt becomes debilitating, ultimately leading the individual to a sort of moral paralysis. But ethics itself provides no grounds for forgiveness, only for judgement. So ethical action requires something the ethical standpoint cannot provide. This looks like a contradiction within the ethical standpoint, one that points towards the religious standpoint as a solution.

As for the second, later in *The Concept of Anxiety* we find remarks to the effect that both guilt (*BA* IV: 377; 4: 410) and sin (*BA* IV: 384; 4: 418) are states of 'unfreedom' and that it is impossible of one's own power to extract oneself from this unfreedom (*BA* IV: 387; 4: 420–1). From these it is easy to infer that what the religious individual expects is to be lifted out of this state of unfreedom by divine

---

[30] Arendt (1989: 236–43).

grace—lifted out of a condition in which he cannot even though he ought, and placed into a new condition in which he can after all. Ethical action ultimately requires divine assistance; the taking up of some religious world view is motivated by the recognition of one's own ethical impotence.[31]

I have three objections to this as an interpretation of the criticism of the ethical standpoint offered by the pseudonyms. The first is that it is too weak to play its appointed role.[32] The natural—and perfectly adequate—response to it is to point out that one has an ethical duty precisely not to allow oneself to become ethically paralysed in the ways described. If one cannot (and it is plausible to think one cannot) of one's own power completely cancel all of one's past guilt, the only *ethical* option is simply to put the past behind one and start afresh. This seems to be Kant's point when he insists on the forward-lookingness of the ethical standpoint (even while embracing the inevitability of moral shortcomings) in *Religion within the Boundaries of Mere Reason*: the most that we can expect from ourselves is 'constant *progress* from bad to better' (*R* 6: 48). Where future guilt seems inevitable, the appropriate response is to insist on the principle of 'ought implies can' and the certainty of conscience's deliverances—again, as Kant does, who remarks in the same discussion that the ethical individual is obliged at least 'to *hope* that, by the exertion of *his own* power, he will attain to the road that leads in this direction [namely, of moral goodness] . . . . For he ought to become a good human being yet cannot be judged *morally* good except on the basis of what can be imputed to him as done by him' (*R* 6: 50). Kant has harsh words, in the same discussion, for the sort of religiousness that sees religion as the way out of the difficulty of the apparent necessity of guilt:

Against this expectation of self-improvement, reason, which by nature finds moral labor vexing, now conjures up, under the pretext of natural impotence, all sorts of impure religious ideas. . . . All religions, however, can be divided into *religion of rogation* (of mere cult) and *moral religion*, i.e. the religion of *good life-conduct*. According to the first, the human being either flatters himself that God can make him eternally

---

[31] For an example of such a reading, one that takes its clue from the discussion in the introduction to *The Concept of Anxiety*, cf. Hannay (1982: 173–4): 'Human imperfection must be a matter of individual responsibility. But again, if the state of perfection cannot even be envisaged, no amount of personal effort can ever guarantee it. The doctrines of salvation and grace correspond formally to a denial of the assumption that human faculty is sufficient to achieve the harmonious reconciliation of particular and infinite in the individual person.' Some commentators (e.g., Whittaker 1988) also read this need for belief in divine forgiveness and a reward not proportional to dessert as the real point of the discussion of the suspension of the ethical in *Fear and Trembling*. I noted in footnote 28 the allusion to sin as evidence of a suspension of the ethical near the end of the third Problema.

[32] Fahrenbach, like Hannay, takes the view that the demise of the ethical is supposed to be the inevitability of guilt—which in Christianity is then explained as the hereditariness of sin, and resolved through divine absolution (1968: 138–53). He goes on to argue that the criticism is a weak one (1968: 168n). I agree that the criticism is weak (and share his reasons for thinking that), but disagree with him in seeing a different, stronger criticism than this one presented in the pseudonymous works. Cf. also Fahrenbach (1979).

happy (through the remission of his debts) without any necessity on his part *to become a better human being*; or else, if this does not seem possible to him, that *God* himself *can make him a better human being* without his having to contribute more than to ask for it. (*R* 6: 51)

Insisting on this line of criticism would put Kierkegaard on the side of the religiousness Kant here criticizes. But—and this is the second objection to the interpretation—that seems profoundly unfair.

For, regardless of what one thinks of the purported criticisms, the purported *solution* has very little to do with anything Kierkegaard has to say about what the Christian life involves. Of course, Kierkegaard does embrace a religious view wherein forgiveness and grace figure ineliminably. But both figure in the wrong sort of way.

First, forgiveness is not portrayed in those works as eliminating past guilt in the sense of making it something that ceases to weigh on one psychologically. Although the religious view makes possible an interpretation of one's past and one's limitations as a task set by God that one is to take up in action, it does not in so doing lift the *burden* of the facticity of agency—at least not according to the description in the main text of *The Concept of Anxiety*: 'Christianity has never assented to giving each particular individual the privilege of starting from the beginning in an external sense. Each individual begins in an historical nexus, and the consequences of nature still hold true. The difference is that Christianity teaches him to lift himself above this "more," and judges the one who does not to be unwilling' (*BA* IV: 342; 4: 376–7). Note here that the 'lifting' is described as the action of the individual rather than of God. Whatever one's past guilt, one is both able and obliged to approach the future as an opportunity to cancel guilt in repentance.

Second, divine grace does not make ethical demands any easier to fulfil on the view presented in the pseudonyms. In fact, Kierkegaard never tires of repeating that being a Christian is infinitely more difficult than being a non-Christian. (This is presumably why the various forms of despair are such tempting alternatives.) And the idea that becoming a Christian lifts some sort of psychological burden imposed by the ethical standpoint is profoundly at odds with the direction of the discussion of existential pathos in *Concluding Unscientific Postscript*. There the progression through the various perspectives to the standpoint of religiousness B (i.e., Christianity) is described as the taking on of ever-*greater* psychological strain—so much so that one is tempted to doubt that there ever has been anyone who was a Christian in the sense described (a doubt that Kierkegaard certainly intended to elicit in his readers). In the discussion of the unanswerable questions about the limitations of finitude and the need for diversion (the amusement park discussion), Climacus cites the mantra 'that a human being is capable of nothing at all, and that we should always keep this in mind' as a doctrine that is *mis*interpreted if it is taken as a reassurance—as he thinks it typically is in the contemporary, *ir*religious, age (*AE* VII: 400–35 *passim*; 7: 417–53 *passim*).[33]

That is the second objection; the third requires a brief detour to explain.

Religiousness A and religiousness B; guilt and sin

The *Postscript* discussion I have just employed in the reconstruction of this interpretation of the criticism of the ethical standpoint does not actually purport to be a description of ethics; instead, the standpoint described there is that of religiousness A. It has been thought appropriate to invoke it in part because it seems to correspond in content to the Ultimatum in *Either/Or*, and the Judge's assertion that the sermon expresses better than the first two letters what he really wanted to say suggests that the ethical standpoint stands in some very close relation with the standpoint of religiousness A. I doubt that relation should be construed as one of identity, but perhaps (among other things) religiousness A is supposed to draw out and make explicit something implicit in the ethical standpoint. Before offering a view of the relation, let me say what I take the moral psychological aspect of the standpoint of religiousness A to be. (I will have more to say about the metaphysics and epistemology of religiousness A in the next chapter.)

The standpoint of religiousness A is described in *Postscript* as based on the idea that 'the individual is capable of doing nothing himself but is nothing before God . . . and self-annihilation is the essential form for the relationship with God' (*AE* VII: 401; 7: 418–19). This view is characterized by a consciousness of necessary guilt, what Kierkegaard calls the 'immanent expression' of the 'terribleness' of the religious: one cannot, of one's own power, make the finite commensurate with the absolute. The religious views grouped under this category share an idea of the good as union with God as a philosophically conceived absolute.[34] They also hold that human beings, as finite creatures, are incapable of attaining to this good. The ideal of religiousness A, the task it sets for the individual, is to overcome those aspects of his being in which finitude consists: not only finite desires and attachment to the world (the task of 'dying to immediacy'), but also existence as a particular individual, and indeed the will itself in so far as it is the

---

[33] A major component of Kierkegaard's late 'attack on Christendom' was his claim that the Church had made Christianity too easy, had eliminated the suffering it involved. An early journal entry whose topic is 'the humorous in Christianity' puts this well: 'The humorous in Christianity shows itself also in the sentence, "my yoke is easy and my burden light"; because it is certainly most heavy indeed, for the world the heaviest that can be thought—self-denial'—Kierkegaard (1909–78: II A 78; 1997–, vol. 17: 216, DD: 6). I will have more to say about the nature of the ethical difficulty of being a Christian in the discussion that follows.

[34] Cf. *AE* VII: 497; 7: 519: Religiousness A 'is not speculation, but it is speculative'. It is not entirely clear which views Kierkegaard means to include under this rubric. Neoplatonic views seem particularly appropriately grouped under this category, but some contemporary approaches—including Schelling's in the 1804 *System*—share features with what Kierkegaard describes. It is often said that religiousness A describes Hegel's view, but I find that a difficult claim to make sense of.

particular will of a particular individual. This is the meaning of the imperative of self-annihilation. In the stage of religiousness A, the individual sets himself aside in order to find God (*AE* VII: 489; 7: 509). What is demanded is a strenuous effort to overcome one's individuality.

Now, since individual agency is among those characteristics of finite existence that one is supposed to attempt to overcome, it is clear that any such effort is doomed to failure. Existence is a trial, but it is the sort of trial that can have only one outcome. The existential pathos of religiousness A is therefore necessary guilt. It is possible to approach, if not to attain, the ideal set up by religiousness A—but not by trying. Rather, the suffering that characterizes existence under the imperative of fulfilling an unfulfilable task brings about a transformation of the individual's existence. 'Religiousness A makes existence as strenuous as possible (outside the sphere of the paradoxically-religious); yet it does not base the relation to an eternal happiness on one's existing but has the relation to an eternal happiness as the basis for the transformation of existence' (*AE* VII: 500; 7: 522). The significance of individual existence is seen not as action, determining the individual's relation to God, but rather as suffering, determined by the relation of the finite to the absolute. 'The "how" of the individual's existence is the result of the relation to the eternal, not the converse, and that is why infinitely more comes out than was put in' (*AE* VII: 500; 7: 522). Infinitely more comes out than was put in, because religiousness A posits a reward for the trial of existence—an eternal happiness—but because the trial cannot be passed it likewise cannot be failed in any sense that entails blame. Religiousness A 'is oriented toward the purely human in such a way that it must be assumed that every human being, viewed essentially, participates in this eternal happiness and finally becomes eternally happy' (*AE* VII: 507; 7: 529). By making guilt a necessary correlate of finite existence, religiousness A removes the burden of responsibility from the individual and transfers it on to a larger order of things. For the individual at the stage of religiousness A, therefore, nothing is really at stake.

One main point of difference between religiousness A and religiousness B seems to be precisely the issue of whether something like guilt can be necessary.[35] This is an easy fact to overlook, obscured by the very peculiar way in which Kierkegaard uses the terms 'sin' and 'guilt'. In ordinary usage 'guilt' is something that is present only if the individual in question freely did (or omitted) something morally reprehensible (or morally required). One cannot ordinarily be guilty for something one did not do, or did not intend or could not have avoided. On the other hand, it is the prevailing view in Christian dogmatics that *sin* is present even in individuals who, morally speaking, have as yet done nothing wrong. This is what it means to say there is 'hereditary' sin: that sin is a sort of necessary guilt. So one would expect Kierkegaard to use the term 'guilt' rather than 'sin' when talking

---

[35] Of course the most central point is that religiousness B, but not religiousness A, involves belief in the incarnation. I examine the relation between these two characteristics of religiousness B in chapter 6.

about responsibility for moral evil in an ordinary sense; and when he discusses 'sin' one would expect the topic to be something like necessary guilt. But just the opposite is the case. It is the hereditary aspect of sin that is denied in *The Concept of Anxiety*. Yet often (though not universally—cf., e.g., *BA* IV: 307; 4: 342) the term 'guilt' is used to refer to a state that an individual can be in of necessity. In *Postscript* the notion of 'essential guilt' is explicitly distinguished from the notion of sin (at *AE* VII: 464; 7: 483)—on the grounds that sin, unlike guilt, is always particular and never essential.[36]

The Concept of Anxiety is a work that deals with the Christian concept of sin from a psychological perspective, and the view that sin is necessary is precisely the view Kierkegaard seeks to avoid in that discussion: 'We have nowhere been guilty of the foolishness that holds that man must sin; on the contrary . . . We have said what we again repeat, that sin presupposes itself, just as freedom presupposes itself, and sin cannot be explained by anything antecedent to it, anymore than can freedom' (*BA* IV: 380; 4: 414). Sin is always particular; it always has its origin in the individual, and can never be traced back to the sinfulness of the race (*BA* IV: 343–4; 4: 378–9) or to the finite condition of human beings. Kierkegaard pushes this point so far in *The Concept of Anxiety* as to deny the doctrine of hereditary sin, claiming that original sin comes into the world anew in every individual, 'by the qualitative leap of the individual' (see, e.g., *BA* IV: 303, 309; 4: 337, 344). This coming-into-existence of sin cannot be explained (*BA* IV: 288, 294; 4: 323, 329); the concept of sin is falsified by an attempt at explanation, because this amounts to a denial that it arises from freedom, a denial which 'perverts ethics' (here ethics in the broader sense that encompasses both forms of religiousness) and 'pay[s] man a compliment at the sacrifice of the ethical' by substituting an explainable occurrence (a 'quantitative determination') for what can only be a free act (*BA* IV: 314; 4: 349).[37]

To draw the last few paragraphs to a point: the concept of necessary or essential guilt, though a core part of religiousness A, does not belong to religiousness B. Instead, the concept of sin belongs to that latter view; sin is non-necessary (if *de facto* universal) guilt. Kierkegaard argues in the main text of *The Concept of Anxiety* that it is a pernicious mistake to treat sin as necessary—pernicious because

---

[36] Of course, like many generalizations about Kierkegaard's works, this one has exceptions. The most difficult seems to me to be the discussion of man's 'essential sinfulness' (VIII: 367) that occurs in the third part of *Upbuilding Discourses in Various Spirits* (1847), a discussion which has much of the flavour of religiousness A as I have characterized it despite purporting to be a discussion of Christian religiousness. It is worth noting, though, that in contrast to the discussions of essential guilt in the problematic sense in *Postscript*, Kierkegaard there emphasizes that despite guilt's being an essential characterization of the relation between God and man, man is nevertheless 'without excuse'. And in any case the relevance of this discourse to the interpretation of *The Concept of Anxiety* and *Concluding Unscientific Postscript*—where the usage is quite consistent—is unclear.

[37] The 'second ethics' of which Kierkegaard speaks in the introduction—the one he opposes to the 'first ethics' which is the object of criticism—is distinguished by its refusal to 'explain' sinfulness. Dogmatics, on which the second ethics is based, presupposes sin but also does not explain it (*BA* IV: 292; 4: 328).

it amounts to exempting people from blame for it. Given these facts, it would be *very* odd—inexplicable, in fact—if the complaint Kierkegaard were making against the ethical standpoint in the introduction to *The Concept of Anxiety* were that it has no resources to deal with the inevitability of guilt and so must be replaced by a religious view which accepts the necessity of guilt and offers individuals a remedy for it. This is my third objection to this second interpretation of Kierkegaard's criticism of the ethical standpoint.

Constitutive ends, autonomy and the possibility of moral evil

I believe the complaint made about the positions grouped under the heading 'first ethics' in the introduction is just the opposite of this, namely that they do not admit the *possibility* of guilt (or, in Kierkegaard's use of the term: the possibility of sin). There are many comments in the introduction to *The Concept of Anxiety* that directly support such an interpretation. '[F]or ethics,' Kierkegaard writes, 'the possibility of sin never occurs' (*BA* IV: 295; 4: 330), and should it occur to ethics to take account of the possibility of sin, this spells the end of the ethical standpoint. 'Sin, then, belongs to ethics only insofar as upon this concept it is shipwrecked with the aid of repentance' (*BA* IV: 289; 4: 324). (Note the subordinate role of repentance in shipwrecking the ethical: the presence of guilt and the unavailability of absolution plays at most a supporting role in the case against the ethical standpoint, but the possibility of sin is the main issue.) The account in the main text, as I have said, provides further support for this interpretation. The work as a whole is primarily concerned with making sense of the possibility of moral evil, and it is linked textually to Schelling's *Freiheitsschrift* and Kant's *Religion* in ways that make it clear that Kierkegaard has these two discussions of moral evil in mind. I will have more to say about these textual links in the next chapter. For now it will suffice to say that the project in *The Concept of Anxiety* mirrors Schelling's project in the *Freiheitsschrift* in a very basic respect—it attempts to explain, in terms of a general theory of human personality, how moral evil is possible. That makes a set of introductory comments about the *lack* of such an account in some ethical views look quite sensible indeed.

But the comments in the introduction really are sketchy, and we still need to look elsewhere to fill out the account. Instead of turning to the description of religiousness A in *Concluding Unscientific Postscript*, I suggest turning to the second of Kierkegaard's primarily moral-psychological works, *The Sickness unto Death*—in particular, to chapters 2 and 3 of the second part (*SD* XI: 199–211). There we find a criticism of the ethical standpoint that precisely mirrors the language and presuppositions of the introduction to *The Concept of Anxiety*.

Socratic ethics is the main target in the first of these chapters, and the criticism is a familiar one: if virtue is knowledge, then sin is ignorance, and this means that there is no sin at all.

If sin is being ignorant of what is right and therefore doing wrong, then sin does not exist. If this is sin, then along with Socrates it is assumed that there is no such thing as a person's knowing what is right and doing what is wrong, or knowing that something is wrong and going ahead and doing wrong. Consequently, if the Socratic definition is sound, then there is no sin at all. (*SD* XI: 200)

Here 'sin' should be taken as referring to moral evil in general, such that to claim that there is sin is simply to claim that there is imputable immorality. For quite apart from the general point about Kierkegaard's use of the terms 'sin' and 'guilt' explained above, local absurdities would result from taking the term 'sin' in this discussion to have its specifically Christian sense. The discussion of a 'Socratic notion of sin' would be meaningless (for there could be no such thing), and the complaint against Socrates would have to be that he lacked a notion it is historically impossible for him to have had. Clearly, the argument presented in this section is not a complaint about pagan ethics that relies on specifically Christian presuppositions. It is instead a rehearsal of a perfectly standard objection to Socratic ethics—that claiming that action's constitutive aim is the good or the perceived good (and that failure to aim at the truly good is caused only by failure to apprehend what it is) amounts to denying individual responsibility for virtue and vice, denying that virtue is a choice. The validity of this standard objection does indeed become clearest when one considers what account of moral evil might be available to someone who takes the view that the moral aim is partly constitutive of action.

As we have seen, the same criticism has other potential targets. Kierkegaard writes that what Socrates lacked for the definition of sin was a conception of 'the will, defiance' (*SD* XI: 201). But the difficulty is better put by saying that he lacked a conception of the agent as *capable* of defiance; merely adding a conception of the will does not help, as Kant's example showed. If the criterion of value is taken to be internal to the will it governs, in the sense of being the law of its operation or the condition of its effectiveness, then wilful defiance of that standard is impossible and the idea of intentional, imputable deviations from it absurd. This seems true no matter what the specific character of the standard, no matter what the conception of the operation of the will. And in fact it is clear that Kierkegaard has Kant in mind in this passage as well (we read, for instance, that the problem with Greek ethics was its embrace of 'an intellectual categorical imperative' (*SD* XI: 201)). This is indeed an issue—perhaps the only issue within the space of Kierkegaard's concerns—on which Kantian and Socratic ethics share a problem (one which, it should be noted, is optional for Socrates in a way it is not for Kant).

The link between ancient and idealist ethics is made explicit towards the end of the chapter, where we read that the ethics of 'modern philosophy' (the reference to 'the system' in this passage makes it clear that the target is German idealism) is at one with Greek ethics in denying the distinction between practical reason and the will.

In pure ideality, where the actual individual person is not involved, the transition is necessary (after all, in the system everything takes place of necessity), or there is no difficulty at all connected with the transition from understanding to doing. This is the Greek mind . . . And the secret of modern philosophy is essentially the very same: *cogito ergo sum*, to think is to be . . .

In the world of actuality, however, where the individual person is involved, there is this tiny little transition from having understood to doing . . . (*SD* XI: 204–5)

Kierkegaard characterizes the common feature of the ethical views that are his target in the chapter as their disregard of the existence of a transition from knowing to doing; they lack 'the courage to declare that a person knowingly does wrong, knows what is right and does the wrong' (*SD* XI: 205). This is the *locus* of the major distinction he sees between Christian and philosophical ethics: 'In this transition Christianity begins; by taking this path, it shows that sin is rooted in willing and arrives at the concept of defiance' (*SD* XI: 204).

If we look at the context of this passage, we find that it is framed by a discussion of constraints on normativity on the one hand and a discussion of the cosmological place of moral evil on the other. It is preceded by a consideration of the relation between the self and the criterion by which it measures itself, in which a contrast is drawn between a relation to a criterion as what defines one and a relation to a criterion as one's ethical goal, and between the two different senses of 'not measuring up' to the criterion that correspond to these two relations:

The criterion of the self is always that before which it is a self . . . everything is qualitatively that by which it is measured, and that which is its qualitative criterion is ethically its goal; the criterion and goal are what define something, what it is, *with the exception of the condition in the world of freedom*, where by not qualitatively being that which is his goal and his criterion a person must himself have merited this disqualification. (*SD* XI: 191— my emphasis)

The idea is that a view of ethics should take care not to cancel the distinction between these two senses of 'criterion' and of 'measuring up' (one naturalistic-teleological; the other properly ethical). And the passage is followed by a brief section titled 'Sin is not a Negation but a Position' which contains a critique of 'speculation' (here the target is clearly idealism) for its 'pantheistic' conception of evil as 'weakness, sensuousness, finitude, ignorance, etc.' (*SD* XI: 207). The order of exposition points to the connection between the substitution of one understanding of 'criterion' for the other and positions in moral psychology and metaphysics on which the will's efficacy is limited to action aimed at satisfying the criterion.

So the criticism of the ethical standpoint found in *The Concept of Anxiety* and *The Sickness unto Death* is that it entails a faulty moral psychology—one wherein moral evil is unintelligible, morally good action the only possible imputable action. It is appropriate that we find the criticism in precisely these two works, since they are the two pseudonymous works that explicitly advertise their 'psychological' character. But when one looks again at *Either/Or* II, one finds that the positive characterization of the ethical view given there is consistent with this critical characterization given in the two psychological works. Kierkegaard has set up this criticism in his characterization of the Judge's ethics of autonomy.[38] According to that position, the standard of duty is something every individual possesses, as a potential, in virtue of having a will at all: 'The task the ethical individual sets for himself is to transform himself into the universal individual . . . But to transform himself into the universal human being is possible only if I already have it within myself *kata dynamin*' (*EE* II: 234; 3: 249). The ethical individual differs from the aesthetic individual in that the latter is 'transparent to himself' (*EE* II: 231; 3: 246), and he becomes transparent to himself by taking choice seriously. The good that is chosen is simply the true self—the self 'in its eternal validity' (*EE* II: 192; 3: 205)—that becomes transparent in this way. Knowing what to choose—indeed, choosing rightly—follows directly from taking choice seriously: 'As soon as a person can be brought to stand at the crossroads in such a way that there is no way out for him except to choose, he will choose the right thing' (*EE* II: 152; 3: 164).[39] In other words, once one pays attention to choice per se, once one takes it absolutely seriously, what one's concrete duty is cannot but become clear, and one cannot but will to do it. Good and evil indeed appear as two possibilities once the ethical as such has been chosen (*EE* II: 153–4; 3: 165–6), but the good appears, in the Judge's view as in Kant's, as simply the most pure expression of the will, the choice that is truly a choice. The Judge's denial of radical evil (*EE* II: 157, 159; 3:170, 171), his view of evil as 'only . . . a weak possibility' (*EE* II: 157; 3: 169) follows from this view. One can allow the energy of one's willing to fade and thereby *fall* back into the aesthetic way of life—but this is not and cannot be a choice in the true sense.[40]

The criticism of autonomy ethics Kierkegaard intends to offer in the pseudonyms, then, is that its account of the source of normativity undermines one of its own presuppositions—that the agent those norms govern be morally responsible.

---

[38] This—that it is an ethics of autonomy, *not* that it fails to leave room for moral evil—is generally acknowledged to be the case. For instance, Disse (2000) argues that the Judge differs from Kant primarily in seeing absolute choice as a matter of pure will rather than as a matter of rational will, and that the Judge's is an ethics of autonomy without being a rationalist ethics. Fahrenbach (1968: 186) also thinks that the Judge relies implicitly on an essentially Kantian/Fichtean view. Like Fahrenbach, I think that a good case can be made for the historical importance of Fichte. But none of these commentators has seen moral evil as a major point of contention between Kantian and Kierkegaardian ethics. In fact the most detailed recent study of Kierkegaard's relation to Kant argues that Kierkegaard fundamentally agrees with Kant's treatment of moral evil (cf. Green 1992: 156–67).

[39] The position in the first of the *Upbuilding Discourses in Various Spirits* (on the topic: 'purity of heart is to will one thing') looks similar. There Kierkegaard argues that willing one thing is necessarily willing the good, that one cannot will evil without a divided will, that good is original and evil derived, a negation. This looks like a constitutivist view, and it might seem odd that it occurs in a religious discourse. In fact Kierkegaard characterized this discourse as 'ethical-ironical' and 'Socratic' at Kierkegaard (1909–78: VIII,1 A 15 10; 1997– vol. 20: NB:129).

[40] The Judge also equates evil with habit and thereby with unfreedom in the first letter (at *EE* II: 115–16; 3: 127).

There is a conflict internal to the ethics of autonomy: it both insists on responsibility and undercuts that insistence by reassuring the agent that he can only be responsible for morally good actions, because these are the only things he does that are *actions* in the true sense. In other words, as ethics it presupposes that moral agents confront an either/or, and as an ethics of autonomy, it denies just this. The denial is one it shares with some ancient ethics, and this is why Kierkegaard includes this under the rubric 'first ethics'.

If what the ethics of autonomy is guilty of is this sort of falsification of the nature of agency, then it, like the aesthetic view of life, should be an example of 'despair' in Kierkegaard's technical sense, and the typology of despair in the first half of *The Sickness unto Death* should include a form that corresponds to it. And it does: the notoriously problematic 'despair of wanting to be oneself'. Kierkegaard calls this 'despair through the aid of the eternal, the despairing misuse of the eternal within oneself to will in despair to be oneself' (*SD* XI: 178). Such an individual desires 'to be master of itself or to create itself' (*SD* XI: 179), to recognize nothing beyond its own sovereign self-determination.

[T]he self is its own master, absolutely its own master, so-called; and precisely this is its despair, but also what it regards as its pleasure and delight. On closer examination, however, it is easy to see that this absolute ruler is a king without a country, actually ruling over nothing; his position, his sovereignty, is subordinate to the dialectic that rebellion is legitimate at any moment. (*SD* XI: 180)

[I]n despair the self wants to enjoy the total satisfaction of making itself into itself, of developing itself, of being itself . . . . And yet, in the final analysis, what it understands by itself is a riddle; in the very moment when it seems the self is closest to having the building completed, it can arbitrarily dissolve the whole thing into nothing. (*SD* XI: 181)

How is it that what look like criticisms of the moral subjectivism of early romanticism are in fact criticisms of the ethics of autonomy? It is possible to develop the notion of autonomy in a number of ways. The fundamental idea is that the rule for conduct is normative in virtue of being partially constituitve of agency itself—this is what makes it the will's *own* rule. But one can tell such a story either by holding the rule fixed and deeming what fails to accord with it not genuine activity, or by holding the activity fixed and deeming whatever rule it fails to accord with not the will's own rule and so not binding on it. Kant developed the idea in the first way, holding the rationality requirement fixed, and this is the way dominant in idealism—Schelling, Hegel, and also, for the most part, Fichte (especially in his later writings on ethics). But the early Fichte's development of the notion of autonomy tended to emphasize the activity over the rule, and the early romantic appropriation of Fichte turned that emphasis into a quite extreme moral subjectivism.[41] Rules of conduct flow from our activity as agents

---

[41] Neuhouser (1990: chapter 4) discusses these two paths in Fichte's ethics—though not quite in these terms. I discuss the connection with the romantics and Kierkegaard in a forthcoming paper. The subjectivist version is the view attributed by Hegel in §140 of the *Philosophy of Right* to Schlegel

in the sense that we *arbitrarily* create the rules that govern our conduct by acting as we do.[42] These romantic views are the specific target in parts of the discussion of the despair of wanting to be oneself. Note, though, that they share the problem of the more standard variant. On them no moral evil is possible, and for the same reason: whatever one does is, by virtue of the fact that one *does* it, morally successful.

How does the reading of *Either/Or* II I gave in §I fare in light of this conclusion? There I distinguished four referents of the Judge's term *det Ethiske* in the second letter: (1) moral responsibility; (2) autonomy; (3) the normative force of social and cultural institutions; and (4) the specific set of ethical duties that the Judge takes to apply to both himself and *A* (namely, to get married, work in a calling, cultivate friendships, etc.). The argument reconstructed in §I was for the acceptance of (1). The argument reconstructed in this section is for the rejection of (2). That (1) and (2) are separable in principle I have tried to show already in my discussion of Kant (in chapter 2). That Kierkegaard viewed them as separable is manifested by the fact that he retains the Judge's criticisms of the aesthetic point of view in later works, even works which take a clear post-ethical stance. Frater Taciturnus in *Stages on Life's Way* is a good example: he accepts the superiority of religious life-views, characterizing the ethical as 'only a transition sphere' (*SLV* VI: 443; 6: 439) and as 'a passageway' (*SLV* VI: 444; 6: 439), but nonetheless accepts (and reiterates) some of the same arguments against the aesthetic view made by the Judge. He can do this because he thinks the Judge's case against the aesthetic view is separable from his positive ethical view—i.e., contra *Groundwork* III, he thinks the claim that the will is free of determination by alien causes is logically separate from the claim that it is the source of the imperatives binding on it.

Ethical optimism as ethical pitfall

It seems to me that this reading of the criticism of the ethical standpoint in the pseudonyms has the advantage over the others I have considered of being one that

---

and others. It implies, he says, 'that objective goodness is something constructed by my conviction, sustained by me alone, and that I, as lord and master, can make it come and go [as I please]. As soon as I relate myself to something objective, it ceases to exist for me, and so I am poised above an immense void, conjuring up shapes and destroying them.' (Hegel 1991: 184). The result according to Hegel is that 'evil is perverted into good and good into evil' (Hegel 1991: 170), which I take to mean that the distinction between good and evil disappears with the disappearance of a normative standard distinct from the will of the agent to which it is supposed to apply. Hegel explicitly exempts Fichte himself from this criticism, but that this sort of conclusion was implicit in Fichte's ethics was widely accepted (also by Kierkegaard, as we learn in the last chapter of *The Concept of Irony*).

[42] This dialectic—in particular the question of whether the construction of norms can be non-arbitrary on such a view—has had a replay in contemporary Kantian ethics. Geuss's comment on Korsgaard (1996b) points to this romantic result as a peril of the emphasis on the activity of norm-creation in Korsgaard's constructivist version of Kantianism.

an inhabitant of the ethical standpoint ought to accept. But I should say something more about that, since it might seem a strange complaint about an account of the source of normativity that it undercuts the possibility of an account of imputable wrongdoing. Why should this be a concern? Two answers present themselves in the pseudonymous works.

The first is simply that to deny that moral evil is a possibility is to be false to the phenomenology of agency and the facts of moral life. Kierkegaard devoted a large proportion of his effort as an author to an extensive typology of moral character, and he did not overlook the varied ways, not only of self-consciously abstaining from pursuing the good, but also of self-consciously pursuing the bad for its own sake.[43] A passage in *The Sickness unto Death*, for instance, describes a form of despair that consists in clinging to one's moral imperfections, insisting upon them, refusing all moral assistance and building one's existence upon such imperfections and the suffering they cause to oneself and others: 'Rebelling against all existence, [such despair] feels that it has obtained evidence against it, against its goodness. The person in despair believes that he himself is the evidence, and that is what he wants to be, and therefore he wants to be himself, himself in his torment, in order to protest against all existence with this torment' (*SD* XI: 184).[44] This sort of rebellion against the moral order is a description of a possible moral stance—one that in less extreme and sustained forms is quite familiar.

Kierkegaard seems to have thought that the denial that individuals can be moved by anything but desire for the perceived good was motivated by a misplaced or exaggerated desire to make ethical duties seem more appealing. But he thought that this was a serious disservice to ethics—and this is his second answer to the question. Kierkegaard often speaks from a sort of ethical public health perspective, and in such moments his diagnosis of the underlying cause of the spiritual poverty of his age is: moral indifference. But it is important to notice that he does *not* see this indifference as the sceptical consequence of a failed

---

[43] For non-Kierkegaardian typologies, cf., e.g., Velleman (1992) and Stocker (1979). Velleman: 'A tendency to desire things under negative descriptions is an essential element of various emotions and moods such as silliness, self-destructiveness, or despair. A mood of playfulness is, in part, a disposition to form desires for things conceived as having no particular value; a self-destructive mood is, in part, a disposition to form desires for things conceived as harms; and so on. None of these desires could retain its characteristic idleness or perversity if it involved an attempt at getting things right' (118). Stocker offers his own typology of more and less self-conscious failures to be motivated by the perceived good, and argues that motivation and evaluation 'need not point in the same direction' because 'they are related only through complex structures of mood, care, energy, interest and the like'—structures whose straightforward operation moral psychologists (illegitimately) assume. Neither Stocker nor Velleman draws the pessimistic conclusion about the ethics of autonomy that Kierkegaard does, however.

[44] Kierkegaard goes on to compare such an individual to an error in an author's writing that becomes conscious of itself as an error, which 'wants to mutiny against the author, out of hatred toward him, forbidding him to correct it and in maniacal defiance saying to him: No, I refuse to be erased; I will stand as a witness against you, that you are a second-rate author' (*SD* XI: 185).

attempt, on the part of enlightenment thinkers, to provide a rational justification of ethical content,[45] and he certainly does not advocate a return to religion as a (second-best) answer that must be relied upon in the absence of such a justification. Instead, he thinks the enlightenment attempt has had, in the eyes of his contemporaries, all too much success, with pernicious results. The major cause of moral indifference is not moral scepticism, but instead excessive moral optimism: the conviction that every answer to the question, 'What should I do?' must come equipped with an explanation that limits what I genuinely can do to the boundaries of what I ought to do.

Kierkegaard's most vivid statements of this view are criticisms of those who portray the life of genuine *religiousness* as somehow inevitable, but the point is the same. There is a characteristically pointed discussion of it at *AE* VII: 349–50; 7: 366–7. Climacus describes a pastor speaking of the paths of vice and virtue, the one wide and easy, the other narrow and difficult, but his enthusiasm for the path of virtue leads him to describe it as ever wider and easier, and the two paths come to resemble one another to the point where 'the sensualist . . . is not only lunatic because he chooses the path of pleasure over the path of virtue, but he is a lunatic sensualist for not choosing the pleasurable path of virtue'. The problem with the pastor's procedure is to have made the path of virtue look so obviously appealing that the listener is convinced he must already be on it. Who could be so dull as not to be?[46] The inclination to rationalize Christianity, to offer 'three good reasons' for being a Christian, both causes and signals lack of enthusiasm (*SD* XI: 213). 'The trouble is not that Christianity is not voiced . . . but that it is voiced in such a way that the majority eventually think it utterly inconsequential' (*SD* XI: 213).

This is a characteristic that the ethical standpoint shares, in fact, with religiousness A, and in closing I would like to return to the question of the relation of these two views in Kierkegaard's thought. There are suggestions—in *Either/Or, Concluding Unscientific Postscript* and in the introduction to *The Concept of Anxiety*—that the first leads into the second after the topic of moral evil is broached. In the introduction to *The Concept of Anxiety*, for instance, we read the following: 'The first ethics was shipwrecked on the sinfulness of the single individual. Therefore, instead of being able to explain this sinfulness, the first ethics fell into an even greater and ethically more enigmatic difficulty,

---

[45] As MacIntyre (1984: chapters 4 and 5) claims.

[46] The worry pressed in this passage and others is far from the centre of contemporary debates, although many contemporary moral theorists produce the same impression as the pastor. If what is required of me morally is just that I be true to myself (my deepest self, of course)—well that seems easy; of course I want to be *that*. But should I really be so confident that being true to my deepest self is something to aspire to? Criticism of, for instance, Korsgaardian constructivism has so far focused on the related problem of arbitrariness (cf., e.g., the comments by Cohen and Geuss in Korsgaard (1996b), but an (equally worrisome) doubt about the possibility of imputable non-moral choices on a Korsgaardian view has been raised by Ginsborg (1998) and Wallace (2001).

since the sin of the individual expanded into the sin of the whole race' (*BA* IV: 293; 4: 328).

In the struggle to actualize the task of ethics, sin shows itself not as something that belongs only accidentally to the accidental individual, but as something that withdraws deeper and deeper as a deeper and deeper presupposition, as a presupposition that goes beyond the individual. Then all is lost for ethics, and ethics has helped to bring about the loss of all. (*BA* IV: 291; 4: 325–6)

I can think of no reason why this *should* be so, but it is very tempting to point, here, to the example of such a transformation in Kant's *Religion within the Boundaries of Mere Reason*. Kant's task in that work should properly be to account for the *possibility* of moral evil, but what he ends up offering is an argument for the *universality* of moral evil—evil as a universal human propensity, 'so deeply rooted in the will that we must say it is found in man by nature' (*R* 6: 35), 'as a natural propensity, inextirpable through human powers' (*R* 6: 37), which 'corrupts the ground of all maxims' (*R* 6: 37). Once evil is possible, it seems, it is unavoidable. Now, Kant's position, even in *Religion*, is still far from matching the characterization of religiousness A that Kierkegaard gives. Further, there are no explicit references to Kant in this discussion. But we should recall once more that *Religion* was one of the works with respect to which Kierkegaard wanted, in *The Concept of Anxiety*, to orient himself—and so to find a sketch of the transformation of Kant's thought in the introduction should come as no surprise.

Whether there exists this genetic relation between the twin targets of this work whose aim is to make room for the possibility of moral evil without thereby committing the author to its necessity, I think it is clear that we should see the ethical standpoint and religiousness A as the optimistic and pessimistic sides of the same coin. According to the first, one cannot become guilty; according to the second, one cannot become anything *but* guilty. Holding either of these views means not taking responsibility seriously, letting oneself off the hook. Climacus summarizes the distinction between the four standpoints in the following passage from *Postscript*:

If in himself the individual is undialectical and has his dialectic outside himself, then we have the *esthetic interpretations*. If the individual is dialectically turned inward in self-assertion in such a way that the ultimate foundation does not itself become dialectical, since the underlying self is used to surmount and assert itself, then we have the *ethical interpretation*. If the individual is defined as dialectically turned inward in self-annihilation before God, then we have *Religiousness A*. If the individual is paradoxical-dialectical, every remnant of original immanence annihilated, and all connection cut away, and the individual situated at the edge of existence, then we have the *paradoxical-religious*. This paradoxical inwardness is the greatest possible, because even the most dialectical qualification, if it is still within immanence, has, as it were, a possibility of an escape, of a shifting away, of a withdrawal into the eternal behind it; it is as if everything were not actually at stake. But the break makes the inwardness the greatest possible. (*AE* VII: 498–9; 7: 519–20)

The 'possibility of an escape' is the possibility of 'a shifting away' of ultimate responsibility, away from the individual and on to something larger—the laws of motion of the cosmos, or of the rational will. A 'withdrawal into the eternal behind it' is, in some form or another, a denial of the freedom of finite individuals, a denial that everything, ethically speaking, is actually at stake. Religiousness B (Christian religiousness) is here portrayed as a standpoint that does not have this characteristic. I now turn to the task of saying why Kierkegaard might have thought that.

6

Religiousness B and Agency

If the argument in the foregoing chapter is correct, the religious view Kierkegaard accepts should come attached either to a non-deterministic metaphysics or at least to a principled scepticism about the possibility of causal explanations of action, and it should account for a theory of normativity that does not tie the force of ethical requirements to the conditions of possibility of genuine action. My goal in §I of this chapter is to explain how religiousness B— Christianity on Kierkegaard's characterization in the pseudonymous works— meets these constraints. It is not my goal (nor, I believe, was it Kierkegaard's) to show that it is the only view that meets them; it is clear from the constraints themselves that it could not be. The constraints as I have construed them do exclude some possible readings of what religiousness B can amount to, however. In particular, the widely held view of Kierkegaard as a voluntarist about religious belief is excluded by them. I find this to be a positive result, and will argue that it is consistent with the passages in the Climacus works that have seemed to force a voluntarist reading in §II. Finally, in §III, I will turn to the positive conception of agency presented in the moral-psychological works *The Concept of Anxiety* and *The Sickness unto Death*, placing Kierkegaard's theory of agency more precisely against the background defined by Kant's, Fichte's, and Schelling's.

I. THE STRUCTURE OF RELIGIOUSNESS B

Philosophical Fragments is the first pseudonymous work dedicated to examining the structural features of religiousness B. Its task is defined, in the first chapter (titled 'Thought-Project') in terms of a contrast with an account of ethico-religious knowledge called 'Socratic'. 'In the Socratic view, every human being is himself the midpoint, and the whole world focuses only on him because his self-knowledge is God-knowledge' (*PS* IV: 181; 4: 220).[1] According to

---

[1] Kierkegaard chooses Socrates as his explicit target, but his formulation emphasizes the parallel between Socratic and idealist philosophical religion, recalling as it does Martensen's depiction of Fichte's equation of self-consciousness with god-consciousness in his *Lectures on the History of Modern Philosophy from Kant to Hegel*: cf. Kierkegaard (1909–78 II: C 25, 300).

Kierkegaard/Climacus, necessary conditions for a view to constitute an alternative to the Socratic one are, in a paragraph, as follows.

A normative criterion ('the truth') would be given to human beings through a revelation by a transcendent and otherwise unknowable god. This would be the communication of a content to which human beings did not have access before. The communication would have not a heuristic, but rather a constitutive role (that is, the communication of the criterion would be at the same time its establishment as a criterion). It would be a historical event, and no one who did not make the right sort of causal contact with it (witnessing it or hearing testimony) could have access to the criterion. Since the content of the truth could not be known by other means (for example, through unaided human reason), and since there are no naturalistically describable marks of divinity, a given historical event could be apprehended as an instance of revelation only with the addition of a 'condition' also given to the human being by the god. This condition would not guarantee that the addressee accepts the criterion; instead it would make the communication look normative (which is equivalent to saying that it would make the revelation look like a revelation). Since such a condition would be both necessary and sufficient for something's seeming like a revelation, there could be no distinction between the epistemic situation of contemporary followers (witnesses) and followers separated in time from the historical events (those who learn of it through testimony). On the other hand, since there would be no objective criteria by which one could assess the communication, there could also be no way to tell the difference between having been given such a condition and being deluded. Two complications of the epistemic situation of the believer follow from all of this: first, even one in possession of the truth (in this ethical/religious sense) cannot know that he is; second, there could in principle be no mechanism through which one could pick out one true revealed religion from a set of pretenders to this position (since to seem to be a pretender is already to seem to have come accompanied by such a condition). This is a very concise statement; I will return to most of these points in the remainder of this section and in the next.

These features of the alternative to the Socratic view are laid out without mention of or appeal to Christianity, though this is the example of such a view the reader is expected to have in mind (as the conversation with the imaginary interlocutor who accuses 'Plagiarism!' at the end of each chapter indicates). The word 'Christianity' is introduced in the final pages, where we read:

As is well known, Christianity is the only historical phenomenon that despite the historical—indeed, precisely by means of the historical—has wanted to be the single individual's point of departure for his eternal consciousness, has wanted to interest him otherwise than merely historically, has wanted to base his happiness on his relation to something historical. . . . To a certain extent, however, I have wanted to forget this, and, employing the unrestricted judgment of a hypothesis, I have assumed the whole thing was a whimsical idea of my own. (*PS* IV: 271; 4: 305)

So Christianity is supposed to be the unique historical example of a view with its particular structure.[2] But that is irrelevant to the project in *Philosophical Fragments*. It is the structural features—the account of the source of normativity and the accompanying moral epistemology—that are of interest, and it is in virtue of these structural features that Christianity, according to the Climacus of *Postscript*, passes the test of 'fit' with existing subjectivity.

Does Kierkegaard think views of the sort outlined in *Fragments* are the only sort that can solve the problem? (Note that this is a distinct question from that of whether Christianity is the only or privileged example of a view of the sort out-lined in *Fragments*.) I find it doubtful that he did. The negative argument against the ethical standpoint is really only an argument against the ethics of autonomy, since only there is the normativity of morality connected in a problematic way with the freedom required for attributing moral responsibility to agents to begin with. The idea that norms might have their source neither in the nature of agency (in the form of constraints on what can constitute genuine action) nor in the will of a higher authority (as in a voluntarist view), but have some other source, is not a view Kierkegaard anywhere seeks to rule out. Nor is the idea that they are simply non-derivative and inexplicable—hardly surprising, since given the nature of the constraints on religious knowledge imposed in *Fragments* it is not clear how very different such a view could be from the one outlined there. (I will return to this issue below.) Nor is the pessimistic alternative—that although we are the sorts of things that can pose questions about what we ought to do, there are no answers to such questions available to us—a view that Kierkegaard anywhere seeks to rule out. In fact he seems to think it cannot be ruled out at all on philosophical grounds and that this is an accurate description of the situation of those not in possession of a condition like the one described.

That Kierkegaard did not seek to rule out these other options (especially the final one) reflects the nature of his project in the pseudonyms. The aim there is not to give an argument for the correctness of Christian belief. If there were such an argument—for example, an elimination argument of the sort we would have if all the other options could be ruled out—Christian belief would be rationally required. But that conclusion would stand in direct contradiction to what Kierkegaard everywhere (directly as well as through pseudonyms) claims about religious belief: that it is *not* rationally required, and indeed that it is highly *ir*rational. So any interpretation of the project in the pseudonyms in which such an elimination argument were proposed would have a lot of explaining to do.

---

[2] How and indeed whether Kierkegaard could actually have thought this is a mystery. Christianity is not the only belief system that purports to be a revealed religion (many religions do that, including the closest relatives to Christianity, Judaism and Islam), to posit an incarnation of the divine (one thinks of Hinduism here) or to posit some form of salvation based on a relation to something historical (especially if one is willing to admit membership in a particular group or race as 'something historical'—which it seems in the relevant sense to be).

In fact the project in the pseudonyms is much more modest. Kierkegaard does think that the problem with the views criticized is visible from a general philosophical perspective and that philosophy can have a negative role in paving the way for the sort of belief that becoming a Christian involves. But this sort of inquiry cannot lead to Christianity in any deductive way; the most it can tell us is that something like a revelation would, if it presented itself, fill a certain existential need—a need that can be described, but not itself filled, from a philosophical standpoint. I take at face value Climacus's comment that philosophy can help one 'seek the leap as a desperate way out, just as Christianity was a desperate way out when it entered the world and will continue to be that for everyone who actually accepts it' (*AE* VII: 85; 7: 103).[3] It is a way out because it passes the test of fit with existing subjectivity, but a desperate way out precisely because of the absence (and, given how the view is explained, the impossibility) of a proof of this kind.

How, then, does the view described in *Philosophical Fragments* pass the test of fit with existing subjectivity? It is a species of theological voluntarism, and in placing the source of value outside the will it governs, it certainly escapes the criticism of the ethics of autonomy as Kierkegaard presents it in the pseudonyms. If the good is what is commanded (or willed) by God, there is no *prima facie* reason to think we are unfree in choosing not to pursue it. Still, not just any species of theological voluntarism will do; Kierkegaard distinguishes the sort of religious belief he takes to be involved in the *Fragments*-style view from a set of alternatives whose fundamental characteristic is that, according to them, the good is apprehensible at least in principle by rational insight into the nature of God's will, rather than solely by revelation and grace. This is part of the distinction between religiousness A and religiousness B. To see what is at issue in Kierkegaard's peculiar species of voluntarism, it is helpful to look more closely at this contrast.

Kierkegaard describes religiousness A as 'immanent' religiousness (for example, in the passage I quoted at the very end of chapter 5, where he also describes the aesthetic and ethical views as 'within immanence'). J. G. Fichte had distinguished dogmatism from the critical philosophy by saying that critical philosophy is 'immanent' because it 'posits everything within the self', while dogmatism is 'transcendent' because it 'goes on beyond the self'.[4] It is this sense of the term that Kierkegaard has in mind when he describes Socrates's god-knowledge as a form of self-knowledge. An immanent view is one that posits nothing higher than the 'self' taken in a broad sense: the contents of human subjectivity. In religiousness

---

[3] This account of the negative relation of philosophy to Christian belief mirrors Schelling's account of the relation of 'negative' to 'positive' philosophy. Negative philosophy paves the way for a philosophy of revelation by presenting a riddle: in the absence of revealed religion, the ethical standpoint is despair, and existence is futile. But negative philosophy cannot provide the answer to this riddle itself. Revelation is an answer to the riddle, but it presents itself, if at all, as an underivable fact.   [4] Fichte (1971: I: 120).

A, the divine is conceived as a place mapped out within the philosophical system: the first principle required for a unified theory of the world. Its god is a 'god within thought' (like that of Schelling's negative philosophy).

Three features are important for making out the contrast between this account of religious belief and Kierkegaard's. First, we know everything there is to know about the god of religiousness A by knowing what systematic place it occupies. From this it follows that nothing that could not be known through human reason is learnable through revelation from a god so conceived. Second, on such a view the finite and the infinite are essentially continuous; it is natural to conceive of such a god pantheistically or in terms of emanation. Human agents are emanations or expressions or proper parts of the absolute; this calls the causal independence of their agency into question. Third, the systematic apparatus that yields a conception of such a god will typically not be such as to admit of causally significant contingency—otherwise the claim to knowledge of the structure of the cosmos (which is the same thing as the knowledge of god, since god is that structure or is a place in it) is undermined. Socrates is the contrast case named in *Philosophical Fragments*, but many examples of views sharing (at least some of) these characteristics were available to Kierkegaard. Spinoza (especially Jacobi's Spinoza) and Plotinus (whose influence on the German idealists and the larger philosophical culture of the time was substantial) were other major historical models. The religion of idealism was of course the most salient example. (Fichte's later religious writings may be particularly significant here, since although Hegel's account of religion fulfils the metaphysical and epistemic constraints of Kierkegaard's description, it wholly lacks the element of existential pathos and emphasis on self-negation as an ethical project that are prominent in *Postscript's* discussion of religiousness A. Fichte's does not.)

Kierkegaard seems to have thought these three features inseparable, such that a denial of one of them (e.g., that the agency of finite beings is an expression of divine agency) must lead to a denial of each of the others (e.g., that the nature of such a god can be known by unaided human reason). The idea of such a connection surfaces at various places in the pseudonyms, for instance at the end of the *Postscript* chapter on 'Possible and Actual Theses by Lessing', where the possibility of complete systematic knowledge of actuality is linked with pantheism and fatalism (*AE* VII: 100–1; 7: 117–18). As we have seen, Schelling believed there to be such a connection, and acceptance of it was common among the opponents of the idealist philosophy of religion that Kierkegaard was reading.

Of course one might reject this sort of account of ethico-religious knowledge without thinking, as Kierkegaard appears to, that there are also no *empirical* criteria for determining what is a revelation and what is an ordinary historical event. But Kierkegaard does seem to hold such a view.

First, he agrees with Kant that there are no naturalistically describable, immediately recognizable, marks of divinity. Recall Kant's remark (in *The Conflict of the Faculties*) that 'It is quite impossible for a human being to apprehend the infinite by his senses, distinguish it from sensible beings, and be acquainted with it as such' (7: 63). His idea is that the divine-making qualities of God can have no direct empirical manifestation. Any spatio-temporal communication that could be apprehended by human beings would be finite; any appearance of God as a human being would be that of something appearing human. Kierkegaard often puts the mismatch between what is to be manifested in a communication of the sort he has in mind and the medium in which it can manifest itself by saying that the idea of the incarnation is paradoxical. The *Fragments* chapter on 'The Absolute Paradox' suggests that the peculiarity of Christian belief is that one is meant to believe what one cannot even think (the finite infinite, the eternal in time, the transcendent God in the world—cf. *PS* IV: 212ff.; 4: 249ff.). The Interlude describes it as requiring one to believe the 'contradiction' that the eternal has come into existence at a particular moment—cf. *PS* IV: 250f.; 4: 285f.). In *Postscript*, we read: 'The eternal has come into existence in time. That is the paradox' (*AE* VII: 175; 7: 191). 'What, then, is the absurd? The absurd is that the eternal truth has come into existence in time, that God has come into existence, has been born, has grown up, etc., has come into existence exactly as an individual human being, indistinguishable from any other human being' (*AE* VII: 176; 7: 193).

The question of the meaning of 'paradox' in the Climacus works has been the object of some discussion.[5] I am in general agreement with those who argue that what Kierkegaard means by 'paradox' and 'contradiction' in these passages must be something short of genuine paradoxicality or logical impossibility.[6] But the point of interest to me here is not whether and in what sense the incarnation might be said to be unthinkable, but the more easily settled question of why it might be thought to be immediately *invisible*. That Kierkegaard also has this in mind emerges most clearly in the discussion, in chapter 5 of *Fragments*, of the follower at second hand. There we are told that historical contemporaneity is no advantage, since there can be no immediate apprehension of the divinity of an individual life: 'divinity is not an immediate qualification' and even the miracu- lousness of the acts of the god-man '*is* not immediately but is only for faith, inasmuch as the person who does not believe does not see the wonder' (*PS* IV: 256; 4: 290–1). Since nothing could in any immediate way look like an appearance of the divine in the world, nothing could count as direct evidence for revelation.

One may, of course, concede that there can be no immediate empirical marks of divinity while nevertheless thinking one could have, *on balance*, sufficient evidence for belief in the divinity of a historical individual—evidence that makes the divinity of that individual look more probable than not. But Kierkegaard

---

[5] This is especially true of English-language Kierkegaard scholarship. Cf. Allison (1966), Conant (1989, 1993), Evans (1989b), Herbert (1961), Lippitt and Hutto (1998), Pojman (1984), Thomas (1980) and Westphal (1971).

[6] Good cases for alternative readings can be found in Evans (1989b) and Westphal (1971).

seems to think that, to the extent that anything at all can be viewed as indirect evidence for the existence (or incarnation) of God, such evidence cannot suffice to convince.[7] Here he adds to the Kantian point a Humean one: that even were one to admit certain sorts of events (miracles, prodigies) as evidence for a religious revelation, one could have no convincing evidence for the occurrence of such events. Since such events are, by their nature, maximally improbable, any report of such an event (or any experience of anything seeming to be such an event)[8] is intrinsically incredible. The falsity of the testimony (or the hallucinatory nature of the experience) would have to be more miraculous than the alleged miracle in order for the testimony (or experience) to count as evidence at all. In Hume's words, 'it appears, that no testimony for any kind of miracle has ever amounted to a probability, much less to a proof; and that, even supposing it amounted to a proof, it would be opposed by another proof; derived from the very nature of the fact, which it would endeavour to establish'.[9] In *Fragments*, Kierkegaard/Climacus ridicules the project of giving a 'probability proof' of the correctness of religious belief, the idea 'of wanting to link a probability proof to the improbable (in order to demonstrate: that it is probable?—but then the concept is changed; or in order to demonstrate: that it is improbable?—but to use probability for that is a contradiction)' (*PS* IV: 257n; 4: 292n).

If there can be neither direct nor indirect empirical evidence for believing some particular historical event to be a revelation, what grounds for such belief can

---

[7] There are complications here, though. Various passages in both Climacus works presuppose that some indirect sign of divinity sufficient to bring about rational belief would be possible, but has been deliberately avoided (cf., e.g, *Fragments*' example of the king courting the lowly maiden at *PS* IV: 195ff.; 4: 233ff.). The emphasis in *Fragments* is on the idea that for a god to appear divine (or as divine as it is possible to appear) is for him to transform, by force, the human being to whom he so appears. The emphasis in *Postscript* is on the claim that objective certainty (whether on the basis of reason alone or on the basis of empirical historical evidence) is incompatible with maximally intense commitment. Objective certainty is incompatible with faith (*AE* VII: 177; 7: 193), since faith is passionate commitment and passion requires risk (*AE* VII: 170; 7: 187), while objective certainty eliminates risk: '[I]f passion is taken away, faith no longer exists, and certainty and passion do not hitch up as a team' (*AE* VII: 18; 7: 36); 'Without risk, no faith. Faith is the contradiction between the infinite passion of inwardness and the objective uncertainty' (*AE* VII: 170; 7: 187). There are suggestions in the *Postscript* discussion that objective uncertainty is something the believer must actively hold on to—as if it could slip away if one were not careful ('If I want to keep myself in faith, I must continually see to it that I hold fast the objective certainty, see to it that in the objective uncertainty I am "out on 70,000 fathoms of water" and still have faith' (*AE* VII: 170–1; 7: 187)). For an examination and criticism of this *Postscript* argument (and a comparison of it to other arguments from the desirability of divine hiddenness) cf. Schellenberg (1993: 152–67). I agree with Schellenberg that this is not an adequate *rationalization* of divine hiddenness, but I do not think Kierkegaard's view is damaged by this criticism, since the presupposition of Schellenberg's endeavour—that it reasonable to ask questions like 'Does God have adequate justification for allowing rational disbelief?' and to take a negative answer to be some sort of argument against theism—is not and cannot be shared by Kierkegaard himself. Adams (1977) offers a more sympathetic reconstruction, and a criticism that is, like Schellenberg's compelling only given an assumption which I think Kierkegaard denies, namely that objective reasoning towards religious belief is an open option.

[8] Of course, Hume's discussion is directed at belief in miracles based on testimony. But the discussion in *Fragments* makes it clear that Kierkegaard thinks a similar case can be made for direct experience of wonders.   [9] Hume (2001: 96).

there be? Nothing, it is clear, that would count as a reason or justification in any ordinary sense; nothing that one could point out to someone else as one's grounds for believing. The only grounds for such beliefs are what Kierkegaard/Climacus calls 'the condition:' 'How, then, does the learner become a believer or a follower? When the understanding is discharged and he receives the condition' (*PS* IV: 228; 4: 265); 'Only the person who personally receives the condition from the god . . . only that person believes' (*PS* IV: 265; 4: 299). Here again Hume's text on miracles stands in the background. Hume had concluded that discussion with these lines:

So that upon the whole, we may conclude, that the Christian Religion not only was at first attended with miracles, but even at this day cannot be believed by any reasonable person without one. Mere reason is insufficient to convince us of its veracity: And whoever is moved by Faith to assent to it, is conscious of a continued miracle in his own person, which subverts all the principles of his understanding, and gives him a determination to believe what is most contrary to custom and experience.[10]

Kierkegaard was introduced to Hume through his early reading of J. G. Hamann, and it is uncontroversial that his view of the relation of Christianity to rationality was definitively shaped by this encounter.[11] In a letter cited by Kierkegaard in an early journal entry, Hamann remarks that while Hume intends this as a criticism, in fact it is just orthodoxy, the truth from the pen of one of its enemies.[12] This was Kierkegaard's view as well.

What is miraculous is the life and teaching of one concrete historical individual *seeming* like the normative standard according to which one ought to live one's life. The life of a historical individual is simply the wrong sort of thing to function as a normative standard—especially when one specifies that it does so not in virtue of being exemplary of any general normative principles one has other reason to endorse (including even the general principle that one should obey the will of God—since even saying that this individual is god is making a claim that one admits can be based neither on direct observation nor *a priori* reasoning nor any reliable form of empirical inference). Kierkegaard found Hume's conclusion— that the only way for a believer to explain his belief is as a sort of miracle—to conform to the phenomenological facts of religious belief: not only the fact that it is rationally unjustified, but also the privacy and (human) incommunicability of its grounds, and the moral tenuousness of the situation of a believer who has every reason to think the condition a delusion. These themes are explored at length in *Fear and Trembling*, and the example of Abraham is appropriate because anything that has the structure of a revealed ethical demand—not only Christianity—raises essentially the same set of issues.

[10] Hume (2001: 99).

[11] Cf. Lowrie (1938: especially 164ff.) and Pojman (1983). For a more comprehensive treatment of the role of Hume in the Climacus works, cf. Popkin (1951).

[12] The journal entry is from September 1836. Kierkegaard (1909–78: I A 100; 1997– vol. 17: 32 AA: 14.1). The source is Hamann (1821–43: I: 406).

II. A BRIEF CASE AGAINST A
VOLUNTARIST UNDERSTANDING OF FAITH
IN THE CLIMACUS WORKS

On the interpretation I have just presented, Kierkegaardian faith rests on the apparent but inexplicable normative force of a set of historical events. Many of Kierkegaard's interpreters disagree with this assessment, in that they see Kierkegaard as offering some further story to explain the normativity of the Gospels for the Christian believer. Interpretations according to which Kierkegaard's version of theological voluntarism is a more standard variety than the one I have described are consistent with my argument in chapter 5 (although I believe they are inconsistent with the text of *Philosophical Fragments*). But interpretations according to which the normative force of the Gospels has its source in a decision on the part of the believer to put credence in them are not consistent with it, because on such interpretations the source of norms rests, ultimately, in the will of the believer— and this idea is the focus of the complaint against the ethical standpoint as I have construed it. There are, however, passages in both Climacus works (most notably the 'Interlude' of *Fragments* and the 'Becoming Subjective' and 'Subjective Truth' chapters of *Postscript*) that have seemed to force a reading of faith as willed belief.[13] In this section, I will sketch the case for such a view, examining what it could amount to and showing it to be incoherent given some of Kierkegaard's assumptions. Then I will show how the two sets of texts that suggest it can (and should) be read in quite different ways.

Scepticism, belief, subjectivity

Fragments and *Postscript* contrast mathematical, logical and some metaphysical propositions on the one hand with existential and historical propositions (with 'historical' including both existential statements about the past and causal explanations of events) on the other. In both works one finds arguments aimed at establishing the distinctness of these sorts of claims and undermining the idea that evidence of the sort that can be offered by the former is able to support claims intuitively of the latter type.[14] A chief concern of both is with the placement of Christianity into the category of 'contingent historical truths' rather than 'eternal truths of reason' (for this distinction, attributed to Lessing, see *AE* VII: 74ff.; 7: 92ff.); another is with establishing the intrinsic uncertainty of historical claims.

---

[13] They once seemed that way to me, too; I thought that Kierkegaard was inconsistent on this point. Cf. Kosch (1999; 2000).

[14] *Fragments'* discussion of *a priori* arguments for the existence of God in chapter III and the discussion of the speculative approach to Christianity in *Postscript's* first part (and throughout the text) are prominent examples.

The result is a sceptical stance towards the possibility of establishing the truth of Christianity by means of evidence or argument.

The Interlude in *Fragments* takes a more radical position, according to which beliefs about matters of fact cannot be rationally justified at all because they rely on forms of inference that themselves rely on unjustifiable assumptions (see, for example, the remark at *PS* IV: 247–8; 4: 283, in the context of a discussion of causality as the basis for inference, that 'I cannot immediately sense or know that what I immediately sense or know is an effect, for immediately it simply is. That it is an effect is something I believe').[15] Climacus concludes that the sceptical doubts adduced rule out all possibilities for adequately justifying historical beliefs. The response to this state of affairs he endorses is not suspension of judgement, but rather belief based on decision: '[B]elief is not a knowledge but an act of freedom, an expression of will' (*PS* IV: 246–7; 4: 282); 'The conclusion of belief is no conclusion but a resolution' (*PS* IV: 247; 4: 283).

The view of belief in *Postscript*, unlike that in *Fragments*' Interlude, admits the possibility that the justification of historical beliefs is at least something that can be approached, even if it can never be obtained (cf., e.g., *AE* VII: 12ff., 177ff.; 7: 30ff., 193ff.). But along with this admission come various warnings to the effect that taking this path to Christian belief in particular is either a danger (because a distraction—cf., e.g., *AE* VII: 35; 7: 52) or comical (because the degree of confidence in the belief so attainable will never be commensurate with the significance of what hangs on such a belief—cf., e.g., *AE* VII: 32ff., 177ff.; 7: 49ff., 193ff.).[16] The prospect of achieving certainty through collection of evidence 'is just an illusion by which the resolving and choosing subject is trapped and he enters the perdition of the parenthesis' (*AE* VII: 35; 7: 52). The sort of agnostic stance that might in principle be possible were mere antiquarianism at issue is not possible where the issue is one of ethical knowledge (that is why the 'parenthesis' is 'perdition'). So the fact that one can have fairly good (or at any rate, better rather than worse) reasons for believing historical claims is not a possible foundation on which one can rest the certainty of one's religious conviction.

The discussion of historical belief in *Fragments* and *Postscript* has seemed to some readers to point to the conclusion that religious belief can be directly willed, and that indeed this is the only way in which it is ever acquired.[17] If this were correct, it would have serious consequences for the sort of normative criterion Christianity could be, since the claims it would make on an individual's conduct

---

[15] The fact that Jacobi is mentioned in this passage is significant, since Kierkegaard's use of the point may have been mediated through Jacobi's *David Hume über den Glauben, oder Idealismus und Realismus* (1815: II: 200ff.).

[16] Adams (1977) discusses these two arguments.

[17] Cf., e.g., Pojman (1984: chapters 5–7; 1990). Of course this reading is far from universal. Among those who contest it—or complicate it in productive ways—are Evans (1989a, 1989b, and 1983: chapter XI), Ferreira (who does think that the will has a major role in Kierkegaardian faith, but whose view is not straightforward voluntarism—cf. Ferreira (1991)), Emmanuel (1996: especially chapter 5) and Wisdo (1987).

would have what force they have on the basis of that individual's decision to put credence in them. On such an interpretation, the individual himself becomes the source of the bindingness of the imperatives that guide his conduct. Further, a set of historical facts is the source of their specific content in a robust sense only if there is a unique historical event or set of events with the surface form of a revelation from a god (which the individual can then render normatively binding by believing it or not). But this is not the case. Given that there is no objective way to distinguish a revelation from a non-revelation, virtually any historical figure must seem as equally plausible a candidate as any other. This gives the individual believer effective control over the content of the criterion as well.[18] Scepticism about historical knowledge seems to close off access to the external criterion of value that Christianity as revealed religion would in principle have made available; combined with a story about willed belief, it seems to commit Kierkegaard to moral subjectivism of just the sort that should be problematic given my reading of the project in the pseudonyms.

There are many passages in *Postscript* that seem explicitly to endorse such subjectivism. Climacus contrasts 'objective truth' with what he calls 'subjective truth', making the following distinction:

When the question about truth is asked objectively, truth is reflected upon as an object to which the knower relates himself. What is reflected upon is not the relation but what he relates himself to is the truth, the true. If only that to which the subject relates himself is the truth, the true, then the subject is in the truth. When the question about truth is asked subjectively, the individual's relation is reflected upon subjectively. If only the how of this relation is in truth, the individual is in truth, even if he in this way were to relate himself to untruth. (*AE* VII: 166; 7: 182; the entire passage is italicized in the original)

This 'how' is likewise called 'faith' at various points (but it is also, alternatively, called 'appropriation', 'passion' and 'inwardness'). So one is 'in the truth' if one has faith, or appropriates the teaching in passionate inwardness. The 'how' of subjective truth has the *structure* of object-directedness, but Climacus goes on to suggest that it is *only* this structure that matters—that the 'how' can be correct regardless of what its object is, even if its object is non-existent. One can be 'in truth' subjectively even if there is nothing at all in the spot at which one's belief is directed:

Now, if the problem is to calculate where there is more truth . . . whether on the side of the person who only objectively seeks the true God and the approximating truth of the God-idea or on the side of the person who is infinitely concerned that he in truth relate himself to God with the infinite passion of need—then there can be no doubt about the answer for anyone who is not totally botched by scholarship and science. If someone who lives in the midst of Christianity enters, with knowledge of the true idea of God, the house

---

[18] He can decide, for example, to take Hitler to have been God on earth (and thus his ethical model), and there would be no more to be said against this than there would be to be said against taking Christ to have been God on earth.

of God, the house of the true God, and prays, but prays in untruth, and if someone lives in an idolatrous land but prays with all the passion of infinity, although his eyes are resting upon the image of an idol—where, then, is there more truth? The one prays in truth to God although he is worshipping an idol; the other prays in untruth to the true God and is therefore in truth worshipping an idol. (*AE* VII: 168; 7: 184)

This passage makes reference to something properly called 'the true God' and acknowledges that it makes sense to talk about whether belief is appropriately directed in addition to whether it is appropriately held (even if it conveys a denial of the relative importance of appropriate directedness). But other passages in the same discussion suggest that such talk might not be sensible. Socrates is held up as a pagan example of 'subjective truth'—the object of his belief the immortality of the soul—and the claim seems to be that his passionate certainty is itself all the demonstration there could be of the truth of that belief:

Let us consider Socrates . . . He poses the question objectively, problematically: if there is an immortality. So, compared with one of the modern thinkers with three demonstrations, was he a doubter? Not at all. He stakes his whole life on this 'if'; he dares to die, and with the passion of the infinite he has so ordered his life that it might be acceptable—*if* there is an immortality. Is there any better demonstration for the immortality of the soul? (*AE* VII: 168; 7: 184–5)

The idea that the manner of the belief itself demonstrates the correctness of the belief looks like the unavoidable reading of these parts of *Postscript*. It can be cashed out in two ways. Either the manner of belief guarantees its truth (such that there is something to that truth over and above its being believed in the right way, but no one who believes in the right way can get that wrong),[19] or the manner of belief constitutes its truth (such that there is nothing else to that truth over and above its being believed in the right way).[20] When combined with the view that

---

[19] This is Pojman's view. Pojman (1984: chapter 3) proposes three readings of the relation between truth and subjectivity in *Postscript* and suggests that the text contains evidence for all three, but claims that the apparent fact that Kierkegaard 'believes we can know that God exists, that we are immortal, and that we are free beings' (149) requires the reading he calls a 'Platonic' of the relation: 'We can know metaphysical truth only through introspection. If people will only look earnestly within themselves, they will find all the truth they need to "get on with" this life and the next' (149–50). On this reading, 'Maximal subjectivity is a sufficient condition for attaining the highest truth. No one who is sufficiently subjective can fail to know the truth about metaphysics and ethics' (64).

[20] Pojman (1984) attributes this view to Mackey and quotes (on 63) an APA presentation in which Mackey argued that the upshot of the *Postscript* discussion is the 'solemn admonition: whatever you believe, remember that your creed has no objective warrant, no *fundamentum in re* save the reality it has in your life'. Mackey (1962) explicates the ethical problem with the subjectivist voluntarist view he believes Kierkegaard holds, points out that on this reading the view runs into the criticism of Kant enunciated at Kierkegaard (1909–1978: X, 2 A 396), and sees no adequate way out. I believe the way around Mackey's problem is not to emphasize the social dimension of Kierkegaard's later signed works (as many contemporary English-language commentators do—cf. Davenport and Rudd (2001) and Pattison and Shakespeare (1998)), but rather to emphasize the element of intuition in Kierkegaard's treatment of the apprehension of divinity.

belief is a matter of arbitrary decision both of these construals lead to highly unorthodox results as well as to contradictions, not only with claims Kierkegaard makes elsewhere in the pseudonyms and in his signed works, but within the very passages themselves. I will examine them briefly before proposing an alternative reading of these chapters.

If maximally passionate commitment guarantees the truth of one's belief (hereafter, 'the guarantee view'), and if the object of such belief is determined by an arbitrary decision on one's own part, the result is the peculiar view that whatever god there is puts himself in the way of passionate belief regardless of where the believer intends to direct it. This seems to me at best a candidate for something a charitable third party could believe about someone dedicated to the worship of what the third party is convinced is a false god.[21] Holding it of one's own belief would require deciding (on no sufficient evidence) to believe that *x* is God, and devoting oneself to worship and emulation of *x*, all the while believing that what one is worshipping and emulating is not (necessarily) *x* at all, but whatever the true god turns out to be. It is hard to see how this agnosticism about the true object of one's belief is even compatible with a determinate belief of the sort hypothesized, much less how it is compatible with maximally passionate commitment.[22] Neither Climacus's idol-worshipper nor his maximally passionate Christian holds this view of *his own* religious belief. One might think that it is possible to be agnostic about the true god's identity but still pray to the true god by directing one's worship to 'the true god (whoever that is)' and letting the facts settle the reference. This is one version of the guarantee view shorn of the decisionism, since the believer does not decide what (in particular) to give credence to. But the elimination of the tension is purchased at the cost of a completely abstract, and therefore contentless, belief. There is no way to live one's life in accordance with such a belief; it entails nothing about what one ought to do, and thus is not even a life-view on Kierkegaard's account (and so *a fortiori* not a religious life-view).

The guarantee view makes sense as a religious view only when attached to the conviction that one's (particular, contentful) belief will be guided in the correct direction.[23] The scepticism and doxastic voluntarism are irrelevant on this interpretation, on which Climacus's claim is simply that the efforts of those who do their best to point their belief in the right direction will be rewarded. The position of the would-be believer on such an account is not at all that of originating or validating the religious source of norms. But even in this form it is inconsistent with the subjective state of the believer described in *Postscript*. Climacus describes religious belief as an 'objective uncertainty held fast through

---

[21] This, I believe, is how these comments should be read—as the hopeful thoughts of a Christian admirer of Socrates.

[22] Note how different this is from the case of doubt about the existence of a *specified* god.

[23] That he takes this to be the right option is presumably why Pojman takes pains to criticize Kierkegaard's voluntarism.

appropriation with the most passionate inwardness' (*AE* VII: 170; 7: 187)—but if the content of the belief includes the guarantee view itself, then objective uncertainty is excluded at the outset. (A believer who holds the guarantee view in any form, including this one, holds a view on which the correctness of her belief is, after all, guaranteed.)

The constitutive view—on which the manner of belief constitutes the truth of its object (such that there is nothing else to that truth over and above its being believed in the right way)—fares even worse on this score. It is naturally coupled with voluntarism about the content or object of belief, since according to it there is no independent religious truth for religious beliefs to track. But it is difficult to see how it is consistent with prayer or worship at all, since it entails that there is nothing to pray to or to worship, and these are activities that are intrinsically object-directed. Once again, it is not a description of the state of the believers actually described in *Postscript*.

If the point of these *Postscript* passages is not to argue that the content of religious belief is validated by the attitude of the believer, how are we to read them? Some interpreters have suggested that the pseudonyms in general and *Postscript* in particular aim at helping the reader to find a way into Christianity by pointing him in a (constructively) wrong direction.[24] On such readings, the proposals just examined are not to be taken literally (even if they are to be taken as interpreted above). Although I have no principled quarrel with such approaches, I do think it is clear that much of *Postscript* can be taken at face value as an accurate description of the fundamental character of Christian belief—including these passages, if we read them correctly.

Reading the 'subjective truth' discussion

How, then, are we to read these two problematic chapters? The first of them, titled 'Becoming Subjective', begins by emphasizing the role of individual responsibility in Christian ethics. The reader is warned against confusing ethical merit with world-historical importance (*AE* VII: 134ff.; 7: 150ff.), and in general against being distracted by considering the results of his actions rather than the quality of the will that produced them (e.g., at *AE* VII: 110; 7: 127: 'if a person cannot by his own efforts, in freedom, by willing the good, become a world-historical figure . . . then it is unethical to be concerned about it'). The reader is also warned about confusing her own ethical fate with that of the generation or the race (especially at *AE* VII: 130ff.; 7: 147ff.), and she is warned against confusing the theoretical project of understanding God with the ethical project of living a good life (*AE* VII: 111, 132ff.; 7: 128, 148ff.). Religious belief, she is told, is not primarily a theoretical stance, but instead primarily a way of acting. Questions of death and immortality are characterized as central ethical concerns in this

---

[24] Allison (1966) is the *locus classicus* of this approach in the English-language literature.

discussion (at *AE* VII: 143ff; 7: 159ff.), and the reason given for this is their capacity to individuate the one who thinks them:

Objectively the question cannot be answered at all, because objectively the question of immortality cannot be asked . . . Socially the question cannot be answered at all, because socially it cannot be enunciated, since only the subject who wills to become subjective can grasp the question and rightly ask: Do *I* become immortal, or, am *I* immortal? (*AE* VII: 144; 7: 160)

Thinking about death and immortality encourages thinking of oneself as an individual, and prevents one from thinking one's ethical standing might somehow be bound up with the standing of the era or collectivity in which one lives. (This is, of course, a major theme of *Two Ages* as well.)

The terms 'ethical' and 'ethics' in this whole section are used of Christian ethics, with 'Christianity', 'ethics' and 'subjectivity' on the same side, opposed to 'the system', 'world-historical significance', 'the race' and 'objectivity'. But subjectivity is not connected with a voluntaristic interpretation of theoretical belief. Instead it is connected with an emphasis on individual responsibility in *action*. The connection between these ideas is best expressed by this passage, which occurs near the beginning of the discussion:

Christianity wants to give the single individual an eternal happiness, a good that is not distributed in bulk but only to one, and to one at a time. Even though Christianity assumes that subjectivity, as the possibility of appropriation, is the possibility of receiving this good, it nevertheless does not assume that as a matter of course subjectivity is all set, as a matter of course has even an actual idea of the significance of this good. This development or remaking of the subjectivity, its infinite concentration in itself under a conception of the infinite's highest good, an eternal happiness, is the developed possibility of the subjectivity's first possibility. Christianity, therefore, protests against all objectivity; it wants the subject to be infinitely concerned about himself. (*AE* VII: 105; 7: 122)

'Subjectivity' here is defined as 'the possibility of appropriation', and what 'appropriation' means, as we learn from the discussion that follows, is not belief viewed as a purely theoretical attitude, but the organization of one's life around a set of ethical injunctions.

The next chapter ('Subjective Truth, Inwardness; Truth is Subjectivity') is the heart of the problem; it is here that the discussion of Socrates and the idol-worshipper is found. This chapter begins with a distinction between two conceptions of knowledge (defined as the 'agreement of thought and being') that correspond to two conceptions of the being that thought agrees with. If 'being' is understood as empirical reality, then 'truth . . . is transformed into a *desideratum*' (*AE* VII: 157; 7: 174) and knowledge a process of approximation. If, on the other hand, being is understood as 'the abstract rendition or the abstract prototype of what being *in concreto* is as empirical being' then 'nothing stands in the way of abstractly defining truth as something finished' (*AE* VII: 158; 7: 174). The latter option seems intended to correspond to the idealist understanding. The criticisms Climacus offers of it there correspond to two of the criticisms of Hegel that Schelling had offered in his lectures: it requires denying the thought-independent existence of both thought's object and its agent.[25] Many of Kierkegaard's most colourful comments on the comical presupposition of speculative thought are really formulations of this second criticism: that it is forgetful of the thinker and therefore of the one existential fact to which we have direct and certain access, namely that we ourselves exist (*AE* VII: 98–9, 286; 7: 116, 303). It leaves thought in 'a mystical suspension', explaining everything within itself except itself, the fact that there is thinking (*AE* VII: 69; 7: 85). 'For existing spirit *qua* existing spirit, the question about truth persists, because the abstract answer is only for that *abstractum* which an existing spirit becomes by abstracting from himself *qua* existing, which he can do only momentarily, although at such moments he still pays his debt to existence by existing nevertheless' (*AE* VII: 158–9; 7: 175). The former option, though not subject to this criticism, involves embarking on a project that can never in principle be finished, and leaves the thinker with no answer to the practical questions that motivated the inquiry to begin with.

At this point, Climacus draws again the conclusion he has already suggested in the first part of the book: that the objective approach to the truth of Christianity is a dead end, and that a different approach is required. Given the fundamentally epistemological character of the discussion so far, it seems natural to suppose that the alternative suggested will be an alternative way of *determining* the truth in ethical/religious matters. Given that the candidates discussed have been characterized as 'objective' it seems to follow that a 'subjective' approach to determining the truth is what is being suggested. Is willed belief—subjective epistemic commitment in the absence of objectively convincing evidence—at issue?

If it were, one would expect Climacus to mention it here. But he does not. Instead, when the nature of subjective truth is discussed, it is explained in terms of 'appropriation', which in turn is described as: the degree to which the believer's life accords with the content of the belief. The demand for objective certainty (that is: immunity from any possibility of doubt) about one's ethical/religious convictions is, we are told, a distraction from the ethical project of conforming one's life to those convictions. This is the meaning of the passage about the 'what' versus the 'how' of belief (at *AE* VII: 166; 7: 182) quoted above, and it is also how we are to read the discussion of the idol-worshipper (which also occurs in these pages). The point is not that where one worships is irrelevant, but rather that how one worships should be one's chief concern as a worshipper, and that excessive concern with the where distracts

---

[25] The characterization of the idealist project in these sections closely follows Martensen's description of that project in his dissertation (cf. Martensen (1837, 1997) and in the lectures on the history of modern philosophy, notes for which are reproduced at Kierkegaard (1909–1978: I C 25). Martensen, unlike Schelling, opposed this theoretical idea for essentially theological reasons; Kierkegaard's criticisms follow Schelling's rather than Martensen's.

one from appropriate concern for the how. This is the sense in which the idol-worshipper, though misled about the direction, is still better off, since at least he knows what to do with the (false) ethical/religious beliefs that he has. The passage about Socrates and immortality (which ends: 'Is there any better demonstration for the immortality of the soul?') continues as follows: 'But those who have the three demonstrations do not order their lives accordingly. If there is an immortality, it must be nauseated by their way of living—is there any better counterdemonstration to the three demonstrations?' (*AE* VII: 168–9; 7: 185). The point in this chapter, then, is an expansion of the point in the preceding one. Looking for objective assurance (in an area in which there can be no objective certainty) can only be an exercise in self-deception, the symptom of a desire to avoid one's ethical task.[26]

What could motivate this sort of self-deception? There are two plausible candidates. The first is the idea that the demand for objective certainty (in the Christian case, about the historical facts behind the scriptural account) justifies one in putting off starting in on the fulfilment of that task. The second is the idea that, were one to attain objective certainty about the nature of that task, that would be all there would be to *do*. In various pseudonymous works Kierkegaard emphasizes that where ethics and religion are concerned it is neither acceptable to put off beginning nor a virtue to finish early. Apart from *Either/Or* (where the emphasis is on not putting off beginning), *Postscript* (especially the discussion of existential pathos late in the book) and *Practice in Christianity* are the two works that come first to mind when one recalls this emphasis on the lifelong nature of the ethical/religious task. The message needs to be got across only because there is no automatic connection between having a theoretical grasp of the truth and living it in the religious life. The appropriation problem is the problem it is because virtue is not knowledge. Construing the ethical task entirely in terms of figuring out (or finding an adequate justification for) the correct ethical/religious view means never beginning on the more challenging task of ordering one's life accordingly. In sum, instead of being seen as an argument to the effect that whatever one believes with utmost passion is the right thing in virtue of the fact that one has believed it with utmost passion (which looks like the Judge's view restated in peculiar new terms), in fact the whole of the 'truth is subjectivity' section should be seen as an extended argument to the effect that knowledge does not suffice for virtue.

This seems to me a reasonable way of dealing with the *Postscript* passages (though it is, necessarily, a brief treatment and may not wholly convince). But it does not address the problem posed by the *Fragments*' Interlude. This second problem can be dealt with by looking more closely at the context of the Interlude and its function in *Fragments*, to which I will now turn.

---

[26] Quite a few commentators agree substantially with the reading I have just given of these passages of *Postscript*. Evans (1998), for example, offers a very convincing account.

Reading the Interlude of *Philosophical Fragments*

The Interlude (we are told at the beginning of the Interlude) serves the function of an intermission in the text. It is placed between a chapter whose topic is the situation of the believer who is a contemporary and a chapter on the topic of the believer at second hand, and it symbolizes the passage of time between the first and the nineteenth centuries. We are told that it is filled with text (rather than blank pages) so that we will not be bored during this interval, in the way that an orchestra may play to fill, and thus shorten, the gap that symbolizes the passage of time between two acts of a comedy (*PS* IV: 235; 4: 272). Kierkegaard/ Climacus fills the time in part by raising issues about historical distance and the possibility of certainty of historical facts. But he concludes the Interlude by drawing a distinction between the claims of revealed religion and the ordinary historical claims that have been the Interlude's topic. In the appendix (which applies the meditation about the historical to the case of a historical revelation), he summarizes the result of the Interlude discussion as being that 'one must not be deluded into thinking that it would be easier to understand that something has come into existence after it has come into existence than before it has come into existence' (*PS* IV: 250; 4: 285). But he goes on to add that since 'that historical fact (the content of our poem) has a unique quality in that it is not a direct historical fact but a fact based upon a self-contradiction', with respect to it 'there is no distinction between an immediate contemporary and someone who comes later, because, face to face with a self-contradiction and the risk entailed in assenting to it, immediate contemporaneity is no advantage at all' (*PS* IV: 250; 4: 285). It is the object not (only) of ordinary belief, but (also) of belief 'in an eminent sense' (*PS* IV: 250; 4: 285), for which there is no distinction between the immediate witness (who encounters the phenomenon directly) and the 'follower at second hand' (who encounters the phenomenon through testimony).

The two chapters that frame the Interlude both contain denials that religious belief can be the result of a decision. In the preceding chapter we are told that belief is not a form of knowledge: 'It is easy to see, then (if, incidentally, the consequences of discharging the understanding need to be pointed out), that belief is not a knowledge, for all knowledge is either knowledge of the eternal . . . or it is purely historical knowledge, and no knowledge can have as its object the absurdity that the eternal is the historical' (*PS* IV: 227; 4: 263–4); and, immediately thereafter, that it is not an act of will, either: 'It is easy to see, then (if, incidentally, the consequences of discharging the understanding need to be pointed out), that faith is also not an act of will, for it is always the case that all human willing is efficacious only within the condition' (*PS* IV: 227; 4: 264). The same point is made in the following chapter: 'Only the person who personally receives the condition from the god . . . only that person believes' (*PS* IV: 265; 4: 299). Neither knowledge nor will but grace is the condition of belief. 'Just as the historical becomes the occasion for the contemporary to become a follower . . . so the report of the contemporaries becomes the occasion for everyone coming later to become a follower—by receiving the condition, please note, from the god himself' (*PS* IV: 263; 4: 297). One person can communicate the existence of this peculiar sort of historical fact to another, 'but, please note, not in such a way that the other believes it' (*PS* IV: 265; 4: 300). 'By means of the contemporary's report (the occasion), the person who comes later believes by virtue of the condition he himself receives from the god' (*PS* IV: 266; 4: 301). In other words, the object of belief is a historical event from which there can be no historical distance; everyone is equally distant from it, 'For one who has what one has from the god himself obviously has it at first hand, and one who does not have it from the god himself is not a follower' (*PS* IV: 263; 4: 297). The final result: 'There is no follower at second hand' (*PS* IV: 266; 4: 301).

Now, if there is no follower at second hand, no problem of historical distance, then the idea that an act of will is required in order for the believer to overcome the uncertainty arising out of historical distance is out of place. It seems, then, that in taking it to recommend willed belief in the religious case, one mistakes the purpose of the Interlude. But if this is not its point, what is? The Interlude is sub-titled, 'Is the past more necessary than the future; or, has the possible, by having become actual, become more necessary than it was?' It begins with a consideration of the proposition that history is necessary, and its claims about the possibility of knowledge of historical propositions are meant to form the basis of a disconfirmation of *that* hypothesis. The first step is to establish that no logical necessity can attach to comings-into and goings-out-of existence: 'Nothing whatever comes into existence by way of necessity. . . . Nothing whatever exists because it is necessary. . . . The actual is no more necessary than the possible. . . . The change of coming into existence is actuality. . . . All coming into existence occurs in freedom, not by way of necessity. . . . Every cause ends in a freely acting cause' (*PS* IV: 238–9; 4: 275). These passages also have the (partially independent) aim of claiming history as the realm of free action:

All coming into existence occurs in freedom, not by way of necessity. . . . As soon as coming into existence is definitively reflected upon, even an inference from natural law is not evidence of the necessity of any coming into existence. So also with manifestations of freedom, as soon as one refuses to be deceived by its manifestations but reflects on its coming into existence. (*PS* IV: 239; 4: 275)

The contingency of history is important not only for the view of religion, but also for the view of human action.

The next step is to establish that the unchangeableness of the past is distinct from the unchangeableness of the necessary.

The future has not occurred as yet, but it is not because of that less necessary than the past. . . . If the past had become necessary, the opposite conclusion could not be drawn with respect to the future, but on the contrary it would follow that the future would also be necessary. If necessity could supervene at one single point then we could no longer speak of the past and the future. (*PS* IV: 241; 4: 277)

Again, a parallel point is made about freedom of action:

If the past had become necessary, then it would not belong to freedom any more. . . . Freedom would then be in dire straits, something to laugh about and to weep over, since it would bear responsibility for something that did not belong to it, would bring forth what necessity would devour, and freedom itself would be an illusion. (*PS* IV: 241; 4: 277)

The primary target in the Interlude seems, then, to be the broadly Hegelian claim that the incarnation is a historical necessity, one step in the necessary developmental path of human consciousness and so both an essentially human (even if also divine) phenomenon and an essentially rational (rather than extra-rational) one. The broader aim of resisting the Hegelian assimilation of history to metaphysics (which gets a fairly decisive treatment in the Interlude at *PS* IV: 235–49; 4: 272–84) is motivated in part by this narrower aim of resisting the assimilation of Christianity to metaphysics on the Hegelian model. A subsidiary point is to attack, again, the idealist compatibilism that had been the target in *Either/Or*. The denial of these claims takes the form of a broader denial of the whole Hegelian philosophy of history,[27] and the point is made precisely here because were the Hegelian interpretation of Christianity true, the incarnation could not be a communication of a criterion of value that human beings could not have had without the communication itself. In claiming to have grasped Christianity according to its necessity, Hegelians assimilate religion to the Socratic model of ethico-religious knowledge.

What, then, is the role of the will in religious belief, according to Kierkegaard? This is a larger topic than I can treat adequately in this context, but any account would need to begin by distinguishing amongst the numerous senses of 'belief' or 'faith' (*Troen*—the difference is not marked in Danish as it is in English) to be found in Kierkegaard's works. Five seem to me minimally necessary. First, Kierkegaard uses 'belief' in the most straightforward sense as an attitude we take towards factual, non-normative propositions (belief$_1$: holding a factual proposition to be true). Beliefs$_1$ are candidates for knowledge but may also remain mere beliefs if they are false or if the believer lacks justification for them. The Climacus works argue that beliefs$_1$ about historical facts can never become knowledge because they can never be adequately justified. Belief$_1$ does not figure in religious questions at all. Kierkegaard also uses 'belief' to mean receipt of the condition (belief$_2$: finding the life and teachings of the biblical Jesus to appear normative).

---

[27] This fact that the focus is on Hegel also explains the (to us, peculiar-sounding) concern with establishing the absence of any asymmetry between the necessity of the future and that of the past, since Hegel thought the philosopher is able to grasp the rationality behind historical events only from the privileged point of one who comes after. This backward-looking character of philosophical understanding is also the target of ridicule in *Either/Or* II (at II: 155ff.; 3: 167ff.).

He also uses it to mean accepting the divine communication as the standard according to which one ought to live one's life—rather than trying to explain it away as a lie or a delusion ($belief_3$: taking the life and teachings of the biblical Jesus to actually be normative). Note that $belief_2$ and $belief_3$ are distinct not because the latter imparts a normativity the object of the former did not have, but instead because of the possibility of various forms of self-deception, and the possibility of offence: The way from $belief_2$ to $belief_3$ is trust and self-transparency. Distinct from these is a sense of 'belief' that designates making an effort to live up to this criterion ($belief_4$: moral effort). Note that $belief_3$ and $belief_4$ are distinct because Kierkegaard does not think that moral judgements issue without further ado in moral motivation sufficient for action. We can genuinely take something to be the criterion according to which we measure our lives without genuinely trying to live our lives in accordance with it. Finally, he uses 'belief' to mean succeeding at this effort if we do make it ($belief_5$: living a blameless religious life), and when he remarks that no one has ever succeeded in having faith, $belief_5$ seems to be what he has in mind.

Kierkegaard is convinced that $belief_3$ is *distinct* from $belief_1$ about the theoretical proposition 'Jesus was the incarnation of God'. Of course the condition, the appearing-normative of a historical individual's life, is also the fact that Jesus seems like the incarnation of God to the Christian.[28] But since this is the sort of claim for which there can be no evidence, one cannot coherently theoretically inquire about it. What an individual in receipt of the condition is faced with, then, is not a set of historical questions, but rather, first, the question of whether to acknowledge the standard it sets or dismiss it as a delusion (whether to $believe_3$) and, second, that of whether and to what extent he will try to live his life in accordance with it (i.e., $believe_4$). One aim of the Climacus works is thus to steer the reader away from looking at religious life as an opportunity to exercise the epistemic virtues attached to $belief_1$ and towards looking at religious life as requiring the exercise of the virtues attaching to $belief_3$ and $belief_4$ (those of self-transparency and trust on the one hand, and the virtues proper to Christian ethics on the other). Belief in these senses is up to the believer in just the way that trust, self-transparency, and moral effort are up to individuals. But only they can be said to involve the will, since where $belief_2$ is concerned, there is nothing for anyone to do (see *PS* IV: 184ff.; 4: 223ff.), and $belief_5$ is not within anyone's power to accomplish.

---

[28] It seems correct, then, to say that the experience that makes belief possible is a private one and that this is what makes, for instance, Abraham's situation inexplicable and non-generalizable, what makes the single individual 'higher' than the universal. There have been powerful challenges to this reading (cf., e.g., Cross (2003)), but it seems to me defensible (although this is not the place for such a defence). The most thorough discussion of this is, of course, in the book on Adler. In the journal entries pertaining to that work the ethical responsibility is described as immediately clear to the one who has actually had a revelation (Kierkegaard 1909–78: VIII B 13, 62) and the only open questions are those of acceptance or rejection (which includes suspending judgement), and of obedience or disobedience (Kierkegaard 1909–78: VIII B 15, 66–7).

III. AGENCY IN *THE SICKNESS UNTO DEATH* AND IN *THE CONCEPT OF ANXIETY*

What remains to be examined is the positive conception of agency and moral choice that Kierkegaard proposes. The demands on such a conception arise out of the double incompatibilism on the one hand and out of the positive account of the source of ethical content on the other. It must be a conception on which free but (morally and immorally) motivated action is possible, one on which both the normative authority of revelation and the psychological possibility of sin are accounted for. The two works aimed primarily at giving such an account are *The Concept of Anxiety* (which is primarily an investigation of the phenomenology of freedom and the psychology of sin) and *The Sickness unto Death* (which contains a general theory of agency and an examination of the psychology of both sin and faith). I will give a brief account of both (in reverse order) in this section.

The structure of the self in *The Sickness unto Death*

The opening pages of *The Sickness unto Death* sketch a theory of agency, and the remainder of the first part of the book fills out that account. The task is to set out the structural features that explain the complex interrelation between freedom and constraint in human action. The main structural features are three. A self is (1) a synthesis 'of the infinite and the finite, of the temporal and the eternal, of freedom [later in the book: possibility] and necessity', which (2) is self-relating and (3) in relating to itself, relates to a power that posited it (*SD* XI: 127). The first two structural features are shared with the conception of subjectivity one finds in Fichte and in both early and later Schelling; the third is the negation of the Fichtean account of self-positing. The character of the rest of the exposition, reminiscent as it is of this discussion of agency in early idealism, only serves to highlight this distinction, and Kierkegaard could only have meant the discussion to be read with this comparison in mind.

For both Kierkegaard and his idealist predecessors, selfhood is defined in part by a characteristic activity—a self-conscious, more or less reflective 'synthesizing' activity. To say that the self is a synthesis is to say that part of its activity involves bringing together and unifying pairs of abstract properties that are meant to be (jointly) exhaustively definitive of agency. The pairs of terms Kierkegaard offers (finitude/infinitude, temporality/eternity, necessity/possibility) might not seem very illuminating. They are meant to point (respectively) to a constraint and that in virtue of which the constraint is not total or determining.[29] The basic

---

[29] I agree with the excellent treatment in Lübcke (1984) on many points in what follows. One of these points concerns his view (52) that the pairs of terms are second-order predicates that qualify properties of individuals' characters or ways of life.

opposition is between an individualizing/concretizing element (finite, temporal, necessity) which is required for existing as an individual (for being at all, for being in a particular situation, and therefore for being free), and an idealizing/ integrating element (infinite, eternal, possibility) that involves an abstraction from and transcendence of individuality/concreteness, and so integration into some ideal structure: some aim of action, some set of goals, some view of life. Note that what is at issue are 'ideals' in a projective, but not in a normative sense.[30] Kierkegaard's characterization of these pairs evokes Schelling's in the *Freiheitsschrift* at many points. His exposition of the finite/infinite opposition comes closest to the idea of opposed expansive/contractive tendencies expressed in Schelling's gravity/light opposition—'the self is the synthesis of which the finite is the limiting and the infinite the extending constituent' (*SD* XI: 144)—and although he is not entirely comfortable with Schelling's naturalistic metaphor, he does reproduce another of Schelling's peculiar analogies: that of consonant/vowel (*SD* XI: 150).

The 'synthesis' is the activity of integrating the givenness of oneself with the set of goals or view of life one has taken up—forming one's concrete embodiment into some ideal shape (again, where 'ideal' is not taken normatively), but also tailoring the ideal to the unchangeables of personal history, social situation, physical and psychological nature, and so on. The description of the self as a synthesis of this sort is supposed to reflect the fundamental structural characteristics of human agency. Such agency is at the same time that of a naturally situated being and that of one not exhaustively defined by its natural situation, a being tied to and constrained by a past which likewise does not exhaustively define it, a being with concrete characteristics which place limits on its powers and at the same time with power to transcend (at least some of) those limits.[31] Human freedom is both in some sense opposed to the constraints upon it and in some sense dependent on them. The constraints, limits and history cannot be ignored—not just because they often cannot be changed in the literal sense and so place limits on possible actions, but also because they provide the context in which actions make sense and so contribute to defining them as actions (as, for example, a betrayal of some part of one's heritage or an overcoming of some physical or psychological challenge). Finally, it is not and cannot be entirely clear where the freedom begins and the constraint leaves off.

[30] Here again I agree with Lübcke (1984: 54), against Taylor (1975), that the 'ideal' pole is never a normative ideal, and that this is evidenced by the fact that one can go too far towards that pole on any of the three measures (cf. *SD* XI: 142–53). An 'ideal' in the sense at issue is something like a complex of intentions.

[31] The characterization so far might seem to make a puzzle of the fact that 'freedom' is listed as one of the elements so synthesized in the passage quoted above; it raises the question of what the 'necessity' in that pair is supposed to amount to. But this puzzle is easily solved. 'Possibility' is substituted for 'freedom' in the more extended discussion later in the text, and in the clarificatory remarks there it is clear that by 'the self's possibility' what is meant are the possibilities offered by a concrete context of action, and that 'the self's necessity' means only a set of limiting physical and psychological constraints rather than a set of determining physical or psychological laws.

The agent is continually faced by the question of what is really possible given the constraints, a question which finds its definitive answer, if anywhere, only in his action (but in any case not in any conclusive deliberation that might precede his action).[32]

Synthesis is not the end of the story, though; a mere synthesis of this sort is not yet a self (*SD* XI: 127). To be a self, the synthesizing activity must bear some relation to itself, must be 'a relation that relates to itself'.[33] This relationship is one of self-consciousness, both immediate consciousness of the content of one's mental states and (potential) reflective consciousness of oneself. Anything that goes on in or with the self is the object of immediate awareness and the possible object of reflective consideration.[34] Immediate self-consciousness and selfhood co-vary, and both admit of degrees (*SD* XI: 142). The activity of synthesis will ordinarily involve some degree of self-reflection as well, though it seems as if the absence of reflective self-consciousness is consistent with selfhood (see, e.g., *SD* XI: 163). There are unclarities in these discussions (relating in part to the ambiguity in 'self-conscious'—it is not always clear whether immediate or reflective self-consciousness is at issue), but what one can say with some assurance is that any normally experienced adult agent will be reflectively conscious of her own activity and, to the extent that she is not, will be so intentionally. Such a refusal to reflect on one's activity is also, of course, a way of relating to oneself (as conceptualizing one's activity deterministically or fatalistically, or as the expression of rational self-determination, and so on, are ways of relating to oneself).[35]

On the Fichtean view, this self-relating synthesizing activity must see itself as absolutely self-positing. This means, at minimum, that it must see itself as

---

[32] Lübcke argues that the 'synthesis' should be seen as a place on a scale with the pairs of terms denoting (unreachable) limit points at each end rather than as a product of the combination of two disparate items. I agree with this characterization in part. It is true that each individual synthesis will end up somewhere on a scale and that what it must mean for an individual to be 'more' finite than another must be something like: the constraints placed by his finitude (as compared with his ability to transcend those constraints) have a determining role in more of his plans and projects than in some comparable individual. But I do not think 'synthesis' can mean simply: placement of oneself on that scale. That is because synthesis is characterized as something agents do directly, but occupying a place on that scale is something they can do only indirectly. But what they do directly is construct plans of action out of the various more concrete material falling under the abstract predicates—plans which, when taken as a whole and given an abstract characterization, will then fall somewhere on that more abstract scale.

[33] This phrase is translated 'relates itself to itself' by the Hongs—but this suggests one too many parties to the relation (a relater and two relata rather than simply two relata), which may be significant even if all the parties are the same (self-relating) self. *Forholder sig* is a reflexive construction; its proper translation in this context is 'relates'. I owe this observation to Fred Neuhouser, who pointed out that translators of Fichte tend to make an analogous mistake with the related German construction. Hannay's translation (Kierkegaard 1989b) gets this right.

[34] What I have in mind here are the two forms of self-awareness that Fichte distinguished: immediate (non-objectifying) consciousness of self and reflection upon oneself as object.

[35] Lübcke (1984) argues, plausibly, that the most basic form of self-relation is interest in one's activity (cf. 56–7).

absolutely spontaneous (its actions having no external causal source) and rationally self-determining (its actions following from its own laws). It has appeared to many readers of the early *Wissenschaftslehre* also to mean that it must see itself as onto-logically *sui generis* (i.e., that something existing as a self cannot see itself as caused to exist in this way by anything outside itself).[36] The Fichtean self relates only to itself, and apparent relations to an other (e.g., an object) are ultimately just rela-tions to itself in another form (since the object is itself posited by the self). The apparent facticity of agency is explained by Fichte (and the early Schelling, in the 'ideal' portion of the system) by appeal to the unconscious character of the self's origin in itself—unconscious because preceding the state in which the self is opposed to an object, an opposition which is taken by both to be required for consciousness.

On the view presented in *The Sickness unto Death*, the self does not posit itself absolutely, but owes its existence as a self to something beyond and above it. This will amount to the denial of the second and third of the three meanings of 'self-positing' just outlined. Here is where the disagreement with Fichte makes itself apparent. The self is spontaneous (its actions do not have their causal source in events preceding them in time). But it is not the source of the laws that govern it; nor is it the source of its own existence as a self (that is, its existence as the sort of thing that has spontaneity and moral responsibility). (Note that this means not only that it does not bring itself into existence but also that it cannot alter its fundamental structure—say, by keeping the self-consciousness but ridding itself of the spontaneity.) Kierkegaard claims (in the spirit of the Schelling of the *Freiheitsschrift*)[37] that the self is not posited as what it is by itself, but by something other than itself, and just as it is (in some way or other) conscious of its own activity, it is also (in some way or other) conscious of that fact. 'The human self is such a derived, established relation, a relation that relates to itself and in relating to itself relates to another' (*SD* XI: 128; translation altered). As in the case of the self-relation, this relation to the power that established it can take a number of forms—including the denial (perhaps philosophically motivated) that there is any such thing, and also including any number of construals of the nature of that thing. Although Kierkegaard clearly intends this claim as one about the relation of human beings to their divine creator, the phenomenological fact that is its basis can be taken (as Heidegger and Sartre take it) as brute. What the condition means is just that the self has some degree of power over what it is or will become, but not

---

[36] The stereotypical reading of Fichte as claiming that selves are literally (ontologically) self-constituting is contested by many interpreters. What is at issue instead is self-constitution as a moral project (a reading that may have more to do with the *Sittenlehre* and later articulations of the *Wissenschaftslehre* than the first and most widely read articulation—cf., e.g., Frank (1997)) or as a phenomenological point (namely, that consciousness does not seem, from the inside, to have its origin in anything outside itself—cf., e.g., Neuhouser (1990)). The stereotypical reading was clearly Kierkegaard's, however, so I assume it here.

[37] One could cite the 'feeling of absolute dependence' Schleiermacher describes in *The Christian Faith* as another relevant antecedent.

over the fact that it is, nor over the fact that it has the sort of structure which gives it power over what it will become.[38]

The forms of despair and the project in *The Sickness unto Death*

As I have said, I believe that the analysis of despair in the first half of *The Sickness unto Death* ought to be read as a catalogue of ways to fail to achieve an appropriate conception of oneself as agent by refusing to take up (in thought and action) the task of synthesis properly construed. This is not the most obvious way to approach the book, but it has the advantage over alternatives of offering a simple way to make sense of the book's most puzzling feature: why it describes precisely the three forms of despair it does.

We have encountered the 'unconscious' form of despair (not recognizing that one is a self to begin with—*SD* XI: 154–8) in chapter 5. The puzzle has to do with the existence of two 'conscious' forms: not wanting (or willing) to be oneself (*SD* XI: 161–77), and wanting (or willing) to be oneself (*SD* XI: 178–85). Obviously there must be *some* equivocation either on 'wanting/willing' or on 'oneself' if these two forms of despair are not to exhaust the options for conscious attitudes one can take towards oneself, and so guarantee that any attitude whatever one takes towards oneself will be despair. That they are not intended to exhaust the options is evidenced by the claim (*SD* XI: 128) that there indeed exists a state of the self free of despair. The difficulty lies in stating what these two formulations can mean consistent with: (1) their surface structure (candidate reformulations must have something recognizable to do with wanting or not wanting to be a self or oneself); (2) the theory of the structure of the self Kierkegaard has offered in the opening pages; and (3) the existence of some fundamental distinctness between the two forms (candidate reformulations must avoid simply reducing one to the other or eliminating one or the other form).

One perennially tempting reading has 'despair' as normative failure, failure to live up to the personal ethical task that has been set for one by God. 'Oneself' means on this reading oneself-as-normative-ideal, and failure to want to be that is despair because it eventuates in failure to achieve the personal fulfilment God has put in the way of those who at least try to achieve their personal ethical tasks. This interpretation makes sense of (is, indeed, strongly suggested by) the announcement that 'despair is sin' with which the second part of the book is introduced. But it has serious difficulties.

---

[38] The descriptive term Heidegger emphasizes in his reading of the *Freiheitsschrift*—'derived absoluteness'—is apt here: 'As freedom, man's freedom is something unconditioned. As man's freedom it is something finite. Thus, the question lying in the concept of human freedom is the question of a finite unconditionedness, more explicitly, of a conditioned unconditionedness, of a dependent independence ("derived absoluteness")' (Heidegger 1988: 71). His suggestion is that there is some fundamental tension in the structure of agency, one that is difficult, if not impossible, to manage. That this description is appropriate to Kierkegaard's view as well is borne out by the remainder of the book, wherein despair (a 'misrelation' in the synthesis) is shown to be a virtually universal condition.

The first is that it can make little sense of the despair of wanting to be oneself. If 'oneself' is oneself-as-normative-ideal, there is no available sense of 'wanting' or 'willing' such that wanting to be oneself *itself* constitutes normative failure. Of course wanting to fulfil one's ethical task is consistent with failing to do so, but it does not all on its own amount to failing to do so. The usual response to this worry is to construe 'wanting to be oneself' as a depiction of the sin of proudly intending to fulfil one's God-given task without relying on God's assistance in any way. I have said already why I think that intending or trying ('wanting') to live up to ethical norms is something that, for Kierkegaard, we are obliged to do all on our own, even if we think that our success in living up to these is not something we can ourselves guarantee. But there are purely textual problems with this response as well. The despair of wanting to be oneself is described as despair 'in defiance' (for instance, at *SD* XI: 154)—but although pride is certainly an element in defiance, proudly intending to fulfil one's God-given task without relying on God's assistance is a form of obedience, not of defiance. Further, the text describes configurations of the despair of wanting to be oneself (the devil's despair, for instance—cf. *SD* XI: 154) that clearly involve the total rejection of the project of adhering to any God-given normative standard. These should, according to this reading, be classified instead as configurations of the despair of *not* wanting to be oneself.

A second problem with this interpretation is that on it the entire discussion of the self's structure in the first part of the book is strictly irrelevant to the characterization of the forms of despair. If there were no reading available on which the account of the possible forms of despair is explained by the account of the structure of the self, this conclusion might be anyway unavoidable. But it *is* possible to explain why despair has the forms that it does given that the self has the structure it does; in fact we find such an explanation in the text of *The Sickness unto Death* itself. Before turning to that explanation, though, I would like to say something about another prominent alternative reading.

I have said (in the context of the discussion of *Either/Or*) that it is tempting to read 'despair' as in the first instance a term denoting a psychological state: a feeling of melancholy or hopelessness, or at any rate some fairly deep dissatisfaction with one's lot. One very prominent interpreter has cast *The Sickness unto Death* as an exercise in depth-psychology aimed at uncovering the sources of this state and building up a theory of the self based on that investigation.[39] Kierkegaard's method, on this reading, is appropriately compared with Freud's: a model of the structure of the psyche is built on the basis of a study of the pathologies to which the psyche is subject—a theory of how the psyche must be in order for it to be susceptible to this sort of pathology. The theory developed then has implications for the understanding of behaviour and mental states that are not pathological in

[39] Theunissen (1991, 1993).

any obvious sense; it provides the paradigm for normalcy, according to which all cases are then judged.

This reading shares with the first alternative the problem of being unable to account for the particular forms of despair outlined. Again, the form described as wanting or willing to be oneself is the sticking point. If despair is taken to be a conscious feeling of hopelessness or a psychological state somehow akin to depression or melancholy, only the first form (that of not wanting to be oneself) makes any sense as a description of despair.[40] It is unclear on such a reading why Kierkegaard should not only insist that there is a form of despair describable as 'wanting to be oneself', but also claim that this is the highest or most extreme form of despair.

A second and equally troubling problem is that this construal is at odds with the moral/theological tone of the work. Although Anti-Climacus does describe despair at various points as an 'illness' and liken himself to a 'physician' out to 'cure' it, he also tells us explicitly that this metaphor should not be taken literally, because despair, unlike physical illness, is something that one brings upon oneself at every moment that one has it (*SD* XI: 130–1). This is the case because despair is 'a qualification of spirit' (*SD* XI: 130), a misrelation in the synthesis (*SD* XI: 130), and cannot even be recognized as such unless the 'ethical-religious' category of spirit is applied (*SD* XI: 158). Despair is a moral category, not a psychological state. Although it may produce certain characteristic feelings—'an unrest, an inner strife, a disharmony, an anxiety about an unknown something' (*SD* XI: 136)—it is not defined in terms of these. The proof of this is the state of the person in unconscious despair, whose condition is best described as a sort of self-assured *lack* of any of the feelings characteristic of conscious despair.[41] Neither is freedom from despair described as the absence of a

[40] This is a consequence of his reading that Theunissen simply accepts. He argues that Kierkegaard has the theoretical resources to explain only one basic type of despair: the despair of not wanting to be oneself. The second form, the despair of wanting to be oneself, is then interpreted as wanting to be some idealized or otherwise altered version of oneself, which in turn is traceable to a more basic not wanting to be the self that one is—i.e., something like the despair of immediacy: not wanting to be oneself because one wants to be *someone else*. If we take 'not wanting to be oneself' to be primarily a sort of revulsion at one's '*vorgegebenes Dasein*,' or a revulsion at the mere fact that one *has* a factical, pre-given existence, as Theunissen does, this reading seems preferable. But then it becomes unclear why Kierkegaard should insist that there *is* a form of despair describable as 'wanting to be oneself' in the first place—not to mention why he should claim that this is the *highest* form of despair. Theunissen acknowledges this difficulty, but points to a remark to the effect that we can see the second form of despair as a version of the first (at *SD* XI: 134) to support his construal. (He ignores a remark to the effect that the opposite reduction is possible as well at *SD* XI: 128.)

[41] The despair of the unconsciously despairing individual is recognized in the same way that 'the anxiety that characterizes spiritlessness is recognized[:] precisely by its spiritless sense of security' (*SD* XI: 156). Theunissen recognizes the problem here, and for that reason rejects the possibility of unconscious despair: '[I]n the case of a despair that has no consciousness of *itself*, [Kierkegaard] differentiates between an inadequate consciousness of *what* despair is, and an unconsciousness of the fact *that* one's state is one of despair. In the latter sense, however, there is no unconscious despair. We can have an inadequate conception of despair, but we cannot be in despair without somehow knowing it' (Theunissen 1993: 30–1).

characteristic mood or feeling, or a state of mental health or proper functioning of the self. If the second part of *The Sickness unto Death* is taken into account, the problems multiply. A discussion of a psychological disorder requires neither a discussion of the problems with the view that virtue is knowledge nor a discussion of the theological problem of the positivity of evil. The characterization of despair as sin is equally perplexing; something that is susceptible of an ultimate characterization as sin must be a moral notion from the beginning.[42]

Finally, although this reading does have the advantage, over the first, of offering some account of the connection between the examination of the self's structure and the examination of the forms of despair in the first part of the book, it gets the relation of dependence backward. That relation of dependence is clearly reflected in the organization of the text, which begins with a highly condensed statement of the structure of the self, and arranges the forms of despair systematically to correspond to the possible misrelations amongst the terms of that definition.

Instead of seeing him as beginning with experienced psychological pathology and deriving from it a conception of the structure of the self, I think we should see Kierkegaard as beginning the work with a set of commitments about the structure of the self in hand (commitments determined by the task of conceiving of the self as it must be in order to be free for good and evil) and deriving a set of possible self-deceptions about the nature of agency from that conception. This makes sense of the moral tone of the work and the concerns of the second part (since it involves seeing it as a work or moral rather than abnormal psychology). It also makes sense of the particular forms of despair Kierkegaard describes, and does so on the basis of the characterization of the structure of the self that opens the discussion. If one's agency is such as to involve something like the structure outlined by Schelling—one wherein the self is responsible *for* itself, but it is not responsible *to* itself—then there ought to be two forms of conscious despair, because there are two things to get wrong.

---

[42] One might think that Kierkegaard's description of the work as a 'psychological exposition' should support Theunissen's reading. It does not. The discipline of psychology as we know it did not exist—and was not on the horizon—in Kierkegaard's time. The words Kierkegaard uses (*psychologisk, psychologie*) were used to indicate something roughly coextensive with Hegelian 'philosophy of (subjective) spirit' (i.e., the philosophy of mind construed broadly enough to include topics ranging from theory of knowledge to philosophy of action). Hegel's *Encyclopaedia* section on subjective spirit included discussions of the soul, the nature of consciousness, reason, representation, thought, inclination and drives. Sibbern's work *Psychologie* (first published in 1843 and reissued several times over the next two decades), though prefaced by a section on general biology, deals with the same set of topics. (There is no reason to think Theunissen is not well aware of the fact that the change in the meaning of the word 'psychology' post-dated Kierkegaard's production; my point is not that his view relies on this sort of mistake, but only that readers unfamiliar with the nineteenth-century context should not be misled by the term's contemporary meaning.) It is worth noting here that some of the very language that makes *The Sickness unto Death* susceptible to the depth-psychological reading is naturalistic language taken over from Schelling's and Schleiermacher's (1963: 286) descriptions of moral evil as an 'illness' or 'disharmony'. Kierkegaard criticizes Schelling for his naturalistic analogies in *The Concept of Anxiety*, but takes over some of them himself in *The Sickness unto Death*.

One can, for instance, take oneself to have no responsibilities at all, or not to have the responsibilities one has. The refusal to see oneself as an agent to begin with was discussed in the preceding chapter under the rubric of aesthetic despair. The refusal to be the self that one is, faced with the particular tasks and challenges that one is faced with, and equipped with the particular equipment one has with which to face them, is the subject of an extended treatment in *The Sickness unto Death*. One example of this is the individual who accepts responsibility for his actions in principle, but thereupon discovers in himself some imperfection with which he is reluctant to deal ethically, and which he uses as an excuse to escape (some of) the particular responsibilities with which he is faced. 'When the self with a certain degree of reflection in itself wills to be responsible for the self, it may come across some difficulty or other in the structure of the self, in the self's necessity. For just as no human body is perfect, no self is perfect. This difficulty, whatever it is, makes him recoil' (*SD* XI: 166–7). This individual views his self as something that could in principle be got away from.

As long as the difficulty lasts, he does not dare, as the saying so trenchantly declares, 'to come to himself,' he does not will to be himself; presumably this will pass, perhaps a change will take place, this gloomy possibility will probably be forgotten. So long as it lasts, he visits himself, so to speak, only occasionally, to see whether the change has commenced. (*SD* XI: 167–8)

If a change does take place, 'he moves home once again, "is himself once again" . . .'; if not, he tries to forget himself in a more permanent way (*SD* XI: 168). This is one example of the despair of not wanting to be oneself; the book contains many others. All are forms of avoidance of personal responsibility.

On the other hand, one can do what is apparently the opposite thing—one can aspire to take total control of oneself and to be not only self-directing, but also self-legislating. This is another type of misconstrual of the nature of agency, 'despair through the aid of the eternal, the despairing misuse of the eternal within oneself to will in despair to be oneself' (*SD* XI: 178). For such a despair to be possible, 'there must be consciousness of an infinite self' (*SD* XI: 179), and this despair is the desire to *be* that infinite self, to sever oneself 'from any relation to a power that has established it, or [to sever] it from the idea that there is such a power' (*SD* XI: 179). The goal of this individual is 'to be master of itself or to create itself' (*SD* XI: 179), to 'fashion out of [this concrete self] a self such as he wants' (*SD* XI: 179). This self is caught up not just in the fantasy of unlimited ability to refashion itself; it is also caught up in the fantasy of being its own lawgiver:

The self is its own master, absolutely its own master, so-called; and precisely this is its despair, but also what it regards as its pleasure and delight. On closer examination, however, it is easy to see that this absolute ruler is a king without a country, actually ruling over nothing; his position, his sovereignty, is subordinate to the dialectic that rebellion is legitimate at any moment. (*SD* XI: 180)

Again, *The Sickness unto Death* offers illustrations of a number of specific configurations of this form of despair; all are instances of refusal to accept an external normative authority.[43]

Anti-Climacus states explicitly that there can be two conscious forms of despair only because the self is a derived or established relation: 'If a human self had itself established itself, then there could only be one form: not to will to be oneself, to will to do away with oneself, but there could not be the form: in despair to will to be oneself' (*SD* XI: 128). Despair takes the forms that it does because human agency has the structure that it has—is something that, in relating to itself (as self-conscious *locus* of agency) simultaneously relates to something outside itself. This relating-to-something-outside has two aspects, ontological and normative. For Kierkegaard as for Schelling, saying that the self is not its own ontological basis and saying that it is not normatively self-sufficient go hand in hand. This is not because the former entails the latter, but instead because the negation of the former seems to entail the negation of the latter: someone committed to a conception of freedom as freedom for good and evil is committed to a non-self-positing self. Of course nothing has been said that requires that the source of norms and the ontological source of the agent be identical, and there is not much to be said in support of this assumption (one Kierkegaard and Schelling share). There does need to be *something* independent of the self and its activity from which norms can come, and this something must also be a plausible source of value, but something can fill those conditions without being the causal source of the agent's existence. So—once again—the theological voluntarist model is not the only one to fit the constraints, even though it is clearly the one that Kierkegaard has in mind.

This account of the structure of the self, by making the self dependent and oriented towards an outside source of norms, makes structurally possible a genuine alternative: turning away from that source and turning towards it. Such a structural possibility was, strictly speaking, all that was required. But Kierkegaard also had some interest in showing that moral evil is a psychological possibility in the motivational sense. His complaint that freedom for evil is literally incoherent or outright excluded often bleeds into a complaint that choosing the (morally) worse is motivationally excluded by a modern conception of agency on which it is nothing beyond practical reason. This worry is addressed at various points in the pseudonyms, but the most concentrated treatment of it is found in *The Concept of Anxiety*'s description of the psychological preconditions of sin.

---

[43] There are further more specific forms of despair that have to do with one's reaction to Christianity specifically. One form is offence, introduced in *The Sickness unto Death* as despair of the forgiveness of sins and in *Practice in Christianity* as a reaction to the person of the god-man. For a discussion of offence cf. Cappelørn (1975).

Phenomenology of freedom and psychology of sin

The Concept of Anxiety is Kierkegaard's most sustained meditation on the psychology of freedom, and, as his account of how a fall into sin is possible, is the work most closely connected both with Schelling's *Freiheitsschrift* and Kant's *Religion*. Its premiss is that the possibility of a basic plurality of outcomes (good and evil) must correspond to something in the phenomenology of agency, and that something (whatever it is) must be what makes a choice of sin a psychological possibility. This is the role Kierkegaard proposes for anxiety, whose ambiguity (*BA* IV: 314, 316, 338, 343, 377; 4: 349, 350, 372, 378, 411) suggests that it is that state of 'restless repose . . . out of which sin constantly arises' (*BA* IV: 294; 4: 329).

Anxiety is the phenomenological companion of freedom, and so a necessary component of human experience. Specifically, human agency is characterized by two features which are necessary, and jointly sufficient, for anxiety. One necessary condition of anxiety is that the agent's future be undetermined (what Kierkegaard calls the 'nothing' of freedom at *BA* IV: 313; 4: 347). Natural necessitation is precluded by this condition, but so is the moral necessitation of the Kantian holy will: 'If a human being were a beast or an angel, he could not be in anxiety' (*BA* IV: 421; 4: 454). The other necessary (and, together with the first, sufficient) condition is the set of constraints that accompany finite freedom. 'How does spirit relate to itself and to its conditionality? It relates itself as anxiety. Do away with itself, the spirit cannot; lay hold of itself it cannot, as long as it has itself outside itself' (*BA* IV: 315; 4: 349). The story here is not simply about the finitude of one's capacities and future lifespan lending a weight of significance to one's choices that would be absent if they could all be made again, or if no substantial consequences could arise from them. Critical to the story Kierkegaard tells is the role played by 'the prohibition'—the fact that the agent is addressed by some demand or set of demands on his conduct that comes from the outside.

According to the view presented in *The Concept of Anxiety*, sin arises in every individual out of an original state of innocence—that is, there is no 'hereditary' sin in the Augustinian sense. ('Just as Adam lost innocence by guilt, so every man loses it in the same way. If it was not by guilt that he lost it, then it was not innocence that he lost; and if he was not innocent before becoming guilty, he never became guilty' (*BA* IV: 307; 4: 342).) So the first part of *The Concept of Anxiety* sets itself the task of explaining how sin can be a possible choice of the innocent individual. The difficulty is that innocence is a state in which the individual is ignorant both of his own capacities and of the difference between good and evil (*BA* IV: 315–16; 4: 349–50). The innocent individual is spirit or selfhood as a mere potentiality—not yet conscious of itself, and so not yet self-relating, and so not yet a genuine self: 'Innocence is ignorance. In innocence, man is not qualified as spirit but is psychically qualified in immediate unity with his natural condition. The spirit in man is dreaming' (*BA* IV: 313; 4: 347). The self's first act is simultaneously an awakening to itself as something capable of acting: 'The real "self" is posited only by the qualitative leap' (*BA* IV: 348; 4: 382). So the innocent individual is brought to the edge of the leap into selfhood, moral knowledge *and* moral determinateness by a voice from the outside. The prohibition and the punishment threatened for its violation awakens in Adam 'freedom's possibility' (*BA* IV: 315; 4: 350) and brings innocence 'to its uttermost' (*BA* IV: 316; 4: 350).[44] Anxiety pushes the individual towards action and so contributes to its becoming morally determinate.[45] (The story about anxiety impelling the agent to (somehow) act is retold in the case of the non-innocent individual as well, the difference being that this individual has a set of more determinate possibilities to be anxious about.)

This moral determinateness can presumably be either that of good or evil. To deny this would be self-defeating, for two reasons. First, the whole purpose of the book is to make sense of the possibility of *sin*—which entails responsibility and could not if it were not avoidable (thus the repeated insistence that sin arises out of anxiety 'not by necessity . . . but by freedom', e.g., at *BA* IV: 294; 4: 329). Second, it would mean that innocence is not anxiety, since no one can be anxious of a predetermined outcome: 'If sin has come into the world by necessity (which is a contradiction) there can be no anxiety' (*BA* IV: 320; 4: 354–5). But Kierkegaard does not consider the possible state of affairs in which Adam anxiously refrains from eating the fruit. Why? The exclusive concern with the origin of sin arises not only out of the fact that the book sets itself the task of saying something about the dogmatic issue of 'hereditary' sin, but also out of the fact that the possibility of sin in an important sense defines human freedom. To say that sin is possible is to say that human beings are partially independent of God; the ground of freedom is also the ground of the possibility of sin, namely the element of independence of the finite self. This picture of partial independence, of self-relating in (and only in) relating to another, has not yet been spelled out explicitly (the publication of *The Sickness unto Death* is five years away), but allusions to that account

---

[44] There is an interesting disclaimer in this part of the discussion. Kierkegaard admits to having assumed that the prohibition comes from without, and claims that this assumption is not necessary: innocence has language, and 'one need merely assume that Adam talked to himself' (*BA* IV: 316; 4: 351). Language has the resources to express the difference between good and evil, and even if the innocent individual does not have the resources to understand that expression (since the difference '*is* only for freedom'), all that is required is that some communication of an enigmatic content be possible. Two pages later Kierkegaard repeats the claim that 'the speaker is language, and it is Adam himself who speaks' (*BA* IV: 318; 4: 353). But in a footnote to that second passage a further step in the dialectic once again produces an appeal to an outside source of language: 'If one were to say further that it then becomes a question of how the first man learned to speak, I would answer that this is very true . . . But this much is certain, that it will not do to represent man himself as the inventor of language' (*BA* IV: 318n; 4: 353n).

[45] Quinn (1990: 238) sees the account of anxiety as helping to explain sin primarily 'preclud[ing] the possibility that the qualitative leap is made from a position of indifference, utterly unmotivated'. The fact that he leaves the source of anxiety's 'ambiguity' unexplained is due, I think, to the fact that he does not consider Schelling alongside Schleiermacher and Kant as a major influence on *The Concept of Anxiety*.

(the description of the self as a self-relating synthesis of the psychical and the physical) are present throughout the text, and the explanation of the psychological possibility of sin relies on it.

So anxiety has the particular ambiguous character that it does for good reason. The good is tempting (for the obvious reasons), but the evil is tempting too, even before the two are fully recognized as such. This is where the influence of Schelling's *Freiheitsschrift*—evident throughout the text[46]—enters in a particularly interesting way. Kierkegaard's central and most striking image of the fall into sin is plainly a meditation upon Schelling's:

Anxiety may be compared with dizziness. He whose eye happens to look down into the yawning abyss becomes dizzy. But what is the reason for this? It is just as much in his own eye as in the abyss, for suppose he had not looked down. Hence anxiety is the dizziness of freedom, which emerges when freedom wants to posit the synthesis and freedom looks down into its own possibility, laying hold of finiteness to support itself. Freedom succumbs in this dizziness. Further than this, psychology cannot and will not go. In that very moment everything is changed, and freedom, when it again rises, sees that it is guilty. Between these two moments lies the leap, which no science has explained and which no science can explain. (*BA* IV: 331; 4: 365–6)

There are several things to note about this passage.

First, the psychic phenomenon described seems to be that of being *tempted* by one's finitude. This is what it means to 'lay hold of finiteness to support [one]self'. The description looks on its face to be one of an individual refusing to recognize his agency because he is anxious about exercising it, anxious about the very fact that he has it to exercise. The innocent individual gets an inkling that there is something he might do, something prohibited, and decides to 'play dead' until the threat passes by. One can certainly imagine a scenario like this—one can even imagine it as a case in which the moral opossum incurs guilt in acting as he does (namely, a situation in which inaction is condemnable). But this is not Adam's situation, which is the one at issue—there, inaction would have been preferable. So 'laying hold of finiteness' here must mean something else. How else can one be tempted by one's finitude?

An answer suggests itself if we recall that the self is a synthesis (of infinite and finite) and we understand those terms as Schelling did in the *Freiheitsschrift* (as indicating an individualizing/concretizing element and an idealizing/integrating element). 'Laying hold of finiteness' is relying upon one's particularity, instead of one's place in a larger order, to guide one's action (taking, to use Schelling's terms, a point on the periphery to be the centre).[47] To be tempted by one's finitude, then, is to be tempted by one's partial independence—tempted into trying to make it a

---

[46] For the most detailed catalogue of the textual references in the *Freiheitsschrift* in *The Concept of Anxiety*, cf. Hennigfeld (1987).

[47] Recall that Schelling thought that, because the ground of freedom is also the ground of the possibility of sin (namely the element of independence of the finite self) the first use of freedom is always a drawing away from God.

total independence (which can include taking the sensuous desires arising out of one's particular embodiment to be sufficient grounds for one's action). This fits Adam's case. It also fits with another part of Kierkegaard's exposition which likewise echoes Schelling: the characterization of sin as selfishness.

The use of the notion of selfishness brings me to the second point I would like to make about the quoted passage. The passage makes it clear that it is intended as a (retrospective) portrayal of the precursors of a case of sin and not a (prospective) portrayal of the necessary outcome of a case of anxiety. This is the function of the disclaimer about the limits of psychology: from anxious innocence to guilt there is no path fully reconstructible by psychology. This claim that choice is a 'leap' which cannot be reconstructed has two motivations.

The first is that choice is not, according to Kierkegaard, an object of possible introspection. There are statements of this view at several points in the pseudonyms. (See, for instance, *AE* VII: 297; 7: 313: 'When existence gives movement time and I reproduce this, then the leap appears in just the way a leap can appear: it must come or it has been', and *EE* II: 148; 3: 160, where the Judge argues that the moment of choice 'is actually not at all'.) Choices appear as future tasks or past deeds; they cannot appear as introspectible psychic events. (This is also, I believe, the motivation behind Kierkegaard's repeated denials that his view presupposes an indifference conception of freedom (twice, in fact, in the course of this short work (*BA* IV: 320, 381; 4: 355, 414)); the same point is made in *Either/Or* (*EE* II: 157; 3: 169). If we can say nothing about the moment of decision, except that it is something that must come or has been, then we also cannot say that it is some state wherein two options, say the 'good' option and the 'evil' option, appear equally worthy of choice or where all inclinations towards one thing or the other are suspended.)

The second motivation for denying that the leap can be psychologically reconstructed is that part of the meaning of the notion of 'choice' relevant in ethical contexts is that it is not subject to 'scientific' explanation—and the context of sin is an ethical context. Kierkegaard is trying to preserve in this account the difficult distinction between making the fall psychologically *plausible* and making it psychologically *explicable*. This is what is required by his conception of freedom, according to which motivations do not determine the will. An analysis of motivations can clarify action, but not explain it.

[Psychology] must guard against leaving the impression of explaining that which no science can explain and that which ethics explains further only by presupposing it by way of dogmatics. If one were to take the psychological explanation and repeat it a number of times and thereby arrive at the opinion that it is not unlikely that sin came into the world in this way, everything would be confused. Psychology must remain within its boundary; only then can its explanation have significance. (*BA* IV: 310–11; 4: 345)

'Psychology comes closest [to sin] and explains the last approximation, which is freedom's showing-itself-for-itself in the anxiety of possibility, or in the nothing of possibility, or in the nothing of anxiety' (*BA* IV: 345; 4: 380). But it does not explain *sin*. 'To want to give a logical explanation of the coming of sin into the world is a stupidity that can occur only to people who are comically worried about finding an explanation' (*BA* IV: 320; 4: 355).

Kierkegaard's criticisms of Schelling's treatment of sin in the *Freiheitsschrift* centre around this issue: Schelling went too far in the direction of explanation, made too many concessions to science. This is a point Kierkegaard makes in the context of admitting the notion of selfishness into the description of sin. He criticizes certain (unnamed, but unmistakable) 'natural philosophers' for finding selfishness in all of nature, for portraying selfishness as 'the centrifugal force in nature'.[48] The conclusion is that selfishness can describe sin, but not in its function as a *natural force*, since that is a theoretical notion:

Although in the newer science sin has so often been explained as selfishness, it is incomprehensible that it has not been recognized that precisely here lies the difficulty of finding a place for its explanation *in any science*. For selfishness is precisely the particular, and what this signifies only the single individual can know as the single individual, because when it is viewed under universal categories it may signify everything in such a way that it signifies nothing at all. The definition of sin as selfishness may therefore be quite correct, especially when it is held that *scientifically* it is so empty of content that it signifies nothing at all. (*BA* IV: 346; 4: 380–1—my emphasis)

Schelling had something right when he pointed to particularity as the ground of the possibility of evil; but he was tempted to generalize particularity into a 'principle of particularity' and turn it into an explanatory notion. This is a legitimate criticism of the *Freiheitsschrift*—Schelling in fact succumbed to the temptation to turn an ethical point into a cosmological one. Kierkegaard, worried as he was that too much concern with the explanation of behaviour is inconsistent with an appropriate conception of and commitment to ethical practice, found this temptation easier to resist.

The two moral psychological works in the pseudonymous corpus present us with a positive picture of the human agent corresponding to the negative arguments against the aesthetic, ethical and immanent-religious standpoints. It is a picture of the agent as a partially independent but partially dependent, a self-determining but not self-legislating being—a moral agent in need of a criterion of value it is unable itself to supply. Can we make any sense of such a picture? I think we can, but one might think this interpretation is subject to a fairly fundamental objection which I will, in concluding, take a moment to address.[49]

Is one actually entitled to use a conception of human freedom as freedom for good and evil (basically ethical categories)—and even to use it *against* certain views of the foundations of ethics—in the absence of an ethical criterion that

---

[48] 'If a concept is brought that far, it might just as well lie down and, if possible, sleep off its drunkenness and become sober again' (*BA* IV: 346–7; 4: 381).

[49] This objection was raised in its most compelling form by Manfred Frank (in conversation).

would specify the content of those notions? If not, then Kierkegaard would have to presuppose some account of that content in order to get his negative arguments off the ground. Otherwise, the negative argument presented in chapter 5 threatens to lead not to the conclusion that we are agents of the sort described in need of a criterion of value, but instead to the quite different conclusion that in the absence of such a criterion, we cannot take ourselves to be agents in the relevant sense to begin with.[50]

The objection makes use of the Kantian notion that some specifiable moral law must be the *ratio cognoscendi* of freedom. Kierkegaard does not share this commitment. He does hold that in the absence of some commitment to a religious source of value, the content of the notions of good and evil cannot be *adequately* specified.[51] But he denies not only that freedom relies ontologically upon the good/evil distinction—a point Kant would agree with—but also that our belief in our freedom relies on beliefs about the content of the notions of good and evil: 'To speak of good and evil as the objects of freedom finitizes both freedom and the concepts of good and evil. Freedom is infinite and arises out of nothing' (*BA* IV: 381; 4: 414–15). Good and evil begin as placeholders for ethical success and failure, and the foundation of the ethical attitude is not the recognition that one stands under some specifiable set of moral injunctions, but is rather the mere raising of the question, 'What am I supposed to do?' Kierkegaard's claim is that this question arises out of the situation of existing subjectivity (cf., e.g., *AE* VII: 365; 7: 383), even if its answer does not. This is what the twentieth-century existentialists saw in Kierkegaard, and to this point, they were quite correct in seeing him as their precursor.[52]

What can be said on behalf of Kierkegaard's commitment here? The objector claims that we cannot see ourselves as free in the sense relevant to moral responsibility at all in the absence of some determinate, specified moral task that we see ourselves as free for. But this makes any sort of fundamental ethical inquiry

---

[50] If the objection is taken to be one about human psychological development—would it be possible for a human being to come to the sort of conception of himself that is described in these two works without ever having thought of himself as subject to specific imperatives?—the right response is to grant it. The presence of *some* evaluative standards—perhaps not correct or even ultimately coherent ones—is required for the development of the agent described in *The Sickness unto Death*. But on this construal, the objection is not interesting, since no one denies that human beings are typically raised in the presence of a set of evaluative standards. It is only once questions are raised, and answers proposed, about the ultimate justification of these norms that the problems Kierkegaard notices arise.

[51] 'Absolutely right. And no *human being* can come further than that [i.e., further than the position that sin is ignorance]; no man of himself and by himself can declare what sin is. . . . That is why Christianity begins in another way: man has to learn what sin is by a revelation from God' (*SD* XI: 205–6).

[52] Sartre at least was importantly wrong about something else he thought he saw in Kierkegaard: the idea that we give rise to what value there is in the world by deciding it is there. This is the subjectivist appropriation of *Postscript* I have argued against in the preceding section. An excellent discussion of this idea as developed in existentialism, which traces its origin to Kant and to this reading of Kierkegaard can be found in Olafson (1967).

problematic. For in order to inquire about our moral task—to ask questions like, 'Are the values I have endorsed up until now really the right ones?'—we must think that there could *be* some such task, and that we could have got its nature quite wrong. But in order to think there could be some such task, we need first to think that we are the sorts of things to which such tasks can be addressed—that we are responsible agents. Now, if the presupposition of the objection is correct, then as soon as we inquire about what the criterion of moral goodness might be, we admit that we lack the required grounds for thinking we are free in the sense that is required to make any such inquiry sensible in the first place. If, in the absence of such a criterion, we have no grounds for believing that we are free, and if, in the absence of such grounds, we are not justified in seeing ourselves as standing under moral imperatives to begin with, it follows that it is senseless to *ask*, 'What is my ethical task in life?' Either we know the answer already, or we lack the presupposition—freedom—that gives it force. So in order to embrace Kant's view that the moral law is the *ratio cognoscendi* of freedom, we also need to embrace Kant's view that we already have the answer to the fundamental normative questions that face us. When we put the matter in those terms, it seems clear that Kant's is the view (on this topic, at least) with less innocuous presuppositions.

Conclusion

This book has been confined to a relatively short list of authors and a relatively narrow range of systematic issues; there are two directions in which the investigation could profitably be expanded.

First, I have confined the historical focus to the individuals who made the major steps along the narrow trajectory I trace. This means that I have left out discussions of several very important figures, a consideration of whom would complicate and enrich the story (though without, I believe, changing its main outlines).

Hegel was, of course, a named target of Kierkegaard's attacks on systematic philosophy and idealist epistemology, but Schelling's early system has been treated alone here instead of alongside Hegel's. There are several reasons for this. Schelling's early system was the historical prototype for the treatment of the reconciliation of freedom and system in Hegel. The criticisms the later Schelling and Kierkegaard make on the topics at issue here apply equally, and in the same way, to the early Schelling and to Hegel (something both well knew, even if Schelling was sometimes reluctant to admit it). Further, although Hegel dominates the period from our historical perspective, things looked rather different in Denmark during Kierkegaard's intellectually formative years. In fact it took Hegel much longer to eclipse Schelling in Denmark than in Germany—it happened in the middle to late 1830s, while Kierkegaard was at the university. (His dissertation adviser Sibbern was a systematician after the Schellingian, not the Hegelian, model.) Kierkegaard's comment that Hegel should be seen as a 'parenthesis' in Schelling[1] should be taken more seriously than it usually is—both as an assessment of the philosophical merits and as an indication of the intellectual situation in Denmark at the time. Finally, it seems to me that the near-exclusive focus on Hegel (and, more recently, on the German and Danish Hegelians) in treatments of Kierkegaard's relation to post-Kantian philosophy has been distorting and that the literature is in need of a corrective. In a book focused on an issue central to Kierkegaard's thought but on which Hegel had nothing new to say, it seemed important to say as little as possible about Hegel.

Hegel is not the only major figure treated only in passing. J. G. Fichte, for instance, seems to have stood on an equal footing with Kant as a model of ethics in the Kantian mode for both Kierkegaard and Schelling, and in many ways Kierkegaard's portrayal of the ethical standpoint is a closer match with Fichte's

---

[1] Cf. Kierkegaard (1909–1978: III A 34; 1997–, vol. 19: 185, Notesbog 5: 18).

ethics than with Kant's.[2] I have concentrated on Kant alone here primarily for the sake of simplicity, but also in order to avoid conveying the impression that Kierkegaard's and Schelling's criticisms of the ethics of autonomy were valid only or primarily for its Fichtean instantiation (and thus that contemporary Kantians have nothing to worry about from these criticisms). In fact they were correct to treat Kant and Fichte as representing the same view of the issue that concerned them. Another important figure in the background of both Schelling's later work and Kierkegaard's whom I have barely mentioned is J. G. Hamann. Hamann's attack on philosophical rationalism and his advocacy of empiricism exercised a strong influence on the later Schelling, even though Schelling never accepted Hamann's scepticism and account of religious belief. Hamann was also enormously influential for Kierkegaard's thinking about Christianity. More work on Hamann's influence on Kierkegaard and the rest of the nineteenth century is certainly in order, but this has not been the place for it. Finally, I have had little to say about the specifically Danish intellectual context, primarily because I have not found original and interesting contributions to the storyline there. Sibbern was a Schelling enthusiast, but principally oriented towards the early Schelling of the *Naturphilosophie*. Martensen's criticisms of the account of autonomy in German idealism have their source in theological rather than moral psychological concerns; in fact his treatment of the problem of moral evil is a fairly standard idealist one. Møller was involved in the late-idealist debate on immortality, but a consideration of his specific contribution would add little of significance to the story. Still, a more historically nuanced treatment would almost certainly result from a consideration of these figures.

The second set of limitations on this study have been systematic; I have confined the focus to the systematic issues as they were raised in this specific historical context, which has meant refraining from pursuing the inquiry as far as it could be pursued in either of two directions.

First, I have not employed the full conceptual apparatus that is at the contemporary philosopher's disposal and have not tried to place the various positions more precisely on the contemporary map than the texts invite and the history demands. For example, since Kierkegaard was not involved in the contemporary debate over internalism, it is rather difficult to place his position precisely on the terrain mapped out in that debate. Certainly, he holds that it is possible to be utterly unmotivated to do what one actually ought to do—normativity is in no way dependent on an agent's existing motivational structure—and just as certainly he thinks it possible to be insufficiently motivated to do what one judges one ought to do. Does a judgement that one ought to imitate Christ necessarily come accompanied by some (albeit possibly insufficient) motivation to do so? *The Sickness unto Death* offers what seem to me to be examples that support an answer of 'no', but they can be read in a number of ways. Since his position can fall on

---

[2] I have argued this in Kosch (forthcoming).

either side of this question while remaining the same on the fundamental problem of autonomy ethics, I have not pushed the investigation all the way to that natural limit. It might be profitable, in another context, to do so. Similarly, I have not attempted to place the late Schelling's concern with the limits of pure rational philosophy on the terrain mapped out in contemporary work on the relation between metaphysical necessity and *a prioricity*, or in modal metaphysics. I am convinced that Schelling's position is sufficiently well thought out to stand up to—and to reward—that sort of detailed examination, but there is no need for it in the story I tell here.[3]

Second, I have not offered any judgements about the state of the debate on this set of issues as it has arisen in contemporary ethics. In fact the resurgence of Kantianism in moral philosophy has led to a renewed discussion of some of the very problems that are central to this book, and the worry pressed by Kierkegaard and Schelling has emerged in recent years as a criticism of contemporary versions of broadly Kantian autonomism.[4] I believe the problem of the imputability of immorality to be a serious one for Kantian ethics in its contemporary manifestations. It is certainly not an adequate response for Kantians to admit that moral evil is unintelligible and leave it at that, since what is unintelligible in the sense at issue cannot be relevant to an agent's practical deliberation and so cannot be, for example, something she sets out to avoid. I have not seen a definitive treatment of these issues—a canvassing of the possible forms the idea of autonomy as a foundation for ethics might take and a demonstration either that the problem arises for all of them, or that it does not arise for some—but such a project is probably worth undertaking, and this study might serve as an indication of where it should begin.

In showing how close—philosophically as well as historically—the Kierkegaardian end-point is to the Kantian beginning, this study ought to go some way towards convincing those attracted to Kantian ethics of the relevance of Kierkegaardian concerns. It is no news that Kant and Kierkegaard gave quite opposed accounts of the relationship between rationality and freedom. Less widely appreciated is the extent to which these two accounts are rooted in the same set of presuppositions, and how very naturally the one arises from problems in the other. From the same narrative I hope students of Kierkegaard will take a more nuanced understanding of his moral psychology, as well as a deeper appreciation of how firmly rooted in the idealist problematic were his concerns, and how deeply and productively engaged with Kant and post-Kantian German philosophy he was. Finally, in tracing the trajectory of the idealist metaphysics of autonomy in its connection with these issues in moral psychology, I hope this study will contribute to the understanding of the history of the nineteenth century by making the decline and replacement of the idealist project nearly as comprehensible as its rise and brief hegemony has been made by the excellent recent work in this field.

---

[3] For a slightly more detailed treatment, cf. Kosch (2003).

[4] It has emerged, for example, in recent criticisms of Korsgaard's treatment of immoral choices in Ginsborg (1998) and Wallace (2001), and a recent criticism of Velleman's autonomism in Clark (2001).

Bibliography

Abicht, J. H. (1789). 'Ueber die Freiheit des Willens'. *Neues philosophisches Magazin* 1(1): 64–85.

Adams, R. M. (1977). 'Kierkegaard's Arguments against Objective Reasoning in Religion'. *Monist* 60: 228–43.

Adams, R. M. (1987). 'Vocation'. *Faith and Philosophy* 4(4): 448–62.

Allison, H. E. (1966). 'Christianity and Nonsense'. *Review of Metaphysics* 20: 432–60.

Allison, H. E. (1983). *Kant's Transcendental Idealism*. New Haven, CT, Yale University Press.

Allison, H. E. (1990). *Kant's Theory of Freedom*. Cambridge, Cambridge University Press.

Allison, H. E. (1996). *Idealism and Freedom*. Cambridge, Cambridge University Press.

Ameriks, K. (ed.) (2000a). *The Cambridge Companion to German Idealism*. Cambridge, Cambridge University Press.

Ameriks, K. (2000b). *Kant and the Fate of Autonomy: Problems in the Appropriation of the Critical Philosophy*. Cambridge, Cambridge University Press.

Ameriks, K. (2000c). *Kant's Theory of Mind*. Oxford, Clarendon Press.

Ameriks, K. (2000d). 'The Practical Foundation of Philosophy in Kant, Fichte and After'. In *The Reception of Kant's Critical Philosophy*. S. Sedgwick, ed. Cambridge, Cambridge University Press: 109–28.

Ameriks, K. (2001). 'Kant and Short Arguments to Humility'. In *Kant's Legacy*. P. Cicovacki, ed. Rochester, NY, University of Rochester Press: 167–94.

Ameriks, K. (2003). *Interpreting Kant's Critiques*. Oxford, Clarendon.

Anscombe, G. E. M. (1958). 'Modern Moral Philosophy'. *Philosophy* 33: 1–19.

Arendt, H. (1989). *The Human Condition*. Chicago, IL, University of Chicago Press.

Ayer, A. J. (1954). 'Freedom and Necessity'. *Philosophical Essays*. London, Macmillan: 271–84.

Baumgarten, H.-U. (2000). 'Das Böse bei Schelling'. *Kant-Studien* 91: 447–59.

Beck, L. W. (1960). *A Commentary on Kant's Critique of Practical Reason*. Chicago, IL, University of Chicago Press.

Beck, L. W. (1978). *Essays on Kant and Hume*. New Haven, CT, Yale University Press.

Beck, L. W. (1987). 'Five Concepts of Freedom in Kant'. In *Philosophical Analysis and Reconstruction*. S. Körner and J. T. J. Srzednick, eds. Dordrecht, Nijhoff: 35–51.

Beiser, F. C. (1987). *The Fate of Reason: German Philosophy from Kant to Fichte*. Cambridge, MA, Harvard University Press.

Beiser, F. C. (2002). *German Idealism: The Struggle against Subjectivism*. Cambridge, MA, Harvard University Press.

Bennett, J. (1966). *Kant's Analytic*. Cambridge, Cambridge University Press.

Bennett, J. (1974). *Kant's Dialectic*. Cambridge, Cambridge University Press.

Bernhardi, A. B. (1796). *Gemeinfaßliche Darstellung der kantischen Lehren über Sittlichkeit, Freyheit, Gottheit und Unsterblichkeit*. Freyberg, Crazischen Buchhandlung.

Bittner, R. and Cramer, K. (eds.) (1975). *Materialien zu Kants Kritik der praktischen Vernunft*. Frankfurt/Main, Suhrkamp.

Bok, H. (1998). *Freedom and Responsibility*. Princeton, NJ, Princeton University Press.

Bowie, A. (1993). *Schelling and Modern European Philosophy*. New York, NY, Routledge.

Brastberger, G. U. (1792). *Untersuchungen über Kants Kritik der praktischen Vernunft*. Tübingen, Cotta.

Cappelørn, N.-J. (1975). 'Et forsøg på en bestemmelse af begrebet forargelse hos Søren Kierkegaard'. *Dansk Teologisk Tidskrift* 38: 197–229.

Carnois, B. (1987). *The Coherence of Kant's Doctrine of Freedom*. D. Booth, trans. Chicago, IL, University of Chicago Press.

Chalybäus, H. M. (1837). 'Philosophie der Geschichte und Geschichte der Philosophie'. *Zeitschrift für Philosophie und spekulative Theologie* 1: 301–38.

Clark, P. (2001). 'Velleman's Autonomism'. *Ethics* 111: 580–93.

Conant, J. (1989). 'Must We Show What We Cannot Say?' In *The Senses of Stanley Cavell*. R. Fleming and M. Payne, eds. Lewisburg, PA, Bucknell University Press.

Conant, J. (1993). 'Kierkegaard, Wittgenstein and Nonsense'. *Pursuits of Reason*. Lubbock, TX, Texas Tech.

Courtine, J.-F. (1990). *Extase de la Raison: Essais sur Schelling*. Paris, Editions Galilee.

Cousin, V. (1834). *Ueber französische und deutsche Philosophie*. H. Beckers, ed. and trans. Stuttgart, Cotta.

Cross, A. (2003). 'Faith and Suspension of the Ethical in *Fear and Trembling*'. *Inquiry* 46: 1–27.

Davenport, J. (2001). 'The Meaning of Kierkegaard's Choice between the Esthetic and the Ethical'. In *Kierkegaard After MacIntyre*. J. Davenport and A. Rudd, eds. Chicago, IL, Open Court: 75–112.

Davenport, J. and Rudd, A. (eds) (2001). *Kierkegaard After MacIntyre*. Chicago, IL, Open Court.

Dempf, A. (1957). 'Kierkegaard hört Schelling'. *Philosophisches Jahrbuch* 65: 147–61.

Disse, J. (1991). *Kierkegaards Phänomenologie der Freiheitserfahrung*. Freiberg, Karl Alber.

Disse, J. (2000). 'Autonomy in Kierkegaard's *Either/Or*'. In *Kierkegaard and Freedom*. J. Giles, ed. New York, NY, Palgrave: 58–69.

Donnelly, J. (1981). 'Kierkegaard's Problem I and Problem II: An Analytic Perspective'. In *Kierkegaard's Fear and Trembling: Critical Appraisals*. R. Perkins, ed. University, AL, University of Alabama Press: 115–40.

Eberhard, J. A. (1792). 'Eine Frage, den Satz der Causalität betreffend'. *Philosophisches Magazin* 4(1): 482–9.

Eberhard, J. A. (1794). 'Ueber das Kantische radicale Böse in der menschlichen Natur'. *Philosophisches Archiv* 2(2): 34–47.

Emmanuel, S. M. (1996). *Kierkegaard and the Concept of Revelation*. Albany, NY, State University of New York Press.

Engstrom, S. (1988). 'Conditioned Autonomy'. *Philosophy and Phenomenological Research* 48: 435–53.

Evans, C. S. (1981). 'Is the Concept of an Absolute Duty toward God Morally Unintelligible?' In *Kierkegaard's Fear and Trembling: Critical Appraisals*. R. Perkins, ed. University, AL, University of Alabama Press: 141–51.

Evans, C. S. (1983). *Kierkegaard's 'Fragments' and 'Postscript'*. Atlantic Highlands, NJ, Humanities Press.

Evans, C. S. (1989a). 'Does Kierkegaard Think Beliefs can be Directly Willed?' *International Journal of the Philosophy of Religion* 26: 173–84.

Evans, C. S. (1989b). 'Is Kierkegaard an Irrationalist? Reason, Paradox and Faith'. *Religious Studies* 25: 347–62.

Evans, C. S. (1998). 'Realism and Antirealism in Kierkegaard's *Concluding Unscientific Postscript*'. In *The Cambridge Companion to Kierkegaard*. A. Hannay and G. Marino, eds. Cambridge, Cambridge University Press: 154–76.

Fahrenbach, H. (1968). *Kierkegaards existenzdialektische Ethik*. Frankfurt/Main, Klostermann.

Fahrenbach, H. (1979). 'Kierkegaards ethische Existenzanalyze (als 'Korrektiv' der Kantisch-idealistischen Moralphilosophie)'. In *Materialien zur Philosophie Søren Kierkegaards*. M. Theunissen and W. Greve, eds. Frankfurt/Main, Suhrkamp: 216–40.

Feder, J. (1788). 'Recension der *Kritik der praktischen Vernunft*'. *Philosophisches Bibliothek* 1: 182–218.

Ferreira, M. J. (1991). *Transforming Vision: Imagination and Will in Kierkegaardian Faith*. Oxford, Clarendon Press.

Ferreira, M. J. (2001). *Love's Grateful Striving: A Commentary on Kierkegaard's Works of Love*. Oxford, Clarendon Press.

Fichte, I. H. (1826). *Sätze zur Vorschule der Theologie*. Stuttgart, Cotta.

Fichte, I. H. (1832–46). *Ueber Gegenzatz, Wendepunkt und Ziel heutiger Philosophie*. 4 vols. Heidelberg, Mohr.

Fichte, I. H. (1833–6). *Grundzüge zum Systeme der Philosophie*. 2 vols. Heidelberg, Mohr.

Fichte, I. H. (1834a). *Die Idee der Persönlichkeit und der individuellen Fortdauer*. Elberfeld, Büchler.

Fichte, I. H. (1834b). 'Religion og Philosophie i deres nærværende gjensidige Forhold'. *Tidskrift for udenlandsk theologisk Litteratur* 2.

Fichte, I. H. (1835). *Ueber die Bedingungen eines spekulativen Theismus*. Elberfeld, Büchler.

Fichte, I. H. (1838). 'Ueber das Verhältnis des Form- und Realprinzipes in den gegenwärtigen philosophischen Systemen'. *Zeitschrift für Philosophie und spekulative Theologie* 2: 21–108.

Fichte, I. H. (1840a). *De principiorum contradictionis, identitatis, exclusi tertii in logicis dignitate et ordine*. Bonn.

Fichte, I. H. (1840b). 'Zur Spekulativen Theologie, Part 1'. *Zeitschrift für Philosophie und spekulative Theologie* 5: 91–113.

Fichte, I. H. (1841). *Beiträge zur Charakteristik der neueren Philosophie*. Sulzbach, Rosenberg.

Fichte, I. H. (1842a). 'Nogle Bemærkninger om Forskjellen imellem den immanente Trinitet og Aabenbaringstriniteten, efter Lücke og Nitzsch, samt med Hensyn til Hegel og Strauß'. *Tidskrift for udenlandsk theologisk Litteratur* 10.

Fichte, I. H. (1842b). 'Die philosophische Literatur der Gegenwart, V'. *Zeitschrift für Philosophie und spekulative Theologie* 9: 93–149.

Fichte, I. H. (1843a). 'Der Begriff des negativen Absoluten und der negativen Philosophie, I'. *Zeitschrift für Philosophie und spekulative Theologie* 10: 25–42.

Fichte, I. H. (1843b). 'Der Begriff des negativen Absoluten und der negativenPhilosophie, II'. *Zeitschrift für Philosophie und spekulative Theologie* 11: 255–90.

Fichte, J. G. (1971). *Werke*. I. H. Fichte, ed. Berlin, De Gruyter.

Figal, G. (1980). 'Schellings und Kierkegaards Freiheitsbegriff'. In *Kierkegaard und die deutsche Philosophie seiner Zeit*. H. Anz, P. Kemp, and F. Schmöe, eds. Munich, Wilhelm Fink: 112–27.

Fischer, C. P. (1839a). *Die Idee der Gottheit*. Stuttgart, Liesching.

Fischer, C. P. (1839b). 'Ueber den spekulativen Begriff der Freiheit'. *Zeitschrift für Philosophie und spekulative Theologie* 3: 101–59.

Fischer, C. P. (1842). 'Forsøg til en videnskabelig Begrundelse af Udødeligheds-Ideen'. *Tidskrift for udenlandsk theologisk Litteratur* 10.

Fischer, K. (1872). *Schellings Leben, Werke und Lehre*. Heidelberg, Winter.

Fischer, N. (1988). 'Der formale Grund der bösen Tat'. *Zeitschrift für philosophische Forschung* 42: 18–44.

Frank, M. (1985). *Eine Einführung in Schellings Philosophie*. Frankfurt/Main, Suhrkamp.

Frank, M. (1992). *Der unendliche Mangel an Sein*. 2nd edition. Munich, Wilhelm Fink.

Frank, M. (1997). *'Unendliche Annäherung'*. Frankfurt/Main, Suhrkamp.

Frankfurt, H. (1969). 'Alternate Possibilities and Moral Responsibility'. *The Journal of Philosophy* 66(23): 829–39.

Franks, P. (2000). 'All or Nothing: Systematicity and Nihilism in Jacobi, Reinhold and Maimon'. In *The Cambridge Companion to German Idealism*. K. Ameriks, ed. Cambridge, Cambridge University Press: 95–116.

Friedman, M. (1992). 'Causal Laws and the Foundations of Natural Science'. In *The Cambridge Companion to Kant*. P. Guyer, ed. Cambridge, Cambridge University Press: 161–99.

Fuhrmans, H. (1940). *Schellings letzte Philosophie*. Berlin, Junker und Dünnhaupt.

Fujino, H. (1994). 'Kontemplativ-äesthetisch oder existentiell-ethisch: Zur Kritik der auf der Stadienlehre basierenden Kierkegaardinterpretation'. *Kierkegaardiana* 17: 66–82.

Garve, C. (1798). *Uebersicht der vornehmsten Principien der Sittenlehre, von dem Zeitalter des Aristoteles an bis auf unsere Zeiten*. Breslau, Korn.

Gass, M. (1994). 'Kant's Causal Conception of Autonomy'. *History of Philosophy Quarterly* 11(1): 53–70.

Gerhardt, V. (1989). 'Selbständigkeit und Selbstbestimmung: zur Konzeption der Freiheit bei Kant und Schelling'. In *Die praktische Philosophie Schellings und die gegenwärtige Rechtsphilosophie*. H.-M. Pawlowski, S. Smid, and R. Specht, eds. Stuttgart, Frommann-Holzboog: 59–105.

Ginsborg, H. (1998). 'Korsgaard on Choosing Nonmoral Ends'. *Ethics* 109: 5–21.

Green, R. M. (1992). *Kierkegaard and Kant: The Hidden Debt*. Albany, NY, State University of New York Press.

Green, R. M. (1998). ' "Developing" *Fear and Trembling*'. In *The Cambridge Companion to Kierkegaard*. A. Hannay and G. Marino, eds. Cambridge, Cambridge University Press: 257–81.

Greve, W. (1990). *Kierkegaards maieutische Ethik*. Frankfurt/Main, Suhrkamp.

Guyer, P. (1998). 'The Value of Reason and the Value of Freedom'. *Ethics* 109: 22–35.

Guyer, P. (2000a). 'Absolute Idealism and the Rejection of Kantian Dualism'. In *The Cambridge Companion to German Idealism*. K. Ameriks, ed. Cambridge, Cambridge University Press: 37–56.

Guyer, P. (2000b). *Kant on Freedom, Law and Happiness*. Cambridge, Cambridge University Press.

Habermas, J. (1954). *Das Absolute und die Geschichte: von der Zweispältigkeit in Schellings Denken*. Dissertation, Philosophy. Bonn, Friedrich-Wilhelms-Universität.

Habermas, J. (1971). *Theorie und Praxis*. Frankfurt/Main, Suhrkamp.

Hamann, J. G. (1821–43). *Schriften*. F. Roth, ed. Berlin, Reimer.

Hannay, A. (1982). *Kierkegaard*. Boston, MA, Routledge & Kegan Paul.

Hannay, A. (2001). *Kierkegaard: A Biography*. Cambridge, Cambridge University Press.

Harper, W. and Meerbote, R. (eds.) (1984). *Kant on Causality, Freedom and Objectivity*. Minneapolis, MN, University of Minnesota Press.

Hegel, G. W. F. (1977). *Phenomenology of Spirit*. A. V. Miller, trans. Oxford, Clarendon Press.

Hegel, G. W. F. (1991). *Elements of the Philosophy of Right*. A. Wood, ed., H. B. Nisbet, trans. Cambridge, Cambridge University Press.

Heidegger, M. (1988). *Schelling: vom Wesen der menschlichen Freiheit*. I. Schüßer, ed. Frankfurt/Main, Klostermann.

Hennigfeld, J. (1987). 'Die Wesensbestimmung des Menschen in Kierkegaards *Der Begriff Angst*'. *Philosophisches Jahrbuch* 94: 269–84.

Henrich, D. (1960). 'Der Begriff der Sittlichen Einsicht und Kants Lehre vom Faktum der Vernunft'. In *Die Gegenwart der Griechen im neueren Denken*. D. Henrich, W. Schulz, and K.-H. Volkmann-Schluck, eds. Tübingen, Mohr: 77–115.

Henrich, D. (1975). 'Die Deduktion des Sittengesetzes'. In *Denken im Schatten des Nihilismus*. A. Schwan, ed. Darmstadt, Wissenschaftliche Buchgesellschaft: 55–112.

Henrich, D. (1989). 'Kant's Notion of a Deduction and the Methodological Background of the First Critique'. In *Kant's Transcendental Deductions*. E. Förster, ed. Stanford, CA, Stanford University Press: 29–46.

Henrich, D. (2003). *Between Kant and Hegel: Lectures on German Idealism*. Cambridge, MA, Harvard University Press.

Herbert, R. (1961). 'Two of Kierkegaard's Uses of "Paradox"'. *The Philosophical Review* 70(1): 41–55.

Heuser-Kessler, M.-L. (1989). 'Schellings Organismusbegriff und seine Kritik des Mechanismus und Vitalismus'. *Allgemeine Zeitschrift für Philosophie* 14: 17–36.

Hill, T. (1985). 'Kant's Argument for the Rationality of Moral Conduct.' *Pacific Philosophical Quarterly* 66: 3–23.

Himmelstrup, J. (1934). *Sibbern*. Copenhagen, Schultz.

Hirsch, E. (1933). *Kierkegaard-Studien*. Gütersloh, Bertelsmann.

Hoffbauer, J. C. (1798). *Anfangsgründe der Moralphilosophie und insbesondere der Sittenlehre*. Halle, Kümmel.

Hoffbauer, J. C. (1799). *Untersuchungen über die wichtigen Gegenstände der Moralphilosophie insbesondere der Sittenlehre und Moraltheologie. Erster Teil*. Dortmund, Blothe.

Horstmann, R.-P. (1991). *Die Grenzen der Vernunft*. Frankfurt/Main, Anton Hain.

Horstmann, R.-P. (2000). 'The Early Philosophy of Fichte and Schelling'. In *The Cambridge Companion to German Idealism*. K. Ameriks, ed. Cambridge, Cambridge University Press: 117–40.

Hudson, H. (1991). 'Wille, Willkür and the Imputability of Immoral Actions'. *Kant-Studien* 82: 179–96.

Hume, D. (2001). *An Enquiry Concerning Human Understanding*. T. L. Beauchamp, ed. Oxford, Clarendon Press.

Hutter, A. (1995). 'Die Spannung zwischen theoretischer und praktischer Vernunft'. *Kant-Studien* 86: 431–45.

Hutter, A. (1996). *Geschichtliche Vernunft: die Weiterführung der Kantischen Vernunftkritik in der Spätphilosophie Schellings.* Frankfurt/Main, Suhrkamp.

Irwin, T. (1984). 'Morality and Personality: Kant and Green'. In *Self and Nature in Kant's Philosophy.* A. Wood, ed. Ithaca, NY, Cornell University Press: 31–56.

Jacobi, F. H. (1815). *Werke.* F. Roth and F. Koeppen, eds. Leipzig, Gerhard Fleischer.

Jakob, L. H. (1794). *Philosophische Sittenlehre.* Halle, Hemmerde und Schwetschke.

Jakob, L. H. (1796). 'Review of Schmid's *Versuch einer Moralphilosophie*'. *Annalen der Philosophie* 2(1): 120–32.

Jenisch, D. (1796). *Ueber Grund und Werth der Entdeckungen des Herrn Profesor Kant in der Metaphysik, Moral und Aesthetik.* Berlin, Bieweg.

Kant, I. (1900–). *Gesammelte Schriften.* Königlich Preußische Akademie der Wissenschaften, ed. Berlin, Reimer and Berlin, De Gruyter.

Kant, I. (1960). *Religion within the Limits of Reason Alone.* T. M. Greene and H. H. Hudson, eds. and trans. New York, NY, Harper Torchbooks.

Kant, I. (1965). *Critique of Pure Reason.* N. Kemp Smith, ed. and trans. New York, NY, St Martin's Press.

Kant, I. (1987). *Critique of Judgment.* W. S. Pluhar, ed. and trans. Indianapolis, IN, Hackett.

Kant, I. (1996). *Religion and Rational Theology.* A. Wood and G. Di Giovanni, eds. and trans. Cambridge, Cambridge University Press.

Kant, I. (1999). *Practical Philosophy.* M. J. Gregor, ed. and trans. Cambridge, Cambridge University Press.

Kant, I. (2000). *Critique of the Power of Judgment.* P. Guyer, ed.; P. Guyer and E. Matthews, trans. Cambridge, Cambridge University Press.

Kierkegaard, S. (1901–6). *Samlede Værker.* A. B. Drachmann, J. L. Heiberg, and H. O. Lange, eds. Copenhagen, Gyldendal.

Kierkegaard, S. (1909–78). *Papirer.* N. Thulstrup, ed. Copenhagen, Gyldendal.

Kieskegaard, S. (1953–64). *Gesammelte Werke.* E. Hirsch, ed. and trans. Düsseldorf, Diederich.

Kierkegaard, S. (1967–78). *Journals and Papers.* H. V. Hong and E. A. Hong, eds. and trans. Bloomington, IN, Indiana University Press.

Kierkegaard, S. (1978). *Two Ages.* H. V. Hong and E. A. Hong, eds. and trans. Princeton, NJ, Princeton University Press.

Kierkegaard, S. (1980a). *The Concept of Anxiety.* R. Thomte and A. B. Anderson, eds. and trans. Princeton, NJ, Princeton University Press.

Kierkegaard, S. (1980b). *The Sickness unto Death.* H. V. Hong and E. A. Hong, eds. and trans. Princeton, NJ, Princeton University Press.

Kierkegaard, S. (1983). *Fear and Trembling* and *Repetition.* H. V. Hong and E. A. Hong, eds. and trans. Princeton, NJ, Princeton University Press.

Kierkegaard, S. (1987a). *Either/Or.* H. V. Hong and E. A. Hong, eds. and trans. 2 vols. Princeton, NJ, Princeton University Press.

Kierkegaard, S. (1987b). *Philosophical Fragments* and *Johannes Climacus.* H. V. Hong and E. A. Hong, eds. and trans. Princeton, NJ, Princeton University Press.

Kierkegaard, S. (1988). *Stages on Life's Way.* H. V. Hong and E. A. Hong, eds. and trans. Princeton, NJ, Princeton University Press.

Kierkegaard, S. (1989a). *The Concept of Irony*. H. V. Hong and E. H. Hong, eds. and trans. Princeton, NJ, Princeton University Press.

Kierkegaard, S. (1989b). *The Sickness unto Death*. A. Hannay, ed. and trans. New York, NY, Penguin.

Kierkegaard, S. (1991). *Practice in Christianity*. H. V. Hong and E. A. Hong, eds. and trans. Princeton, NJ, Princeton University Press.

Kierkegaard, S. (1992). *Concluding Unscientific Postscript to* Philosophical Fragments. H. V. Hong and E. A. Hong, eds. and trans. Princeton, NJ, Princeton University Press.

Kierkegaard, S. (1993). *Upbuilding Discourses in Various Spirits*. H. V. Hong and E. A. Hong, eds. and trans. Princeton, NJ, Princeton University Press.

Kierkegaard, S. (1995). *Works of Love*. H. V. Hong and E. A. Hong, eds. and trans. Princeton, NJ, Princeton University Press.

Kierkegaard, S. (1997–). *Skrifter*. N. J. Cappelørn, J. Garff, J. Knudsen, J. Kondrup, and A. McKinnon, eds. Copenhagen, Gad.

Koeller, D. (1989). *The Physics of Freedom: The Beginnings of Schelling's Philosophy of Nature*. Dissertation, History. Berkeley, CA, University of California.

Koktanek, A. (1962). *Schellings Seinslehre und Kierkegaard*. Munich, Oldenbourg.

Korsgaard, C. (1989). 'Morality as Freedom'. In *Kant's Practical Philosophy*. Y. Yovel, ed. Dordrecht, Kluwer: 23–48.

Korsgaard, C. (1996a). *Creating the Kingdom of Ends*. Cambridge, Cambridge University Press.

Korsgaard, C. (1996b). *The Sources of Normativity*. Cambridge, Cambridge University Press.

Korsgaard, C. (2003). 'Realism and Constructivism in 20th Century Moral Philosophy'. *Journal of Philosophical Research* APA Centennial Supplement: 99–122.

Kosch, M. (1999). *Choosing Evil: Schelling, Kierkegaard, and the Legacy of Kant's Conception of Freedom*. Dissertation, Philosophy. New York, NY, Columbia University.

Kosch, M. (2000). 'Freedom and Immanence'. In *Kierkegaard and Freedom*. J. Giles, ed. New York, NY, Palgrave: 121–41.

Kosch, M. (2003). ' "Actuality" in Schelling and Kierkegaard'. In *Kierkegaard und Schelling*. J. Hennigfeld and J. Stewart, eds. Berlin, De Gruyter: 235–51.

Kosch, M. (forthcoming). 'Kierkegaard's Ethicist: Fichte's Role in Kierkegaard's Construction of the Ethical Standpoint'. *Archiv für Geschichte der Philosophie*.

Krabbe, O. (1837). 'Ueber die Stellung der philosophischen und der Christlichen Ethik zueinander'. *Zeitschrift für Philosophie und spekulative Theologie* 1: 202–31.

Küppers, B.-O. (1992). *Natur als Organismus: Schellings Frühe Naturphilosophie und ihre Bedeutung für die moderne Biologie*. Frankfurt/Main, Klostermann.

Lavin, D. (2004). 'Practical Reason and the Possibility of Error'. *Ethics* 114: 424–57.

Leese, K. (1929). *Philosophie und Theologie im Spätidealismus*. Berlin, Junker und Dünnhaupt.

Lichtenberger, H. P. (1993). 'Ueber die Unerforschlichkeit des Bösen nach Kant'. *Studia Philosophica* 52: 117–31.

Lippitt, J. (2003). *Kierkegaard and* Fear and Trembling. New York, NY, Routledge.

Lippitt, J. and Hutto, D. (1998). 'Making Sense of Nonsense: Kierkegaard and Wittgenstein.' *Proceedings of the Aristotelian Society* 98: 263–86.

Lowrie, W. (1938). *Kierkegaard*. New York, NY, Oxford University Press.

Lübcke, P. (1984). 'Selvets ontologi hos Kierkegaard'. *Kierkegaardiana* 13: 50–62.

Lübcke, P. (1991). 'An Analytical Interpretation of Kierkegaard as Moral Philosopher'. *Kierkegaardiana* 15: 93–103.

Lübcke, P. (2003). 'F. C. Sibbern: Epistemology as Ontology'. In *Kierkegaard and His Contemporaries*. J. Stewart, ed. Berlin, De Gruyter: 25–44.

McCarthy, V. (1985). 'Schelling and Kierkegaard on Freedom and Fall'. In *International Kierkegaard Commentary: The Concept of Anxiety*. R. Perkins, ed. Macon, GA, Mercer University Press: 89–109.

McFarland, J. (1970). *Kant's Concept of Teleology*. Edinburgh, Edinburgh University Press.

MacIntyre, A. (1966). *A Short History of Ethics*. New York, NY, Macmillan.

MacIntyre, A. (1984). *After Virtue*. Bloomington, IN, Notre Dame.

MacIntyre, A. (2001). 'Once More on Kierkegaard'. In *Kierkegaard After MacIntyre*. J. Davenport and A. Rudd, eds. Chicago, IL, Open Court: 339–55.

Mackey, L. (1962). 'The Loss of the World in Kierkegaard's Ethics'. *Review of Metaphysics* 15: 602–20.

Mackie, J. L. (1977). *Ethics: Inventing Right and Wrong*. New York, NY, Penguin.

Marquet, J. F. (1973). *Liberté et existence: Étude sur la formation de la philosophie de Schelling*. Paris, Gallimard.

Marquet, J. F. (1974). 'Schelling et la tentation hegelienne'. *Les Études Philosophiques*: 187–96.

Martensen, H. L. (1837). *De autonomia conscientiæ sui humanæ in theologiam dogmaticam nostri temporis introducta*. Copenhagen, Hauniæ.

Martensen, H. L. (1997). *Between Hegel and Kierkegaard*. C. L. Thompson and D. J. Kangas, eds. and trans. Atlanta, GA, Scholars Press.

Marx, W. (1977). *Schelling: Geschichte, System, Freiheit*. Munich, Karl Alber.

Mavrodes, G. (1986). 'Religion and the Queerness of Morality'. In *Rationality, Religious Belief, and Moral Commitment*. R. Audi and W. Wainwright, eds. Ithaca, NY, Cornell University Press: 213–26.

Mehl, P. (1995). 'Moral Virtue, Mental Health and Happiness: The Moral Psychology of Kierkegaard's Judge Wilhelm'. In *International Kierkegaard Commentary: Either/Or Part II*. R. Perkins, ed. Macon, GA, Mercer University Press: 155–82.

Moore, G. E. (1912). *Ethics*. London, Williams and Norgate.

Møller, P. M. (1837). 'Tanker over Muligheden af Beviser for Menneskets Udødelighed'. *Maanedskrift for Litteratur* 17: 1–72, 422–53.

Nelkin, D. (2000). 'Two Standpoints and the Belief in Freedom'. *Journal of Philosophy* 97(10): 564–76.

Neuhouser, F. (1990). *Fichte's Theory of Subjectivity*. Cambridge, Cambridge University Press.

Neuhouser, F. (2000). *Foundations of Hegel's Social Theory: Actualizing Freedom*. Cambridge, MA, Harvard University Press.

Olafson, F. (1967). *Principles and Persons*. Baltimore, MD, Johns Hopkins University Press.

O'Neill, O. (1989). *Constructions of Reason*. Cambridge, Cambridge University Press.

Pattison, G. and Shakespeare, S. (eds.) (1998). *Kierkegaard: The Self in Society*. New York, NY, St Martin's Press.

Peetz, S. (1995). *Die Freiheit im Wissen: eine Untersuchung zu Schellings Konzept der Rationalität*. Frankfurt/Main, Klostermann.

Pinkard, T. (2002). *German Philosophy 1760–1860: The Legacy of Idealism*. Cambridge, Cambridge University Press.

Pippin, R. (1997). *Idealism as Modernism: Hegelian Variations*. Cambridge, Cambridge University Press.

Pojman, L. (1983). 'Christianity and Philosophy in Kierkegaard's Early Papers'. *Journal of the History of Ideas* 44(1): 131–40.

Pojman, L. (1984). *The Logic of Subjectivity*. University, AL, University of Alabama Press.

Pojman, L. (1990). 'Kierkegaard on Faith and Freedom'. *International Journal of the Philosophy of Religion* 27: 41–61.

Popkin, R. (1951). 'Hume and Kierkegaard'. *The Journal of Religion* 31(4): 274–81.

Prauss, G. (1983). *Kant über Freiheit als Autonomie*. Frankfurt/Main, Klostermann.

Quinn, P. (1990). 'Does Anxiety Explain Original Sin?' *Nous* 24(2): 227–44.

Railton, P. (2003). 'On the Hypothetical and Non-Hypothetical in Reasoning about Belief and Action'. *Facts, Values and Norms*. Cambridge, Cambridge University Press.

Rawls, J. (1999). 'Kantian Constructivism in Moral Theory'. In *Collected Papers*. S. Freeman, ed. Cambridge, MA, Harvard University Press.

Reath, A. (1994). 'Legislating the Moral Law'. *Nous* 28(4): 435–64.

Reinhold, C. L. (1790 and 1792). *Briefe über die kantische Philosophie*. Leipzig, Göschen.

Reinhold, C. L. (1796–7). *Auswahl vermischter Schriften*. Jena, Mauke.

Rivelaygue, J. (1990). *Leçons de Métaphysique Allemand*. Paris, Grasset.

Rohde, H. P., (ed.) (1967). *Auktionsprotokol over Søren Kierkegaards Bogsamling*. Copenhagen, Den Kongelige Bibliotek.

Romang, J. P. (1835). *Ueber Willensfreiheit und Determinismus*. Bern, Jenni & Sohn.

Rosenau, H. (1993). 'Wie kommt ein Aesthet zur Verzweiflung? Die Bedeutung der Kunst bei Kierkegaard und Schelling'. *Kierkegaardiana* 16: 94–106.

Rosenkranz, K. (1843a). *Schelling: Vorlesungen*. Danzig, Gerhard.

Rosenkranz, K. (1843b). *Ueber Schelling und Hegel*. Königsberg, Bornträger.

Rossi, P. J. and Wreen, M. J. (1991). *Kant's Philosophy of Religion Reconsidered*. Bloomington, IN, Indiana University Press.

Rudd, A. (1993). *Kierkegaard and the Limits of the Ethical*. Oxford, Clarendon Press.

Rudd, A. (2001). 'Reason in Ethics: MacIntyre and Kierkegaard'. In *Kierkegaard After MacIntyre*. J. Davenport and A. Rudd, eds. Chicago, IL, Open Court: 131–50.

Sandkühler, H. J. (ed.). (1984). *Natur und Geschichtlicher Prozeß: Studien zur Naturphilosophie F. W. J. Schellings*. Frankfurt/Main, Suhrkamp.

Scheler, M. (1973). *Formalism in Ethics and Non-Formal Ethics of Values*. M. S. Frings and R. L. Funk, trans. Evanston, IL, Northwestern University Press.

Schellenberg, J. L. (1993). *Divine Hiddenness and Human Reason*. Ithaca, NY, Cornell University Press.

Schelling, F. W. J. (1809). *F. W. J. Schellings Philosophische Schriften: Erster Band*. Landshut, Philipp Krüll.

Schelling, F. W. J. (1830). *Vorlesungen Über die Methode des akademischen Studiums*. Stuttgart, Cotta.

Schelling, F. W. J. (1841). *Schellings erste Vorlesung in Berlin*. Stuttgart, Cotta.

Schelling, F. W. J. (1842). *Bruno, oder, über das göttliche und natürliche Prinzip der Dinge: ein Gespräch*. 2nd edition. Berlin, Reimer.

Schelling, F. W. J. (1856–61). *Sämmtliche Werke*. K. F. A. Schelling, ed. 14 vols. Stuttgart, Cotta.

Schelling, F. W. J. (1927–8). *Werke*. M. Schröter, ed. 6 vols. Munich, Beck and Oldenbourg.

Schelling, F. W. J. (1946). *Die Weltalter*. M. Schröter, ed. Munich, Biederstein und Leibniz.

Schelling, F. W. J. (1954–9). *Werke*. M. Schröter, ed. 6 supplementary vols. Munich, Beck.

Schelling, F. W. J. (1969). *Initia Philosophiae Universae: Erlanger Vorlesungen WS 1820/21*. H. Fuhrmans, ed. Bonn, Bouvier.

Schelling, F. W. J. (1972). *Grundlegung der Positiven Philosophie: Münchener Vorlesungen WS 1832/33 und SS 1833*. H. Fuhrmans, ed. Turin, Bottega D'Erasmo.

Schelling, F. W. J. (1977). *Philosophie der Offenbarung*. M. Frank, ed. Frankfurt/Main, Suhrkamp.

Schleiermacher, F. (1963). *The Christian Faith*. H. R. MacIntosh and J. S. Stewart, eds. and trans. New York, NY, Harper and Row.

Schmid, C. C. E. (1790). *Versuch einer Moralphilosophie*. Jena, Cröker.

Schulz, E. G. (1975). *Rehbergs Opposition gegen Kants Ethik*. Cologne, Böhlau.

Schulz, W. (1975). *Die Vollendung des deutschen Idealismus in der Spätphilosophie Schellings*. Pfullingen, Neske.

Schwab, J. C. (1792). 'Ueber die zweyerley Ich, und der Begriff der Freyheit in der kantischen Moral'. *Philosophisches Archiv* 1: 69–80.

Schwab, J. C. (1794a). 'Ueber den intelligiblen Fatalismus in der kritischen Philosophie.' *Philosophisches Archiv* 2: 26–33.

Schwab, J. C. (1794b). 'Wie beweiset die kritische Philosophie, daß wir uns als absolut-frey denken müssen?' *Philosophisches Archiv* 2: 1–9.

Sellars, W. (1971). '. . . this I or he or it (the thing) which thinks . . .' *Proceedings & Addresses of the American Philosophical Association* 44: 5–31.

Silber, J. (1960). 'The Ethical Significance of Kant's Religion'. In *Religion within the Limits of Reason Alone*. G. A. Hudson and T. M. Greene, eds. New York, NY, Harper Torchbooks: lxxix–cxxxiv.

Snow, D. (2000). 'The Evolution of Schelling's Concept of Freedom'. In *Schelling: Zwischen Fichte und Hegel*. C. Asmuth, A. Denker, and M. Vater, eds. Amsterdam, Gruner: 317–32.

Stahl, F. (1830–3). *Philosophie des Rechts nach geschichtlichem Ansicht*. 2 vols. Heidelberg, Mohr.

Steffens, H. (1846). *Nachgelassene Schriften*. Berlin, Schröder.

Stewart, J. (2003a). 'Kierkegaard and Hegelianism in Golden Age Denmark'. In *Kierkegaard and His Contemporaries*. J. Stewart, ed. Berlin, De Gruyter: 106–45.

Stewart, J. (2003b). *Kierkegaard's Relations to Hegel Reconsidered*. Cambridge, Cambridge University Press.

Stocker, M. (1979). 'Desiring the Bad: An Essay in Moral Psychology'. *Journal of Philosophy* 72(12): 738–53.

Strawson, P. F. (1966). *The Bounds of Sense*. New York, NY, Routledge.

Taylor, M. (1975). *Kierkegaard's Pseudonymous Authorship*. Princeton, NJ, Princeton University Press.

Taylor, M. (1980). *Journeys to Selfhood: Hegel and Kierkegaard*. Berkeley, CA, University of California Press.

Theunissen, M. (1958). *Der Begriff Ernst bei Søren Kierkegaard*. Munich, Karl Alber.

Theunissen, M. (1964–5). 'Die Dialektik der Offenbarung'. *Philosophisches Jahrbuch* 72: 134–60.

Theunissen, M. (1965). 'Schellings anthropologischer Ansatz'. *Archiv für Geschichte der Philosophie* 47: 174–89.

Theunissen, M. (1991). *Das Selbst auf Grund der Verzweiflung*. Frankfurt/Main, Anton Hain.

Theunissen, M. (1993). *Der Begriff Verzweiflung: Korrekturen an Kierkegaard*. Frankfurt/Main, Suhrkamp.

Thielst, P. (2003). 'Poul Martin Møller: Scattered Thoughts, Analysis of Affectation, Struggle with Nihilism'. In *Kierkegaard and His Contemporaries*. J. Stewart, ed. Berlin, De Gruyter: 45–61.

Thomas, J. H. (1980). 'Paradox'. *Concepts and Alternatives in Kierkegaard*. M. Thulstrup. Copenhagen, Reitzel: 192–219.

Thulstrup, N. (1972). *Kierkegaards Verhältnis zu Hegel und zum spekulativen Idealismus*. Stuttgart, Kohlhammer.

Tilliette, X. (1970). *Schelling: une Philosophie en Devenir*. Paris, J. Vrin.

Tilliette, X. (1975). 'Die Freiheitsschrift'. In *Schelling: Einführung in seine Philosophie*. H. M. Baumgartner, ed. Munich, Karl Alber.

Timmermann, J. (2000). 'Warum scheint transzendentale Freiheit absurd?' *Kant-Studien* 91: 8–16.

Timmons, M. (1994). 'Evil and Imputation in Kant's Ethics'. *Jahrbuch für Recht und Ethik* 2: 113–41.

Tuschling, B. (1990). 'Intuitiver Verstand, absolute Identität, Idee'. In *Hegel und die Kritik der Urteilskraft*. H. F. Fulda and R.-P. Horstmann, eds. Stuttgart, Klett-Cotta: 174–88.

Tuschling, B. (1991). 'The System of Transcendental Idealism: Questions Raised and Left Open in the *Kritik der Urteilskraft*'. *Southern Journal of Philosophy* 30 Supplement: 109–27.

Velleman, J. D. (1992). 'The Guise of the Good'. *Nous* 26: 3–26.

Velleman, J. D. (1996). 'The Possibility of Practical Reason'. *Ethics* 106: 694–726.

Wallace, R. J. (2001). 'Normativity, Commitment, and Instrumental Reason'. *Philosophers' Imprint* 1(3): 1–26.

Warda, A. (1922). *Immanuel Kants Bücher*. Berlin, Breslauer.

Weiße, C. (1833). *Die Idee der Gottheit*. Dresden, Grimmer.

Weiße, C. (1837). 'Die drei Grundfragen der gegenwärtigen Philosophie'. *Zeitschrift für Philosophie und spekulative Theologie* 1: 67–114 and 161–201.

Weiße, C. (1838a). 'Den evangeliske historie, kritisk og filosofisk behandlet'. *Tidskrift for udenlandsk theologisk Litteratur* 5.

Weiße, C. (1838b). 'Om den evangeliske histories troværdighed'. *Tidskrift for udenlandsk theologisk Litteratur* 5.

Weiße, C. (1840). 'Ueber die geschichtliche Entwicklung der Philosophie als Wissenschaft'. *Zeitschrift für Philosophie und spekulative Theologie* 5: 235–55.

Westphal, M. (1971). 'Kierkegaard on the Logic of Insanity'. *Religious Studies* 7: 193–211.

Westphal, M. (1996). *Becoming a Self*. West Lafayette, IN, Purdue University Press.

White, A. (1983a). *Absolute Knowledge: Hegel and the Problem of Metaphysics*. Athens, OH, Ohio University Press.

White, A. (1983b). *Schelling: An Introduction to the System of Freedom*. New Haven, CT, Yale University Press.

Whittaker, J. H. (1988). 'Suspension of the Ethical in *Fear and Trembling*'. *Kierkegaardiana* 14: 101–13.

Wieland, W. (1967). 'Die Anfänge der Philosophie Schellings und die Frage nach der Natur'. In *Natur und Geschichte*. K. Löwith, ed. Stuttgart, Kohlhammer: 237–79.

Wirth, J. U. (1843). 'Ueber den Begriff Gottes, als Prinzip der Philosophie'. *Zeitschrift für Philosophie und spekulative Theologie* 11: 235–92.

Wisdo, D. (1987). 'Kierkegaard on Belief, Faith and Explanation'. *International Journal of the Philosophy of Religion* 21: 95–114.

Wood, A. (1970). *Kant's Moral Religion*. Ithaca, NY, Cornell University Press.

Wood, A. (1978). *Kant's Rational Theology*. Ithaca, NY, Cornell University Press.

Wood, A. (1984). 'Kant's Compatibilism'. In *Self and Nature in Kant's Philosophy*. A. Wood, ed. Ithaca, NY, Cornell University Press: 73–101.

Wood, A. (1990). *Hegel's Ethical Thought*. Cambridge, Cambridge University Press.

Wood, A. (1999). *Kant's Ethical Thought*. Cambridge, Cambridge University Press.

Wood, A. (2000). 'The "I" as Principle of Practical Philosophy'. In *The Reception of Kant's Critical Philosophy*. S. Sedgwick, ed. Cambridge, Cambridge University Press: 93–108.

Index

34717152R00136

Printed in Great Britain
by Amazon